Thomas Nicolas Burke

Sermons and Lectures on Moral and Historical Subjects

Thomas Nicolas Burke

Sermons and Lectures on Moral and Historical Subjects

ISBN/EAN: 9783337112400

Printed in Europe, USA, Canada, Australia, Japan

Cover: Foto ©Lupo / pixelio.de

More available books at **www.hansebooks.com**

THE
IRISH-AMERICAN LIBRARY.
VOLUME III.

SERMONS,

AND

LECTURES ON MORAL AND HISTORICAL SUBJECTS.

BY

Very Rev. THOMAS N. BURKE, O.P.

NEW YORK:
LYNCH, COLE & MEEHAN, 57 MURRAY STREET.
1873.

Entered according to Act of Congress, in the year 1873, by
LYNCH, COLE & MEEHAN,
In the Office of the Librarian of Congress, at Washington.

Stereotyped and Printed at the
NEW YORK CATHOLIC PROTECTORY,
West Chester, N. Y.

INTRODUCTION.

THE discourses contained in the present volume comprise the most important and beautiful of the Sermons delivered in the United States by the Very Rev. Thomas N. Burke, O.P., as well as of his Lectures on moral and historical subjects,—all of which possess an interest for the Irish-American element of the community, not only as magnificent and praiseworthy efforts of one of the most gifted living orators of their race, but also on account of the testimony which they bear to the fidelity to faith, religious fervor, and national virtue exhibited by the Irish people in every vicissitude of fortune. As specimens of pulpit oratory, nothing can be imagined finer or more impressive than those discourses; while the enlightened spirit, and broad, comprehensive views characterizing the Lectures,—in which the great wants and deficiencies of society, in the present day, are analyzed with the acumen of a master-mind and the learning of a true Christian philosopher,—render them doubly valuable, even from a purely humanitarian point of view.

The secret of Father Burke's influence over his auditors, (and, indeed, over his readers, also,) lies not so much in his eloquence—great as are his natural gifts in that particular—as in the convincing force of his sincerity, and the intensity of his zeal for the enlightenment, elevation, and sanctification of all his fellow-creatures. On this point, one of the most eminent and well-known of American Catholic writers has said of the great Irish Dominican:—

"Father Thomas Burke is known all over Europe, as a great apostolic preacher. It is especially in Rome, where most of his life has been passed, that his reputation is so great. Wherever he goes, after he has preached once, the faithful flock around the pulpit and around the church, if he preaches a second time, as bees gather round a bed of jessamines. * * * What is the power by which he holds, hushed and breathless, each one in a crowded congregation; alike the most learned and critical, and the rough men with little either of sentiment or education? A natural gift of oratory no one can mistake in him. He has the richness of voice, and the persuasiveness of accent, that God has lavished so largely on his countrymen. But these are 'tricks of the tongue,' that the man of trained intellect can arm himself against, even while he admires them. But Father Burke *disarms* this trained, intellectual listener; because, in him, it is neither *trick* nor *art*. It is the *gift* God has given him, *and that he has consecrated to God!* The honey-dew that drops from his lips is distilled from a soul consecrated to God, and an intellect saturated and *steeped* in the learning and piety of the Saints and Doctors of the Church."

All the discourses given in this volume have been taken down by competent stenographers, with the utmost accuracy and fidelity, as delivered by Father Burke, and, in the course of compilation have been carefully revised, in order that they should not only be correct as to the text, but should, in every way, accord with the high reputation of the illustrious Dominican, who, as a preacher, stands to-day without a superior, and with scarce a rival.

CONTENTS.

	PAGE
THE CHRISTIAN MAN, THE MAN OF THE DAY	9
THE CATHOLIC CHURCH, THE FOSTER-MOTHER OF LIBERTY	25
THE CHURCH, THE MOTHER AND INSPIRATION OF ART	48
ST. JOHN THE EVANGELIST	70
CHRIST ON CALVARY	87
THE CATHOLIC CHURCH, THE SALVATION OF SOCIETY	110
THE RESURRECTION	133
THE CATHOLIC MISSION	145
THE CONSTITUTION OF THE CATHOLIC CHURCH	158
THE ATTRIBUTES OF CATHOLIC CHARITY	180
THE CATHOLIC CHURCH, THE TRUE EMANCIPATOR	200
THE MONTH OF MARY	219
THE POSITION AND DIGNITY OF THE MOTHER OF GOD	231
MARY, THE IMMACULATE MOTHER OF GOD	240
THE POPE'S TIARA, ITS PAST, PRESENT, AND FUTURE	250
THE IMMACULATE CONCEPTION	272
CATHOLIC EDUCATION	288
THE BLESSED EUCHARIST	306
THE DIVINE COMMISSION OF THE CHURCH	325

LECTURES AND SERMONS.

THE CHRISTIAN MAN THE MAN OF THE DAY.

[*A Discourse Delivered by the Very Rev. T. N. Burke, O.P., in St. Paul's Church, Brooklyn, March 22, 1872.*]

MY FRIENDS: I have selected, as the subject on which to address you, the following theme :—" The Christian Man the Man of the Day." You may, perhaps, be inclined to suppose that I mean by this, that, in reality, the Christian man was the actual man of the day ; that he was the man whom our age loved to honor; that he was the man who, recognized as a Christian man, received, for that very reason, the confidence of his fellow-men and every honor society could bestow upon him. Do not flatter yourselves, my friends, that this is my meaning. I do not mean to say that the Christian man *is* the man of the day. I wish I could say so. But what I do mean is, that the Christian man, and he alone, must be the man of the day ; that our age cannot live without him ; and that we are fast approaching to such a point, that the world itself will be obliged, on the principle of self-preservation, to cry out for the Christian man. But to-day he is not in the high places ; for the spirit of the age is not Christian. Now, mark you, there is no man living who is a greater lover of his age than I am : and, priest as I am, and monk as well, coming here before you in this time-honored old habit; coming before the men of the nineteenth century, as if I were a fossil dug out of the soil of the thirteenth century, I still come before you as a lover of the age in which we live, a lover of its freedom, a lover of its laws, and a lover of its material progress. But I still assert that the spirit of this nineteenth century of ours is not Catholic. Let me prove it. At this very moment, the Catholic Church, through her bishops, is engaged in a hand-to-hand and deadly conflict, in England, in Ireland, in Belgium, in France, in

Germany, aye, and in this country, with the spirit of the age; and for what? The men in power try to lay hold of the young child, to control that child's education, and to teach him all things except religion. But the bishops come and say: "This is a question of life and death, and the child must be a Christian. Unless he is taught of God, it is a thousand times better that he were never taught at all; for knowledge without God is a curse, and not a blessing." Now, if our age were Christian, would it thus seek to banish God from the schools, to erase the name of God clean out of the heart of that little one, for whom Christ, the Son of God, shed his blood?

Another proof that the spirit of our age is anti-Christian,—for whatever contradicts Christ is anti-Christian:—Speaking of the most sacred bond of matrimony, which lies at the root of all society, at the fountain-head of all the world's future, Christ has said: "What God hath joined together, let no man put asunder." But the Legislature—the "spirit of the age," as it is called—comes in and says: "I will not recognize this union as being from God: I reserve to myself the right to separate them." They have endeavored to substitute a civil marriage for the holy Sacrament which Christ sanctified by His presence, and ratified by His first miracle,—the sacrament which represents the union of Christ with His Church. "I will not let God join them together," says the State; "let them go to a magistrate or a registrar." Let God have nothing to do with it. Let no sanctifying influence be upon them; leave them to their own lustful desires, and to the full enjoyment of wicked passions, unchecked by God.

Thus the State rules, in case of marriage, and says: "I will break asunder that bond." And it made the anti-Christian law of "divorce." "Whom God joins together," says the Master of the world, whose word shall never pass away, though heaven and earth shall pass away,—"let no man separate." God alone can do it: the man who dares to do it shakes the very foundation of society, and takes the keystone out of the arch. But the State comes and says: "I will do it." This is the legislation—this is the spirit of our age. I do not mean to say that there were not sins and vices in other ages; but I have been taught, from my earliest childhood, to look back, full six hundred years, to that glorious thirteenth century, for the bloom and flower of sanctity prospering upon the earth. Still, I have been so taught as not to shut my eyes to its vices; and yet the spirit of that age was more Christian than the spirit of this. The spirit that had faith enough to declare that, whatever else was touched by profane hands, the sanctity of the marriage Sacrament was to remain inviolate; when all recognized its living author as the Son of God. It had faith enough to move all classes of men as one individual, and as possessing one faith and one lofty purpose. And this is not the spirit of our age. Whom do we hear spoken of as the men who invent and make our telegraphs and railroads, and all the great works of the day? We hear very little about Catholics being any thing generally but lookers-on in these great matters; that Catholics had nothing to do with them, and that they came in simply to profit by the labor of others. And yet do we not know that nearly every great discovery made upon this earth was made by some Catholic man or other; and some of the greatest of them all made by old monks in their cloisters? Therefore, as the spirit of the day makes the man of the day, I cannot congratulate you, my friends, that the man of the day is a Christian man.

Now, I am here this evening, to prove to you, and to bring home to your intelligence, two great facts: remember them always: First—The man the world makes independent of God, is such an incubus and curse, that the world itself cannot bear him, that the world itself cannot endure him; for, if he leaves his mark upon history, it is a curse, and for evil. Secondly—The only influence that can purify and save the world, is the spirit of that glorious religion which alone represents Christianity. Call me no bigot, if I say that the Catholic Church alone is the great representative of Christianity. I do not deny that there is goodness outside of it, nor that there are good and honest men who are not of this Church. Whenever I meet an honest, truthful man, I never stop to inquire if he is Catholic or Protestant; I am always ready to do him honor, as " the noblest work of God." But this I do say—all this is, in reality, represented in the Catholic Church. And I further assert that the Catholic Church alone has the power to preserve in man the consciousness that God has created him.

And now, having laid down my opening remarks, let us look at the man of the day, and see what he is. Many of you have the ambition to become men of the day. It is a pleasant thing to be pointed at and spoken of as a man of the day. "There is a man who has made his mark." "There is a man of whom every one speaks well; the intelligent man, the successful man, the man who is able to propound the law by expressing his opinion; able to sway the markets; the man whose name is blazoned everywhere." You all admire this man. But let us examine him in detail—for he is made for mere show, a mere *simulacrum* of a man. Let us pick him in pieces, and see what is in this man of the day; whether he will satisfy God or man; see whether he will come up to the wants of society or not.

Man, I suppose you will all admit, was created by Almighty God for certain fixed, specific purposes and duties. Surely, the God of wisdom, of infinite love,—a God of infinite knowledge and freedom,—never communicated to an intelligent human being power and knowledge like His own, without having some high, grand, magnificent, and God-like purpose in view. A certain purpose must have guided Him. Certain duties must have attached to the glorious privileges that are thus imprinted on man's soul as the image of God. And hence, my friends, there are the duties man owes to the family; the duties of the domestic circle; the duties he owes to society, to those who come within the range of his influence, and within the circle of his friendship; the duties he owes to his country and native land,—his political duties; and, finally, over them all, permeating through them all, overshadowing all that is in him, there is his great duty to Almighty God, who made him.

Now, what are man's duties in the domestic circle? Surely, the first virtue of man in this circle is the virtue of fidelity, representing the purity of Christ in the man's soul; the virtues of fidelity, stability, and immovable loyalty to the vows he has pledged before high heaven, and to all the consequences these vows have involved. God created man with a hearty disposition to love and to find the worthy object of his love; and to give to that object the love of his heart, is the ordinary nature of man. A few are put aside—among them the priest and the monk and the nun, to whom God says, "I myself will be your love:" and they know no love save that of the Lord Jesus Christ. Yet they have the same craving for love, the same desire, and the same necessity. But to them the Lord says: "I myself will be your love, your portion, your inheritance." These, I say, are those who are wrapt in the love of the Lord Jesus Christ. This is not the time nor the occasion for me to dwell upon the infinite joy and substantial happiness of the days of those who have fastened their hearts upon the great heart of Jesus Christ; but, for the ordinary run of mankind, love is a necessity; and the Almighty has created that desire for love in the hearts of all men; and it has become sanctified and typical of the union of Christ with His Church; typical of the grace that Christ poured abroad upon her: and this love must lie at the very fountain-head of society; it must sanctify the very spring whence all our human nature flows; for it is out of this union of two loving hearts that our race is propagated, and mankind continued to live on earth. What is that grace which sanctifies it? I answer, it is the grace of fidelity. Understand me well; there is nothing more erratic, nothing more changeable than this heart of man; nothing wilder in its acts, in its propensities, than this treacherous heart of man. I know of no greater venture that a human being can make than that which a young woman makes, when she takes the hand of a young man, and hears the oath from his lips that no other love than hers shall ever enter his heart. A treacherous, erratic heart is this of man; prone to change, prone to evil influences, excited by every form of passing beauty. But from that union spring the obligations of father and mother to their progeny. Their children are to be educated; and as they grow up and bloom into the fulness of their reason, the one object of the Christian father and mother is to bring out in these children the Christianity that is latent in them. Christ enters into the young soul by Baptism; but He lies sleeping in that soul, acting only upon the blind animal instincts of infancy; and, as the child wakes to reason, Christ that sleeps there must be awakened and developed, until that child comes to the fulness of his intellectual age, and the man of God is fully developed in the child of earth.

Now, how does the man of the day fulfil this end? how does he fulfil these duties to his wife and to his children, these duties which we call the domestic duties? This "clever" man of the day—how does he fulfil them? He, perhaps, in his humbler days, before he knew to what meridian the sun of his fortune would rise, took to himself a fair and modest wife. Fortune smiled upon him. The woman remained content only with her first and simple love, and with fidelity to the man of her choice, and the duties which that love brought with them. But how is it with the man of the day? Shall I insult the ears of the Christian by following the man of the day through all the dark paths of his iniquity? Shall I describe to you the glance of his lustful eye, forgetful of the vows he has made to the one at home? Can I tell you of the man of the day, following every passing form,—a mere lover of beauty; without principle, without God, without virtue, and without a thought of the breaking hearts at home? Shall I tell you of the man of the day trying to conceal the silvering hand of age as it passes over him, trying to retain the shadow of departed youth—and why? Because all the worst vices of the young blood are there, for they are inseparable from the man of the day. Sometimes, in some fearful example, he comes out before us in all his terrible deformity. The world is astonished—the world is frightened for a moment; but men who understand all these things, better than you or I, come to us, and say: "Oh! this is what is going on; this is the order of the day." There is no vestige of purity, no vestige of fidelity. Mind and imagination corrupted; the very flesh rotting, defiled by excess of unmentionable sin. Children are brought forth to him in all innocence, in all the magnificence of God-like purity: but the time comes when the State assumes that which neither God nor man ever intended it should assume—namely, the office of instructor; when the State comes and says: "I will take the children; I will teach them every thing excepting God; I will bring them up clever men, but infidels, without the knowledge of God." Then the man of the day turns round to the State, and says, "Take the labor off our hands; these children are incumbrances; we don't want to educate them: you say you will." But the Church comes in, like a true mother,—like the mother of the days of Solomon; and, with heartbreaking accents, says to the father, "Give me the child; for it was to me that Christ said: 'Go and teach; go and educate.'" But the father turns away. He will not trust his child to that instructor who will bring up this child as a rebuke to him in his old age for his wickedness, by its own virtue and goodness. The "spirit of the age" not only tolerates this, but actually assists all this. This man may tell his wife that she is not the undisturbed mistress of her house. He may come in with a writing of "divorce" in his hand, and turn his wife out of doors. Yes; when her beauty and accomplishments are not up to the fastidious taste of this man of the day, he may call in the State to make a decree of "divorce," and depose the mother of his children, the queen of his heart.

Let us now pass from the domestic to the social circle. He is surrounded by his friends and has social influence. He has a duty, to lay at least one stone in the building up of that society of which the Almighty created him a member, and of which He will demand an account in the hour of death. Every man is a living member of society. He owes a duty to that society. What is that duty? It is a duty of truthfulness to our friends, a good example to those around us, a respect and veneration for every one, old and young, with whom we come in contact. Even the pagans acknowledge this in the maxim, "*Maxima debetur puero reverentia.*" The man of the day opens his mouth to vomit forth words of blasphemy, or sickening obscenity; and before him may be the young boy, growing into manhood, learning studiously, from the accomplished jester's lips, the lesson of iniquity and impurity that will ruin his soul. Hear him, and follow him into more refined and general society. What a consummate hypocrite he is, when he enters his own house, dressed for the evening! With a smile upon his face, and with words of affection upon his adulterous lips, he addresses himself to his wife, or to his daughter, or to his lady friends. What a consummate hypocrite he is! Ah! who would imagine that he knows every mystery of iniquity and defilement, even to its lowest depths! Who would imagine that this smiling face has learned the smile of contempt for every thing that savors of virtue, of purity, and of God! Who would imagine that the man who takes the virgin hand of the young girl in his, and leads her with so much confidence and so much gladness to the altar,— who would imagine that that man's hand is defiled by contact with every thing abominable that the demon of impurity could present to him? Take him in his relations with his friends. Is he a trustworthy friend? Is he a reliable man? Will he not slip the wicked publication into the hands of his young friend, to instruct him in vice? Will he not pass the obscene book from hand to hand, with a pleasant look, as though it were a good thing, although he knows the poison of hell is lurking between its leaves? Is he a reliable man? Is he trustworthy? Go and ask his friends will they trust him; and they will turn and laugh in your face, and tell you he is as "slippery as an eel."

This is the man of the day,—this boasted hero of ours,—in a social way. Pass a step farther on. Take him in his relations to his country, to its legislature, to its government. Take him in what they call the political relations of life. What shall I say of him? I can simply put it all in a nut-shell. I ask you, my friends, in this our day, suppose somebody were to ask you to say a good word for him, as for a friend; suppose somebody were to ask you the character of the man; and suppose you said: "Well, he is an honest man; a man of upright character in business; a man of well-ascertained character in society; a good father, a good husband,—but, you know—he is a politician;"—I ask you, is there not something humiliating in the acknowledgment, —"he is a politician?" Is it not almost as if you said something dishonorable, something bad? But there ought to be nothing dishonorable in it. On the contrary, every man ought to be a politician,—especially in this glorious new country, which gives every man a right of citizenship, and tells him: "My friend, I will not make a law to bind and govern you without your consent and permission;"—why, that very fact makes every man a politician among us. But if it does, does it not also recognize the grand virtue which underlies every free government; which makes every man a sharer in its blessings, because he enhances them by his integrity; which makes politics not a shame and a disgrace, but something to be honored and prized as the aim of unselfish patriotism? What is that? It is a love, but not a selfish love, of one's country; a love, not seeking to control or share its administration for selfish purposes—not to become rich—not to share in this, or take that—but to serve the country for its good, and to leave an honorable and unblemished name in the annals of that country's history. Is this the man of the day? I will not answer the question. I am a stranger amongst you; and it would be a great presumption in me to enter upon a dissertation on the politics of America. But this I do know, that, if the politicians of this country are as bad, or half as bad as their own newspapers represent them, it is no credit to a man to be a politician. Some time ago a fellow was arrested in France for having committed a robbery. He was taken before a magistrate and jury, and the prosecuting officer said: "The crime of the man indicted before you is this: That on such a night he went to such a house for the purpose of robbery." "Yes," said he, "it is so; but remember, there is an extenuating circumstance." "What is it?" "I am no Jesuit." "Did you rob the house?" "Yes, I did." "Did you rob the house and set fire to it?" "Yes, I did; but, thank God, I am no Jesuit." This man had been reading the French infidel newspapers; and he selected a priest as something worse than himself. Bad as he was, in order to make it appear that there was something still worse, it was necessary to say, "he was not a Jesuit." So if a man were arraigned for any conceivable crime, he might urge, as an extenuating circumstance, "It is true; I did it; but I am no politician!" Thank God, there are many and honorable exceptions. If there were not many honorable exceptions, what would become of society? Why, society itself would come to a standstill. But there are honest and independent men, and no word of mine can be regarded as, in the slightest degree, reflecting on any man, or class of men. True, I know no one: I speak simply as a stranger coming amongst you, and from simply reading the accounts that your daily papers give.

Now, I ask you, if the man of the age, or the day, be such—and I do not think that I have overdrawn the picture; nay more, I am convinced that, in the words I have used, you have recognized the truth, perhaps something less than the whole truth, of "the man of the day" in his social, political, and domestic relations—I ask you—not as a Catholic priest at all, but as a man—as a man not without some amount of intelligence—as one speaking to his fellow-men, as intellectual men—can this thing go on? Should this go on? Are you in society prepared to accept that man as a true man of the day? Are you prepared to multiply him as the model man? Are you prepared to say: "We are satisfied; he comes up to the requirements of our mark?" Or, on the other hand, must you say this: "It will never do: if this be the man of the day there is an end to society; if this be the man of the day, it will never do; we must seek another style—another stamp of man, with other principles of conduct, or else society comes to a deadlock and standstill?" And to those two propositions I will invite your attention.

Go back three hundred years ago. When Martin Luther inaugurated Protestantism, one of the principles upon which he rested his fallacy was to separate the Church from all influence upon human affairs. His tenets said: "Let her teach religion, but let her not be mixing herself up with this question or that." The Church of God, my dear friends, not only holds and is the full deposit of truth, not only preaches it, not only pours forth her sacramental graces, but the Church—the Catholic Church—mixes herself up with the thousand questions of the day—not as guiding them, not as dictating or identifying herself with this policy or that, but as simply coming in to declare, in every walk of life, certain principles and rules of conduct. Here let me advert to the false principle that, outside of the four walls of her temples, she has nothing to do with man's daily work. This principle was followed out in France in 1792-3, when not only was the Church separated from all legitimate influence in society, but she was completely deposed for the time being. And now, the favorite expression of this day of our is: "Oh, let the Catholic priests preach until they are hoarse; let them fire away until they are black in the face; but let us have no Catholicity here, Catholicity there, the priest everywhere! We will not submit to it; like the Irish, getting the priest into every social relation; taking his advice in every thing; acting under his counsel in every thing. We will not submit to be a priest-ridden people. We will not submit to have the priest near us at all, outside of his church. If he stays there, well and good: if not, every one can do as he likes." For the last century all the Catholic nations of Europe—in fact, the whole world—have, more or less, acted upon this principle. Let us see the advantage of all this. Have the world, society, governments, legislatures, gained by it? To the Church they say: "Stand aside; don't presume to come into the Senate or the Parliament. We will make laws without you. Don't be preaching to me about God; I can get along without you." The world has "got along" for some hundreds of years; and it has produced only that beautiful man I have described to you—the man of the day—the accomplished man—the gentleman—the man in kid gloves—the man who is well dressed—

the man with the gemmed watch and gold chain—the man with the lacquered hair and well-trimmed whisker. Do not trust his word—he is a liar! Do not trust him. Oh, fathers, oh, children, do not have any thing to say to him! He is a bad man. Keep away from him. Close the doors of your government-house—of your House of Representatives—against him. This is the man whom the Church knows not as of her; whom the world and whom society have to fear. If this is the best thing that the world has created, surely it ought to be proud of its offspring! Society lives and can only live upon the purity that pervades the domestic circle and sanctifies it; upon the truthfulness and integrity that guard all the social relations of life and sanctify them; and upon the pure and disinterested love of country upon which alone true patriotism depends. Stand aside, man of the day! You are unfit for these things. Stand aside, *O simulacrum!* O counterfeit of man, stand aside! Thou art not fit to encumber this earth. Where is the truthfulness of thy intellect, thou scoffer at all religion? Where is the purity of thy heart, thou faithless husband? Where is the honesty of thy life, thou pilfering politician? Stand aside! If we have nothing better than you, we must come to ruin. Stand forth, O Christian man, and let us see what we can make of thee! Hast thou principles, O Christian man? He advances, and says: "My first principle is this: that the Almighty God created me responsible for every wilful thought, and word, and act of my life. I believe in that responsibility before God. I believe that these thoughts, and words, and acts shall be my blessedness or my damnation for eternity." These are the first principles of the Christian man. Give me a man that binds up eternity with his thoughts, and his words, and his acts of to-day: I warrant you he will be very careful how he thinks, how he speaks, and how he acts. I will trust that man, because he does not love honesty for the sake of man, but for the love of his own soul; not for the love of the world, but for the love of God. Stand forth, O Christian man, and tell us what are thy principles in thy domestic relations, which, as father and husband, thou hast assumed. He comes forth and says: "I believe,—and I believe it on the peril of my eternal salvation,—that I must be as true in my thought and in my act to the woman whom I made my wife, as you, a priest, are to the altar of Christ. I believe that, as long as the Angel of Death comes not between me and that woman, **she is** to be the queen of my heart, the mother and mistress of my household; **and that no power,** save the hand of God, can separate us, or break **the tie that binds us."**

Well said, thou faithful **Christian man! Well** said! Tell us about thy **relations to thy children.** The Christian man answers and says: "I believe and I know that, if one of these children **rises up in judgment** against me, and cries out **neglect and bad education and bad** example against me, that that alone will weigh me down and cast me into hell for ever." Well said, **O Christian father!** You are the man of the day so far. With you the domestic hearth and circle will remain holy. When your shadow, after your **day's** labor, falls across your humble threshold, it is the **shadow of a man** loving the God of all **fidelity, and of all** sanctity, in his soul. What are your relations to your friends, O Christian man? He answers: "I love my friend in Christ, my **Lord**; I believe that when I **speak of** my friend, or of my fellow-man, every word I utter goes forth into eternity, there to be registered for or against me, as true or false. I believe that when my friend, or neighbor, and fellow-man, is in **want or** in misery, and that he sends forth the cry for consolation or for relief, I am bound to console him, or to relieve him, as if I saw my Lord himself lying prostrate and helpless before me." Who are thy enemies, O man of faith? He answers: "Enemies I have none." Do you not hold him as an enemy who harms you? "No, I see him in my own sin, and in the bleeding hands and open side of my Saviour; and whatever I see there I must love in spite of all injustice." What are your political relations? He answers and says: "If any one says of another, he is a man who fattened upon corruption, no man can say so of me. I entered into the arena of my country's service, and came forth with unstained hands. Whatever I have done, I have done for love of my country; because my country holds upon me the strongest and highest claims, after those of God." Heart and mind are there. Oh, how grand is the character that is thus built upon Faith and Love! How grand is this man, so faithful at home, so truthful abroad, so irreproachable in the **senate or the forum! Where shall we find him?** I answer, the Catholic Church alone can produce him. This is a bold assertion. I do not deny that he **may exist** outside the Catholic Church; but if he does it is as an exception; and the exception only proves the rule. I do not deny much of what I have said, if not all, to that glorious name that shall live for ever as the very type of patriotism, and honor, and virtue, and truth,—the grand, the majestic, the immortal name of George Washington, the Father of his country. But, just as a man may find a rare and beautiful flower, even in the field, or by the roadside, and he is surprised and says, " How came it to be here? How came it to grow here?" when he goes into the garden, the cultivated spot, he finds it as a matter of course, because the soil was prepared for it, and the seed was sown. There is no surprise, no astonishment, to find the man of whom I speak—the Christian man—in the Catholic Church. If you want to find him, as a matter of course—if you want to find the agencies that produce him—if you want to find the soil he must grow in, if he grows at all, you must go into the Catholic Church, decidedly. Nowhere out of the Catholic Church is the bond of matrimony indissoluble. In the Catholic Church, the greatest ruffian, the most depraved man that ever lived, the most faithless woman that ever cursed the world, if they are faithless to every thing, they must remain joined by the adamantine bonds that the Church will not allow any man to break.

Secondly, the only security you have for all I have spoken of as enriching man in his social and political relations, is in conscience. If a man has no conscience, he can have no truth: he loses his power of discerning the difference between truth and falsehood. If a man has no conscience, he loses all knowledge and all sense of sin. If a man has no conscience, he loses by degrees even the very abstract faith that there is for good in him. Conscience is a most precious gift of God; but, like every other faculty in the soul of man, unless it be exercised, it dies out. The conscience of man must be made a living tribunal within him, and he must bring his own soul and his own life before that tribunal. A man may kneel down and pray to God; he may listen to the voice of the preacher attentively, seriously; but in the Catholic Church alone there is one Sacrament, and that Sacrament the most frequent, and the most necessary, after Baptism,—and that is the Sacrament of Penance; the going to confession; an obligation imposed under pain of mortal sin, and of essential need to every Catholic at stated times: an obligation that no Catholic can shrink from without covering himself with sin. This is at once a guarantee for the existence of a conscience in a man, and a restraining power, which is the very test, and the crucial test, of a man's life. A Catholic may sin, like other men; he may be false in every relation of life; he may be false in the domestic circle; he may be false socially; he may be false politically; but one thing you may be sure of,—that he either does not go to confession at all, or, if he goes to confession, and comes to the holy altar, there is an end to his falsehood, there is an end to his sin; and the whole world around him, in the social circle, the domestic circle, the political circle, receives an absolute guarantee, an absolute proof, that that man must be all that I have described the Christian man to be,—a man in whom every one, in every relation of life, may trust and confide. This is the test. Do not speak to me of Catholics who do not give us this test. When a Catholic does not go to the Sacraments, I could no more trust in him than in any other man. I say to you, do not talk to me about Catholics who do not go to the Sacraments. I have nothing to say of them, only to pray for them, to preach to them, and to beseech them to come to this holy Sacrament, where they will find grace to enable them to live up to the principles which they had forsaken. But give me the practical, intellectual Catholic man, the man of faith: give me the man of human power and intelligence, and the higher power, divine principle, and divine love. With that man, as with the lever of Archimedes, I will move the world.

Let me speak to you, in conclusion, of such a man. Let me speak to you of one whose form, as I beheld it in early youth, now looms up before me; so fills, in imagination, the halls of my memory, that I behold him now as I beheld him years ago; majestic in stature, an eye gleaming with intellectual power, a mighty hand uplifted, waving, quivering with honest indignation; his voice thundering like the voice of a god in the tempest, against all injustice and all dishonor. I speak of Ireland's greatest son, the immortal Daniel O'Connell. He came, and found a nation the most faithful, the most generous on the face of the earth; he found a people not deficient in any power of human intelligence or human courage; chaste in their domestic relations, reliable to each other, and truthful;

and, above all, a people who, for centuries and centuries, had
lived, and died, and suffered to uphold the faith and the
Cross. He came, and he found that people, after the rebellion of '98, down-trodden in the blood-stained dust, and
bound in chains. The voice of Ireland was silent. The
heart of the nation was broken. Every privilege, civil and
otherwise, was taken from them. They were commanded, as
the only condition of the toleration of their existence, to lie
down in their blood-stained fetters of slavery, and to be grateful to the hand that only left them life. He brought to that
prostrate people a Christian spirit and a Christian soul. He
brought his mighty faith in God and in God's holy Church.
He brought his great human faith in the power of justice,
and in the omnipotence of right. He roused the people from
their lethargy. He sent the cry for justice throughout the
land, and he proved his own sincerity to Ireland and to her
cause, by laying down an income of sixty thousand pounds a
year, that he might enter into her service. He showed the
people the true secret of their strength himself. One day
thundering for justice in the halls of the English Senate, on
the morrow morning he was seen in the confessional, and
kneeling at the altar to receive his God: with one hand
leaning upon the eternal cause of God's justice; with the other
leaning upon the Lord Jesus Christ. Upheld by these and
by the power of his own genius, he left his mark upon his
age: he left his mark upon his country. This was, indeed,
the "Man of his Day!" the Christian man, of whom the
world stood in awe—faithful as a husband and father; faithful as a friend; the delight of all who knew him; faithful in his disinterested labors; with an honorable, honest
spirit of self-devotion in his country's cause! He raised that
prostrate form, he struck the chains from those virgin arms,
and placed upon her head a crown of free worship and
free education. He made Ireland to be, in a great measure,
what he always prayed and hoped she might be, "The
Queen of the Western Isles, and the proudest gem that
the Atlantic bears upon the surface of its green waters."
Oh, if there were a few more like him! Oh, that our race
would produce a few more like him! Our O'Connell was
Irish of the Irish, and Catholic of the Catholic. We are
Irish and we are Catholic. How is it we have not more
men like him? Is the stamina wanting to us? Is the

intellect wanting to us? Is the power of united expression in the interests of society wanting to us? No. But the religious Irishman of our day refuses to be educated; and the educated Irishman of to-day refuses to be religious. These two must go hand in hand. Unite the highest education with the deepest and tenderest practical love of God and of your religion, and I see before me, in many of the young faces on which I look, the stamp of our Irish genius. I see before me many who may be the fathers and legislators of the Republic, the leaders of our race, and the heroes of our common country and our common religion.

THE CATHOLIC CHURCH THE FOSTER-MOTHER OF LIBERTY.

[*A Lecture delivered by the Very Rev. T. N. Burke, O.P., in St. Paul's Church, Brooklyn, March 3, 1872.*]

MY FRIENDS: On last Tuesday evening, when I had the honor of addressing you, I proposed to you a subject for your consideration which, perhaps, may have struck a good many among you as strange. We are such worshippers of this age of ours, that when the "man of the day," as he is called, is put before us in any other than an amiable light, no matter how true it may be, it seems strange. It is a hazardous thing for me to attempt;—and there are many among you that will consider the thing I have undertaken to do this evening a still more hazardous attempt—namely, to prove to you that the Catholic Church is the foster-mother of human liberty. Was there ever so strange a proposition heard?— the Catholic Church the mother of human liberty! If I undertook to prove that the Catholic Church was the instrument chosen by Almighty God to save Christianity, I might do it on the testimony of Protestant historians. I might quote, for instance, Guizot, the French statesman and historian, who repeatedly and emphatically asserts that only for the organization of bishops, priests, monks, etc.,—what is called "the Church,"—the Christian religion would never have been preserved; never have been able to sustain the shock of the incursions of the barbarians of the North upon the Roman Empire; and never have been preserved through the following ages of confusion, and, some people say, of darkness. I could quote the great German historian, Neander, who was not only a Protestant, but bitterly opposed to the Catholic Church, and who repeats, again and again, the self-same proposition: "Were it not," he says, "for the Church, the Christian religion must have perished during the time that elapsed between the fifth and the tenth centuries." I might, I say again, find it easy to prove any one of these propositions, with less fear of cavil. Ah, but this is quite another thing, you will say in your own minds! This man tells us that he is prepared to prove that the Catholic Church is the foster-mother of human liberty. Why, the "man of the day," whom we were considering on a previous evening, is not a very amiable character. He has a great many vices; there are a great many moral deformities about him—this boasted man of the nineteenth century. But there is one thing that he lays claim to: he says,—and he claims that it is something which no man can gainsay,—that he is a freeman; that he is not like those men who lived in the ages when the Catholic Church had power, when she was enabled to enforce her laws. "Then, indeed," he says, "men were slaves; but now, whatever our faults may be, we have freedom. Nay, more," he will add, "we have freedom in spite of the Catholic Church. We are free because we have succeeded in disarming the Catholic Church; in taking the power out of her hands. We are free because our legislation and the spirit of our age is hostile to the Catholic Church. How then, Monk, do you presume to come here and tell us, the men of the day, that this Church of yours—this Church whose very name we associate with the idea of intellectual slavery—that she is the foster-mother of human liberty?"

Well, I need not tell you, my friends, that there is nothing easier than to make assertions; that there is nothing easier than to proclaim such and such things; lay them down as if they were the law; tumble it out as if it was gospel. It may be a lie. Out with it. Assert it strongly. Repeat it. Do not let it be put down. Assert it again and again. Even though it be a lie, a great many people will believe it. Nothing is easier than to make assertions without thinking well on what we say. Now, let me ask you this evening to do what very few men in this age of ours do at all; and that is, to reflect a little. It is simply astonishing, considering the powers that God has given to man,—the power of thought, the power of reflection, the power of analyzing facts and weighing statements, the power of reducing things to their first principles, —I say it is astonishing to think of that and to look around us and see how few the men are who reason at all,—who reflect, —who take time for thought; how many there are who use words of which they do not know the meaning. Take, for instance, that word "liberty." I need hardly tell you that I must explain it to you before I advance the proposition that the Catholic Church is the mother of liberty.

What is the meaning of the word "liberty,"—so dear to us all? We are always boasting of it; the patriot is always aspiring to it; the revolutionist makes it justify all his wiles and all his conspiracies. It is the word that floats upon the folds of the nation's banners, as they are flung out upon the breeze over the soldier's head; and he is cheered in his last moments by the sacred sound of liberty! It is a word dear to us all,—the boast of all of us. What is the boast of America? That it is the Land of Freedom. Yes; but I ask you, do you know what it means? Liberty! Just reflect upon it a little. Does liberty mean freedom from restraint? Does liberty, in your mind, mean freedom from any power, government, or restraint of legislation? Is this your meaning of liberty? For instance: Is this your meaning of liberty—that every man can do what he likes? If so, you cannot complain if you are stopped by the robber on the roadside, and he puts his pistol to your head and says: "Your money or your life!" You cannot complain; he is only using his liberty in doing what he likes. Does liberty mean that the murderer may come and put his knife into you? Does liberty mean that the dishonest man is to be allowed to pilfer? Is this liberty? This is freedom from restraint. But is it liberty? Most certainly not. You will not consider that you are slaves because you live under laws that tell you that you must not steal; that you must not murder; that you must not interfere with or violate each other's rights; but that you must respect those of each other; and if you do not do that, you must be punished. You do not consider you are slaves because you are under the restraint of law. Whatever liberty means, therefore, it does not, in its true meaning, imply simple and mere freedom from restraint. Yet, how many there are who use this word, and who attach this meaning to it. What is liberty? There are in man—in the soul of man—two great powers,—God-like, angelic, spiritual,—viz.: the intelligence of the mind and the will. The intelligence of the human mind, the soul, and the will are the true fountains and the seat of liberty. What is the freedom of the intelligence? What is the freedom of the will? There are no other powers in man capable of this freedom except these two. If you ask me in what does the freedom of the intelligence and of the will of man consist, I answer: The freedom of the intellect consists in being free from error,—from intellectual error. The freedom of man's intelligence consists in its being perfectly free from the danger and liability of believing that which is false. The slavery of the intelligence in man is submission in mind and in belief to that which is a lie. If, for instance, I came here this evening, and if, by the power of language, by plausibility of words, by persuasiveness, I got any man among you to believe a lie, and take that lie as truth and admit it into his mind as truth, and admit it as a principle that is right, and just, and true, when it is false, and unjust, and a lie,—that man is intellectually a slave. Falsehood is the slavery of the intelligence.

Reflect a little upon this. It is well worth reflecting upon. It is a truth that is not grasped or held by the men of this century of ours. There was a time when it was considered a disreputable thing to believe a lie. There was a time when men were ashamed of believing what, even by possibility, could be a lie. Nowadays, men glory in it. It was but a short time ago a popular orator and lecturer in England referred to the multitude of religions sects that are there— of those people who assert that Christ is God, and of those who assert that He is not God; of those who assert that there are three persons in the Trinity, and of those who assert that there is no Trinity—the Unitarians; of those who assert that good works are necessary for salvation, and of those who assert that good works are not necessary at all; of those who assert that Christ is present on the altar, and of those who say it is damnable heresy to assert that He is there at all;—speaking of all these,—how, we ask, can any one of them be true and all the rest not be false? This lecturer said: "The multitude of sects and churches in England is the glory of our age and of our people; for it shows what a religious people we are." My God! A man believes a lie; a man takes a lie to him as if it were the truth of God; a man takes an intellectual falsehood—a thing that is false in itself—a thing that has no real existence in fact—a thing that God never said, and never thought of saying; and he lays that religious lie upon the altar of his soul, and he bows down and does homage to it as if it were the truth! And then he says: "It may be a lie! but you know it is a religious lie; and it is so respectable and religious to have a multitude of sects; and it shows what a good people we are!" This is our age. The very definition of the intellectual freedom of man, which I am about to give you, I take from the highest authority. I will not quote for you, my friends, the words of man; but I will quote to you the Word of God—of God himself—who ought to know best; of God himself, who made man and gave him his intelligence and his freedom—of God himself, who has declared that the freedom of the human intellect lies in the possession of the truth—the knowledge of the truth—the grasping of the truth—the exclusion, by that very fact, of all error. Christ, our Lord, said:—"You shall know the truth and the truth shall make you free." You shall know the truth, and, in the knowledge of that truth, will lie your freedom. Mind you, He did not say: "I will send you groping after the truth." No! But you shall know it—you shall have it—no doubt about it! He did not say: "Here is a book; here is My word; take it and look for the truth in it, and if you happen to find it, well and good; if not, you are still a religious man!" He did not say: "Your duty is to seek for the truth, to look for it;" no, but He said: "You shall have it, and you shall know it; and that shall make your freedom; the truth shall make you free!" I lay it down, therefore, as a first principle, that the very definition of intellectual freedom lies in the possession of the truth.

Now, my friends, before I go any further, I may as well at once come home to my subject, and that is, that the Catholic Church alone is the foster-mother of intellectual freedom. Afterwards we will come to the freedom of the will. We will ask what it is, and apply the same principles in answering it. There is in the Catholic Church a power which she has always exercised; and, strange to say, it is the very exercise of that power which forms the world's chief accusation against her. And that is, the power of defining, as articles of faith and dogma—as what we are to believe beyond all doubt, all cavil, beyond all speculation, what she holds and knows to be true. There is this distinguishing feature between the Catholic Church and all sects that call themselves religions,—that she always speaks clearly. Every child that belongs to her, every man that hears her voice, knows precisely what to believe, knows precisely what the Church teaches. Never does she leave a soul in doubt. What can be more striking than the contrast which Protestantism presents to the Catholic Church in this respect,—its leaders lost in utter perplexity, not knowing what to say. Some time ago a deputation of clergymen of the Church of England waited upon the Archbishop of Canterbury, and propounded a very simple question, indeed, to him: viz.,— Whether the Protestant Church allowed its ministers, or taught them, to preach their sermons, with surplices on, or without. Well, there was not much in that: about half a yard of calico was all of it; the most of it was not as much as would make a surplice for a little boy. They came and asked the Archbishop if he would kindly tell them what was the discipline of the Church. The Archbishop knew and remembered very well that there was a party in England that could not bear to see a surplice on a clergyman. The very sight of such a thing is like the shaking of a red rag before a bull: it makes them mad. It is a singular thing. Now, when you come in here to your devotions, you do not mind much whether the alb the priest wears be a long one or a short one; whether the surplice be plain or embroidered; or whether the fringes of the lace are long or short. But, in the Protestant Church, in England, if a minister goes up before a certain congregation with a surplice on, one-half of them stand up and walk out of the house. The Archbishop knew this; he also knew that there is a strong party in the Protestant Church who not only favor surplices, but would like to see all kinds of vestments worn. Mournfully he turns round, and what is the answer that he gives? He answers them as if he had nothing to say, as if there was nothing in it. What was the answer his Grace of Canterbury gave? What answer do you suppose he gave them? He rubbed his hands—(I don't know whether he took a pinch of snuff or not)—but he rubbed his hands and said: "It was—a—really—a—a—a—very—serious question; that we lived in times when the Church uses a caution and prudence that was most admirable and most necessary;—that the fact of it is, that those who wear surplices in performing the functions of the Church,—that, no doubt, they were actuated by the purest of motives and the best of feelings; that he honored them; and that, in fact, he felt that, according to circumstances, the surplice might be worn; and that when a man had it on him—why—he had it on him! There was no mistake about it. Then, that there were others who did not wear surplices—and, of course, as to those who did not wear them—why, they were not in the habit of putting them on; and that, really, he must say that, on this question, the discipline of the Church was such that it was very hard precisely to say whether the wearing of a surplice, or the not wearing of a surplice, was precisely the most convenient;" and, to use a vulgar phrase, he bamboozled them.—and, under Heaven, they did not know what he meant. One minute he told them it was right; the next minute he told them it might be wrong. And that on the mere question of a surplice! The Catholic Church comes out on a question affecting the existence of God; Heaven; the Revelation of Scripture; the Divinity of Jesus Christ. It is a question affecting an article of faith. She gives to the Church, on this or that article of faith, language as clear as a bell—language so clear and decided that every child may know what God has revealed; that this is what God teaches;—that this is the truth. But the "Man of the Day" says: "What right has the Church to impose this on you? Are you not a slave to believe it?" I answer at once: "If it be a lie, you are a slave to believe it. If it be not a lie, but the truth,—in the very belief of it, then,—in the knowledge of it lies your freedom, according to the words of Christ: 'You shall know the truth, and the truth shall make you free.'"

The whole question hinges upon this: Has the Church the power and the authority to teach you what is the truth? She at once falls back upon the Scriptures and lays her hand upon the words of Jesus Christ, saying—"Go and teach all nations; teach them all truth; I will send the Spirit of truth upon you to abide with you, and I Myself will be with you all days to the end of the world; and the gates of hell,—that is to say, the spirit of error,—shall never, never, never prevail against My Church!" If that be true, the whole question is settled. If that word be true—if Jesus Christ be the God of truth, as we know Him to be, then the whole controversy is at an end. He commands us to hear the Church, to accept her teachings, to grasp them, being the truth, with our minds as though we heard them immediately from the lips of our Lord God Himself—who is the very quintessence of truth and of intellectual freedom—for intellectual freedom lies in a knowledge of the truth. And now, let me give you a familiar proof of this. Let me suppose, now, that instead of being what I am—a Catholic priest and a monk—that I was—(God between us and harm!)—a Methodist, a Presbyterian, or that I was a Baptist, an Anabaptist, or any thing of that kind, or a Quaker, or a Shaker, or any thing that you like. And suppose that I came here, a man of a certain amount of intellect and originality, and that I had taken up, or that I had dreamt, last night, some crooked view of the Scriptures, and that I said in my own mind: "Well, perhaps, after all, Christ did not die on the cross; perhaps that was one of those fictions that we find in history;" and that I then came up here, on this altar, and put that lie plausibly,—perhaps dogmatically,—and told you how many other lies were thus told,—how this thing thus said was proved to be false, and that that thing thus said was proved to be false;—and that then I said to you: "What evidence have we of the crucifixion of our Lord but historical evidence? Perhaps, after all, it was only a myth?" When we look into ourselves, and see how much there is in us of evil and how little of good, and then think of Christ coming to die for us and save us!—indeed, they say, there is a question whether He came at all or not. If I were only to put that question plausibly to you, what is to hinder me from deceiving you? What is to hinder me, if I am able to do it eloquently and forcibly? What is to save some of you from being imposed upon, and some of you from believing me? You are at my mercy. So far as I can raise a doubt in your minds, I can put an intellectual chain upon you. You are at my mercy; and I am at the mercy of my own idle dreams. Well, let us take things as they are. I came here as a Catholic priest to you, who are Catholics. If I were here, this evening, to breathe one breath—one word—against the real presence of our Lord,—or against the infallibility of the Pope,—or against the indefectibility of the Church,—or against the power of the priest to absolve from sin,—or any other doctrine of the Catholic Church;—if I was just to approach it with the faintest touch;—is there a man among you—is there one in this Church—who would not rise up and say: "You lie! You are a heretic! You are a false teacher! You are a heathen and an infidel!" If I dared to do it, could I have the slightest influence on any one of you? No. And why? Because you know the truth. Why? Because the Church of God has thrown the shield of dogma between you and every false teacher—between you and every one who would try to make you believe a lie. Is not this freedom?

Some time ago, a poor man from the county of Galway—my own county—went over to England, to earn the rent by reaping the harvest. He went down into the southwest of England—into Gloucestershire. And, now, you must know that the Protestants of that part of England are what they call "Puseyites,"—men who are fond of being as like Catholics as possible, without being actually Catholics. And so this poor fellow went in one Sunday morning;—to be sure, it was a very strange place in which he found himself;—but he heard the bells ring; he walked along; he saw a cross; he saw, as he supposed, a church; he went in, and (sure enough) saw a cross, found an altar, and the candles on it; and three men—young men—attending, if you please, on the altar. There were a priest, and his deacon, and sub-deacon, and a congregation—all kneeling down as the service went on; and he thought he was all right. He knelt down, blessed himself, and every thing went on smoothly, to all appearance; and the mock Mass went on until the time came for the priest to preach, and the deacons and sub-deacons sat down in their chairs. The priest took off his vestments and laid aside his stole. He then blessed himself. There were many distinguished personages there—all Protestants. In his beautiful sermon he called the Blessed Virgin Mary, the mother of God. All this time the poor Galway man was beating his breast. Every thing went off delightfully until the man came to talk to the people that were coming in: "Now," said he, "some of you, my dear brethren,"—(he was an elegant English Protestant, highly educated)—"Now, my dearly beloved brethren," said he, "some among you, no doubt, are going to approach the holy communion;—of course, I do not wish to force my opinion upon you;—but you must remember that faith is required, and I humbly hope that as many of you as go to the altar will believe that you are about really to receive the Lord. I do not want to say, for an instant, that this is absolutely necessary, or that I put it upon you under the awful penalty of excommunication; but still I hope you will approach it in the right faith." "God bless my soul!" said the poor Galway man; "this is too bad! I have never seen the like of this before!" So he stoops down, takes up his hat, and goes for the door; for, as soon as he heard the hesitating, faltering, almost apologetic assertion of the preacher, he at once understood that he was in a Protestant and not in a Catholic Church. When he was telling it to me, he said: "Why, your reverence, it was only when he got to the end of the sermon that he let the cat out of the bag!" Now, I ask you who was the free man in that church? Was it not the man whose intelligence, humble as he was, uneducated as he was in worldly learning—but with the knowledge of the Catholic Church in his soul—was it not he whose intelligence instantly rose up, rejected the false doctrine, and shook off the slavery of the lie?

Need I say any more? Before I end, I will come to vindicate the Church, my mother, as is my duty, from any charge of ever fostering slavery, or of ever riveting one fetter upon the intelligence of man. But I think I have so far sufficiently brought it home to the intellect of every one among you that, if the knowledge of the truth, the possession of the truth, the grasping of the truth, creates freedom of the intellect, according to the definition of it by the word of our Lord and Saviour, Jesus Christ,—that man alone can have that freedom who receives the truth knowing it to be the truth, from the mouth of one whom Christ, the Son of God, declares to be incapable of teaching man a lie!

But now we pass to the second great stronghold of freedom or of slavery in the soul of man; and that is, the will. For you know that, strictly speaking, the will of man—that free will that God gives us - is really and truly the subject-matter either of freedom or of slavery. If a man has the freedom of his will, he is free; if a man's will is coerced, he is a slave. I grant you that. But when is that will coerced? What is the definition of the word "freedom," so far as it touches human will? I answer at once, and define the freedom of the human will to be, on the one side, obedience to recognized and just law, and, on the other side, freedom from over-ruling or coercive action of any authority, or of any power that is not legitimately appointed to govern and rule the will. We are slaves, if we are bound to observe laws that are, in themselves, unjust,—laws that involve an immoral act; and no man but a slave is bound to obey them. Thus, for instance, if the law of the land tells me that what I have heard from any one of my Catholic children in the confessional, I am to go and make a deposition of it, that is, to use it as evidence against him—if the law said that—(and the law has sometimes said it)—the Catholic priest knows, and every Catholic knows, that the observance of that law would make a slave of the priest—it would destroy his over-ruling conscience that dictates to his will; —so that if he observed that law he would be a slave; but if he died rather than observe it, he would be a martyr and an apostle of freedom.

Secondly, the freedom of the will lies in being free from every influence, from every coercing power that has no right or title whatever to command our wills. Who has a right to command the will of man? Almighty God, who made it. Every human law that tells us, do this or do that, has authority only inasmuch as it is the echo of the eternal voice, commanding or prohibiting. I will only obey the law because St. Paul tells us, "the law comes from on high"— that all power, all law, comes from Almighty God. Any other power that is opposed to God, any other power that upsets the reasons of God, has nothing whatever to say to the will of man; and if the will of man submits to the persuasion or coercion of that power, by that very fact it becomes a slave.

Now, what are the great powers that assert themselves in this our age upon the will of man? What are the great powers that make slaves of us? I answer, they are the world around us and its principles;—our own passions within us, and our sinful inclinations. Reflect upon it. We live in a world that has certain principles, that lays down certain maxims and acts upon them. The world has its own code of laws; the world has its own sins, greater or lesser. For instance, a man is insulted. The world tells him to go, take a revolver, and wipe out the insult in the blood of the man who dares to insult him. This is the world's law; but it is opposed to God's law, which says: "Love your enemies, and pardon them for My sake!" The world says to a man, "You are in a good position; you have place, power, influence, patronage; you have it in your power to enrich yourself. Ah! don't be so squeamish; don't be so mealy-mouthed; shove a friend in here. Let a man have a chance of taking up his own pickings. Put another man to do the same there. Take something for yourself." The world says this; and I believe you have evidence of it every day. The world says to the man of pleasure: "You are fond of certain sins of impurity. Ah! but my dear friend, you must keep that thing very quiet. Keep it under the rose as long as you can. There is no great harm in it. It is only the weakness of our nature. You may go on and enjoy yourself as much as you choose; only be circumspect about it. Keep it as quiet as possible, and do not let your secret be found out." The great sin is in being found out. This is the way of the world. It thus operates upon men. It thus influences our will, and makes us bow down and conform to the manners and customs of those around us. How true this is! Is there any thing more common? I have heard it said, over and over again, since I came to America: "Oh, Father, we are very different in this country from what we were in the old country. In the matter of going to Mass, in this country, on Sunday, you cannot go unless you are well dressed. In the old country they go no matter how they are. In this country people would look on it as queer if you did not go as well dressed as your neighbor. In the old country they were very particular about stations, and about going to confession. They used all to go to their duty at Christmas or Easter—and often more frequently;—but in this country scarcely anybody goes at all." This is the language I have heard. It is not uncommon. Now, what does all this mean? What has this country or that, this portion of the world or that, this maxim of the world or that,—what has it to do with your will? Where, in reason,—where, in faith,—where, in Scripture, can you find me one word from Almighty God to man: "Son of man, do as those around you do; conform your life to the usages of the world around you—to the maxims of the world in which you live." But Christ has said: "Be not conformed to this world; for the friendship of this world is enmity before God." The passions within us,—those terrible passions!—the strong, the unreasoning, the lustful desires of youth—the strong, unreasoning, revengeful pride and passion of man;—the strong, unreasoning desire to be enriched before his time by means which are accursed; —the strong passions within him, whatever they may be, that rise up, like giants, in his path,—these are the most terrible tyrants of all, when they assume dominion over man; and, above all, when they assume the aggravated and detestable dominion of habit. Let me say a word to you about this. There is not a man among us who has not his own little world of iniquity within him. Not one! There is not a man among us, even of those who are within the sanctuary, that must not work out his salvation with fear and trembling. And why? Because he has great enemies in his own passions. Now, the Almighty God's design is that those passions should become completely subject to the dominion of reason by the free will of man. So long as man is able to keep them down, to subdue them—so long as a man is able to keep humble, pure, chaste, temperate, in spite of them, —that man is free; because he controls and keeps down those servants, his passions, which the Almighty God never intended should govern him.

Now, the intention of Almighty God is that we should keep down those passions. The second intention of Almighty God is, therefore, that if they rise,—as rise they do, in many cases,—and, for a time, overpower the soul, and induce a man to commit this sin or that,—that he must at once rise up out of that sin, put down that passion, and chain it down under the dominion of reason and will; because, if he lets it remain and allows it to subdue him, and seduce him into sin again, in an inconceivably short time that passion will become the habit and the tyrant of his life. For instance, if a man gets drunk,—if there is any one among you that was ever drunk,—I would ask that man, and say: "My dear friend, try to recall the first time you got drunk. Do you remember next morning in what a state your head was, splitting as if it would go asunder? You felt that you would give half of all you were worth for a drink of water. Your tongue was dry and parched, and a coarse fur on it. Do you remember how you got up in the morning and did not know what to do with yourself for the whole day, going about here and there, afraid to eat, your stomach being so sick; afraid to lie down, and not able to remain up or go to work; moaning and shaking and not able to get over the headache of the preceding night? That was the first time; and you made vows it should be the last. Next day a friend came along and said: "Let us go out and take a glass of toddy?" He wanted you to take it as medicine. I remember once, I heard of a man in this particular state; and when he saw brandy and water before him, he said: "No, sir; I would rather take Epsom salts." And why? Because the habit is not yet formed; the habit is not yet confirmed. But go on, my friend. Do not mind that. When that headache and that first sickness go away, go on; and after awhile, when you have learned to drink, the headache does not trouble you any more; you get used to it; the poison assimilates to the system;—but the habit is come; the physical weakness is gone, and the habit of sin is come. Now, I would like to see you, if you were drunk yesterday evening, to be able to resist "taking your morning." You could not do it? I have seen a man, I was at his bedside, and the doctor was there after taking him over six long days of delirium tremens; and the doctor said to him, "As sure as God created you, if you take brandy or whiskey for the next week, you will be a dead man! It will kill you!" I was present; I was trying to see if the poor fellow would go to confession. There was the bottle of brandy near him on the table; for they had had to give him brandy. And while the doctor was yet speaking to him, I saw his eyes fastened on it, and the hand creeping up towards it; and if ever you saw a hungry horse or mule looking at oats, it was he, when, with his eyes devouring the bottle, he reached out, clutched it, and put it to his head, after hearing that, as surely as God made him, so surely would he die if he drank of it! He could not help it. Where, then, was that man's freedom? It had perished in the habit of sin. Look at Holofernes, as we read of him in Scripture,—the profane, the impure man! What does the Scripture say of him? That when Judith came into his tent, the moment he looked upon her, the moment he cast his eyes upon the woman, he loved her. He could not help it. His senses had enslaved him. His will! He had no will. Speak to me of the freedom of the will of a thirsty animal going to the water to drink, and I may believe it. Speak to me of the freedom of will of a raging lion, hungering for days, and seeing food and leaving it, and I will believe in it as soon as I will believe in the freedom of the will of the man who has enslaved himself in the habit of sin.

Therefore, Almighty God intends either that we should be free from sin altogether, keeping down the habit of all those passions; or if they, from time to time, rise up, taking us unawares, taking us off our feet, not to yield to them, but to chain them down again, and not by indulgence to make them grow into habits.

Now, the essence of freedom in the will of man lies not in the restraint of legitimate authority but in the freedom from all care, and from those powers and influences that neither God, nor man, nor society intended should influence or govern his will. Here I come home again to the subject of my lecture. Now I invite you again to consider where shall we find the means of emancipating our will from these passions and other bad influences? Where shall we find the means? Will knowledge do it? No. Will faith do it? No. It is a strange thing to say, but knowledge, no matter how extensive, no matter how profound, gives no command over the passions; no intellectual motives influence them. "Were it for me," says a great orator of the present day, Dr. Wilberforce, in his "Earnest Cry for a Reformation;" "when you can moor a vessel with a thread of silk, then you may hope to elevate this human knowledge, and, by human reason, to tie down and restrain those giants—the passions and the pride of man." I know as much of the law of God as any among you—more probably than many—for we are to teach it. Does my knowledge save me from sin? Will that knowledge keep me in the observance of the sacred vows I took at the altar of God? Is it to that knowledge that I look for the power and strength within me to keep every sinful passion down in sacerdotal purity—every grovelling desire down in monastic poverty—every sin—every feeling of pride down, in religious obedience? Is it to my knowledge I look for that power? No: I might know as much as St. Augustine, and yet be imperfect. I might be a Pilate in atrocity, and yet as proud a man! There is another question involving the great necessity of keeping down these passions. I would like to know where, in history, you could find a single evidence of knowledge restraining the passions of man, and purifying him. No; the grace of God is necessary—the grace of God coming through fixed, specific channels to the soul. The actual participation of the holiness and the infinite sanctity of Christ is necessary. Where is that to be found? Where is that to be found that will save the young from falling into sin, and save the sinner from the slavery of the habit of sin? Where is that to be found which will either tie down the passions altogether, or, if they occasionally rise up, put them down again and not allow them to grow into the gigantic, tyrannical strength of habit? Where, but in the Catholic Church? Take, for example, the Sacrament of Penance. These children are taught, with the opening of reason, their duty to God. You may say the Church is very unreasonable, because to-day she tells you that she will not allow these children to go to your common schools, or to any other schools where they are not taught of God—where they are not taught the holiness of God, the things of God, the influence of God, mixed up with every addition of knowledge that comes to their minds. You may say the Church is unreasonable in that. No: because she tries to keep them from sin? She tries to give them the strength that will bind these passions down, so as to make moral men, truthful men, pure-minded men of them,—and to give them complete victory, if possible, over these passions. But if, as age comes on, as temptations come on, if the Catholic man goes and gets drunk, if the Catholic man falls into any sin, this or that one, at once the Church comes before him, and at the moment he crosses the threshold of the sanctuary, and his eyes fall upon the confessional, that moment he is reminded of the admonition, "Come to me! and wash your soul in the blood of the Lamb! Come and tell your sin!" The very consciousness of the knowledge of having to confess that sin; the humiliation of being obliged to tell it in all its details— to tell it with so much self-accusation, and sense of self-degradation for having committed it,—is, in itself, a strong check to prevent it, and a strong, powerful influence, even humanly speaking, against again falling into it, or repeating it. As the confessional saves from the tyranny of the passions, and above all, breaks up the means and does not allow the habit of sin to become a second nature in the life of man, what is the consequence? The Catholic man, if he only observes his religion, if he only exercises himself in its duties, if he only goes to confession, if he only partakes in its Sacraments and uses them; the Catholic man is free in his will, by Divine grace, as he is free in his intelligence, by love. Knowledge of the truth is freedom of the intellect—freedom from every agency, from every power that might control the freedom of the will;—and that is effected by Divine grace. So far, we have seen that Almighty God has reproduced in the Church the elements of true freedom. I do not say that the Catholic Church was the "mother" of human freedom. I said she was "the foster-mother;" for, to use a familiar phrase, we are literally and truly "put out to nurse," as it were, to the Church. The freedom which we possess came to us, not from the Church, but from God. He came down from Heaven, after man had been four thousand years in sin—after man had lost his noble inheritance of knowledge, of light, of freedom, and power, and self-restraint. He came in the darkness; and He gave the light. He came in slavery; and he gave freedom. Having thus restored in man what he had lost in Adam, He then, as He himself tells us in the parable of the Good Samaritan, gave us to the Church, and said—"Take care of this race; preserve them in this light of knowledge and freedom of truth. Preserve them till I come back again, and I will pay thee well for thy care." Now, my friends, if there were one here to-night who is not a Catholic, he might smile in his own soul and say: "This Friar is a very cunning fellow. He dresses up things plausibly enough so long as he is arguing in the clouds about freedom and the elements of freedom, and the soil of freedom. He is quite at home there. But when he comes down from the clouds to find how this Church, this terrible Church, this enslaving Church, has dealt with society, then let him look out! Then let us hear what he has to say for himself!"

Again, what are those charges that are laid against the Catholic Church? The first charge alleged against her is that she does not allow people to read every thing that is published. It is quite true. If the Church had her will, there are a great many books, that are considered now by many people very nice reading, that would all be put in the fire. I acknowledge that; I admit it. Tell me, my friends, —and are there not a great many fathers of families among you?—if one of you found with your little boy some blackguard book, some filthy, vile, immoral book, would you let your child read it? Would you consider that you were enslaving his mind by taking that book from him and putting it in the fire before his face? If you found one of your sons reading some very beautiful passage of Voltaire, in which he makes a laughing-stock of faith, and tries to raise a laugh against Christ on the cross, would you consider you were doing badly for your child—would you consider yourself enslaving him—by taking that book from him and putting it in the fire?

Now, this is what the Catholic Church does. She declares that people have no right to read that which is against faith and morals; that which is against the truth of Christ; that which is against the divinity of Christ—that in which the pride of the unregenerated mind of man rises up and says: "I will not believe:" and, not content with this, he writes a book, and tries to make everybody believe and say the same thing. The Church says: "Do not read it." There are some whom she allows to read it. She lets me read it. She lets my fellow-priests read it. Sometimes she even obliges us to read it. Why? Because she knows we have knowledge enough to see the falsity of it, and she allows us to read it that we may refute it. She does not allow you to read it. And why? I do not care to flatter you, my friends. Nothing is more commonly used to lead people astray than a plausible lie. I declare to you that, although I think "the truth is great and must prevail;" that if I had my choice given to me, and I could do it without sin.—if it were given to me to come out and try to enforce the truth or to make you believe a lie—I really believe I would be able sooner to do the second; it is so much easier for us to flatter—especially with a lie to flatter your pride—to tell you you are the finest fellows in the world—to tell you you must not be governed by a certain class—that you must not be paying taxes;—that you have no right to support an army and navy;—that you have no right to pay a class of men to govern you;—and thus they go on, playing into your hands, playing on your love of money and your love of yourself. There is no lie among the whole catalogue of lies that, if I were like them, I would not tell you; and I could make you believe it. The Church says: "There is, in a certain book, an immoral lesson or a lie, and I will not allow my children to read it." There are books published, and I have seen them in the hands of Protestant boys and girls, and the very Pope of Rome has not leave to read them. They are books that contain direct appeals to immorality, direct appeals to the passions—books against both faith and morals, that the Church does not allow to be read by any one. But is this slavery?

But the argument against Catholicity is that the men who make scientific discoveries—the men who said that the world was round, for instance,—men who said that the world was round when it was generally believed to be a great flat plain, —were put in prison. There is one answer to that: There is not a single instance in history of the Church joining issue with any minister on any purely scientific subject, and persecuting him for it. If there was not any question of faith or morals involved, she bade him "God speed!" and told him to go on with his discoveries, if there was any thing useful in them, and nothing hostile to religion in them. I will give you an instance: In the sixth century there was an Irish Saint who was called Virgilius—(in his own country his name was Feargil)—and this man was a great Culdee monk, and a great scholar. The result of his speculations was that he became satisfied in his own mind that this world was a globe—round—as it is,—and that there must, therefore, be antipodes—one on this side and one on the other side, and that there must be seas between one land and another. He announced this; and it came among the scientific men of the day, and fell among them, really and truly, as if a bombshell had burst at their feet. The scholars of the day, the universities of the day, appealed to Rome against him for having pronounced so fearful a theory: they said it was heresy. What did the Pope do? Remember, you can consult the authorities for yourselves. I can give you chapter and verse, if you want them. What did that Pope do? He summoned this man to Rome. He said: "You are charged with teaching a strange doctrine,—with saying that the world is a sphere—a globe. Tell us all about it?" He did so. What answer did Feargil get? The Pope took him by the hand. "My dear friend," he said, "go on with your astronomical discoveries;"—and he made him Archbishop of Salzburg, and sent him home with a mitre on his head. This is how the Catholic Church dealt with intellectual liberty when that intellectual liberty did not claim for itself any thing bad, and was void of any thing that interfered with or was opposed to Christian faith or morals. Do you wish to make us out slaves because we ought not to get a knowledge of evil? One of the theories of the day is that it is better to let little boys and girls read every thing, good and bad; to know every thing. Is it better? Do you think you know better than Almighty God? There was one tree in the garden of Eden, and Almighty God gave a commandment to Adam and Eve, that they should neither taste of it nor touch it. What tree was it? It was the "tree of the knowledge of good and evil." Did Almighty God intend to exclude from Adam the knowledge of good? No; but He intended to exclude from him the fatal knowledge of evil. A prohibition against reading a very bad book was the first and only prohibition that Almighty God gave to the first man. "Do not touch that tree," said He, "because, if you do, you will come to the knowledge of that which is evil." "When ignorance is bliss, 'tis folly to be wise." So says Pope.

Now, my friends, who are they that make this charge against the Catholic Church, that she enslaves her children? Who are they that tell us that the historical mother of all the great universities in the old world is afraid of knowledge? Who are they who tell us that the Church, whose monks, in her cloisters, preserved art and science for a thousand years—preserved all the ancient relics that we have of ecclesiastical learning, and of the learning of Greece and Rome;—that Church that set her monks, her alchemists, and students experimentalizing in their cloisters, in the Middle Ages, until most of what are called the modern discoveries were made or anticipated by them;—who are they who tell us that the Church is the enemy of light and knowledge and of freedom? Who are they? They are the Freemasons of the day. Freemasons.

Now, you will allow me, if you please, to retort the assertion on my friends the Masons—Mazzini and Garibaldi and Bismarck;—for all these are Freemasons. They all say: "Oh, let us wash our hands clean of this old institution—the Catholic Church. She would make slaves of us all. We must give the people freedom; we must give them liberty." And then they lay on taxation. Then they tell every citizen in the land that he must lay aside his spade and become a soldier. They tell every man who is eighteen years of age, that he is to fight for freedom; and they thrust him into the army. Call you this freedom? Yet this is what they give for the liberty of the Church! Are they free themselves, these Freemasons? I will give you one answer—and one is as good as a thousand. Last December twelvemonth, when I was in the city of Dublin, a man came to me. He had attended a series of sermons I was preaching in our church there. He was an intellectual man, a well-educated man.

He came to me and said : " I ought to be a Catholic; but the fact of it is, I have been so long away from the Sacraments and every thing religious that I can scarcely say I am, even in name, a Catholic. But now," he says, " I feel and I know that I must do something to save my soul." Well, I took him, and instructed him in the holy Sacraments, gave him the Holy Communion, and sent him away. He said that he had never, for years upon years, known such happiness; and he went on his way. That man received Confirmation, and was constant in his duty from December until the month of April. Then I waited for him; but, instead of his coming, he wrote a letter to me. " My Rev. friend," he said, " you will, no doubt, be disappointed to find I am not coming to you on Saturday. The fact of it is, I cannot come. I find that I cannot shake off Freemasonry. I have got several notices from my Masonic brethren that I must either adhere to them or give up my religion. My religion has brought me more happiness than I ever experienced in my life, and it is with bitter regret I tell you that my business is falling off; that they are turning away my customers from me;—and they tell me they will bring me to a beggar's grave—a wretched end; and they can and will do it. Therefore I hope you will not forget me; but I must give up the happiness I have had!" Was that man free, I ask you?

Who are the men who turn round and tell me I am not free?—who tell me I am not free, because, indeed, I am not fettered like a slave, bound by every filthy passion! Who are they that tell me I am not free, because I do not, of my own free will, incline myself and pollute my mind with every species of evil and impurity? Who are they who tell me I am not free, because in the Church I have to believe that what she teaches is true? But I tell them it is true. Who are the gentlemen who told my friend that, at the peril of his life, he must return to them, and give up his religion? These are the men who turn round, nowadays, and tell us that in the Catholic Church a man is not free! But this is the Church that has brought me from the slavery of sin into the freedom of God, and the glorious liberty of an heir of Heaven. As long as you pursue any scientific research, as long as you extend your mind in any legitimate, healthy, moral course of literature, or in any intellectual pursuit, you have the blessing and encouragement of the Church upon you. Do not mind the world if it call you a slave. If you come to a certain point, if you read certain books, the Church says you must become either an impure man or an infidel. Do not read them, in God's name! It is not slavery for the intellect to repudiate a lie. It is not slavery for the will to reject that which, if once accepted, asserts the dominion of the slavery of sin and of habit over the souls of men. This do I say with truth: that our mother, the Church, in the principles which our Lord established, in her daily sacerdotal exercises, is the foster-mother of human freedom. It is a historical and a remarkable fact, that the kings of Europe—the King of Spain, the Emperor of Germany, the King of England, the King of France—exercised the most absolute and irresponsible power precisely at the time when the Catholic Church was weakened in her influence over them by the heresy of Martin Luther. It is most remarkable that so absolute in England was Henry the Eighth, (and never was there a king whose absolute manner of governing and whose conduct recalls more the days of the Grand Turk,) that he married a woman one day, he killed her the next; and who was to call him to account? So absolute a king could not have done this as a Catholic; and he threw aside his allegiance. If a Catholic king had done these things—if Henry's father had done them—if any one of Henry's Catholic predecessors had done so, his excommunication would have come from Rome. He would have been afraid of his life to do it. He would have been afraid of the Pope. What was this but securing the people's liberty?

Thus do we see that, so long as the Catholic Church had power to exercise, and exercised that power, she exercised it to coerce kings into justice, into respect for their subjects and for law, for property and for life. This is a historical fact, that the Tudors assumed an absolute sovereignty as soon as they shook off the Pope, and declared to the people that they were the lords and rulers of the consciences, as well as of the civil obedience of men. We also know that Gustavus, the Protestant King of Sweden, assumed absolute power. We also know that that power grew into iron fetters under Charles the Fifth, who, though not a Protestant himself, but a good Catholic, yet governed a people who were divided in their principles of allegiance; and he forsook the world for the Church. We can bring home history to prove that the weakening of the Catholic Church in her temporal power over society has been the cause of the assumption of more power, more absolute dominion, and more tyrannical exercise of that dominion on the part of every ruler in Europe. And, therefore, I say that, historically, as well as in principle, the Catholic Church is the foster-mother of human liberty.

And now, my friends, you will be able, by word of mouth, to answer all those who call you slaves because you are Catholics. You may as well call a man a slave because he obeys his father. You may as well say the child is a slave because there are certain laws and rules that govern him. You may as well say that the citizen is a slave because he acknowledges the power of the State to legislate for him, and he bows to the power of that legislation.

THE CHURCH THE MOTHER AND INSPIRATION OF ART.

[*A Lecture delivered by the Very Rev. T. N. Burke, O.P., in the Church of St. Vincent Ferrer, New York, March 10, 1872.*]

DEARLY BELOVED BRETHREN: This morning I told you the Holy Catholic Church was the spouse of the Lord Jesus Christ, so described to us in Scripture as "dear to the Lord," the interior beauty of which the Psalmist says is "like the beauty of the king's daughter," and of the exterior of which he spoke when he said: "The queen stood at His right hand, in golden garb, surrounded with variety." We saw, moreover, this morning, that the interior beauty and ineffable loveliness of the Church consists, above all, in this, that she holds enshrined in her tabernacles the Lord, the Redeemer of the world, as the Blessed Virgin Mary, His mother, held Him in her arms in Bethlehem, as the cross supported Him on Mount Calvary; that she possesses His everlasting truth, which He left as her inheritance, and which it is her destiny not only to hold, but to proclaim and propagate to all the nations; and, finally, that she holds in her hands the sacramental power and agencies by which souls are sanctified, purified, and saved. In these three features we saw the beauty of the Church of God; in these three we beheld how the mystery of the Incarnation is perpetuated in her, for Christ our Lord did not for ever depart from earth, but, according to His own word, came back and remained. "I will not leave you orphans," He said, "but I will come to you again, and I will remain with you all days, even to the consummation of the world." We see in these three wonderful features of the Church's interior beauty how she is truly "the city of the Living God," "the abode of grace and holiness:" and, therefore, that all the majesty, all the beauty, all the material grandeur with which it is in our power to invest her, it becomes our duty to give to her, that she may thus appear before the eyes of men a fitting tabernacle for our Divine

Lord Himself. We have seen, moreover, how the Church of God, acting upon the instincts of her divinely infused life and perpetual charity, has always endeavored to attest and to proclaim her faith by surrounding the object of that Faith, her God, with all that earth holds as most precious and most dear. I then told you (if you remember) this morning, that the subject for our evening's consideration would be the exterior beauty of the Holy Church of God—some other features that belong to her distinct from, though not independent of, the three great singular graces of God's abiding presence, of God's infallible truth, and of the unceasing stream of sacramental grace that, through her, flows onward;—those features of divine beauty which we recognize upon the face of our Holy Mother, the Church. Therefore, dearly beloved, the things that are indicated by the exterior garb with which the Prophet invested the spouse of Christ: "The queen stood on the right hand, in golden garb, surrounded with variety,"—every choicest gem, every celestial form of beauty embroidered upon the heavenly clothing of Heaven's Queen, every rarest jewel let into the setting of that golden garment, every brightest color shining forth upon her.

What is this exterior beauty of the Church? I answer that it consists in many things—in many influences—in the many ways in which she has acted upon society. Ever faithful to the cause of God and to the cause of humanity,—ever faithful to her heavenly trust,—after more than eighteen hundred years of busy life, she stands to-day before the world, and no man can fix upon her virgin brow the shame of deception, the shame of cruelty, the shame of the denial of the food of man's real life, the Word of Truth. No man can put upon her the taint of dishonor, of a compromise with hell or with error, or with any power that is hostile to the sovereignty of God or to the interests of man. Many, indeed, are the ways in which the Church of God has operated upon society. Of these many ways, I have selected as the subject for our evening's illustration, the power reposed in the Catholic Church, and attested by undoubted historical evidences,—the power which she exercised as the mother and inspirer of the fine arts. And, here, let me first of all say, that, besides the useful and necessary arts which occupy men in their daily life,—the arts that consist in maintaining the essential necessaries, and in providing the comforts of life;

the arts that result in smoothing away all the difficulties that meet us in our path in life, as far as the hand of man can materially affect this;—besides these useful and necessary arts, there are others which are not necessary for our existence,—nor, perhaps, even for our comfort,—but which are necessary to meet the spiritual cravings and aspirations of the human soul, and that fling a grace around ourselves. There are arts and sciences which elevate the mind, soothe the heart, and captivate the understanding and the imagination of man. These are called "the fine arts." For instance: it is not necessary for your life or for mine that our eyes should rest with pleasure upon some beautiful painting. Without that we could live. Without that we could have all that is necessary for our existence—for our daily comfort. Yet, how refining, how invigorating, how pleasing to the eye, and to the soul to which that eye speaks, is the language that appeals to us silently, yet eloquently, as from the lips of a friend, from works of architecture, or sculpture, or painting! It is not necessary for our lives, nor for the comfort of our lives, if you will, that our ears should be charmed with the sweet notes of melodious music; but is there one among us that has not, at some time or other, felt his soul within him soothed, and the burden of his sorrow lightened, the pleasure he enjoyed increased and enhanced, when music, with its magic spell, fell upon his ear? It is not necessary for our lives that our eyes should be charmed with the sight of some grand majestic building; but who, among us, is there who has not felt the emotion of sadness swell within him as he looked upon the ivy-clad ruin of some ancient church? Who is there among us that has not, at some time or other, felt the softening, refining, though saddening influences that crept over him when, entering within some time-honored ruin of an abbey, he beheld the old lance-shaped windows, through which came streams of sunshine like the "light of other days;" and beheld the ancient tracery on that which stood behind the high altar, and had once been filled with legends of angels and saints, but now open to every breeze of heaven;—when he looked upon the place as that in which his imagination pictured to him holy bishops and mitred abbots officiating there and offering up the unbloody sacrifice, while the vaulted arches and long-drawn aisles resounded with the loud hosannas of the long-lost monastic song? Who is there among us who has not felt, at times, elevated, impressed,—aye, filled with strong feelings of delight,—as his eye roamed steadily and gradually up to the **apex of some grand cathedral,** resting upon niches of saints and angels, **and gliding from** beauty to beauty, until, at length straining **his vision, he** beheld, **high among the** clouds of heaven, the **saving sign of** the **Cross of Christ,** upheld in triumph, **and flinging its** sacred **shadow over the** silent graves? It is thus **these arts,** called **the Liberal or the Fine Arts, fill a great place, and accomplish a great work in the designs of God, and in the history of God's Holy Church.**

My friends, the theme which I have propounded to you contains two grave truths. The first of these is this: I claim for the Catholic Church that she is the mother of the arts; secondly, I claim for her the glory that she has been and is their **highest inspiration.** What is it that forms the peculiar attraction, that creates the peculiar influence of art upon the soul of man, through his senses? What is it that captivates the eye? It is the ideal that speaks to him through art. In nature there are many beautiful things, and we contemplate them with joy, with delight;—the faint blushes of the morning, as the rising sun, with slanting beams, glides over the hills and through the glades, filling the valleys with rosy light, and revealing the slopes of the hillsides, so luxuriant and so bold, rising up towards the majestic, towering mountains, flinging the shadows of their snow-crowned summits to Heaven. All this is grand, all this is beautiful. But, in nature,—because it is nature,—the perfectly beautiful is rarely or never found. Some one thing or other is wanting that would lend an additional feature of loveliness to the scene which we contemplate, or to the theme, the hearing of which delights us. Now, the aim of the Catholic soul of art is to take the beautiful, wherever it is found, to abstract it from all that might deform it, or to add all that might be wanting to its perfect beauty; to add to it every feature and every element that can fulfil the human idea of perfect **loveliness, and to** fling over all the still higher loveliness which is caught from Heaven. This is called "the Ideal" in art. We rarely find it in nature. Do we often find it in art? We do not find that perfect **beauty** in the things around us. We look upon a picture, and there we behold portrayed, with supreme power, all the glory **of the** light that the sun can lend from Heaven—all the glory of material beauty;—but in vain do we look for inspiration. It is dead form and color. It has no soul. Among the ancient nations—the great fountains of the ancient civilization—Egypt, Assyria, Greece, and, finally, Rome,—during the four thousand years that went before the coming of the Redeemer,—these arts and sciences flourished. We have still the remains of the Coliseum, for instance, in Rome, combining vastness of proportion with perfect symmetry; and the mind is oppressed at the immensity of size, while the eye is charmed with the beauty of proportion. But, in the fourth and fifth centuries,—after the foundation of the Church,—after the promulgation of the Christian religion,—when the Roman Empire had bowed down her imperial head before the glory of the cross of Christ,—it was in the designs of God that all that ancient civilization, all these ancient arts and sciences, should be broken up and perish. From Egypt, Syria, and the far East they came; their glory concentrated itself in Greece; and later, and most of all, in Rome. All the wealth of the world was gathered into Rome. All the glory of earth was centralized in Rome. Whatever the world knew of painting, of sculpture, of architecture, of music, was found in Rome, in the highest perfection to which the ancient civilization had brought it. Then came the moment when the Church was to enter upon her second mission,—that of creating a new world and a new civilization. Then came the moment when Rome and her ancient empire gravitated to a climax by her three hundred years of religious persecution of the Church of God, and her crimes were about to be expiated. Then came the time when God's designs became apparent. Even as the storm-cloud bursts forth and sweeps the earth in its resistless force, so, in these centuries of which I speak, from the fastnesses of the North came forth dreadful hordes of barbarians—men without civilization, men without religion—men without mercy—men without a written language—men without a history—men without a single refining element of faith among them;—and they came, Goths and Visigoths, Huns and Vandals, sweeping onward in their resistless might,—almost countless thousands of warriors, carrying slavery and destruction in their hands;—and thus they swept over the Western world. Rome went down before them. All her glory departed; and so the civilization of Greece and Rome was completely destroyed. Society was overthrown, and reduced to the first chaotic elements of its being. Every art, every science, every splendid monument of the ancient world was destroyed; and, at the close of the fifth century, the work of the four thousand preceding years had to be done over again. Mankind was reduced to its primal elements of barbarism. Languages never before heard, barbaric voices, were lifted up in the halls of the ancient palaces of Italy, and in the Forum of Rome. All the splendors of the Roman Empire disappeared, and, with them, almost every vestige of the ancient arts and civilization of the preceding times. No power of earth was able to withstand the hordes of Attila. No army was able to make front against them. All went down before them, save and except one—one organization, one power in the world,—one power, founded by Christ and compacted by the very hand of God; —founded upon an immovable foundation of knowledge and of truth;—one power which, for divine purposes, was allowed a respite from persecution for a few years, in order that she might be able to present to the flood of barbarism that swept away the ancient civilization, a compact and well-formed body, able to react upon it;—and that power was the Holy Church of God. She boldly met the assault; she stemmed the tide; she embraced and absorbed in herself nation after nation, million after million of those rude children of the Northern shores and forests. She took them, rough and barbarous as they were, to her bosom; and, at the end of the fifth century, the Church of God began her exterior, heroic mission of civilizing the world, and laying the foundations of modern civilization and of modern society.

So it went on until the day when the capital of Rome was shrouded in flames, and the ancient monuments of her pride, of her glory, and of her civilization, were ruined and fell; and almost every vestige of the ancient arts disappeared. The Church, on the one hand, addressed herself, first and most immediately, to the Christianizing of these Northern nations. Therein lay her divine mission; therein lay the purpose for which she was created—to teach them the truths of God. While she did this she carefully gathered together all that remained of the traditions of ancient Pagan science and art. While all over Europe the greater part of the nations were engaged in the war between Northern barbarism and civilization, and the land was one great battle-field, overflowing with blood, the Church gathered into her arms all that she could lay her hands on, of ancient literature, of ancient science and art, and retired with them into her cloisters. Everywhere over the whole face of Europe, and in Africa and Asia,—everywhere the monk was the one man of learning,—the one man who brought with him, into his cloister, the devotion to God that involved the sacrifice of his life, the devotion to man that considers a neighbor's good, and makes civilization and refinement the purpose and study of his life. Where, to-day, would be the literature of ancient Greece and Rome, if the Church of God, the Catholic Church, had not gathered their remnants into her cloisters? Where, to-day, would be (humanly speaking) the very Scriptures themselves, if these monks of old had not taken them, and made the transcribing of them, and multiplying copies of them, the business of their lives? And so, all that the world has of science, of art,—all that the world has of tradition—of music, of painting, of architecture—all that the world has of the arts of Greece and Rome, was treasured up for a thousand years in the cloisters of the Catholic Church.

And, now, her twofold mission began. While her preachers evangelized,—while they followed the armies of the Vandal and the Goth, from field to field, and back to their fastnesses of the North; while they converted those rude and terrible sons of the forest into meek, pure-minded Christians, upon the one hand, on the other the Church took and applied all the arts, all the sciences, all the human agencies that she had,—and they were powerful,—to the civilizing and refining of these barbarous men. Then it was that in the cloisters there sprang up, created and fostered by the Church of God, the fair and beautiful arts of painting, music, and architecture. I say *created* in the Church. There are many among you as well informed as I am in the history of our civilization; and I ask you to consider that, among the *debris* of the ruin of ancient Rome and of ancient Greece,—although we possess noble monuments of the ancient architecture,—we have only the faintest tradition of their music, or their paintings? Scarcely any thing. I have visited the ruined cities of Italy. I have stood within the walls of Ostium, at the mouth of the Tiber, when, after hundreds of years, for the first time the earth was removed, and the ancient temples were revealed again. The painting is gone, and nothing but the faintest outline remains. Still less of the music of the ancients have we. We do not know what the music of ancient Greece or of ancient Rome was. All we know is that, among the ancient Greeks, there was a dull monotone or chorus, struck into an alternating strain. What the nature of their music was we know not. Of their sculpture, we have abundant remains; and, indeed, on this it may be said that there has not been any modern art which has equalled, scarcely approached, the perfection of the ancient Grecian model. But the three sciences of architecture, painting, and music, have all sprung from the cloisters of the Church. What is the source of all great modern song? When the voice of the singer was hushed everywhere else, it resounded in the Gregorian chant that pealed in loud hosannas through the long-drawn aisles of the ancient Catholic mediæval churches. It first came from the mind—it came from out the loving heart of the holy Pope, Gregory, himself a religious, and consecrated to God as a monk. Whence came the organ, the prince, the king of all instruments, the faithful type of Christianity—of the Christian congregation —so varied yet so harmonious, made up of a multitude of pipes and stops, each one differing from the other, yet all blending together into one solemn harmony of praise, just as you, who come in here before this altar, each one full of his own motives and desires—the young, the old,—the grave, the gay,—rich and poor—each with his own desire and experience of joy, of sorrow, or of hope,—yet before this altar, and within these walls do you blend into one united and harmonious act of faith, of homage, and of praise before God. Whence came the king of instruments to you,—so majestic in form, so grand in its volume,—so symbolical of the worship which it bears aloft upon the wings of song? In the cloisters of the Benedictine monks do we hear it for the first time. When the wearied Crusader came home from his Eastern wars, there did he sit down to refresh his soul with sacred song. There, during the solemn Mass of midnight, or at the Church's office at matins,—while he heard the solemn, plaintive chant of the Church, while he heard the low-blended notes of the accompanying organ, skilfully touched by the Benedictine's hand,—then would his rugged heart be melted into sorrow and the humility of Christian forgiveness. And thus it is the most spiritualizing and highest of all the arts and sciences—this heaven-born art of music. Thus did the Church of God make her divine and civilizing appeal; and thus her holy influence was brought out during those stormy and terrible times when she undertook the almost impossible task of humbling the proud, of purifying the unchaste, of civilizing the terrible, the fierce, and the blood-stained horde of barbarians that swept, in their resistless millions, over the Roman Empire.

The next great art which the Church cultivated in her cloisters, and, which, in truth, was created by her, as it exists to-day, was the art of painting. Recall the circumstances of the time. Printing was not yet invented. Yet the people had to be instructed,—and not only to be instructed but influenced; for mere instruction is not sufficient. The mere appeal to the power of faith, or to the intellect of man, is not sufficient. Therefore did the Church call in the beautiful art of painting; and the holy, consecrated monk, in his cloister, developed all the originality of his genius and of his mind to reproduce the captivating forms—to reproduce, in silent but eloquent words, the mysteries of the Church,—the mysteries which the Church has taught from her birth. Then did the mystery of the Redemption, the Incarnation of the Son of God, the Angel coming down from Heaven to salute Mary,—then did all these greet the eye of the rude, unlettered man, and tell him, in language more eloquent than words, how much Almighty God in Heaven loved him. But it was necessary for this that this art of painting should be idealized to its very highest form. It was necessary that the painter's hand should fling round Mary's head a halo of virginity and of the light of Heaven. It was necessary that the angelic form that saluted her should have the transparency of Heaven, and of its own spiritual nature, floating, as it were, through it in material color. It was necessary that the atmosphere that surrounded her, should be as that cloudless atmosphere which is breathed before the throne of the Most High. It was necessary that the man who looked upon this should be lifted up from the thoughts of earth, and engaged wholly in the contemplation of objects of Heaven. Therefore, glimpses of beauty the most transcendent, aspirations of Heaven, lifting up the soul from all earthliness—from worldliness,—were necessary. For all this the monk was obliged to fast and pray while he painted. The monk was obliged to lift up his own thoughts, his own imagination, his own soul, in contemplation, and view, as it were, the scene which he was about to illustrate, with no earthly eye. The Church alone could do this: and the Church did it. She created the art of painting. There was no tradition in the Pagan world to aid the painter; no beauty—the beauty of no fair forms, in all the fulness of their majestic symmetry, before his eyes to inspire him. He must look altogether to Heaven for his inspiration. And so faithfully did he look up to Heaven's glories, and so clear was the vision that the painter-monk received of the beauties he depicted on earth, that, in the thirteenth century, there arose, in Florence, a Dominican monk, a member of our Order, beatified by his virtues, and called by the single title of "The Angelic Painter." He illustrated the Holy Trinity. He put before the eyes of the people all the great mysteries of our faith. And now, after generations of ages,—after six hundred years have passed away,—whenever a painter or lover of art stands before one of those wonderful angels and saints, painted by the hand of the ancient monk, now in Heaven, it seems to him as if the very Angels of God had descended from on high and stood before the painter while he fixed their glory in colored form, as they appear to the eye of the beholder. It seems as if we gazed upon the blessed angelic hosts; and as if Gabriel, standing before Mary, mingled the joy of the meeting with the solemnity of the message which the painter represents him as announcing. It seems as if Mary is seen receiving the message of man's redemption from the Angel, not as a woman of earth, but as if she was the very personification of the woman that the inspired Evangelist, at Patmos, saw, "clothed with the sun, and the moon under her feet, and on her head a crown of twelve stars." Michael Angelo, the greatest of painters, gazed in wonder at the angels and saints the Dominican monk had painted. Astonished he knelt down, gave thanks to God, and said: "'The man that could have painted these must have seen them in Heaven!"

The architecture of the ancient world, of Greece and of Rome, remained. It was inspired by a Pagan idea, that never rose above the idea that inspired it. The temples of Athens and of Rome remain in all their shattered glory, and in all the chaste beauty of their proportions. Very remarkable are they, as architectural studies, for this,—that they spread themselves out, and covered as much of the earth's space as possible; that the pillars were low and the arches low; and every thing seemed to cling to and tend towards earth. For this was the idea, and the highest idea of architecture that ever entered into the mind of the greatest of the men of ancient civilization. The monk in his cloister, designing to build a temple and a house for the living God, looking upon the models of ancient Greece and Rome, saw in them a grovelling and an earthly architecture. His mind was heavenward in aspiration. His thoughts, his affections were all purified by the life which he led. Out of that upward tendency of mind and heart sprang the creation—the invention—the new creation—of a new style of Christian architecture, which is called the Gothic: as little in it of earth as may be—just sufficient to serve the purpose of a superstructure. The idea was to raise it as high as possible towards Heaven—to raise a monument to Almighty God—a monument revealing in every detail of its architecture the Divine idea, and the upward tendency of the regenerated heart of the Christian man. Now, therefore, let every arch be pointed; now, therefore, let every pillar spring up as loftily as a spire; now, therefore, let every niche be filled with angels and saints,—some who were tried in love—others who maintained the faith,—teaching the lesson of their sanctity;—now pronouncing judgment, now proclaiming mercy. Now, therefore, let the high tower be uplifted, on which swings the bell, consecrated by the blessing of the Church, to fling out upon the air around, which trembles as it receives its message, the notes of Christian joy and of Christian sorrow. And, high above that tower, let the slender, pointed spire seek the clouds, and rear up, as near to Heaven as man can go, the symbol of the Cross on which Christ redeemed mankind. Such is the Church's idea; and such is the architecture of which she is the mother. Thus we behold the glorious churches of the middle ages. Thus we behold them, in those ancient and quaint towns of Belgium and of France. We behold on their transepts, for instance, a tracery as fine as if it were wrought and embroidered by a woman's hands, with a strength that has been able to defy the shocks of war and the action of ages. If the traveller seeks the sunny plains of Italy, he climbs the snow-crowned, solitary

Alps, and there, after his steep and rugged ascent, he beholds on one side the valleys of Switzerland, with its cities and lakes; and he turns to the land of the noonday sun, and sees before him the fair and widespread plains of Lombardy. The great rivers flow through these plains, and look as if they were of molten silver. The air is pure; the sky is the sky of Italy. Majestic cities dot the plains at his feet. But, among them all, as the sun flings his Italian light upon the scene,—among them all, he beholds one thing that dazzles his eyes with its splendor. There, far away in the plains, within the gates of the vast city of Milan, he sees a palace of white marble rising up from the earth; ten thousand statues of Saints around it; with countless turrets, and a spire with a pinnacle rising towards Heaven, as if in a riot of Christian joy. The sun sparkles upon it as if it were covered with the rime of a hoar frost, or as if it were made of molten silver. Possibly his steps are drawn thither, and it pleases him to enter the city. Never before—never, even with the eye of the mind—has the traveller seen so grand an idea of the sacred humanity of Jesus Christ. Here He reigns. Who can deny the historical facts which I have narrated? Who can deny that, if to-day our ear is charmed with the sound of music—our eye delighted with the contemplation of paintings,—if our hearts within us are lifted up at the sight of some noble monument of architecture,—who can deny, with such facts before him, that it was the Church that created these,—that she is the mother of these,—and that she brought them forth from out the chaos and the ruin that followed the destruction of the pagan civilization.

Thus, while the Church was their mother, she was also their highest inspiration. For, remember, that the zeal in art may be taken from earth, or drawn from Heaven. Art may aspire to neither more nor less than "to hold the mirror up to nature." The painter, for instance, may aspire to nothing more than to render faithfully, as it is in nature, a herd of cattle, or a busy scene in the town. The musician may aspire to nothing more than the pleasure which his music will give to the sense of the voluptuous in man. The architect may aspire to nothing more than the creation, in a certain space, of a certain symmetry of proportion, and a certain usefulness in the work of his hands. They may "hold a mirror up to nature;" but this is not a perfect idealization of art. The true ideal holds the mirror of its representation not only up to nature, to copy that nature faithfully, but—higher still—to God, to catch one ray of divine inspiration, one ray of divine light, one ray of heavenly instruction, and to fling that pure heavenly light over the earthly productions of his art. This pious inspiration is only to be found in the Catholic Church. It is found in her music —those strains of hers which we call the "Gregorian chant," —which, without producing any very great excitement or pleasure, yet fall upon the ear, and, through the ear, upon the soul, with a calming, solemn influence, and seem to speak to the affections in the very highest language of worship. Plaintively do they fall,—yes, plaintively,—because the Church of God has not yet shone over the earth in the fulness of her glory: plaintively, because the object of her worship is mainly to make reparation to an offended God for the negligence of the sinner: plaintively, because the words which this music breathes are the words of the penitent, and the contrite of heart: plaintively,—because, perhaps, my brethren, the highest privilege of the Christian here is a holy sadness, according to the words of Him who said: "Blessed are they who mourn and weep, for they shall be comforted."

In the lapse of years, the Church again brought forth another method and gave us another school, which expresses to-day the pious exultation, the riot of joy, with which, on Christmas day, Palæstrina sung before Pope Marcellus in Rome. Hear, for instance, the "Magnificat," as it resounds within the Catholic Cathedrals at the hour of prayer. Hear, for instance, some of the hymns, time-honored and ancient, in which she breaks in on an Easter morning, and which she sets to the words—the triumphant words—of the "Alleluia!" Who cannot say—who is there with trained, sympathetic ear who hears them, who cannot say—that the inspiration which is in them is altogether of Heaven—heavenly:—and that it lifts up the soul to the contemplation of heavenly themes, and to the triumph of Jesus Christ. The highest inspiration comes through faith.

Let us turn to the art of painting. So long as this noble art was in the hands of the Monk—the man of God—so long had we masterpieces of painting, such as have never been equalled by any that since came forth—masterpieces by men who fasted and prayed, and looked upon their task, as painters, to be a heavenly and a holy one. We read of the Blessed Angelico, the Dominican painter, whose works are the glory of the world to-day,—we read of him, that he never laid his brush to a painting of the Mother of God, or of Our Lord, except on the day when he had been at Holy Communion. We read of him that he never painted the infant Jesus, or the Crucifixion, except on his knees. We read of him that, while he brought out the divine sorrow in the Virgin Mother for the Saviour on the cross,—while he brought out the God-like tribulation of Him who suffered there,—he was obliged to dash the tears from his eyes—the tears of love—the tears of compassion—which produced the high inspiration of his genius. Nay, the history of this art of painting teaches us that all the great masters were eminent as religious men, and that when they separated from the Church, as we see, their inspiration left them. The finest pictures that Raphael ever painted were those which he painted in his youth, while his heart was yet pure, and before the admiration of the world had made him stain the integrity of his soul by sin. The rugged, the almost omnipotent genius of Michael Angelo was that of a man deeply impressed with faith, and most earnestly devoted to the practice of his religion. Whether in the Vatican of Rome, or over the high altar of the Sistine Chapel, he brings out all the terrors of the Divine Judgment, which he puts there, in a manner that makes the beholder tremble to-day,—the Lord in the attitude, not of blessing, but of sweeping denunciation over the heads of the wicked,—he took good care, by prayer, by frequenting the Sacraments, by frequent confession and communion, and by the purity of his life, to avert the punishments that he painted from falling on his own head. The most glorious epoch in the history of architecture was precisely that in the thirteenth and fourteenth centuries, when there arose the minsters of York, of Westminster; of Notre Dame, in Paris; of Rouen, and all the wonderful old churches that, to-day, are the astonishment of the world for the grandeur and majesty of their proportions, and the beauty of design they reveal. These churches sprang up at the very time that the Church alone held undisputed sway; when all the arts were in her hands, and when the architects who built them were nearly all consecrated sons of the cloister. It is worthy of remark that we do not know the name of the architect that built St. Patrick's or Christ Church, in Dublin. We do not know the name of the architect that built Westminster Abbey, nor any one of those great and mighty mediæval churches throughout Europe. We know, indeed, the name of the architect who built St. Paul's in London, and of him who built St. Peter's, in Rome. They were laymen. The men who laid the foundations (that rarely appear to the eye) were Monks, and are now in the dust; and, in their humility, they brought the secret of their genius to the grave, and no names of theirs are emblazoned on the annals of the world's fame.

Thus we see the highest civilization, the highest inspiration of the arts,—music, painting and architecture,—came from the Catholic Church,—and that the most attractive of them all was created in her cloisters. The greatest painters that ever lived had come forth from her bosom, animated by her spirit. The greatest churches that ever were built were built and designed by her consecrated children. The grand strains of ecclesiastical music, expressing the highest ideas resounded in her cathedral churches. The world had grown under her fostering care. Young Republics had sprung up under the Church's hand and guidance. The Italian Republics—the Republics of Florence, of Pisa, of Venice, of Genoa,—all gained their municipal rights and rights of citizenship—(rights that were established for protection, and to insure equality of the law,)—under the Church's protection. Nay, more. The Church was ever willing and ready, both by legislation and by action, to curb the petty tyrants that oppressed the people; to oblige the rugged castellan to emancipate his slaves. The Church was ever ready to send her highest representatives, Archbishops and Cardinals, into the presence of Kings, to demand the people's rights. And the very man who wrung the first principles of the British Constitution from an unwilling and tyrannical king, was the Catholic Archbishop of Canterbury—the only man who would dare to do it; for (and well the tyrant knew it) he could not touch the Archbishop, because the arm of the Church was outstretched for his protection. Society was formed under her eyes and under her care. Her work now seemed to be nearly completed, when the Almighty God, in His wisdom, let fall a calamity upon the world; and I think you will agree with me,—even such among you (if there be any) who are not

Catholics,—that a calamity it was; a calamity fell upon the world in the sixteenth century, which not only divided the Church in faith and separated nations from her, but which introduced new principles, new influences, new and hostile agencies which were destructive of the most sacred rights. I am not here this evening so much as a preacher as a lecturer. I am not speaking to you so much as a priest as a historian; and I ask you to consider this:—We are accustomed to hear on every side that Protestantism was the emancipation of the human intellect from the slavery of the Pope. To that I have only to answer this one word: Protestantism substituted the uncertainty of opinion instead of the certainty of faith which is in the Catholic Church. Protestantism declared that there was no voice on earth authorized or empowered to proclaim the truth of God; that the voice that had proclaimed it for fifteen hundred years had told a lie; that the people were not to accept the teaching of the Catholic Church as an authoritative and time-honored law, but that they were to go out and look for the faith for themselves, —and in the worst way of all. Every man was to find a faith for himself; and when he had found it, he had no satisfactory guarantee, no certainty, that he had the true interpretation of the truth. If this be emancipating the intellect— if this changing of certainty into uncertainty, dogma into opinion, faith into a search after faith, be emancipation of the intellect, then Christ must have told a lie when He said: "You shall know the truth; and the truth shall make you free!" The knowledge of the truth He declared to be the highest freedom: and, therefore, I hold, not as a priest, but simply as a philosopher, that the assertion is false which says that the work of Protestantism was the emancipation of the intellect. All the results of modern progress—all the scientific success and researches that have been made—in a word, all the great things that have been done—are all laid down quietly at the feet of Protestantism as the effects of this change of religion. In England nothing is more common than for good Protestants to say that the reason why we are now in so civilized a condition is because Martin Luther set up the Protestant religion. Protestantism claims the electric telegraph. The Atlantic cable does not lie so much in a bed of sand as on a holy bed of Protestantism that stretches from shore to shore! They forget that there is a philosophical axiom which says: "One thing may come after another, and yet it may not be caused by the thing that went before." If one thing comes after another, it does not follow that it is the effect of the other. It is true that all these things have sprung up in the world since Protestantism appeared. It is perfectly true that the many have learned to read since Protestantism gained ground. But why? Is it because the Catholic Church kept the people in ignorance? No: it was because of a single want. It was about the time Protestantism sprung up that the art of printing was invented. Of course the many were not able to read when they had no books. The Catholic Church, as history proves, was even far more zealous than the Protestant new-born sect, in multiplying copies of the Scripture and in multiplying books for the people. Now, one of the reproaches that is made to us to-day is, that we are too busy in the cause of education. Surely if the Catholic Church is the mother of ignorance, that reproach cannot be truly made. Now, Protestants are making a noise and saying that the Church, in every country and on every side, is planning and claiming to educate. But all this is outside of my question. My question deals with the fine arts.

Now, mark the change that took place! Protestantism undoubtedly weakened the Church's influence upon society. Undoubtedly it took out of the Church's hands a great deal of that power which we have seen the Catholic Church exercise, for more than a thousand years, upon the fine arts. They claim, or they set up a rival claim of fostering the arts of music, of architecture, and of painting, so that these may no longer claim to receive their special inspiration from the Church, which was their mother and their creator, and through which they drew their heavenly genius. Well, the arts were thus divided in their allegiance, and thus deprived of their inspiration, by the institution of this new religion. I ask you to consider, historically, whether that inspiration of art, that high and glorious inspiration, that magnificent ideal, was not destroyed the moment it was taken from under the guidance and inspiration of the Catholic Church. I say that it was destroyed; and I can prove it. Since the day that Protestantism was founded, the art of architecture seems to have perished. No great cathedral has been built. No great original has appeared. No new idea has been expressed from the day that Luther declared schism in the Church, and warred against legitimate authority. No Protestant has ever originated a noble model in modern architecture. It has sunk down into a servile imitation of the ancient, grovelling forms of Greece and Rome. Nay, whenever the ancient Gothic piles—majestic and inspiring Christian churches—fell into their hands, what did they do? They pulled them down in order to build up some vile Grecian imitation; or else they debased the ancient grandeur and purity of the Gothic cathedral, by mixing in a servile imitation of some ancient heathen or pagan temple.

As to the art of painting, the painter no longer looked up to Heaven for his subject. The painter no longer considered that his pious idea was to instruct and elevate his fellow-man. The painter no longer selected for his subject the Mother of God, or the sacred humanity of our Lord, or the Angels and Saints of Heaven. The halo of light that was shed upon the brush of the blessed Angelico,—the halo of divine light that surrounded the Virgin's face as it grew under the creative hand of the young Christian painter,—the halo of heavenly light that surrounded the Judge upon his throne, in the fresco of Michael Angelo,—this is to be found only in Christian art. The highest ambition of the painter, now, is to sketch a landscape true to nature. The highest excellence of art seems now to be to catch the colors that approach most faithfully to the flesh tints of the human body. And it is a remarkable fact, my friends, that the art of animal painting,—painting cows and horses, and all these things,—began with Protestantism. One of the very first animal painters was Roos, a German Protestant, who came to Rome; and the reproach of his fellow-painters was, "There is the man that paints the cows and horses." Even sacred subjects were dealt with in this debased form,—in this low and empty inspiration. How were they dealt with? Look, for instance, at the Magdalens; look at the Madonnas of Rubens. Rubens, himself, was a pious Catholic; yet his paintings displayed the very genius of Protestantism. If he wanted to paint the Blessed Virgin, he selected some corpulent and gross-looking woman, in whom he found some ray of mere sensual beauty that struck his eye; and he put her on the canvas, and held her up before men as the Virgin, whose prayer was to save, and whose power was above that of the angels! The artist who would truly represent her on canvas, must have his pencils touched with the purity and grandeur of Heaven.

Music lost its inspiration when it fell from under the guidance of the Church. No longer were its strains the echoes of Heaven. No longer is the burden of the hymn the heavenly aspiration of the human soul, tending towards its last and final beatitude. Oh, no! but every development that this high and heavenly science receives is a simple degradation into the celebration of human passion; into the magnifying of human pride: into the illustration of all that is worst and vilest in man: and the highest theme of the musician to-day is not the "*Dies Iræ*,"—an expression, as it were, of the prayers of the Angels in Heaven for the dead;—it is not the "*Stabat Mater*," the wailing voice of the Virgin's sorrow; it is not the "*Alleluia*," to proclaim to the world the glories of the risen God: no, the highest theme of the musician to-day is to take up some story of sensual, and merely human, love; to set that forth with all the charms and all the meretricious embellishments of art.

Thus do we behold, in our own experience of to-day, how the arts went down and lost their inspiration, as soon as there were taken from them the genius and the inspiring influence of the Church that created them, and through them civilized the world, and brought to us whatever we have of civilization and refinement in this nineteenth century. Thank God, the reign of evil cannot last long upon this earth. It is one of the mysterious circumstances that the coming of our Lord developed. Before the Incarnation of the Son of God, an evil idea seemed to be in the nature of man. It propagated itself, it found a home, and an abiding dwelling among the children of men. But since the Incarnation of the Son of God, since the Eternal Word of God vouchsafed to take a human soul, a human body, human sensibilities, and, I will add, human genius,—since that time the base and the vile, and the ephemeral, and the degraded, may come; may debase art and artists, may spoil the spirit of art for a time; but it cannot last very long. There is a native force, a nobleness in the soul of man that rises in revolt against it.

And to-day, even to-day, the hour of revival seems to be coming,—almost arrived,—is already come. The three arts, of Painting, of Music, and Architecture, seem to be rising with their former inspiration, and seem to catch again a little of the departed light that was shed on them and flowed through them, from religion. Architecture revives, and the glories of the thirteenth century, though certainly they may not be eclipsed, yet they are almost equalled by the glories of the nineteenth. But a short distance from this, you see, in the middle of this great city, rising in its wonderful beauty, that which promises to be, and is to be, of all the glories of this city, the most glorious,—the great Cathedral. Across the water, you see in the neighboring city of Brooklyn the fair and magnificent proportions of that which will be, in a few years, the glory of that adjacent shore, when on this side, and on that, each tower and spire and pinnacle upholding an Angel or Saint, the highest of all will uphold the Cross of Jesus Christ.

Music is reviving again,—catching again the pure spirit of the past. A taste for the serene, the pure, the most spiritual songs of the Church, is every day gaining ground, and taking hold of the imagination. Painting, thank God, is reviving again, and of this you have here abundant proof. Look around you! No gross, earthly figure stands out in the bare proportions of flesh and blood. No vile exposure of the mere flesh invites the eye of the voluptuous to feast itself upon the sight. The purity of God is here. The purity of the Church of God overhangs it; and the story of these scenes will go home to your hearts and to the hearts of your children, as the story that the blessed Angelico told in Florence six hundred years ago. Thanks be to God, it is so! Thanks be to God, that, when I lift up my eyes, I may see so much of the purity of the face down which flow the last tears of blood! When I lift up mine eyes here, it seems to me as if I stood bodily in the holy society of these men. It seems to me that I see in the face of John the expression of the highest manly sympathy that comforted and consoled the dying eyes of the Saviour. It seems to me that I behold the Blessed Virgin, whose maternal heart consented, in that hour of agony, to be broken for the sins of men. It seems to me that I behold the Magdalen, as she clings to the Cross, and receives, upon that hair with which she wiped His feet, the drops of His blood. It seems to me that I behold that heart, humbled in penance and inflamed with love—the heart of the woman who had loved much, and for whom He had prayed. It seems to me that I travel step by step to Calvary, and learn, as they unite in Him, every lesson of suffering, of peace, of hope, of joy, and of divine love! Thank God, it is fitting, in a Dominican Church, that this should be so! It is fitting, in a temple of my Order, that, when I look upon the image of my holy Father over that entrance, in imagination, and without an effort, I travel back to the spot where I had the happiness to live my student's days, and where, in the very cell in which I dwelt, I beheld, from Angelico's own hand, one glorious specimen of his art. These are the gladness of our eyes, the joy of our hearts. They give us reason to rejoice with Him who said: "I have loved, O Lord, the beauty of Thy house, and the place where Thy glory dwelleth." They give us reason to rejoice because they are not only fair and beautiful in themselves, but they are also the guarantee and the promise that the traditions of ecclesiastical painting, sculpture, architecture and music in this new country, shall yet come out and rival all the glories of the nations that for centuries and centuries have upheld the Cross. They are a cause of gladness to us; for, when we shall have passed away, our children, and our children's children shall come here, and, in reviewing these pictures, shall learn to feel the love of Jesus Christ.

Among the traditions of one of the old cities of Belgium, there is one of a little boy, who grew up, visiting every day the Cathedral of the city. One day he stood with wondering and childlike eyes before a beautiful painting of the infant Jesus. According as time went on, and reason grew upon him, his love for the picture became greater and greater; and when he became a man, his love for it was so great that he spent his days in the Cathedral as organist, pealing forth the praises of the Son of God. His manhood went down into the vale of years; but his love for the picture was still the one child-love—the young love and passion of his heart. And so he lived, a child of art, and died in the odor of sanctity, a child of God. And that art had fulfilled its highest mission, for it had sanctified the soul of a man. Oh, may these pictures, that we look upon with so much pleasure, teach to you, and to your children after you, the lesson they are intended to teach, of the love, of the charity, of the mercy of Jesus; that—loving Him and loving the beauty of His house, and catching every gleam that faith reveals of her higher beauty, and every thing that speaks of Him for ever—you may come to behold Him as He shines in the uncreated light and majesty of His glory!

ST. JOHN THE EVANGELIST.

[*A Sermon delivered by the Very Rev. T. N. Burke, O.P., in the Dominican Church, New York, on Sunday, March* 24, 1872.]

I TOLD you this morning, my brethren, that we should confine our attention, during the next few days, to the groupings that surrounded our Blessed Lord upon the Hill of Calvary. I then intended, this evening, to put before you the various characters and classes of men who were there as the enemies of God. I must, however, alter somewhat this programme. To-morrow will be the Feast of the Annunciation of the Blessed Virgin—one of the greatest festivals of the Christian year—commemorating a mystery from which all the mysteries of our redemption have flown. It will be held, as you are aware, as of obligation; and, therefore, I shall be obliged so far to depart from my original design, as to let in, to-morrow evening, a sermon on the great festival of the day—the Annunciation of the Blessed Virgin. Thus far I must interfere with the plan I have laid down, and this will oblige me, this evening, simply to notice briefly the different groups and classes by which the enemies of our Divine Lord were represented upon Calvary. We shall pass, at once, to the consideration of the man who stood there as the friend of his dying Lord and Saviour.

There were many classes of men surrounding our Blessed Lord on that fearful and terrible journey, when, starting from the house of the High Priest, Annas, He turned His face towards Calvary, and set out upon the dolorous "Way of the Cross." The men who, sitting in that tribunal, had condemned Him, were not satisfied with that sentence; but, in the eagerness of their revenge, they would fain witness His execution; following out the expressed word of the Evangelist, that the Scribes and Pharisees followed our Lord, and fed their revengeful eyes upon the contemplation of His three hours of agony on the Cross. The immediate agents of this terrible act of execution were the Roman soldiers of the cohort who had scourged Him, who had crowned Him with thorns, and who accompanied Him with stolid indifference to the place of his execution. They were the pagans. They were men who had never heard of the name of God. They were men who, had they heard of it, must have heard of it, if at all, in a language which they scarcely understood, and which was the medium of the common record of what were called "the wonders,"—that is, of the miracles of Christ. But it scarcely stirred up in them even a natural curiosity; and, therefore, they brought him to execution, as they would have dragged any other criminal; with this one exception, that, by a strange, diabolical possession, they looked upon this man, of whom they knew nothing,—upon this man who had never injured them in word or in deed,— with intense abhorrence, and hated him with an inexplicable hatred. They thus typified the nations which, in the old law, knew not the Lord of Truth. In paganism, in the darkness of the wickedness of their infidelity, they know not the name of God. When that name is pronounced in their presence, it falls upon their ears rather as the name of an enemy than that of a friend. They cannot explain why they hate Him. No more can we explain the hatred of the Roman soldiers. The missionary goes forth to-day in all the power of the priesthood of Christ. He stands in the presence of the people of China or of Japan. As long as he speaks to them of the civilization, of the immense military power, of the riches and of the glory of the country from which he comes, they hear him willingly and with interested ears. As long as he reveals to them any secret of human science, they make use of him, they are glad to receive him. Thus it is, we know, that some of the Jesuit missionaries held the very highest places at the court of the Emperor of China. But as soon as ever the missionary mentions the name of Christ, they not only refuse to hear him, but they are stirred up on the instant with diabolical rage; hate and anger flash from their eyes; they lay hold of the messenger who bringeth them the message of peace and love, and of eternal life; and they imagine they have not fulfilled their duty until they have shed his heart's blood upon the spot. Oh, how vast is the crowd of those who, for centuries, have thus greeted the Son of God and every man who speaks in His name! Think of the outlying millions, to whom, for eighteen hundred years and more, the Church—the messenger of God—has preached and appealed, but in vain! Behold the class that was represented round the Cross, lifting up indifferent, stolid, or, if any thing, scowling faces, amid the woes of Him who, in that hour of His agony and of His humiliation, mingled His prayers for forgiveness with the last drop of blood that flowed through His wounds from His dying heart!

There is another class there. It is made up of those who knew Him well, or who ought to have known Him. They had seen His miracles; they had witnessed His sanctity; they had disputed with Him upon the laws, until He had convinced them that His was the wisdom that could not belong to man, but to God. He had silenced them. He had answered every argument that foolhardy and audacious men made to Him. He had reduced them to such shame that no man ever wanted to question Him again. But He interfered with their interests and their pride. That pride revolted against submitting to Him. That self-love and self-interest prompted the thought that, if He lived, His light would outshine theirs, and their influence with the people would be gone. These were the Scribes and the Pharisees. They were the leaders of the people. They were the magistrates of Jerusalem. They were the men whose loud voice and authoritative tones were heard in the Temple. They were the men who walked into that house as if it was not the house of God, but *their* house. They were the men who walked fearlessly up to the altar, to speak words of blasphemous pride, and call them prayers. They were the men who despised the humble Publican making his act of contrition. They were the men who lifted their virtuous hands and hypocritical eyes to Heaven to lament over the weakness of human nature. They were the men who hated Christ, because they could not argue with Him—because they could not uphold their errors against His truth—because they could not hold their own, but were struck dumb at the sight of His sanctity and the sound of His powerful voice. What did they do? They began to tell lies to the people. They began to tell the people how He was an impostor and a blasphemer. They began to mislead the people,—to warp the estimate that people might make of Christ! They endeavored to find false witnesses to bring them to swear away, first, His character and, then, His life. Ah! need I say whom they represent? Need I tell a people in whose memories is fresh to-day the ever recurring lie that is flung in the face of the Catholic Church, —the ever-recurring false testimony that is brought against her,—the burning of her churches, the defiling of her altars, the outrages on her priests,—the insults heaped upon her holy nuns, the people inflamed against the very name of Catholicity itself, so that the word might be fulfilled of Him who said: "They shall cast out your very name as evil for My sake"? The men who made the very name of a Monk, or a Friar, or a Jesuit mean something awfully gross, or sensual, or material, were naturally worldly and deceitful. I need not point out to you that, in the midst of you, and every day, from their pulpits, from their conventicles, through their daily press—every day we are made familiar with the old lie, shifted and changed, tortured, distorted, and twisted, and the false testimony brought out in a thousand forms of falsehood.

And there were others who believed in Christ—who knew Him—who had enjoyed His conversation and His friendship, and who were afraid to be seen in His company in that dark hour, and upon that hill of shame. Where were the Apostles? Where were the Disciples? They had fled from their Master because it was dangerous to be seen with Him! Judas, the representative of the man who sells his religion and his God for this world; who sells his conscience in order to fill his purse; who sells every thing that is most sacred when that demand is made upon him for temporal profit and pelf; who seals his iniquity by a bad communion, in order to save appearances; while with one hand he was taking money from the Pharisees, with the other hand he was taking Christ to his breast;—the man who played a double part—the man who did not wish to break utterly with his Lord, nor to sacrifice the good opinion of his fellow-apostles; and, therefore, he received damnation to himself in a bad communion;—*he* does not dare to climb the rugged steep of Calvary; but he stands afar off: and the vision that he sees, of so much sorrow, so much suffering;— the vision that he sees passing before his eyes is his Lord, his Master in whom he still believes, though he has betrayed Him; his Lord, his Master, torn with scourges from head to foot; crowned with thorns; disguised in His own blood; blinded with the blood that was flowing down from every wound in His sacred brow:—his Lord and his Master, who had so often spoken to him words of friendship and of love; passed before the eyes of the renegade and traitor. As he looked, and his eyes caught, for an instant, the countenance of that figure tottering along in weakness and in pain,—the sight brought back remembrance of the days that were gone, with no glimmering of hope, no light of consolation to his soul, but only the feeling that he had betrayed his God, and that he held then, in his infamous purse, the money for which he had sold his soul and his conscience. He stood aghast and pale. He tore his hair and wrung his hands. He found that he could not live to see the consummation of his iniquity; and, before the Saviour had sent forth the last cry for a redeemed world, the soul of the suicide Judas had gone down to hell! "It were better for him had he never been born!" Does he represent any class? Are there not in this world men who are almost glad to have something to barter with the world, when they give up their holy faith and religion in order to clutch this world's possessions? Have we not read in the history of the nations—in the history of the land from which most of us sprang—have we never read of men selling their faith for this world's riches and this world's honors? Have we never read, in the history of the world, of men who, in order to save appearances, approached the holy altar and received the holy communion? Of monarchs who, in order to stand well with their Catholic subjects, made a show of going to holy communion? And of sycophants and courtiers who, in order to please a king, in a fit of piety or a fit of repentance, went to holy communion? But time will not permit me to linger in the contemplation of the many classes of the worldly-minded; the false friend, the bitter, though conscious, enemy; the heartless executioners; the exact representatives of those who crowded round the Cross in that terrible hour.

But there was one there;—and it is to that one that my thoughts and my heart turn this night,—there was one there who was destined to be, through all ages, and unto all nations, a type of what the true Christian man—the friend of Christ, must be; a true representative of the part that he must play, in the sacrifice that, from time to time, he must make, to test the strength and the tenderness of his love. There was one there, young and beautiful, who did not flinch from his Mas-

ter and Lord in that hour; who walked by His side; who
shared in the reproaches that were showered upon the head
of the Son of God, and took his share of the grief and the
shame of that terrible morning of Good Friday. There was
one there, whom the Master permitted to be there, that he
might, as it were, lean upon the strength of his manhood and
the fearlessness of his love. That one was John, the Evangelist. Behold him, as with virginal eyes, he looks up as a
man to his fellow-man on the Cross! Behold him as he seems
to say: "Oh, Master! Oh, Lover of my soul and heart! can I
relieve you of a single sorrow by taking it up and making it
my own?" This was John. Consider who he was, and
what. Three graces surrounded him as he stood at the foot
of the Cross. Three divine gifts formed a halo of heavenly
light around his head. They were the grace of Christian
purity, the grace of divine love, and the manliness of the
bravery that despises the world, when it is a question of giving testimony of love and of fidelity to his God and his
Saviour;—three noble gifts, with which the world is so ill-supplied to-day! Oh, my brethren, need I tell you that, of
all the evils in this our day, there is one which has arrived
at such enormous proportions that it has received the name
of "The Social Evil!"—the evil which finds its way into
every rank and every grade of society; the evil which, raising
its miscreated head, now and again frightens us, and terrifies
the very world by the evidence of its widespread pestilence;
—the evil that, to-day, pollutes the hearts, destroys the souls
of the young, and shakes our nature and our manliness to its
very foundations, and brings down the indignant and the
sweeping curse of God upon whole nations? Need I tell
you that that evil is the terrible evil of impurity,—the unrestrained passion, the foul imagination, the debased and
degraded cravings of this material flesh and blood of ours,
rising up in rebellion, and declaring, in its inflamed desires,
that nothing of God's law, nothing of God's redemption shall
move it; that all, all may perish, but that it must be satiated
and gorged with that food of lust, of which, says the holy
Apostle, "the taste is death." Of this I have already spoken
to you, and also of the opposite virtue, the "index" virtue,
as it is called—the virtue of virtues; of that I have also
spoken to you, that by which lost man is raised up to the
very perfection of his spiritual nature; by which the Divine

effulgence of the highest resemblance to Christ is impressed upon the soul; by which the brightness of the Virgin, and of the Virgin's Son, seems to pass forth, even from His body, and sink into the soul's tissues, until it becomes divine. Such virtue of angelic purity did Christ, our Lord, come to establish upon earth. Such virtue did He lay as the foundation of His Church, in a chaste and a virginal priesthood; in the foundations of society, in a chaste and pure manhood, preserving the integrity of the soul in the purity of the body. Such virtue belonged to John, "the Disciple of love;" and it belonged to him in its highest phase; for, as the Holy Fathers,—and the interpreters of the Church's traditions from the very beginning, and notably, St. Peter Damascus, tell us,—John the Evangelist was a virgin from the cradle to the grave. No thought of human love ever flashed through his mind. No angry uprising of human passion ever disturbed the equable nature of his heavenly-tempered soul and body. He was the youngest of all the Apostles; and he was little more than a youth when the virgin-creating eyes of Christ fell upon him. Christ looked upon him, and saw a virginal body, fair and beautiful in its translucent purity of innocence. He, the Creator and Redeemer, saw a soul pure, and bright, and unstained,—a soul just opening into manhood, and in the full possession of all its powers, and a tender, yet a most pure heart, unfolding itself. Even as the lily bursts forth and unfolds its white leaves to gather in its calyx the dews of Heaven, like diamond drops in its heart of glorious innocence,—so did our Lord behold the fair soul of John. In his earliest youth, the words of invitation dropped in that virgin ear; and in that virgin soul those graces of apostleship, of love, of tenderness, and of strength, that lay there, among these petals of glory, brought forth, in the soul of the young man, all that was radiant with the most Christ-like virtue. A virgin—that is to say, one who never let a thought of his mind, nor an affection of his heart stray from the highest form of divine love,—thus was he before he had beheld the face of his Redeemer. But when, to that virginal purity, which naturally seeks the love of God in its highest form, that God made Himself visible to it in the shape of the sacred humanity of our Lord: when the virgin's King, the Prince, and the leader of the virgin's choir in Heaven, presented Himself to the eyes of the young Apostle;—oh, then, with the instinct of purity, his heart seemed to go forth from him, and to seek the heart of Christ. And so it was for three years, under the purifying eyes of our Lord. He lived for three years, in the most intimate communion of love with his Master; distinguished from all the other Apostles, of whom we do not know that any one of them was a virgin, but only John; distinguished from them, by being admitted, through his privileged, virginal purity, into the inner chambers of the heart of Christ. Thus, when our Lord appeared to the Apostles upon the waters, all the others shrank from Him, terrified; and they said to each other, "It is a ghost! It is an appearance!" John looked, and instantly recognized his Master; and said to Peter; "Do not be afraid! It is the Lord." Whereupon, St. Jerome says:—"What eyes were those of John, that could see that which others could not see? Oh, it was the eye of a virgin recognizing a virgin!" So it was that a certain, tacit privilege was granted to John, as is seen in the conduct of the Apostles themselves. Peter, certainly, was honored above all the others by getting precedence and supremacy; by being appointed the Vicar and Representative of his Master; in other words, "the Head of the Apostles." But this was preceded by the severest tests. He was tried,—nay more, the heart of Peter was sounded to the very depths of its capacity and of its love, before Christ, our Lord, appointed him as His representative. Three times did he ask him, "Simon, son of John, lovest thou Me?" Again in the presence of John, "Lovest thou Me, Peter, more than these?" "More than these; more than the men who are present before Me, and of whom I speak to you." And Peter was confirmed in that hour, and rose, by divine grace, to a height in the sight of his Divine Master, greater than any ever attained by man. It is not the heart of the man loving the Lord; but it is the heart of the Lord loving the man. So, Peter was called upon to love his Lord more than the others; but the tenderest love of his Divine Master was the privilege of John. He was "the disciple whom Jesus loved." And well did his fellow-Apostles know it. What a privilege was not that which was given to John at the Last Supper, because of his virginal purity! There was the Master, and there were the disciples around Him. There was the man whom he destined to be the first Pope,—the representative of His power and the head of His followers. Did Peter get the first place? No. The first place,—the place next to the left side,—nearest the dear heart-side,—was the privilege of John. And,—oh! ineffable dignity vouchsafed by our Saviour to His virgin friend!—the head of the Disciple was laid upon the breast of the Master! and the human ear of John heard the pulsations of the virginal heart of Christ, the Lord of earth and Heaven! Between those two, in life, you may easily see in this and other such traits recorded in the Gospel,—between these two—the Master and the "disciple whom He loved,"—there was a silent inter-communion—an intensity of tender love of which the other Apostles seem not to have known. Out of this very purity of John sprang the love of his Divine Lord and Master. It was after His resurrection that our Lord asked Peter, "Dost thou love Me more than these?" Before the suffering and death of the Son of God, Peter only loved Him as a man. John's love knew no change. Peter's love had first to be humbled, and then purified by tears, and the heart broken by contrition before he was able to assert: "Lord, Thou knowest all things: Thou knowest that I love Thee!" But, in the love of St. John, we find an undoubting, an unchanging love. What his Master was to him in the hour of His glory, the same was He in the hour of His shame. He beheld his Lord, shining on the summit of Tabor, on the day of His Transfiguration; yet he loved Him as dearly when he beheld Him covered with shame and confusion on the Cross. What was the nature of that love? Oh, my friends, think what was the nature of that love! It had taken possession of a mighty but an empty heart. Mighty in its capacity of love is the heart of man—the heart of the young man—the heart of the ingenuous, talented, and enlightened youth. Would you know of how much love this heart is capable? Behold it in the Saints of the Catholic Church. Behold it in every man who gives his heart to God wholly and entirely. Behold it even in the sacrifices that young hearts make, when they are filled with merely human love. Behold it in the sacrifice of life, of health, of every thing which a man has, which is made upon the altar of his love, even when that human love has taken the base, revolting form of impurity. Look at it. Measure it, if you can. I address the **heart** of the young man, and **he** cannot see it! The truth lies here, that the **most** licentious and self-indulgent sinner on the earth has never yet known, in the indulgence of his wildest excesses, the full **contentment, the complete enjoyment, the mighty faculty of love which is in the human heart.**

Such was the **heart** which our Lord called to him. Such was the heart **of** John. It was a capacious **heart. It was** the heart **of a young man.** It was empty. **No human love was there.** No previous affection came in to cross or counteract the designs of God in the least degree, or to take possession of even the remotest corner of that heart. Then, finding it thus empty in its purity, thus capacious in its nature, **the Son of God filled the heart of the young Apostle with His love.** Oh, it was the rarest, the grandest friendship that ever existed on **this earth: the friendship that bound together two virgin hearts—the** heart **of the beloved disciple, John; the** grand virgin love which absorbed **John's affections,** filling his young heart and intellect with **the beauty and** the highest appreciation of **his Lord and Master, filling his senses with** the charms **ineffable produced by the sight of the face of the Holy One.** He looked upon the beauty of that sacred and Divine **humanity; and he saw, with the penetrating eyes of the intellect, the fulness of the Divinity that** flashed upon him. **He, at least, had listened to the voice of** the Divine Master, **and sweeter it was than the music which** he heard in **Heaven, and which he describes in the Apocalypse,** where he **says: " I heard the sound of many voices, and** the harpers **harping upon many harps."** Far sweeter than the echoes **of Heaven that descended into his soul on the** Isle of **Patmos, was the** noble, **manly voice of his Lord** and Master,—now pouring forth blessings **upon the** poor,—now telling those who weep that they shall **one day be** comforted,— **now whispering** to the widow of Naim, **" Weep no** more;" now telling the penitent Magdalen, " Thy **sins are** forgiven thee because thou **hast** loved much **;"—now,** thundering in the temple of Jerusalem until **the very stones** resounded to the God-like manifestation of **Him who said :** " It is written that My house is a house **of prayer;** but you have made it a den of thieves **;"**—it **was still the loftiest** music and melody **—the harmonious roll of the** voice of God—as it fell upon the charmed ears of the **enraptured** Evangelist,—the young man who followed his Master and fed his soul upon that divine love.

Out of this love sprang that inseparable fellowship that bound him to Christ. Not for an instant was he voluntarily absent from his Master's side. Not for an instant did he separate himself from the immediate society of his Lord. And herein lay the secret of his love;—for love, be it human or divine, craves for union, and lives in the sight and in the conversation of the object of its affection. Consequently, of all the Apostles, John was the one who was always clinging around his Master—always trying to be near Him—always trying to catch the loving eyes of Christ in every glance. This was the light of his brightness,—the divine wisdom that animated him!

How distinct is the action of John,—in the hour of the Passion,—from that of Peter! Our Divine Lord gave warning to Peter. "Peter," He said, "before the cock crows you will deny me thrice." No wonder the Master's voice struck terror into the heart of the Apostle! And yet, strange to say, it did not make him cautious or prudent. When our Lord was taken prisoner, the Evangelist expressly tells us that Peter followed Him. Followed Him? Indeed, he followed Him; but he followed Him "afar off." He waited on the outskirts of the crowd. He tried to hide himself in the darkness of the night. He tried to conceal his features, lest any man might lay hold of him, and make him a prisoner, as the friend of the Redeemer. He began to be afraid of the danger of acknowledging himself to be the servant of such a master. He began to think of himself, when every thought of his mind, and every energy of his heart should have been concentrated upon his Lord. He followed Him; but at some distance. Ah! at a good distance! John, on the other hand, rushed to the front. John wanted to be seen with his Master, John wanted to take the Master's hand,—even when bound by the thongs,—that he might receive the vivifying touch of contact with Christ! John wanted to hear every word that might be said, whether it were for or against Him. John wanted to feast his eyes upon every object which engaged the attention of his Lord, and by whose look it was irradiated; a type, indeed, of a class of Christian men, seeking the society and the presence of their Master, and strengthened by that seeking and that presence. He is the type of the man who goes frequently to holy communion, preparing himself by a good confession, and so laying the basis of a sacramental union with God, that becomes a large element of his life;—the man who goes to the altar every month;—the man who is familiar with Christ, and who enters somewhat into the inner chambers of that Sacred Heart of infinite love;—the man who knows what those few minutes of rapture are which are reserved for the pure,—for those who not only endeavor to serve God, but to serve Him lovingly and well. Those are the men who walk in the footsteps of John; those are his representatives. Peter is represented by the man who goes to holy communion once or twice in the year;—going perhaps, once at Easter or Christmas, and then returning to the world again. God grant that neither the world, nor the flesh, nor the devil will take possession of the days, or weeks, or years of the rest of his life!—he who gives,—twice in the year, perhaps,—an hour or two to earnest communion with God, and, for all the rest, only a passing consideration, flashing momentarily across the current of his life. And what was the consequence? John went up to Calvary, and took the proudest place that ever was given to man. Peter met, in the outer hall, a little servant-maid; and she said to him: "Whom seekest thou?—Jesus of Nazareth?" The moment that the child's voice fell upon his ear, he denied his Master, and he swore an oath that he did not know Him.

Now, we come to the third grand attribute of John; and it is to this, my friends, that I would call your attention especially. Tender as the love of this man was for his Master—his friend,—mark how strong and how manly it was at the same time. He does not stand aside. He will allow no soldier, or guard, or executioner, to thrust him aside or put him away from his Master. He stands by that Master's side, when he stood before His accusers in the Prætorium of Pilate. Christ comes out. John receives Him into his arms, when, fainting with loss of blood, He returns, surrounded by soldiers, from the terrific scene of His scourging. And, when the cross is laid upon the shoulders of the Redeemer,—with the crowd of citizens around him,—at His right hand, so close that He might lean upon him if He would,—is the manly form of St. John the Evangelist. Oh, think of the love that was in his heart, and the depth of his sorrow, when he saw his Lord, his Master, his Friend, his only love, reduced to so terrible a state of woe, of misery, and of weakness! This was the condition of our Divine Lord, when they laid the heavy cross upon His shoulder. How the Apostle of Love would have taken that painful and terrible crown, with its thorns, from off the brows to which it adhered, and set the thorns upon his own head, if they had only been satisfied to let him bear the pains and sufferings of his Master and his God! Oh, how anxious must he have been to take the load that was placed upon the unwilling shoulders of Simon of Cyrene! Oh, how he must have envied the man who lifted the cross from off the bleeding shoulders of the Divine Victim, and set it on his own strong shoulders, and bore it along up the steep side of Calvary! With what gratitude must the Apostle have looked upon the face of Veronica, who, with eyes streaming with tears, and on bended knees, upheld the cloth on which the Saviour imprinted the marks of His divine countenance! Yet, who was this man?—who was this man, who received the blow as the criminal who was about to be executed? Who is this man who takes the place of shame? Who is this man who is willing to assume all the opprobrium and all the penalty that follows upon it? He is the only one of the Twelve Apostles that is publicly known. We read in the Gospel that the Apostles were all humble men,—poor men, taken out of the crowd by our Lord. The only one among them who had made some mark, who was noted, who was remembered for something or another, was St. John. And by whom was he known? He was known,—says the Evangelist,—he was known to the High Priest. He was so well known to him, and to the guards and to the officers, and to the priests, that, when our Lord was in the house of Annas, John entered as a matter of course; and when Peter, with the rest, was shut out, all that John had to do was to speak a word to the officers:— because, says the Evangelist, "he was well-known to the High Priest"—well-known to the chief magistrates—well-know to the men in power—well known to the chief senators. "Oh, John! John! be prudent! Remember that you are a noted man, so that you will be set down by the men in power, for shame perhaps, or indignity, or even death. Consult your own interests. Do not be rash. There is no knowing when your aid or your authority may be wanted." This is the language of the world. This is the language which we hear day after day. "Prudence and caution!"

"No necessity to parade our religion!" "No necessity to be thrusting our Catholicity before the world!" "No necessity to be constantly unfurling the banner on which the Cross of Christ is depicted—the Cross on which He died to save the souls of men." "No necessity for all this. Let us go peacefully with the world! Let us worship in secret. Let us go quietly on Sunday, to divine service; and let the world know nothing about it!" This is self-love! This is cowardice! Oh, how noble the answer of him whom all the world knew! How noble the soul of him who stood by his Lord, when he knew that he was a noted man, and that, sooner or later, his fidelity, on that Good Friday morning, would bring him into trouble! How glorious the action of the man who knew he was compromising himself!—that he was placing his character, his liberty, his very life in jeopardy!—that he was suffering, perhaps, in the tenderest intimacy and friendship!—that he was losing himself, perhaps, in the esteem of those worldly men who thought they were doing a wise, a proper, and a prudent thing when they sent the Lord to be crucified. John stands by his Master. He says, in the face of the whole world: "Whoever is His enemy, I am His friend. Whatever is His position to-day, I am His creature: and I recognize Him as my God!"

And so he trod, step by step, with the fainting Redeemer, up the rugged sides of Calvary. We know not what words of love and of strong, manly sympathy he may have poured into the afflicted ear of the Redeemer. We know not how much the drooping humanity of our Lord may have been strengthened and cheered in that sad hour by the presence of the faithful and loving John! Have you ever been in great affliction, my friends? Has sorrow ever come upon you with a crushing and an overwhelming weight? Have you ever lacked heart and power in great difficulty, and seen no escape from the crushing weight of anxiety that was breaking your heart? Do you not remember that such has been the daily experience of your life? Do you not know what it is to have even one friend—one friend on whom you can rely with perfect and implicit confidence—one friend who, you know, believes in you and loves you, and whose love is as strong as his life?—one friend who, you know, will uphold you even though the whole world be against you? Such was the comfort, such was the consolation that it was the Evangelist's privilege to pay to our Lord on Calvary. No human prudence or argument dissuaded him. He thought,—and he thought rightly,—that it was the supreme of wisdom to defy, to despise, and to trample upon the world, when that world was crucifying his Lord and Master. Highest type of the man, saying, from out the depths of his own conscience, "I am above the world!" Let every man ask himself this night, and answer the question to his own soul: "Do I imitate the purity, do I imitate the love, do I imitate the courage or the bravery of this man, of whom it is said that he was 'the disciple whom Jesus loved?'" He got this reward, exceeding great. Ah, how little did he know—great as was his love—how little did he know the gift that was in store for him—and that should be given him through the blood that flowed from that dying Lord! Little did he know of the crowning glory that was reserved to him at the foot of the Cross! How his heart must have throbbed with the liveliest emotions of delight, mingled in stormy confusion with the greatness of his sorrow, when, from the lips of his dying Master, he received the command: "Son, behold thy Mother!" —and, with eyes dimmed with the tears of anguish and of love, did he cast his most pure, most loving, and most reverential glance upon the forlorn Mother of the dying Son! What was his ecstasy when he heard the voice of the dying Master say to Mary: "O Mother, look to John, My brother, My lover, My friend! Take him for thy son!" To John he says: "Son, I am going away. I am leaving this woman, the most desolate of all creatures that ever walked the earth. True, she is to me the dearest object in Heaven or on earth. Friend, I have nothing that I love so much! Friend, there is no one for whom I have so much love as I have for her! And to you do I leave her! Take her as your mother, O dearly beloved!" John advances one step,—the type and the prototype of the new man, redeemed by our Lord;—the type of the man whose glory it was to be that he was Mary's son;—he advances a step, until he comes right in front of his dying and blessed Lord. John advances one step,—the type—the prototype of the new man, redeemed by the Saviour,—and whose glory it was henceforth to be that he was to be Mary's son. He advances a step, until he comes right in front of his dying Lord; and he approaches Mary, the Mother, in the midst of her sorrow, and flings himself into her loving arms. And the newly-found son embraces his heavenly Mother, while, from the crucified Lord, the drops of blood fall down upon them and cement the union between our human nature and His, and fulfil the promise He had made to His Heavenly Father in the adoption of our humanity.

The scene at Calvary I will not touch upon, or describe. The slowly passing minutes, of pain, of anguish, and of agony that stretched out these three terrible hours of incessant suffering;—of these I will not speak. In your estimation and in mine they do not need to be spoken of. But, when the scene was over;—when the Lord of glory and of love sent forth His last cry;—when the terrified heart of the Virgin throbbed with alarm as she saw the Centurion draw back his terrible lance and thrust it through the side of our Divine Lord;—when all this was over, and when our Lord was taken down from the Cross and His body placed in Mary's arms;—after she had washed away the stains with her tears, and purified His face;—after she had taken off the crown of thorns from His brow, and when they had laid Him in the tomb—the desolate Mother put her hands into those of her newly-found child, St. John, and with him returned to Jerusalem. The glorious title of "The Child of Mary" was now his; and with this precious gift of the dying Redeemer he rejoiced in Mary's society and in Mary's care. The Virgin was then, according to tradition, in her forty-ninth year. During the twelve years that she survived with John, she was mostly in Jerusalem, while he preached in Ephesus, one of the cities of Asia Minor, and founded there a church, and held the chair as its first Apostle and Bishop. He founded a church at Philippi, and a church at Thessalonica, and many of the churches in Asia Minor. His whole life, for seventy years after the death of his divine Lord, was spent in the propagation of the Gospel and in the establishing of the Church. But, for twelve years of it, the Virgin Mother was with him, in his house, tenderly surrounding him with every comfort that her care could supply. Oh, think of the raptures of this household that we read of so much! Every glance of her virginal eyes upon him reminded her of Him who was gone,—for John was like his Divine Master. It was that wonderful resemblance to Christ which the highest form of grace brings out in the soul. Picture to yourselves, if you can, that life at Ephesus, when the Apostle, worn down by his apostolic preaching,—fatigued and wearied from his constantly proclaiming the victory and the love of the Redeemer,—returned to the house and sat down, while Mary, with her tender hand, wiped the sweat from his brow, and these two, sitting together, spoke of the Lord, and of the mysteries of the life in Nazareth; and from Mary's lips he heard of the mysteries of the thirty years of love in the humble house of Nazareth; and of how Joseph had died, she holding his head, and the Son of God standing by his side. From Mary's lips he heard the secrets—the wonderful secrets—of her Divine Son;—until, filled with inspiration, and rising to the highest and most glorious heights of divinely-inspired thought, he proclaimed the Gospel that begins with the wonderful words, "In the beginning was the Word," denoting and pointing back to the eternity of the Son of God. Picture to yourselves, if you can, how Mary poured out to John, years after the death of our Lord, her words of gratitude for the care with which he surrounded her, and of her gratitude to him for all that he had done in consoling and upholding her Divine Child in the hour of His sorrow! Oh, this surpasses all contemplation! Next to that mystery of Divine Love, the life in Nazareth with her own Child, comes nearest the life she lived in Ephesus with her second, her adopted son, St. John the Evangelist.

He passed to Heaven,—first among the virgins, says St. Peter Damian,—first in glory as first in love, enshrined to-day in the brightest light that surrounds the virgin choirs of Heaven! Now, now he sings the songs of angelic joy and angelic love;—and he leaves to you and to me,—as he stands, and as we contemplate him upon the Hill of Calvary,—the grand and the instructive lesson of how the Christian man is to behave towards his Lord and his God; living in Christian purity,—in the Christ-given strength of divine love,—and in that glorious, world-despising assertion of the divinity and of the love of Christ, which, trampling under foot all mere human respect, lives and glories in the friendship of God and in the possession of His holy faith and the practice of His holy religion;—not blushing for Him before man; and thus gaining the reward of Him who says: "And he that confesses Me before men, the same will I confess before My Father in Heaven."

CHRIST ON CALVARY.

[*A Sermon delivered by the Very Rev. T. N. Burke, O.P., in the Dominican Church of St. Vincent Ferrer, New York, on Good-Friday, March 29, 1872.*]

"All you that pass this way, come and see if there be any sorrow like unto my sorrow."

DEARLY BELOVED BRETHREN: These words are found in the Lamentations of the Prophet Jeremiah. There was a festival ordained by the Almighty God, for the tenth day of the seventh month of the Jewish year; and this festival was called the "Day of Atonement." Now, among the commandments that the Almighty God gave concerning the "Day of Atonement," there was this remarkable one: "Every soul," said the Lord, "that shall not be afflicted on that day, shall perish from out the land." The commandment that He gave them was a commandment of sorrow, because it was the day of the atonement. The day of the Christian atonement is come,—the day of the mighty sacrifice by which the world was redeemed. And if, at other seasons, we are told to rejoice,—in the words of the Scripture—"Rejoice in the Lord; I say to you again, rejoice,"—to-day, with our holy mother, the Church, we must put off the garments of joy, and clothe ourselves in the raiment of sorrow. If, at other times, we are told to be glad in the Lord,—according to the words of Scripture, "Rejoice in the Lord and be glad,"—to-day the command is that every soul shall be afflicted; and the soul that is not afflicted shall perish.

And now, before we enter upon the consideration of the terrible sufferings of our Lord Jesus Christ,—all that He endured for our salvation,—it is necessary, my dearly beloved brethren, that we should turn our thoughts to the Victim, whom we contemplate this night dying for our sins. That Victim was our Lord and Saviour Jesus Christ, the Son of God. When the Almighty God, after the first two thousand years of the world's history, resolved to destroy the whole race of mankind, on account of their sins, He flooded the earth; and, in that universal ruin, He wiped out the sin by destroying the sinners. Now, in that early hour of God's first terrible visitation, the water that overwhelmed the whole world, and destroyed all mankind, came from three sources. First of all, we are told, that God, with his own hand, drew back the bolts of Heaven, and rained down water from Heaven upon the earth. Secondly, we are told that all the secret springs and fountains that were in the bosom of the earth itself, burst and came forth:—"The fountains of the great abyss burst forth," says Holy Writ. Thirdly, we are told that the great ocean itself overflowed its shores and its banks; "and the sea uprose, until the waters covered the mountain tops." Thus, dearly beloved brethren, in the inundation, the flood of suffering and sorrow that came upon the Son of God made man, we find that the flood burst forth from three distinct sources. First of all, from Heaven,—the Eternal Father sending down the merciless hand of justice to strike His own Divine Son. Secondly, from Christ our Lord himself. As from the hidden fountains of the earth sending forth their springs; so, from amid the very heart and soul of Jesus Christ,—from the very nature of His being, —do we gather the greatness of His suffering. Thirdly, from the sea rising,—that is to say, from the malice and wickedness of man. Behold, then, the three several sources of all the sufferings that we are about to contemplate. A just and angry God in Heaven; a most pure, and holy, and loving Man-God upon earth, having to endure all that hell could produce of most wicked and most demoniac rage against Him. God's justice rose up,—for, remember, God was angry on this Good-Friday;—the Eternal Father rose up in Heaven, in all His power;—He rose up in all His justice. Before Him was a Victim for all the sins that ever had been committed; before Him was the Victim of a fallen race; before Him, in the very person of Jesus Christ himself, were represented the accumulated sins of all the race of mankind. Hitherto, we read in the Gospel, that, when the Father from heaven looked down upon His own Divine Child upon the earth, He was accustomed to send forth His voice in such language as this:—" This is my beloved Son, in whom I am well pleased." Hitherto, no sin, no deformity, no vileness was there, but the beauty of Heaven itself in that fairest form of human body,—in that beautiful soul, and in the fulness of the divinity that dwelt in Jesus Christ. Well might the Father exclaim—"This is my beloved Son, in whom I am well pleased!" But, to-day,—oh, to-day!—the sight of the beloved Son excites no pleasure in the Father's eyes,—brings forth no word of consolation or of love from the Father's lips. And why? Because the all-holy and all-beloved Son of God, on this Good-Friday, took upon Him the garment of our sins,—of all that His Father detested upon this earth; all that ever raised the quick anger of the Eternal God; all that ever made Him put forth His arm, strong in judgment and in vengeance:—all this is concentrated upon the sacred person of Him who "became the Victim for the sins of men." How fair He seems to us, when we look up to that beautiful figure of Jesus!—how fair He seemed to His Virgin Mother, even when no beauty or comeliness was left in Him!—how fair He seemed to the Magdalen, again, who saw Him robed in His own crimson blood! The Father in Heaven saw no beauty, no fairness, in His Divine Son in that hour. He only saw, in Him and on Him, all the sins of mankind, which He took upon Himself that He might become for us a Saviour. Picture to yourselves, therefore, first, this mighty fountain of divine wrath that was poured out upon the Lord. It was the Father's hand,—the hand of the Father's justice,—outstretched to assert His rights, to restore to Himself the honor and the glory of which the sins of all men, in all ages, in all climes, had deprived Him! Picture to yourselves that terrible hand of God drawing back the bolts of Heaven, and letting out on His own divine Son the fury of this wrath that was pent up for four thousand years! We stand stricken with fear in the contemplation of the anger of God, in the first great punishment of sin, the Universal Deluge. And all the sins that in every age roused the Father's anger were actually visible to the Father's eyes on the person of His Divine Son. We stand astonished and frightened when we see, with the eyes of faith and of revelation, the living fire descending from Heaven upon Sodom and Gomorrha,—the balls of fire floating in the air, thick as the descending flakes in the snowstorm;—the hissing of the flames as they came rushing down from Heaven, like the hail that comes down in the hailstorm; the roaring of these flames as they filled the atmosphere;—their terrible, lurid light;—the shrieks of the people, who are being burned up alive;—the lowing of the tortured beasts in the fields;—the birds of the air falling, and sending forth their plaintive voices, as they drop to earth, their plumage scorched and burned! All the sins that Almighty God, in heaven, saw in that hour of His wrath, when he rained down fire,—all these did He see, on that Good-Friday morning, upon His own Divine Son. All the sins that ever man committed were upon Him, in the hour of His humiliation and of His agony, because He was truly man; because He was a voluntary victim for our sins; because He stepped in between our nature, that was to be destroyed, and the avenging hand of the Father lifted for our destruction: and these sins upon Him became an argument to make the Almighty God in Heaven forget, in that hour, every attribute of His mercy, and put forth against His son all the omnipotence of His justice. Consider it well; let it enter into your minds;—the strokes of the Divine vengeance that would have ruined you and me, and sunk us into hell for all eternity, were rained by the unsparing hand of Omnipotence, in that hour, upon our Lord Jesus Christ.

The second fountain and source from which came forth the deluge of His sorrow and His suffering was His own divine heart, and His own immaculate nature. For, remember that He was as truly man as He was God. From the moment Mary received the Eternal Word into her womb, from that moment Christ, the Second Person of the Blessed Trinity, was as truly man as He was God; and, in that hour of His incarnation, a human body and a human soul were created for Him. Now, first of all, that human soul that He took was the purest and most perfect that God could make,—perfect in every natural perfection;—in the quickness and comprehensiveness of its intelligence;—in the large capacity for love in its human heart; in the great depth of its generosity and exalted human spirit. Nay more, the very body in which that blessed soul was enshrined was so formed, that it was the most perfect body that was ever given to man. Now, the perfection of the body in man lies in a delicate organization,—in the extreme delicacy of fibre, muscle, and nerve; because they make it a fitting instrument in order that the soul within may inspire it. The more perfect, therefore, the human being is, the more sensitive is he to shame, the more deeply does he feel degradation, the more quickly do dishonor and humiliation, like a two-edged sword, pierce the spirit. Nay, the more sensitive he is to pain, the more does he shrink away naturally from that which causes pain; and that which would be merely pain to a grosser organization, is actual agony, is actual torment to the perfect man, formed with such a soul that, at the very touch of his body the sensitive soul is made cognizant of pleasure and of pain, of joy and of sorrow. What follows from this? St. Bonaventure, in his "Life of Christ," tells us that so delicate was the sacred and most perfect body of Our Lord that even the palm of His hand, or the sole of His foot, was more sensitive than the inner pupil of the eye of any ordinary man; that even the least touch caused him pain; that every ruder air that visited that Divine face brought to Him a sense of exquisite pain that ordinary men could scarcely experience. Add to this, that in Him was the fulness of the God-head, realizing all that was beautiful on earth; realizing with infinite capacity the enormity of sin; realizing every evil that ever fell upon nature in making it accessible to sin; and above all, taking in, to the full extent of its eternal duration, the curse, the reprobation, the damnation that falls upon the wicked. Oh, how many sources of sorrow are here! Here is the heart of the man—Jesus Christ:—here is the fulness of the infinite sanctity of God,—here, the infinite horror that God has for sin. For this man is God! Here, therefore, is at once the indignation, the infinite repugnance, the actual sense of horror and detestation which, amounting to an infinite, passionate repugnance, absorbed the whole nature of Jesus Christ in one act of violence against that which is come upon Him. Now, every single sin committed in this world comes, and actually effects, as it were, its lodgment in the soul and spirit of Jesus. At other times he may rest, as He did rest, in the Virgin's arms;—for she was sinless · at other times He may allow sin and the sinner to come to His feet and touch Him; but, by that very touch, that sinner was made as pure as an angel of God. But to-day this infinitely holy heart,—this infinitely tender heart must open itself to receive,—no longer simply to purify, but to assume and atone for,—all the sins of the world.

The third great source of His suffering was the rage and the malice of men. They tore that sacred body; they forgot every instinct of humanity; they forgot every dictate, every ordinance of the old law, to lend to their outrages all the fury of hell, when they fell upon him, as the Scripture says, "Like hungry dogs of chase upon their prey." He is now approaching the last sad day of His existence; He is now about to close His life in sufferings which I shall endeavor to put before you. But remember that this Good-Friday, with all its terrors, is but the end of a life of thirty-three years of agony and of suffering! From the moment when the Word was made flesh in Mary's womb,—from the moment when the Eternal God became man,—even before He was born,—the cross, the thorny crown, and all the horrors that were accomplished on Calvary were steadily before the eyes of Jesus. The Infant in Bethlehem saw them; the Child in Nazareth saw them; the Young Man, toiling to support his mother, saw them; the Preacher on the mountain side beheld them. Never, for a single instant, were the horrors that were fulfilled on Good-Friday morning absent from the mind or the contemplation of Jesus Christ. Oh, dearly beloved brethren, well did the Psalmist say of Him, "My grief, my sorrow is always before me;" well the Psalmist said, "I have, during my whole life, walked in sorrow! I was scourged the whole day!" That day was the thirty-three years of His mortal life. Picture to yourselves what that life of grief must have been. There was the Almighty God in the midst of men, hearing their blasphemies, beholding their infamous actions, fixing His all-pure and all-holy eyes on their licentiousness, their ambition, their avarice, their dishonesty, their impurity. And, so, the very presence of those He came to redeem was a constant source of grief to Jesus Christ. Moreover, He knew well that He came into the world to suffer, and only to suffer. Every other being created into this world was created for some joy or other. There is not, even in hell, a creature whom Almighty God intended, in creating, for a life and eternity of misery; if they are there, they are there by their own act, not by the act of God. Not so with Christ. His sacred body was formed for the express and sole purpose that it might be the victim for the sins of man, and the sacrifice for the world's redemption. "Sacrifice and oblation," He said, "Thou wouldst not, O God; but Thou hast prepared a body for me." "Coming into the world," says St. Paul, "He proclaimed, 'for this I am come, that I may do Thy will, O Father.'" The Father's will was that He should suffer; and for this was He created. Therefore, as He was made for suffering,—as that body was given to Him for no purpose of joy, but only of suffering, of expiation, and of sorrow,—therefore it was that God made him capable of a sorrow equal to the remission He was about to grant. That was infinite sorrow.

And now, dearly beloved, having considered these things, we come to contemplate that which was always before the mind of Christ,—that from which He knew there was no escape,—that which was before Him really, not as the future is before us, when we anticipate it and fear it, but which still comes indistinctly and confusedly before the mind. Not so with Christ. Every single detail of His Passion, every sorrow that was to fall upon Him, every indignity that was to be put upon His body,—all, in the full clearness of their details, were before the eyes of the Lord Jesus Christ for the thirty-three years of His life.

As the sun was sloping down towards the western horizon on the evening of the vigil of the Pasch, behold our Divine Lord with His Apostles around Him: and there, seated in the midst of them, he fulfilled the last precept of the law, in eating the Paschal lamb; and He then changed the bread and wine into his own Body and Blood, and fed His Apostles with that of which the Paschal lamb was but a figure and a promise. Now they are about to separate in this world. Now, the greatest act of the charity of God has been performed. Now the Lord Jesus Christ is living and palpitating in the heart of each and every one of these twelve. Now,—horror of horrors!—He is gone into the heart of Judas! Arising from the tables our Lord took with Him Peter, and James, and John; and He turned calmly and deliberately to enter the red sea of His Passion, and to wade through His own blood, until He landed upon the opposite shore of pardon, and mercy, and grace, and brought with Him, in His own sacred humanity, the whole human race. Calmly, deliberately, taking his three friends with Him, He went out from the supper-hall, as the shades of evening were deepening into night; and He walked outside the walls of Jerusalem, where there was a garden full of olive trees, that was called Gethsemane. The Lord Jesus was accustomed to go there to pray. Many an evening had He knelt within those groves; many a night had He spent under the shade of these trees, filling the silent place with the voice of His cries and petitions, before the Lord, His Father, to obtain pardon and mercy for mankind. Now, He goes there for the last time; and as He is approaching,—as soon as ever He catches sight of the garden,—as soon as the familiar olives present themselves to His eyes, He sees—what Peter, and James, and John did not see,—He sees there, in that dark garden, the mighty array—the mighty, tremendous array —of all the sins that were ever committed in this world, as if they had taken the bodily form of demons of hell. There they were now—waiting silently, fearfully, with eyes glaring with infernal rage! And he saw them. And was He, the Lord God, to go among them! Among them must He go! No wonder that the moment He caught sight of that garden He started back, and turning to the three Apostles, He said: "Stand by Me now, for My soul is sorrowful unto death." And, leaning upon the virgin bosom of John, who was astonished at this fearful trial of his Master, He murmured unto him: "My soul is sorrowful unto death! Stand by me," He says, "and watch with me—and pray!" The man!—the man proving his humanity! proving his humanity which belonged to him as truly as his divinity! The man, turning to, and clinging to his friends! Gathering them around Him at that terrible moment when he was about to face His enemies, He cries again and again:—"Stand by me! stand by me! and support me, and watch, and pray with me!" And then, leaving them, alone He enters the gloomy place. Summoning all the courage of God,—summoning to His aid all the infinite resources of His love,—summoning the great thought that if He was about to be destroyed, mankind was to be saved, He dashes fearlessly into the depths of Gethsemane; and when He was as far from His Apostles as a man could cast a stone,—there, in the dark depths of the forest, the Lord Jesus knelt down and prayed. What was His prayer! Oh, that army of sins was closing around Him! Oh, the breath of Hell was on His face! There did He see the busy demons marshalling their forces,—drawing closer and closer to Him all the iniquities of men. "Oh, Father!" He cries—"Oh, Father, if it be possible, let this chalice pass away from me!" But He immediately added— "Not My will but Thine be done!" Then turning—for the Father's will was indicated to him in the voice from Heaven, with the first tone of anger upon it; the first word of anger that Jesus ever heard from His Father's lips, saying: "It is My will to strike Thee! Go!" He turned; He bared his innocent bosom; He put out His sinless hands; and, turning to all the powers of hell, allowed the ocean-wave of sin to flow in upon Him and overwhelm Him. The lusts and wickedness of men before the Flood, the impurities of Sodom and Gomorrha, the idolatries of the nations, the ingratitude of Israel;—all the sins that ever appeared under the eyes of God's anger—all—all!—like the waves of the ocean, coming in and falling upon a solitary man, who kneels alone on the shore,—all fell upon Jesus Christ. He looks upon Himself, and He scarcely recognizes Himself now. Are these the hands of Jesus Christ, scarcely daring to uplift themselves in prayer, for they are red with ten thousand deeds of blood? Is this the heart of Jesus, frozen up with unbelief, as if He felt—what He could not feel—that He was the personal enemy of God? Is this the sacred soul of Jesus Christ, darkened for the moment with the errors and the adulteries of the whole world? In the halls of His memory nothing but the hideous figures of sin!—desolation, broken hearts, weeping eyes, cries of despair, dire blasphemies;—these are the things that He sees within Himself, that He hears in His ears! It is a world of sin around Him. It is a raging of demons about Him. It is as if sin had entered into His blood. Oh, God! He bears it as long as a suffering man can bear. But at length, from out the depths of His most sacred heart, —from out the very divinity that was in Him,—the fountains of the great deep were moved, and forth came a rush of blood from every pore! His eyes can no longer dwell on the terrible vision! He can no longer look upon these red scenes of blood and impurity! A weakness comes mercifully to His relief. He gazes upon the fate that God has put upon Him; and then He falls to the earth, writhing in His agony; and forth from every pore of His sacred frame streams the blood! Behold Him! Behold the blood as it oozes out through His garments, making them red as those of a man who has trodden in the wine press! Behold Him, as His agonizing face lies prone upon the earth. Behold Him, as, in the hour of that terrible agony, His blood reddens the soil of Gethsemane!—behold Him as he writhes on the ground,— one mass of streaming blood,—sweating blood from head to foot,—crying out, in His agony, for the sins of the whole world! A mountain of the anger of God is upon Him! Behold Him in Gethsemane, O Christian man! Kneel down by His side! Lie down on that blood-stained earth, and, for the love of Jesus Christ, whisper one word of consolation to Him! For, remember that you and I were there; were there; and He saw us,—even as He sees us in this hour, gathered under the roof of this church. He saw us there, in our quality of sinners, as—with every sin that ever we committed—as if, with a stone in our uplifted hand, we flung it down upon His defenceless form! When Acan was convicted of a crime, Joshua gave word that every man of the Jewish nation should take a stone in his hand, and fling it at him; and all the people of Israel came and flung them upon him, and put him to death. So every son of man, from Adam down to the last that was born on this earth,—every son of man—every human being that breathed the breath of God's creation in this world, was there, in that hour, to fling his sins, and let them fall down upon Jesus Christ. All, all,—save *one*. There was *one* whose hand was not lifted against Him. There was one who, if she had been there, could be only there to help Him and to console Him. But no help could come, no consolation in that hour! Therefore Mary, the only sinless one, was absent.

He rises after an hour. No scourge has been yet laid upon that sacred body. No executioner's hand has profaned Him as yet. No nail had been driven through His hands. And yet the blood covered His body;—for His Passion began from that source to which I have alluded—His own divine spirit: His Passion—His pain began from within. He rises from the earth. What is this which we hear? There is a sound, as of the voices of a rabble. There are hoarse voices filling the night. There are men with clubs in their hands, and lanterns lighted. They come with fire and fury in their eyes, and the universal voice is, "Where is He? Where is He?" Ah there is one at the head of them! You hear his voice:—"Come cautiously! I see Him. I will point Him out to you! There are four of them. There He is, with three of His friends. When you see me take a man in my arms and kiss him, He is the man! Lay hold of Him at once, and drag Him away with you;—and do what you please!" Who is he that says this? Who are they that come like hell-hounds, thirsting for the blood of Jesus Christ? that come with the rage of hell in their blood, and in their mouths? They are come to take Him and to tear Him to pieces. Who is this that leads them on? Oh, friends and men! it is Judas, the Apostle! Judas, who spent three years in the society of Jesus Christ! Judas, that was taught by Him every lesson of piety and virtue, by word and by example! Judas, who received the priesthood! Judas, upon whose lips, even now, blushes the sacred blood received in holy communion! Oh, it is Judas! And he has come to give up his Master, whom he has sold for thirty pieces of silver. He went after his unworthy communion to the Pharisees, and he said: "What will you give me, and I will sell Him to you?—give Him up?" He put no price upon Jesus. He thought so little of his Master, that He was prepared to take any thing they would offer. They offered him thirty small pieces of silver; and he clutched at the money. He thought it was a great deal, and more than Jesus Christ was worth! Now he comes to fulfil his portion of the contract; and he points the Lord out by going up to him—putting his traitor lips upon the face of Jesus Christ, and sealing upon that face the kiss of a false-hearted, a wicked, and a traitorous follower. Behold him now. The Son of God sees him approach. He opens his arms to him. Judas flings himself in his Master's arms, and he hears the gentle reproach,—oh, last proof of love!—oh, last opportunity to him to repent—even in this hour!—"Judas, is it with a kiss thou betrayest the Son of Man!"

Now, the multitude rush in upon Him and seize Him. We have a supplement to the Gospel narrative in the revelations of many of the Saints, and of holy souls who, in reward for their extraordinary devotion to the Passion of our Lord, were favored with a closer sight of His sufferings. We are told by one of these,—whose revelations, though not yet approved, are tolerated by the Church,—that when our Divine Lord gave Himself into the hands of His enemies, they bound His sacred arms with a rope and rushed towards the city, dragging along with them, forcibly and violently, the exhausted Redeemer. Exhausted, I say, for His soul had just passed through the agony of His prayer, and His body was still dripping with the sweat of blood. Between that spot and Jerusalem flowed the little stream called the

Brook of Kedron. When they came to that little stream, our Saviour stumbled and fell over a stone. They, without waiting to give Him time to rise, pulled and dragged Him on with all their might. They literally dragged Him through the water, wounding and bruising His body by contact with the rocks that were in its bed. It was night when they brought Him into Jerusalem. That night a cohort of Roman soldiers formed the body-guard of Pilate. They were called "The Archers;" men of the most corrupt and terrible vices; men without faith in God or man: men whose every word was either a blasphemy or an impurity. These men, who were only anxious for amusement, when they found the prisoner dragged into Jerusalem at that hour, took possession of Him for the night; and they brought Him to their quarters: and there the Redeemer was put sitting in the midst of them. During the whole of that long night, between Holy-Thursday and Good-Friday morning, the soldiers remained sleepless, employed in loud revel, and in their derision and torture of the Son of God. They struck Him on the head. They spat upon Him. They hustled Him, with scorn, from one to another. They bruised Him. They wounded Him in every conceivable form. Here,—silent as a lamb before the shearer,—was the Eternal Son of God, looking out, with eyes of infinite knowledge and purity, upon the very vilest men that all the iniquity of this earth could bring around Him.

He was brought before the High Priest. He was asked to answer. The moment the Son of God opened His lips to speak—the moment he attempt to testify—a brawny soldier came out of the ranks, stepped before our Divine Lord, and saying to him: "Answerest thou the High Priest thus?" drew back his clenched mailed hand, and, with the full force of a strong man, flinging himself forward, struck Almighty God in the face! The Saviour reeled, stunned by the blow.

The morning came. Now He is led before Pilate, the Roman Governor, who alone has power to sentence Him to death, if He be guilty,—and who has the obligation to protect Him and set Him at liberty, if He be innocent. The Scribes and Pharisees and the Publicans were there,—the leaders of the people, and the rabble of Jerusalem were with them: and in the midst of them was the silent, innocent Victim who knew that the sad and terrible hour of His crucifixion was upon Him. Brought before Pilate, He is accused of this crime and that. Witnesses are called; and the moment they come—the moment they look upon the face of God,—they are unable to give testimony against Him. They could say nothing that proved Him guilty of any crime; and Pilate enraged turned to the Pharisees, turned to the learned men, turned to the people themselves, and said: "What do you bring this man here for? Why is he bound? Why is he bruised and maltreated? What has he done? I find no crime, or shadow of a crime in him." He is not only innocent, but the judge declares, before all the people, that the man has done nothing whatever to deserve any punishment, much less death. How is this sentence received? The Pharisees are busy among the people, whispering their calumnies, and prompting them to cry out, and say: "Crucify Him! crucify Him! We want to have Jesus of Nazareth crucified! We want to do it early, because the evening will come and bring the Sabbath with it! We want to have His blood shed! Quick! Quick! Tell Pilate he must condemn Jesus of Nazareth, or else he is no friend to Cæsar!" The people cry out: "Let Him be crucified! If you let Him go, you are no friend of Cæsar!" What says Pilate? "Crucify your king! He calls himself 'King of the Jews.' You yourselves wished to make Him your king: and you honored Him. Am I to crucify Him whom you would have for king? Am I to crucify your king?" And then,—then, in an awful moment, Israel declared solemnly that God was no longer her king; for the people cried out: "He is not our king! We have no king but Cæsar! We have no king but Cæsar!" The old cry of the man who, committing sin, says: "I have no king but my own passions; I have no king but this world; I have no king but the thoughts of money, or of honors, or of indulgence!" So the Jews cried: "He is no king of ours; we have no king but Cæsar!" Pilate, no doubt, in a spirit of compromise, said to himself: "I see this man cannot escape. I see murder in these people's eyes! They are determined upon the crucifixion of this man; and, therefore, I must try to find out some way or another of appealing to their mercy." Then he thought to himself: "I will make an example of Him. I will tear the flesh off His bones. I will cover Him with blood. I will make Him such a pitiable object that not one in all that crowd will have the heart to demand further punishment, or another blow for Him." So he called his officers, and said: "Take this man, and scourge Him so as to make Him frightful to behold; let Him be so mangled that when I show Him to the people, they may be moved to pity and spare his life: for he is an innocent man."

In the cold early morning, the Lord is led forth into the court-yard of the Prætorium; and there sixty of the strongest men of the guard are picked out,—chosen for their strength; and they are told off into thirty pairs, and every man of the sixty has a new scourge in his hand. Some have chains of iron; some cords knotted, with steel spurs at the end of them; others, the green, supple twig, plucked from the hedge in the early morning;—long, and supple, and terrible, armed with thorns. Now these men come and close around our Lord. They strip Him of His garments; they leave Him perfectly naked, blushing in His infinite modesty and purity, so that He longs for them to begin in order that they may robe Him in His blood. They tie His hands to a pillar; they tie Him so that He cannot move, nor shrink from a blow, nor turn aside. And then the two first advance; they raise their brawny arms in the air; and then, with a hiss, down come the scourges upon the sacred body of the Lord! Quicker and quicker these arms rise in the air with these terrible scourges. Each stroke leaves its livid mark. The flesh rises into welts. The blood is congealed and shows purple beneath the skin. Presently, the scourge comes down again, and it is followed by a quick spurt of blood from the sacred body of our Lord;—the blows quickening, and without pause, and without mercy; the blood flowing after every additional blow;—till these two strong men are fatigued and tired out,—until their scourges are sodden and saturated, and dripping with His blood, do they still strike Him,—and then retire, exhausted, from their terrible labor; then, in comes another pair,—fresh, vigorous; fresh arms and new men come to rain blows upon the defenceless body of the Lord, upon His sacred limbs, upon His sacred shoulders! Every portion of His sacred body is torn: every blow brings the flesh from the bones, and opens a new wound and a new stream of blood. Now He stands ankle deep-in His own blood,—hanging out from that pillar, exhausted, with head drooping, almost insensible. He is still beaten,—

even when the very men who strike Him think, or suspect, that they may have killed Him. It was written in the Old Law, "If a man be found guilty," says the Lord in Deuteronomy, "let him be beaten, and let the measure of his sin be the measure of his punishment; yet so that no criminal receive more than forty stripes, lest thy brother go away shamefully torn from before thy face!" These were the words of the law. Well the Pharisees knew it! Well the Publicans and Scribes knew it! And there they stood around, in the outer circle, with hate in their eyes, fury upon their lips; and even when the very men who were dealing out their revenge thought they had killed the victim they were scourging, still came forth from these hardened hearts the words of encouragement: "Strike Him still! Strike Him still!" And there they continued their cruel task until sixty men retired, fatigued and worn out with the work of the scourging of our Lord!

Now, behold Him as, senseless, He hangs from that pillar, one mass of bruised and torn flesh!—one open wound, from the crown of His head to the soles of His feet!—all bathed in the crimson of His own blood, and terrible to behold! If you saw Him here, as He stood there; if you saw Him now, standing upon that altar,—there is not a man or woman among you that could bear to look upon the terrible sight. They cut the cords that bound Him to the pillar; and the Redeemer fell down, bathed in His own blood, and senseless upon the ground. Behold Him again, as at Gethsemane; now, no longer the pain from within, but the pain from the terrible hand of man—the instrument of God's vengeance. Oh, behold Him! Mary heard those stripes and yet she could not save her Son. Mary's heart went down with Him to the ground, as He fell from that terrible pillar of His scourging! Behold Him, you mothers! You fathers, behold the Virgin's Child, your God—Jesus Christ! The soldiers amused themselves at the sight of His sufferings, and scoffed at Him as He lay prostrate. Recovering somewhat, after a time He opened His languid eyes and rose from the ground,—rose, all torn and bleeding. They throw an old purple rag around His shoulders, and they set Him upon a stone. One of them has been, in the meantime, busily engaged in twisting and twining a crown made of some of those thorns, which they had prepared for the scourging,—a crown in which seventy-two long thorns were put, so that they entered into the sacred head of our Lord. This crown was set upon his brow. Then a man came with a reed in his hand, and struck those thorns deep into the tender forehead. They are fastened deeply in the most sensitive organ, where pain becomes maddening in its agony. He strikes the thorns in, till even the sacred humanity of our Lord forces from Him the cry of agony! He strikes them in still deeper!—deeper! Oh, my God! Oh, Father of Mercy! And all this opens up new streams of blood!—new fountains of love! The blood streams down, and the face of the Most High is hidden under its crimson veil. Now, now, indeed, O Pilate,—O wise and compromising Pilate,—now, indeed, you have gained your end! You have proved yourself the friend of Cæsar. Now, there is no fear but that the Jews, when they see Him, will be moved by compassion!

They bring Him back and they put Him standing before the Roman governor. His rugged pagan heart is moved within him with horror when he sees the fearful example they have made of Him. Frightened when he beheld Him, he turned away his eyes; the spectacle was too terrible. He called for water and washed his hands. "I declare before God," he says, "I am innocent of this man's blood!" He leads Him out on the balcony of his house. There was the raging multitude, swaying to and fro. Some are exciting the crowd, urging them to cry out to crucify Him; some are preparing the Cross, others getting ready the hammer and nails, some thinking of the spot where they would crucify Him! There they were arguing with diabolical rage. Pilate came forth in his robes of office. Soldiers stand on either side of him. Two soldiers bring forth our Lord. His hands are tied. A reed is put in His hand in derision. Thorns are on His brow. Blood is flowing from every member of His sacred body. An old tattered purple rag is flung over him. Pilate brings him out, and looking round on the multitude says: "*Ecce homo!* Behold the man! You said I was no friend to Cæsar. You said I was afraid to punish Him! Behold Him now! Is there a man among you who would have the heart to demand more punishment?" Oh, Heaven and earth! Oh, Heaven and earth! The cry from out every lip—from out every heart is: "We are not yet satisfied! Give Him to us! Give Him to us! We will crucify Him!" "But,"

says Pilate, "I am innocent of His blood!" And then came
a word—and this word has brought a curse upon the Jews
from that day to this. Then came the word that brought
the consequences of their crime on their hard hearts and
blinded intellects. They cried out: "His blood be upon us
and upon our children! Crucify Him!" "But," says Pilate,
"here is a man in prison; he is a robber and a murderer!
And here is Jesus of Nazereth whom I declare to be innocent! One of these I must release. Which will you have—
Jesus or Barrabas?" And they cried out "Barrabas! give
us Barrabas! But let Jesus be crucified!" Here is the
Son of God compared to the robber and the murderer! And
the robber and murderer is declared fit to live, and Jesus
Christ, the Son of God, is declared fit only to die! The
vilest man in Jerusalem declared in that hour that he would
not associate with our Lord, and that the Son of God was
not worthy to breathe the air polluted by this man! So
Barrabas came forth rejoicing in his escape: and, as he
mingled in the crowd, he too, threw up his hands and cried
out, "Oh, let Him be crucified! let Him be crucified!"

He is led forth from the tribunal of Pilate. And now,
just outside of the Prefect's door, there are men holding up a
long, weighty, rude cross, that they had made rapidly; for
they took two large beams, put one across the other, fastened
them with great nails, and made it strong enough to uphold
a full-grown man. There is the cross! There is the man
with the nails! And there are all the accompaniments of
the execution. And He who is scarcely able to stand,—He,
bruised and afflicted,—the Man of Sorrows, almost fainting
with infirmity, He is told to take that cross upon his bleeding, wounded shoulders, and to go forward to the mountain
of Calvary. Taking to him that cross, holding it to His
wounded breast, putting to it, in tender kisses, the lips that
were distilling blood, the Son of God, with the cross upon His
shoulders, turns His faint and tottering footsteps towards the
steep and painful way that led to Calvary. Behold Him as
He goes forth! That cross is a weight almost more than a
man can carry; and it is upon the shoulders of one from
whom all strength and manliness and courage are gone!
Behold the Redeemer, as He toils painfully along, amid the
shouts and shrieks of the enraged people! Behold Him as he
toils along the flinty way, the soldiers driving Him on, the

people inciting them, every one rushing and hastening to Calvary, to witness the execution. John, the beloved disciple, follows Him. A few of His faithful disciples toil along. But there is one who traces each of His blood-stained footsteps; there is one who follows Him with a breaking heart: there is one whose very soul within her is pierced and torn with the sword of sorrow. Oh, need I name the Mother, the Queen of Martyrs? In that hour of His martyrdom, Mary, the mother of Jesus, followed immediately in His footsteps, and her whole soul went forth in prayer for an opportunity to approach Him to wipe the blood from His sacred face. Oh, if they would only let her come to Him, and say, "My child! I am with you!" If they would only let her take in her womanly arms, from off the shoulders of her dear Son, that heavy cross that He cannot bear! But no! She must witness His misery; she must witness His pain.

He toils along: He takes the first few steps up the rugged side of Calvary. Suddenly His heart ceases to beat; the light leaves His eyes; He sways, for a moment, to and fro; the weakness and the sorrow of death are upon Him; He totters, falls to the earth; and down, with a heavy crash, comes the weighty cross upon the prostrate form of Jesus Christ! Oh, behold Him, as for the third time He embraces that earth which is sanctified and redeemed by His love! Mary rushes forward; Mary thinks her child is dead: she thinks that terrible cross must have crushed Him into the earth. She rushes forward; but with rude and barbarous words the woman is flung aside. The cross is lifted up and placed on the shoulders of Simon of Cyrene; and, with blows and blasphemies, the Saviour of the world is obliged to rise from that earth; and, worn with the sorrows and afflictions of death, He faces the rugged steep on the summit of which is the place destined for His crucifixion. Arrived at the place, they tear off His garments; they take from Him the seamless garment which His mother's loving hands had woven for Him; they take the humble clothing in which the Son of God had robed Himself,—saturated, steeped as it is in His blood; and, in removing them, they open afresh every wound, and once again the saving blood of Christ is poured out upon the ground. With rude, blasphemous words the God-man is told to lie down upon that cross. Of His own free will He stretches His tender limbs, puts forth His hands, and stretches out His feet at their order. The executioners take the nails and the hammer, and they kneel upon His sacred bosom; they press out His hands till they bring the palms to where they had made the holes to fit the nails. They stretch Him out upon that cross, even as the Paschal Lamb was stretched out upon the altar; they kneel upon the cross; they lay the nails upon the palms of His hands. The first blow drives the nail deep into his hands, the next blow sends it into the cross. Blow follows blow. They are inflamed with the rage of hell. Earnestly they work,—and hell delights in the scene,—tearing the muscles and the sinews of His hands and feet. Rude, terrible blows fall on these nails, and reëcho in the heart of the Virgin, until that heart seems to be broken at the foot of the cross. And, now, when they have driven these nails to the heads, fastening Him to the wood, the cross is lifted up from the ground. Slowly, solemnly, the figure of Jesus Christ, all red with blood, all torn and disfigured, rises into the air, until the cross, attaining its full height, is fixed into its socket in the earth. The banner of salvation is flung out over the world; and Jesus Christ, the Son of God, and the Redeemer of mankind, appears in mid-air, and looks out over the crowd and over Jerusalem, over hill and valley, far away towards the Sea of Galilee, and all around the horizon; and the dying eyes of the Saviour are turned over the land and the people for whom He is shedding His blood. Uplifted in mid-air,—the eternal sacrifice of the Redeemer for everlasting,—hanging from these three terrible nails on the cross,—for three hours He remained. Every man took up his position. Mary, His Mother, approaches, for this is the hour of her agony; she must suffer in soul what He suffers in body. John, the disciple of love, approaches, and takes his stand under his Master's outstretched hands. Mary Magdalen rushes through the guards, to the feet of her Lord and Master; they are now bathed with other tears—with the tears of blood that save the world,—the feet which it was her joy to weep over! And now she clasps the cross, and pours out her tears, until they mingle with the blood which flows down His feet. There are the Pharisees and the Scribes, who had gained their point; they come and stand before the cross; they look upon that figure of awful pain and misery; they see those thorns sunk deeply into that drooping head; with no love in their hearts, they see the agony expressed in the eyes of the Victim who is dying; and then looking up exultingly, they rejoice and say to Him: "You said you could destroy the Temple, and build it up in three days; now, come down from the cross, and we will believe in and worship you." The Roman soldier stood there, admiring the courage with which the man died. The third hour is approaching. The penitent thief on His right hand had received his pardon. A sudden gloom gathers round the scene.

Before we come to the last moment, I ask you to consider Jesus Christ as your God. I ask you to consider the sacrifice that He made, and to consider the circumstances under which He approached that last moment of His life. All He had in the world was some little money: it was kept to give to the poor; Judas had that, and he had stolen it. Christ had literally nothing but the simple garments with which He had been clothed; these the soldiers took, and they raffled for them under His dying eyes. What remained for Him? The love of His mother; the sympathy of John? But He, uplifted on the cross, said to Mary: "Woman, behold thy son!" And to John He said; "Son, behold thy mother!" Thus I give one to the other; let that love suffice: and leave Me all alone and abandoned to die." What remained to Him? His reputation for sanctity, for wisdom, and for power. His reputation for sanctity was so great, that the people said; "This man never could do such things if He had not come from God." And as to His wisdom: His reputation for wisdom was such that we read, not one of the Pharisees or Doctors of the Law had the courage to argue with Him. His reputation for power was such that all the people said: "This man speaks and preaches, not as the Pharisees, but as one having power." Christ had sacrificed and given up His reputation for sanctity, for He was crucified as a blasphemer and a teacher of evil. His reputation for wisdom was sacrificed in the course of His Passion, when Herod declared that He was a fool. Clothed in a white garment, in derision, He was marched through the streets of Jerusalem, from Herod's palace to Pilate's house, dressed as a fool; and men came to their doors to point the finger of scorn and laugh at Him, and reproached each other for having listened to His doctrine. His reputation for power was gone. They came to the foot of the cross and said: "Now, if you have the power, come down from that cross and we will believe you." Now, all the man's earthly possessions are gone: His few garments are gone; Mary's love and sustaining compassion are gone; His reputation is gone; He is one wound, from head to foot; the anger of man has vented itself upon Him. What remains for Him? The ineffable consolations of His divinity; the infinite peace of the Godhead, the Father! Oh, Man of Sorrow! Oh, Lord Jesus Christ, cling to that! Whatever else may be taken from you, that cannot be taken away. Oh, Master, lean upon Thy Godhead! Oh, crucified, bleeding, dying Lord, do not give up that which is Thy peace and Thy comfort,—Thy joy in the midst of all this suffering! But what do I see? The dying head is lifted up; the drooping eyes are cast heavenwards; an expression of agony absorbing all others comes over the dying face; and a voice breaks forth from the quivering, agonized lips—"My God! My God! why hast Thou forsaken Me!" The all-sufficient comfort of the divinity and the sustaining power of the Father's love are put away from Him in that hour! A cloud came between Jesus Christ upon the cross, the victim of our sins, and the Father's face in Heaven; and that cloud was the concentrated anger of God which came upon His divine Son, because of our sins and our transgressions. Not that His divinity quitted Him. No; He was still God; but by His own act and free will, He put away the comfort and the sustaining power of the divinity for a time, in order that every element of sorrow, every grief, every misery of which the greatest victim of this earth was capable, should be all concentrated upon Him at the hour of His death. And then, having used these solemn words, He waited the moment when the Father's will should separate the soul from the body.

Now, Mary and John have embraced: Judas is struggling in the last throes of his self-imposed death: Peter has wept his tears. The devil for a moment triumphs; and the man-God upon the cross awaits the hour and the moment of the world's redemption. The sun in the Heavens is withdrawn behind mysterious clouds: and though it was but three o'clock in the day, a darkness like that of midnight came upon the land. Men looked upon each other in horror and in terror. Presently a rumbling noise is heard: they look around and see the hills and the mountains tremble on their bases: the very ground seems to rock beneath them; it groans as though the earth were breaking up from its centre; the rocks are splitting up; and round them strange figures are flitting here and there; the graves are opened, and the dead entombed there are walking in the dark ways before them. "What is this? Who is this terrible man that we have put on that cross?" The earth quakes; darkness is still upon it; perfect silence reigns over Calvary, unbroken by the cry of the dying Redeemer,—unbroken by the voice of the scoffers,—unbroken by the sobs of the Magdalen. Every heart seems to stand still. Then, over that silence, in the midst of that darkness, is heard the terrible cry—"O Father, into Thy hands I commend My spirit!" The head of the Lord Jesus Christ droops; the man upon the cross is dead! And the world is saved and redeemed! The moment the cry came forth from the dying lips of Jesus Christ, the devil, who stood there, knew that it was the Son of God who was crucified, and that his day was gone. Howling in despair, he fled from the Redeemer's presence into the lowest depths of hell. The world is saved! The world is redeemed! Man's sin is wiped out! The blood that washed away the iniquity of our race has ceased to flow from the dead and pulseless heart of Jesus. Wrapt in prayer, Mary bowed down her head under the weight of her sorrows! the Magdalen looked up and beheld the dead face of her Redeemer. John stretched out his hands and looked upon that face. The Roman soldier lays hold of his lance, under some strange impulse. Word comes that the body was to be taken down; they did not know whether our Lord was dead; there might yet some remnant of life remain in Him. The question was to prove that he was dead; and this man approaches. As a warrior, he puts his lance in rest, rushes forward with all the strength of his arm, and drives the lance right into the heart of the Lord! The heavy cross sways; it seems as if it is about to fall; the lance quivers for an instant in the wound; the man draws it forth again; and forth from the heart of the dead Christ stream the waters of life and the blood of redemption! The soldier drew back his lance, and the next moment, on his knees, before the Crucified, with the lance dripping with the blood of the Lord still in his hand, he cried out: "Truly this Man was the Son of God!" Then the earthquake began again; the dead were seen passing in fearful array, turning the eyes of the tomb upon the faces of those Pharisees who had crucified the Lord. And the people, frightened, became conscious that they had committed a terrible crime, when they heard Longinus, the Roman soldier, cry out,—" This Man is truly the Son of God, whom you have crucified." Then came down from Calvary the crowds, exclaiming—" Yes, truly this is the Son of God." And they went down the hillside, weeping and beating their breasts! Oh, how much we cost! Oh, how great was the price that He paid for us! Oh, how generously He gave all He had—and He was God—for your salvation and mine! It is well to rejoice and to be here; it is well to come and contemplate the blessings which that blessed, gracious Lord has conferred on us. It is, also, well to consider what He paid and how much it cost Him. And if we consider this, then, with Mary the mother, and Mary the Magdalen, and John the Evangelist and friend—then will our hearts be afflicted. For the soul that is not afflicted on this day shall be wiped out from the pages of the Book of Life.

THE CATHOLIC CHURCH THE SALVATION OF SOCIETY.

[*A Lecture delivered by the Very Rev. T. N. Burke. O.P., in the Church of St. Charles Borromeo, Brooklyn, April 2, 1872.*]

My Friends: The subject which, as you know, has been announced to you, and which I purpose to treat before you this evening, is the proposition that "The Catholic Church is the Salvation of Society." Perhaps there are some among you who think I am an unusually courageous man to make so wild and so rash an assertion. But it must be acknowledged, indeed, that, for the past eighteen hundred years that the Catholic Church has existed, Society has aways endeavored to get away from her grasp and to live without her. People who admit the action of the Church, who allow it to influence their history, who let it influence their lives—if they rise to the height of their Christian elevation, if they conform themselves to the teachings of what is true, if they avail themselves of the graces of the Church, are very often scoffed at and called a priest-ridden and besotted people. Nowadays, it is the fashion to look upon that man as the best of his class who has succeeded the most completely in emancipating himself from every control of religion, or of the Catholic Church. In one sense, it is a great advantage to a man to have no religion,—to shake off the influence of the Church. Such a man remains without a conscience and without remorse of mind. He saves himself from those moments of uneasiness and self-accusation that come to most men until they completely lose all reverence for God; and the consequence is that, if he is a sinner, and in the way of sin, he enjoys it all the more; and he can make the more use of his time in every pathway of iniquity, if he has no obstacles of conscience or of religion to fetter him. So far, it is an advantage to be without religion. The robber, for instance, can rob more confidently if he can manage to forget that there is a God above him. The murderer can wash his hands with more serenity, no matter how deeply he stains them,—if there is no condemning record, no accusing voice, no ear to hear the voice of the blood that cries out against him for satisfaction. He can pursue his misdeeds all the more at his own ease. And so, for this, among many other reasons, the world is constantly trying to emancipate itself from the dominion of God, and from the control of the Church, the messenger of the Saviour of the world.

It would seem, therefore, at first sight rather a hazardous thing to stand up in the face of the world, and in the face of society to-day—this boasted society—and say to them: "You cannot live,—you cannot get on without the Catholic Church! She can do without you! A coterie here! A tribe there! A nation elsewhere! A race beyond! Of what account are you to her, speaking humanly? She can do without you. But you, at your peril, must let her in, because you cannot do without her!" Now, this is the pith and substance of all that I intend to say to you here to-night; but not to say it without proof: for I do not ask any man here to accept one iota of what I say, on my mere assertion, until I have proved it.

My proposition, as you perceive, is that the Catholic Church is the salvation of society—and it involves three distinct propositions, although it may appear to you to be only one: First, it involves the proposition that society requires to be saved,—that it requires something for its salvation. Then, it involves the proposition that the Catholic Church, so far, has been the salvation of the world in times past;—out of which grows the third proposition; namely, that she is necessary to the world in all future time; and it is her destiny to be, in time to come, what she has been in time past,—the salvation of society. These are three distinct propositions.

The man who admires this century of ours and who serenely glories in it,—who calls it "the Age of Progress" —the "Age of Enlightenment;"—who speaks of his own land,—be it Ireland or America, or Italy or France,—as a country of enlightenment, and its people as an enlightened people,—this man stands amazed, when I say to him that this boasted society requires salvation. Somebody or other must save it. For, consider what it has done? What has it produced without the saving influence of the Catholic

Church? We may analyze society, as I intend to view it, from an intellectual stand-point. Then we shall see the society of learning,—the society of art and of literature. Or we may view it from a moral stand-point,—that is to say, in the government of the world, and how the wheels of society work in this boasted progress of ours,—emancipated from the Catholic Church, as this society has been mainly for the last three hundred years; in some countries more, in some countries less, in some countries entirely. Now, I ask you, what has this society produced, intellectually, morally, politically? Intellectually, it has produced a philosophy that asks us, at this hour of the day, to believe in ghosts! The last climax of the philosophy of this nineteenth century of ours is "Spiritualism," of which you have all heard. The philosopher of to-day, unlike even the philosopher of the Pagan times of old, does not direct his studies, nor the labors of his mind, to the investigation of the truth and of the development of the hidden secrets of nature—of the harmonies of the soul of man—of the wants of the spirit of man. To none of these does the philosopher of to-day direct his attention. But this man,—this leader of mind in society,—gets a lot of his friends round a table; and there they sit and listen until "the spirits" begin to "knock:" that is the pith and substance of his philosophy. Another man— one of another great school; and, indeed, these two schools may be said to have divided the philosophical empire of our age;—this disciple of another school stands up in our churches and pulpits, and says: "O man! son of the children of men,—since thou hast received a commission to sound the Scriptures—to mend the 'Word of God,' as it is called,— believe me when I tell you that our common ancestor was an ape,—and that it was by the merest accident,—the accident of progression; eating a certain kind of food; endeavoring, by degrees, to walk erect instead of crawling on our hands and feet,—it was by the merest accident,—a congeries of accidental circumstances,—that we happen to be men, and have not tails!" This is the philosophy of the nineteenth century! This is the intellectual grandeur and "Progress of the Age" that says: "I do not require salvation!"

The moral progress of this society, which has emancipated itself from the Catholic Church,—what is it? It has produced, in this our society, sins, of which, as a priest and a man, I am ashamed to speak. It has produced in the city of New York the terrible insult to a crucified Lord,—that a woman, pretending to be modest, should have chosen Good-Friday night to advocate impurity! Just as the "intellectual" development of our society, emancipated from the Church, has arrived at the glorious discovery of "Spiritualism," so the "moral" development of this age of ours has arrived at the deep depth of "free love."

What is the political spirit of society, and the perfection to which it has attained since it has been emancipated from the Church? Why, it has produced the "politician" of our day. It has produced the ruler who imagines that he is set up, throughout all the nations, only to grasp,—justly, if he can, unjustly, if he has no other means,—every privilege of power and of absolutism. It has produced in the people an unwillingness to obey even just laws. I need not tell you; you have the evidence of your own senses; you have records of the daily actions of the world laid before you every morning. This is the issue of the dominant spirit of society, when society emancipates itself from the Church, and, by so doing, endeavors to shake off God. Now we come to the great question: *Quis medecabitur?* Who shall touch society with a scientific and healing hand? What virtue can we infuse into it? That must come, I assert, from God, and from Him alone, of whom the Scriptures say that "He made the people healthy" (*fecit populum sanabilem*); that He has made our nature so that, even in its worst infirmity, it is capable of cure. He came and found it in its worst infirmity; society rotten to its heart's core; and the interior rottenness—the obscurity of the intellect—the corruption of the heart—manifesting itself in the actions and sins of which St. Paul the Apostle says, "*Nec nominabitur in vobis*,"—that they must not be even mentioned among Christian men. Christ, the Son of God, because He was God—equal to the Father—girding Himself up to the mighty work of healing this society, came down from Heaven and cured it, when no other hand but His could have touched it with healing; when no other virtue or power save His could, at all, have given life to the dead world, purity to the corrupt world, light to the darkened intellect of man. From Him came life to the dead—and that life was light to the darkened and strength to the weak,—because He was God.

Then the nations of Greece and Rome appeared in the strength of their power,—proud in their mental culture,—proud in the grandeur of their civilization;—and contemptuously put away and despised the message of the Divine Faith which was sent to them; and for three hundred long years persecuted the Church of God. This great instructress, who came to talk in a language that they knew not, and to teach them things that they never heard of—both the things of Heaven and the things of earth;—this great instructress, for three hundred years, lay hid in the caves and catacombs of the earth, afraid to show her face; for the whole world—all the power of Pagan Rome—was raised against her. There was blood upon her virgin face; there was blood upon her unspotted bosom—the blood of the innocent and of the pure; and all the world knew of Christianity was the strong testimony which, from time to time, was given of it, by youth and maiden, in the arena of Rome, or in the amphitheatres of Antioch or of Corinth. Then, in punishment for their pride,—as an act of vengeance upon them for their rejection of His gospel,—the Almighty God resolved to break up their ancient civilization; to sweep away their power; to bring the hordes of barbarous nations from the North of Europe into the very heart of Rome, the centre of the world's empire, and to crush and destroy it with fire and sword, and utterly to break up all that society which was formed, of old, upon the literature and the philosophy of Greece and of Rome. Consequently, we behold, in the fifth century, all the ancient civilization completely destroyed, and the world reduced again almost to the chaos of barbarism from which the Pagans of old had elevated it. Arts and sciences perished, when the Goth and Vandal, Visigoth, and Ostrogoth, and Hun swept down, like a swarm of locusts, over the old Roman Empire, and all the lands subject to Roman sway. Alaric, at the head of his Visigoths, was swooping over Rome. He was asked to spare the city out of respect to the civilization of the world and the tombs of the Apostles! "I cannot withhold," exclaimed the Visigoth, "I cannot withhold. I hear within me a mysterious voice which says: 'Alaric! Alaric! On! on to Rome!'" And so he came and sacked the city, burned and destroyed its temples, its palaces, its libraries, and its glories of painting and sculpture—hurled them all into the dust! And the desolation spread world-wide wherever a vestige of ancient civilization was found; until, at the end of that fatal century, the Church of God found herself standing upon the ruins of a world that had passed away. Before her were the countless hordes of the savage children of the North, out of which rugged material it was her destiny and her office to form the society of modern times. Hard, indeed, was the task which she undertook— not only to evangelize them—to teach them the things of God, but, also to teach them the beauties of human art and human science—to soften them with the genial influences and the tender appliances of learning;—to gain their hearts and soften their souls, and mollify their manners and refine them by every human appliance as well as by every Divine influence. For this task did she gather herself up. She, in that day, collected with a careful and a venerating hand all that remained out of the ruin of ancient literature, of ancient poetry, of ancient history, in the languages of Greece and of Rome. She gathered them lovingly and carefully to her bosom. She laid them up in her sacred recesses,—in her cloisters. She applied diligently to the study of them, and to the diffusion of them, the minds of the holiest and best of her consecrated children; until, in a few years, all that the world had of refinement, of learning, of all that was refining and gentle was concentrated in the person of the lowly monk who,—full of the lore of Greece and Rome—full of ancient learning as well as of that of the time,—an artist— a painter—a musician—a man of letters,—covering all with the humility of his profession, and hiding all in the cloister, —yet treasured all up for the society that was to come after him, and for the honor and glory of God and of His Church. And so, by degrees, the Church was enabled to found schools and, then, colleges,—and thence to form, gradually, universities—and to obtain for them and to ensure unto them civic and municipal rights, as we shall see farther on.

By degrees she founded the great mediæval universities, gathering together all those who wished to learn, and sending forth from her cloisters her Benedictines and Cistercians, her Dominicans, her Franciscans to teach philosophy and theology, while they illustrated the very highest art in the beauty of their paintings and the splendor which they threw around the Christian sciences. Universities were founded by her, into which she gathered the youth of various nations;

and then sending them home, among their rude and rugged fellow-citizens, she spread gradually the flame of human knowledge, as well as the fire of divine faith and sanctity. And thus, for many a long century, did the Church labor assiduously, lovingly, perseveringly; and so secured unto us whatever blessings of learning we possess to-day. In this way she saved society for the time, by drawing forth its rude chaotic elements, and by her patient action in creating the light of knowledge where the darkness of ignorance was before,—with patient and persevering effort bringing forth order out of disorder—until her influence over the world was like the word of God, when, upon the first day of creation, He made all things, and made them to exist where nothing but void and darkness were before. Nor can the history of bygone times be disputed in this; nor can any man allege that I am claiming too much for the Catholic Church, when I say that she alone has presented to us all the splendor of the Pagan literature of the ancient times,—all the arts and sciences; that she alone has founded the great schools and universities of Christendom and of the civilized world—even in Protestant countries to-day;—nay more, that nearly all the great scholars who shone as stars in the firmament of learning were her children,—either consecrated to her in the priesthood, or attached to her by the strongest and the tenderest bonds of faith. Lest my word in this matter be considered exaggerated, let me read for you the testimony of a Protestant writer to what I say. He says to us:

"If the Catholic Church had done nothing more than to preserve for us, by painful solicitude and unrewarded toil, the precepts and intellectual treasures of Greece and Rome, she would have been entitled to our everlasting gratitude. But her hierarchy did not merely preserve these treasures. They taught the modern world how to use them. We can never forget that at least nine out of every ten of all the great colleges and universities in Christendom were founded by monks or priests, bishops or archbishops. This is true of the most famous institutions in Protestant as well as in Catholic countries. And equally undeniable is the fact that the greatest discoveries in the sciences and in the arts (with the sole exception of Sir Isaac Newton) have been made either by Catholics, or by those who were educated by them. Our readers know that Copernicus, the author of our present system of astronomy, lived and died a poor parish priest, in an obscure village; and Galileo lived and died a Catholic. The great Kepler, although a Protestant himself, always acknowledged that he received the most valuable part of his education from the monks and priests. It were easy to add to these illustrious names many equally renowned in other departments of science as well as literature and the arts, including those of statesmen, orators, historians, poets, and artists."

This is the testimony of a Protestant writer, confirmed by the voice of history, to which I fearlessly appeal, when I lay down the proposition that, if the intellectual darkness, if the barbarism of ignorance be a disease in society, then history proves that the Catholic Church has been the salvation of society in the cure of that disease. I might go deeper here. I might show you here, in the beautiful reasoning of the great St. Thomas Aquinas, how, in the Catholic Church alone, is the solid basis of all intellectual knowledge. "For," observes the Saint, "every science, no matter how different it may be from others,—every science rests upon certain principles that are taken for granted—certain axioms that are accepted, without being proved. Now," he goes on to say, "the principle of acknowledged certainty, of some kind or other, lies at the base and at the foundation of every science, and of every form of intellectual power." But, in the sciences and in the intellectual world, we find the same order, the same exquisite harmony, which, in the works of God, we find in the material and physical creation. The principle, therefore, of all the arts and sciences, each with its respective power, is that all go up in regular order from the lowest form of art to the highest of human sciences,—astronomy,—until they touch divine theology, which teaches of God and of the things of God. Upon the certainty of that First Science depends the very idea of "certainty," upon which every other science is based. And, therefore, the keynote of all knowledge is found in the science of divine theology, which teaches of God. Now, outside of the Catholic Church, there is no theology, as a science; because science involves certain knowledge—and there is no certain knowledge of divine things outside the Catholic Church. There is no certain knowledge of Divine things where truth is said to consist in the inquiry after truth, as in Protestantism, where religion is reduced from the principle of immutable faith to the mere result of reasoning, amounting to a strong opinion. There is no certainty, therefore, outside of that Church that speaks of God in the very language of God; that gives a message sent from the very lips of God; that puts that message into the Godlike form of immutable dogma before the minds of His children, and so starts them in the pursuit of all human knowledge, with the certain light of divinely-revealed truth, and with the principle of certitude deeply seated in their minds.

Now, we pass from the intellectual view of society to the moral view of it. In order to understand the action of the Church here as the sole salvation of society, I must ask you to consider the dangers which threaten society in its moral aspect. These dangers are the following :—First of all, the libertinism, the instability, the inconstancy, and the impurity of man. Secondly, the absence of the element of holiness and sanctity in the education of childhood. Thirdly, the sense of irresponsibility, or a personal liberty which not only passes us over from under the control of the law, but cuts off our communication with God, and makes us forget that we are responsible to God for every action of our lives; and so, gradually brings a man to believe that liberty and freedom mean irresponsible licentiousness and impurity. These I hold to be the three great evils that threaten society. The inconstancy of man;—for man is fickle in his friendship, is unstable in his love, is inconstant in his affections, subject to a thousand passing sensations;—his soul laid open to appeals from every sense,—to the ebb and flow of every pulse; and every sense of his for ever palpitating with a quick response to every impression telling the eye to look with pleasure upon this object, as amusing; to the ear, telling it to drink in with pleasure such and such a sound of melody; —and so on. Need I tell you, my friends, what your own heart has so often told you—how inconstant we are; how the thing that captivates us to-day, we will look coldly upon to-morrow, and the next day, perhaps with eyes of disgust? Need I tell you how fickle is that love, that friendship of the human heart, against which, and its inconstancy, the Holy Ghost seems to warn us? " Put not thy trust in Princes, nor in the children of men, in whom there is no salvation." To guard against this inconstancy, it is necessary to call in divine grace and help from Heaven. For it is a question of confirming the heart of man, in the steadiness, in the unchangeableness, and in the purity of the love that is to last all his life long. Therefore it is that the Catholic Church sanctifies the solemn contract by which man promises to his fellow-creature that he will love her; that he will never allow that love for her to grow cold in his bosom; that he will never allow even a thought of any other love than hers to cross his imagination or enter his soul, that he will love her in the days of her old age as he loves her to-day in the freshness of her beauty as she stands by his side before the altar of God, and puts her virgin hand into his. And she swears to him a corresponding love. But ah! who can assure to her that heart which promises to be hers to-day—who can insure to her that love, ever inconstant in its own nature, and acted upon by a thousand influences,—calculated, first to alienate, then to destroy it? How can she have the courage to believe that the word that passes from that man's lips, at the altar, shall never be regretted—never be repealed? I answer, the Catholic Church comes in and calls down a special sacramental grace from Heaven; lets in the very blood of the Saviour, in its sacramental form, to touch these two hearts, and by purifying them, to elevate their affection into something more than gross love of sense, and to shed upon those two hearts, thus united, the rays of divine grace, to tinge their lives somewhat with the light of that ineffable love that binds the Lord to His Church. And so, in that sacrament of matrimony, the Church provides a divine remedy for the inconstancy of the heart of man; and she also provides a sanctifying influence which, lying at the very fountain-head, and source, and spring of our nature, sanctifies the whole stream of society that flows from the sacramental and sanctifying love of Christian marriage.

Do you not know that this society, in separating itself from the Church, has literally destroyed itself? If Protestantism, or Unitarianism, or any other form of error, did nothing else than simply to remove from the Sacrament of Matrimony its sacramental character—its sanctifying grace —by that very act, that error of religious unbelief, it destroys society. The man who destroys, in the least degree, the firmness of the bond that can never be broken,—because it is bound by the hand of God, and sealed with the sacramental seal,—the man that touches that bond, the man that takes from that Sacrament one single iota of its grace, makes himself thereby the enemy of society, and pollutes the very fountain-head from which the stream of our life comes. When the prophet of old came into the city of Jericho, they showed him the stream that ran by the city walls; and they told him: "Here is a stream of water: whoever drinks of that water dies; our people are dying either of thirst or of the poisoned waters." He did not attempt to heal the stream as it flowed thereby; but he took to himself salt, and he blessed that salt, and he said to the people—"Bring me to the fountain out of which this river cometh." And they brought him up into the mountain; and they showed him the fountain-head of the stream. "Here," he said, "here must we heal it." He put the blessed salt into the fountain, the spring from which the stream came, and he said: "Thus saith the Lord, I have healed these waters, and there shall no more be in them death or bitterness." Thus he purified the fountain-head of the spring of the waters of Jericho. Such is the Sacrament of Marriage to human society. The future of the world, the moral future of mankind—of the rising generations—depend upon the purity and the sanctity of the matrimonial tie. There does the Church of God throw, as it were, her sacramental salt of grace into the fountain-head of our nature, and so sanctifies the humanity that springs from its source.

The next great moral influence of society which requires the Church's action, is Education. "The child," as you know, "is father to the man;" and what the child is to-day the man will be in twenty or thirty years' time. Now, the young soul of the child is like the earth in the Spring season. The time of childhood is the time of sowing and of planting. Whatever is put into that young heart in the early days of childhood, will bring up, in the Summer of manhood, and in the Autumn of old age, its crop, either of good or evil. And, therefore, it is the most important time of life. The future of the world depends upon the sanctity of education. Now, in order that education may be bad, it is not necessary, my friends, to teach the child any thing bad. In order to make education bad, it is quite enough to neglect the element of sanctity and of religion. It is quite enough to neglect the religious portion of the education. By that very defect the education becomes bad. And why? Because, such is our nature, such the infirmity of our fallen state, such is the atmosphere of the scenes in which we live in this world, such the power of the infernal agencies that are busily at work for our destruction, that, educate the child as carefully as you may, surround him with the holiest influences, fill him with the choicest graces, you still run great risks that, some day or other, the serpent of sin will gain an entrance into that young soul, in spite of you. How much more if that young heart be not replenished with divine grace! How much more if that young soul be not fenced around by a thousand appliances and a thousand defences against its enemies! And thus do we see that the principle of bad education is established the moment the strong religious element is removed. Hence it is that, out of the sanctity of marriage, springs the sanctity of education in the Catholic Church. And why? Because the Church of God proclaims that the marriage bond no man can dissolve; that that marriage bond,—so long as death does not come in to separate the man and wife,—that that marriage bond is the one contract which no power on this earth can dissolve. Consequently, the Catholic woman, married to the Catholic man, knows that the moment their lips mutually pronounce their marriage vows, her position is defined and established for evermore: that no one can put her down from the holy eminence of wife or of mother, and that the throne which she occupies in the household, she never can live to see occupied by another; that her children are assured to her, and that she is left in her undisputed empire and control over them. She knows that —no matter how the word may prosper or otherwise with her —she is sure, at least, of her position as a wife, and of her claims to her husband's love, and of the allegiance of his worship. She knows that even though she may have wedded him in the days of poverty, and that should he rise to some great and successful position,—even if he became an emperor, —she must rise with him, and that he can never discard her; and, consequently, she feels that her position and her children are her own for ever. Now, the element of sanctity in the family, even when the husband is a good man,—even when he is a sacrament-going man, as every Catholic man ought to be,—yet the element of sanctity in the family, and for the family, lies with the woman. It is the duty and privilege of the mother. She has the children under her eye and under her care the livelong day. She has the formation of them,—of their character—their first sentiments, thoughts, and works, either for good or evil. The seed to be planted,—the formation of the soul,—is in the mother's hands; and therefore it is that the character of the child mainly depends on the formation which the mother gives it. The father is engaged in his office, in keeping his business, or at his work all the day long. His example, whether for good or bad, is not constantly before the eyes—the observant eyes—of the child, as is the example of the mother. And so it is, my friends, that all depends upon the mother; and it is of vital importance that that mother should blend in herself all that is pure, holy, tender, and loving, and that she be assured of the sanctity of her position, of which the Church assures her by the indissoluble nature of the marriage tie.

Again the Church of God follows the child into the school, and she puts before the young eye, even before reason has opened—she puts before the young sense the sight of things that will familiarize the mind of the child with Heaven and with heavenly thoughts. She goes before the world, anticipates reason, and tries to get the start of that "mystery of iniquity" which, sooner or later, lying in the world, shall be revealed to the eyes and the soul of this young child. Hence it is that, in her system of education, she endeavors to mix up sacramental graces, lessons of good, pictures of divine things, holy statues, little prayers, singing of hymns,—all these religious appliances,—and endeavors to mingle them all, constantly and largely, with every element of human education, that the heart may be formed as well as the mind, and that the will may be strengthened as well as the intellect and the soul of man. If, then, the evil of a bad education be one of the evils of society, I hold that the Church, in her scheme and plan of education, proves that she is the salvation of society by touching that evil with a healing hand.

The next great evil affecting the morals of society, is the sense of irresponsibility. A man outside the Catholic Church is never expected to call himself to account for his actions. If he speaks evil words, if he thinks evil thoughts, if he does wrong things, the most that he aspires to is a momentary thought of God. Perhaps he forms a kind of resolution not to do these things any more. But there is no excruciating self-examination; there is no humiliating confession; there is no care or thought upon motives for sorrow; there is no painstaking to acquire a firm resolution; there are none of the restraints against a return to sin with which the sacramental agencies of the Catholic Church, especially through the Sacrament of Penance, have made us all familiar. The Catholic man feels that the eye of God is upon him. He is told this every time the Catholic Church warns him to prepare for confession. He is told this every time his eyes, wandering through the church, rest upon the confessional. He is told this every time he sees the priest standing there, with his stole on, and the penitent going in with tearful eyes, and coming forth with eyes beaming with joy and with the delight of forgiveness. He is told this in a thousand ways; and it is brought home to him by the precepts and Sacraments of the Church at stated times in the year. The consequence is that he is made to believe that he is responsible to Almighty God; and therefore this obligation, creating a sense of responsibility, arouses and excites this watchfulness of his own conscience. The man who feels that the eye of God is upon him will also feel that the eye of his own conscience is upon him. For watchfulness begets watchfulness. If the master is looking on while a servant is doing any thing, the servant will endeavor to do it well, and he will keep his eye upon the master while the master is present. So, a soldier, when he is ordered to charge, turns his look upon his superior officer, while he dashes into the midst of the foe. And so it is with us. Conscience is created; conscience is fostered and cherished in the soul by a sense of responsibility which Almighty God gives us through the Church and through her Sacraments. What follows from this? It follows that the Catholic man, although in conscious freedom, is conscious that he must always exercise that freedom under the eye of God and under the dominion of His law; so that in him, even although he be a sinner for a time, the sense of freedom never degenerates into positive recklessness or license.

Finally,—in the political view of society,—the dangers that threaten the world from this aspect, are, first of all—absolutism and injustice, and oppression in rulers; and, secondly, a spirit of rebellion, even against just and established government, among the governed. For the well-ordering of society lies in this: That he who governs respects those whom he governs; and that those who are governed by him recognize in him only the authority that comes to him from God. I say *from God*. I do not wish here, or now, to enter into the question as to the source of power, and how far the popular element may or may not be that source; but I do say that where the power exists,—even where the ruler is chosen by the people,—that he exercises that power, then, as an official of the Almighty God, to whom belongs the government of the whole system which He has created. If that ruler abuses his power,—abuses it excessively;—if he despises those whom he governs;—if he has not respect for their rights, their privileges and their consciences,—then the balance of power is lost, and the great evil of political society is inaugurated. If, on the other hand, the people,—fickle and inconstant,—do not recognize any sacredness at all in their ruler; if they do not recognize the principle of obedience to law as a divine principle,—as a necessary principle, without which the world cannot live; if they think that among the rights of man—of individual man—is the right to rise in rebellion against authority and law,—the second great evil of political society is developed, and the whole machinery of the world's government is broken to pieces. What is necessary to remedy this? A power—mark my words—a power recognized to be greater than that of the people or than that of the people's government. A power, wielded not only over the subject, but over the monarch. A power, appealing with equal force and equal authority to him who is upon the throne, to him who is at the head of armies and empires, and to the meanest and the poorest and the lowest of his subjects. What power has that been in history? Look back for eighteen hundred years. What power is it that has been exercised over baron and chieftain, king and ruler, no matter how dark the times,—no matter how convulsed society was,—no matter how confused every element of government was,—no matter how rude and barbarous the manners of men,—no matter how willing they were to assert themselves, in the fulness of their pride and savage power, in field and in council? What power was it that was acknowledged and obeyed by them, during twelve hundred years, from the close of the Roman persecutions till the outbreak of Protestantism? What power was it that told the monarchs of the middle ages that, if they imposed an oppressive or unjust tax upon the people, they were excommunicated? What power was it that arose to tell Philip Augustus of France, in all the lust of his greatness and his undisputed sway, that, if he did not respect the rights of his one wife, and adhere to her chastely, he would be excommunicated by the Church, and abandoned by his people? What power was it that confronted the voluptuous tyrant seated on the Tudor's throne in England, and told him that, unless he were faithful to the poor persecuted woman, Catherine of Arragon, his lawful wife, he should be cut off as a rotten branch, and cast—by the sentence of the Church—into hell-fire? What power was it that made the strongest and most tyrannical of these rude mediæval chieftains, kings, and emperors, tremble before it? Ah, it was the power of the Vatican. It was the voice of the Church, upholding the rights of the people; sheltering them with its strong arm, proclaiming that no injustice should be done to them; that the rights of the poorest man in the community were as sacred as the rights of him who sat upon the throne; and, therefore, that she would not stand by and see the people oppressed. An ungrateful world is this of ours to-day, that forgets that the Catholic Church was the power that inaugurated, established, and obtained all those civic and municipal rights, all those rights, respecting communities, which have formed the basis of what we call our modern civilization! Ungrateful age! that reflects not, or chooses to forget, that the greatest freedom the people ever enjoyed in this world, they enjoyed so long as they were under the ægis of the Church's protection; that never were the Italians so free as they were in the mediæval Republics of Genoa, Pisa, Lucca, and Florence; that never were the Spaniards so free as when their Cortes, as the ruling voice of the nation, was heard resounding in the ears of their monarchs, and respected by them; that never were the English so free as when a Saint was their ruler; or, that when a demon in mortal shape clutched the sceptre, an Archbishop of Canterbury, with the knights of the realm closed around him, told him they would abandon him and depose him, unless he gave to the people that charter which is the foundation of the most glorious constitution in the world. And thus, I answer, the Church maintained the rights of the people, whenever those rights were unjustly invaded by those who were in power.

But, to the people, in their turn, this Church has always preached patience, docility, obedience to law, legitimate redress, when redress was required. She has always endeavored to calm their spirits, and to keep them back, even under great and sore oppression, from the remedy which the world's history tells us has always been worse than the disease which it has attempted to cure—viz.: the remedy of rebellion and revolution.

Such is the history of the Church's past. Have I not said with truth, that the Church is the salvation of society; that she formed society; that she created what we call the society of our day; and that, if it had not been for her, a large percentage of all that forms the literature of our time, would not now be in existence? The most powerful restraints, the most purifying influences that have operated upon society for so many centuries, would not have sent down their blessings to us; blessings that have been inherited, even by those who understood them so little that their very first act, in separating from the Church, was to lay the axe at the very root of society, by depriving the Sacrament of Matrimony of its sacramental and indispensably necessary force. In like manner, have I not proved that, if there be a vestige of freedom, with the proper assertion of right, in the world to-day, it can be traced distinctly to the generating and forming action of the Catholic Church during those ages of faith when the world permitted itself to be moulded and fashioned by her hands? And, as she was in the past, so must she be in the future. Shut your eyes to her truths: every principle of human science will feel the shock; and the science of sciences will feel it first,—the science of the knowledge of God, and of the things which He has given us. What is the truth? Is it not a mere matter of fact, known by personal observation to many among us, that the Protestant idea of sin involves infidelity,—that is to say, a denial of the divinity of Christ, of the inspiration of the Scriptures, and of the existence of God? What is the Protestant idea of the sinner? We have it, for instance, in their own description of the Elder's death-bed. His son was a sinner. He comes to the father's bedside. He is broken with grief, seeing that his father is dying before his eyes. The father seizes the opportunity to tell the erring son: " Remember that Christ died for our sins, and that Christ was the son of God." He begins then to teach what a Catholic would consider the very first elements of the catechism. But to him they were the conclusions of a long life of study; and he has arrived, now, at the end of his days, at the very point at which the little Catholic child starts when he is seven years of age. Now, in the Catholic Church, these things,—which are the result of careful inquiry, hard study, the conclusions of years, perhaps, —being admitted as first principles, the time which is lost by the Protestant in arriving at these principles, is employed by the Catholic in applying them to the conduct and the actions of his daily life,—in avoiding this danger or that, repenting of this sin or that, praying against this evil or that,—and so on. Shut your eyes to the truths of Catholic teaching, and the divine Scriptures themselves, on which you fancy, perhaps, that you are building up your religion, are shaken from their pedestal of a sure definition, and nothing remains but her reassuring power—even to the inspiration of God's written word. Is not this true? Where, during the fifteen hundred years that preceded Protestantism,—where do we read of the inspiration of the Scriptures being called in question? Where do we read of any theologian omitting this phrase, leaving out that sentence, because it did not tally with his particular views? He knew that he might as well seek to tie up the hands of God as to change one iota or syllable of God's revealed truth. But what do we see during the last three hundred years? Luther began by rejecting the Epistle of St. James, calling it "an epistle of straw," because there were certain doctrines there that did not suit him. From his time, every Protestant theologian has found fault with this passage or that of Scripture, as if it was a thing that could be changed and turned and forced and shaped to answer this purpose or that;—as if the word of God could be made to veer about, north, east, south, and west—according to human wishes;—until at length, in our own day, they have undertaken a new version of the Scriptures altogether. And this is quietly going on in one great section of the Church of England; while another great section of the

Church of England disputes its authority altogether, and tells you that the doctrinal part of it is only a rule to guide, and that the historical part of it is nothing more than a myth, like the history of the ancient Paganism of Greece and of Rome! They discard the Church's action upon the morality of society; tell her that they do not believe her when she says: "Accursed is the man or woman that puts a divorce into his or her partner's hand." They tell her that they do not believe her when she says: "No matter what the conduct of either party is, I cannot break the bond that God has made;—no matter what may be the difference of disposition;—no matter what the weariness that springs from the union, I cannot dissolve it, I cannot alter it." If you dissolve it, I ask you in all earnestness to what you reduce yourselves? To what does the married woman reduce herself? She becomes (I blush to say it,) a creature living under the sufferance and the caprices of her husband. You know how easy it is to trump up an accusation! You have but to defame that which is so delicate and so tender as a woman's name;—a gentle and a tender and a pure woman's good name is tainted and destroyed by a breath. No matter how unfounded the calumny or the slander, how easy it is first to defame and then to destroy it! At the time when the Protestant Church was called upon by the people in England to admit the lawfulness of divorce, the Catholic Church raised up her voice in defence of truth, and warned England that she was going into a deeper abyss,—warned the people that they were going to destroy whatever sanctity of society remained among them, —warned them that there was an anathema upon the measure —upon those who proposed it—upon those who aided it. I remember at that time a poor woman in Ireland,—indeed she was almost a beggar in her poverty,—asking of me; "Is it true, your Reverence, they are going to make a law in England to let the husband and wife separate from one another and go and marry other people?" "Yes," I said. "Well, I hope," she said, "we will not be included in that law?" "Oh, no; not at all," I said. "You are all right." "Glory be to God!" she said, "I never knew before the happiness of being a Catholic. I would rather be married to my Jimmy, and be sure of him, than to the first nobleman in England: for he might come to me to-morrow and tell me to go out and take the children with me!"

Such is the Church's action on the morale of society. Tell her to shut up her confessionals; tell her that her priests, sitting in those tribunals, are blasphemous usurpers of a power that God has never given to man. What follows from this? O my friends, do you think that you, or that any of you would be better men if you were absolved to-morrow from all obligation of ever going to confession again? Do you think you would draw nearer to God? Would you look more sharply after yourselves? Do you not think that even those very human agencies—the humiliation, the painstaking of preparation, the violent effort to get out whatever we must confess,—do you not think all these things are a great restraint upon a man, and that they help to keep him pure, independent altogether of the higher argument of an offended God,—of the crucified Lord bleeding again at the sight of our sins? Most assuredly they are. Most assuredly that man will endeavor to serve God with greater purity, with greater carefulness,—will endeavor to remember the precept of the Saviour, "You must watch and pray, that you enter not into temptation,"—when he is called from time to time to sweep the chambers of his own soul, to wash and purify every corner of his own heart, to analyze his motives, call himself to account, even for his thoughts and words;—examine his relations in regard to honesty, in regard to charity with his neighbor;—examine himself how he fulfils his duties as a father, or as a husband, as the case may be;—that the man, who is obliged to do this, is more likely to serve God in purity and watchfulness, than the man who never, from the cradle to the grave, is asked even to consider the necessity of taking a few minutes' thought and asking himself, "How do I stand with God?" Remove this action of the Church upon the good conduct of society; and then you will have, indeed, the work which was accomplished, and which is reaping its fulfilment to-day,—the work of the so-called great Reformer, Martin Luther, who has brought it to this pass, that the world itself is groaning under the weight of its own iniquities; and society rises up and exclaims that its very heart within it is rotted by social evil.

Disturb the action of the Church upon political society, and what guarantee have you for the future? You may see from the past what is to be in the future; for, when Luther broached his so-called "Reformation," the principle upon which he went was that the Catholic Church had no business to be an universally Catholic body; that she should break herself up into national Churches,—the Church of Germany, the Church of England, the Church of France, the Church of America, and so on. And, in fact, Protestantism, to this day, in England, is called the Church of England.— The necessary consequence that immediately followed was that the King, if it was a Kingdom, or the President, if it was a Republic,—no matter who he may be,—became the head of the Church—if it was a national Church—as well as the head of the nation. The two powers were concentrated in him—one as Governor—head of the State; the other as the head of the national Church. He became king over the consciences of the people, as well as ruler of their external actions. He was to make laws for the soul as well as for the body. He was to tell them what they were to believe and how they were to pray, as well as to tell them their duties as citizens. He was to lead them to Heaven! The man who led his armies in the battle-field was then to persuade his people that the way to Heaven lay through rapine and through blood! But so it was. And, strange to say, in every nation in Europe that accepted Protestantism, the monarch became a tyrant at once. The greatest tyrant that ever governed England was the man who introduced Protestantism. So long as Henry the Eighth was a Catholic,— although he was a man of terrible passions,—still, the Church, reminding him of his soul, bringing him occasionally to the Confessional, trying to shake him out of his iniquities,—had some control over him; and he conquered his passions, and kept himself honorable and pure. The moment that this man cast off his allegiance to the Church,—the very day he proclaimed that he was emancipated from the Pope, and did not believe in the Pope or acknowledge him any more,—that very day he turns to Anne Boleyn, takes and proclaims her his wife,—Catherine, his rightful wife, still living; and, in a few days, when his heart grew tired of Anne, and his eyes were attracted by some other beauty, he sent Anne to the block, and had her head cut off;—and he took another lady in her place: and, in a short time, he cut off her head, also. And so, Gustavus Vasa, of Sweden, when he became a Protestant, at once assumed and became the head of an absolute monarchy. The very kings of the Catholic countries imitated their Protestant confreres in this respect; for we find the Catholic monarchs of Spain cutting off the ancient privileges of the people in the Cortes, saying :—" I am the State; and every man must obey!" It is quite natural. The more power you give into a man's hand, the more absolute he becomes. The more you concentrate in him the spiritual as well as the temporal power, the more audaciously will he exercise both temporal and spiritual power, and the more likely is it that you are building up in that man a tyrant—and a merciless tyrant—to oppress you. From the day that society emancipated itself, by Protestantism, from the action of the Church, revolution, rebellion, uprising against authority, became the order of the day; until at length society is honeycombed with secret associations which swear eternal enmity, not only to the altar, but to the throne.

And so, my dear friends, we see that we cannot move without the Church of God; that nations may go on for a time, and may be upheld by material prosperity; but without a surer basis they will certainly be overthrown. The moments are coming, and coming rapidly, when all the society of this world, that wishes to be saved, will have to cry out with a mighty voice to the Catholic Church. Persecuted, despised, to-day, she will yet come,—with her light of truth—with her sanctifying influences,—with her glorious dominion over king and subject,—to save them from the ruin which they have brought upon their own heads. Then will be the day of grace for man,—the day of the world's necessity. And when that day comes,—and I behold it now in my mental vision,—this uprising of the whole world in the hands of the Church,—it will bring peace, security, and joy to society. I see thee, O glorious spouse of Christ!—O Mother Church, I see thee seated once more, in the councils of the nations, guiding them with a divinely-infused light —animating them with thy spirit of justice! I see, O mother, as, of old, I saw a glorious city rise out of the ruins of the Goth and Visigoth and Vandal: so out of the men of this day,—relapsing into chaos through neglect of thee,—do I behold thee forming the glorious city that shall be; a society in which men shall be loyal and brave, truthful, pure, and holy; a city in which the people shall grow up formed by thee for God; a city in which all men, governors and governed, shall admit the supremacy of law, the sanctity of principle, the omnipotence of justice! And, O Mother, in the day when that retribution comes—in that day of the world's necessity—the triple crown shall shine again upon the brows of thy chief,--Peter's successor and the Vicar of Christ; upon that honored brow shall shine forth again the triple crown,—the most ancient and the holiest in the world; the Prince of Peace shall extend his sceptre over the nations; and every man shall rejoice in a new life!

THE RESURRECTION.

[*A sermon preached by the Very Rev. T. N. Burke, O.P., in the church of St. Vincent Ferrer, New York, on Easter Sunday, April 7, 1872.*]

"And when the Sabbath was past, Mary Magdalen, and Mary, the mother of James and Salome, bought sweet spices, that, coming, they might anoint Jesus. And very early in the morning, the first day of the week, they came to the sepulchre, the sun being now risen. And they said one to another, Who shall roll us back the stone from the door of the sepulchre? And, looking, they saw the stone rolled back; for it was very great. And entering into the sepulchre, they saw a young man sitting on the right side, clothed with a white robe. And they were astonished. And he said to them: Be not affrighted. You seek Jesus of Nazareth, who was crucified. He is risen; He is not here. Behold the place where they laid Him. But, go; tell His disciples and Peter, that He goeth before you into Galilee. There you shall see Him, as He told you."

DEARLY BELOVED BRETHREN: We are told, in the history of the Passion of our Lord Jesus Christ, which we have been considering during the past few days, that, after our Saviour had yielded up His spirit upon the cross, Joseph of Arimathea went to Pilate and demanded the body of the Lord. Pilate was surprised to hear that our Divine Lord was already dead. And yet, if he had only consulted his own memory, and remembered how the life was almost scourged out of the Saviour by the hands of the soldiers, it would not have seemed to him so wonderful that the three hours of agony should have closed that life. He sent to inquire if He was already dead; and gave orders that, in case He was dead, Joseph of Arimathea and Nicodemus were to take possession of His body. They came, sorrowing, and again climbed the Hill of Calvary; and, lest there might be any doubt that the Master was dead, the soldier drove his lance once through the heart of our Lord Jesus Christ. Then the body was taken down from the cross. They took out the nails, gently and tenderly; and they handed them down, and they were put into the hands of the Virgin Mother. They took the body reverently from its high gibbet, and laid the thorn-crowned head upon the bosom of the Virgin, who waited to receive it. With her own hands she removed these thorns from His brow; and the fountain of tears, that had been dried up because of the greatness of her sorrow, flows now, and rains the Virgin's tears upon the stained and disfigured face of her child. Then they brought Him to a garden in the neighborhood; and there they laid Him in the tomb. It was another man's grave; and He, the Lord, had no right to it. But He died so poor, that, even in death, He had no place whereon to lay His head, until charity opened another man's tomb for Him. There they laid Him down; covered with blood and with wounds—all disfigured and deformed, they laid Him down, like the patriarch of old, with a stone for His pillow; and upon that stone they laid the wounded and the blessed head of the Lord. They closed the sepulchre. Mary, the mother, gathered up the thorns, the nails, the instruments with which her child was so cruelly maimed and put to death; and with them pressed to her heart, and leaning upon her newly-found son, John, she returned to her sad home in Jerusalem; and all, having adored, silently dispersed; for the evening was coming that brought the Sabbath. One only remained. The heart-broken Magdalen lay down outside the tomb, and laid her head upon the stone which they had rolled against the Master's grave. There, she knew, He lay; and the instinct of her love, and of her sorrow, was so strong that she could not go away from the tomb of her Lord, but remained there, weeping and alone. Whilst she wept, evening deepened into night; and alone, the heart-broken lover of Jesus Christ saw that she must rise and depart. She rose. She kissed, again and again, that great stone that enclosed her Divine Saviour; and, turning to the city, she heard the heavy, measured tread of the soldiers, who came with the night to guard the tomb. They closed around the tomb. With rudeness and with violence they drove the woman away—wondering at her tears, and the evidence of her broken heart. And then, piling their arms and their spears, they settled down to the night-watch, cautioned not to sleep—cautioned to take care not to let a human being come near that grave until the morning light. Excited by their own superstitious fears and emotions (for it was, indeed, a strange office for these warriors to be set on guard over a dead man), agitated by the strangeness of their position, excited by their fears, they slept not, but, waiting the night, watchfully, diligently, and with vigilance, they guard on the right hand and on the left; scarcely knowing who was to come; fearing with an undefined fear; thinking that, perhaps, it was to be a phantom, a spirit, an evil thing of the night coming upon them; and ever ready to grasp their arms, and put themselves on their defence.

The night fell, deep and heavy, over the tomb of Jesus Christ. The whole of that night, and of the following day, they kept their watch. Mary, the mother, was in Jerusalem. Kneeling before these instruments of the passion, she spent the whole of that night, and the whole of the following Sabbath-day, weeping over those thorns and over those nails; contemplating them, examining them, and seeing, from the evidence of the blood that was upon them, how deeply they had been struck into the brow, and into the hands and feet of Jesus, her divine child; her heart breaking within her, as every glance at these terrible instruments of the Passion brought up all the horrors which she had witnessed on that morning of Friday, on the Mount of Calvary. The women kept watch and ward round her; and so terrible was the mother's grief, that even the Magdalen was silenced and hushed, and dared not obtrude one word of consolation upon the Virgin's ear.

The Sabbath passed away. Dull and heavy the black cloud that had settled over Calvary and over Jerusalem, was lifted up. Men walked about with fear and with trembling. The sun seemed to have scarcely risen that Sabbath morning. The dead who started from their graves the moment Jesus gave his last cry on the cross, flitted in the darkening night to and fro in the silent streets of Jerusalem. Men beheld the awful vision of these skeleton bodies that rose from the grave. A fire, as of vengeance and of fury, seemed to glare in the empty sockets in their heads. They showed their white teeth, gnashing, as it would seem, over the crime that the people had committed. They flitted to and fro. All Jerusalem was filled with fear and terror. No man spoke above his breath, and all was silent during that long Sabbath day, that brought no joy, because the people had called down the blood of the Saviour upon their heads.

The Sabbath day and evening had closed; and again night was recumbent upon the earth. The guard is relieved.

Fresh soldiers are put at the doors. They are again cautioned that this is the important night when they must watch with redoubled vigilance, because this night will seal the Redeemer's fate. He said: "I will rise again in three days;" and, if the morning sun of the first day of the week—the Sunday—rose upon the undisturbed grave of the dead man, then all that He had preached was a lie, and all the wonders that He wrought were a deception upon the people. Therefore the guards were trebly cautioned to keep watch. Then, filled with fear and with an undefined alarm, they close around the sepulchre, resolved that so long as hand of theirs can wield a spear, no human being shall approach that grave.

The Magdalen lingered round, fascinated by the knowledge that her Redeemer and her Lord was there in that tomb which she was not allowed to approach. And the guards watched patiently, vigilantly, with sleepless eyes; and the night came down, and all the city was silent and darkened. Hour followed hour. Slowly and silently time rolls away. The night was deepening to its deepest gloom. The midnight hour approached. The moment comes when the third day in the tomb is accomplished. The moment comes when the Sabbath was over—the Sabbath of which it was written, that "the Lord rested on the seventh day from all his works." That Sabbath had Jesus Christ made in that dreary, silent tomb. Wounds and blood were upon Him. The weakness of death had fastened upon Him. Those lifeless limbs cannot move. The sightless eyes cannot open to behold the light of day. Death, indeed, seems to have rioted in its triumph over the Eternal Lord of life, and hell appears victorious in the destruction of the victim. The midnight hour approaches. The guards hear the rustling of the coming storm. They see the trees bow their heads in that garden, and wave to and fro, as by a violent trembling. They see them bending as if a storm was sweeping over them. They look. What is this orient light that blushes upon the horizon? What is this light which bursts upon them, bright, bright as the sun of heaven, bright as ten thousand suns? And while the light flashes upon them, and, dazzled, they close their eyes, they hear a riot of voices: "*Gloria in excelsis!* Alleluia to the risen Saviour!" What is this that they behold? The great stone comes rolling back from the mouth of the monument into the midst of them! Save yourselves, O men! Save yourselves, or it will crush you! The men are frightened and alarmed. Is it the power of Heaven? Or is it a force from hell? Presently, forth from that tomb bursts the glorified and risen Saviour. Their eyes are dazzled with the spectacle of the Man that lay in that cold, dark, silent grave. A voice was heard: "Arise, for I am come for thee!" And the glorified soul of the Saviour, entering, that moment, into His body, bursts triumphant from the grave! Death and hell fly from before His face. Fly, for a power is here that you cannot command! Fly, you demons, who rejoiced in your triumph, for death and hell are conquered. Arise, glorious sun, from the tomb! Oh, what do I behold? Where, O Saviour, is the sign of Thy agony? Where is the disfigurement of blood? Where is the sign of the executioner's hand upon Thee? It is gone—gone! No longer the bloodstained thorn defiles Thy brows! No longer Thy sacred flesh hangs torn from the bones! No! But now, triumphant, glorified, incorruptible, impassible, He has resumed the grandeur and the glory which He put away from Him on the day of His Incarnation; and He rises from the tomb, the conqueror of death and hell, the God and Redeemer of the world!

Behold, my brethren, how sorrow is changed into joy! Bursting forth in the light of His divinity, He went His way—the way of His eternity. The mountains, the hills of Judea—of Jerusalem—bowed down before Him. The mountains moved and rocked on their bases before the assertion of Thy sovereignty, O God! He went His way, and left behind Him an empty grave, and the clothing in which His disfigured body had been wrapped up. An empty grave! But all the angels in Heaven were looking on at that moment. At that moment, when the form of the glorified Saviour burst from the grave, all the angels of Heaven put forth alleluias of joy and of praise. The heart of the Father in Heaven exulted. Rising upon His eternal throne, He sent forth a cry of joy over the glory of His Son. All the angels in Heaven exulted; and, triumphing, they came down to earth, and gazed upon the sacred spot wherein their Master and their God had lain.

The morning came, and the dark clouds had disappeared. The very brows of Olivet seemed to shine with a solemn gladness, and the cedars of Lebanon seemed to lift their heads with a new instinct of life—almost of love and joy. Calvary itself seemed to rejoice. The morning rose, and the sun gladly came up from his home in the east, and his first rays fell upon the empty grave. And behold the Magdalen, and the other pious followers of our Lord, coming with ointment and sweet spices to anoint Him. They came; and questioning—as we have seen—questioning each other. How could Mary, with nothing but her woman's strength, how could Mary move that stone? But see; it is moved. And beneath they behold an angel of God. His light fills the tomb. There is no darkness there, no sign of sadness, no sign of death. Robed in transparent white—even as the garments of our Lord shone upon Tabor—so did the Angel shine as he kept guard over the death-bed of his Lord and Master. Then, speaking to the woman, he says: "Woman, whom seekest thou?" "Jesus of Nazareth, who was crucified." "Why seekest thou the living among the dead? He is not here. He is risen!" And then their hearts were filled with a mighty joy; for the Master is risen; while the soldiers, frightened and crestfallen, went into Jerusalem, proclaiming the appearance to the Pharisees and to the people, and that He whom they were set to guard was the Lord of light and life, and the Son of God.

The eyes that were oppressed with the weariness of death are now lifted up, shining in the glory of His resurrection. The hands that were nailed helplessly to the cross, wield again the omnipotence of God. The heart that was broken and oppressed, now enters into the mighty ocean of the ages of His divinity, undisturbed, unfettered, unencumbered by any sorrow. "Christ, risen from the dead, dies no more. Death has no more dominion over Him." He died once, and He died for sin. "Therefore," says St. Augustine, "by dying on Calvary, He showed that He was man; by rising from the grave, He proved that He was God."

If, therefore, dearly beloved brethren, during the past forty days, the Church has called upon us for fasting and mortification, has called upon us to chastise our bodies and humble our souls ("*humiliabam in jejunio animam meam*,") "In my fast I will humble my soul"—if the Church during the past weeks called upon us to be afflicted, and to shed our tears at the feet of Jesus crucified—if we have done this—above all, if we have purified our souls so as to let His light, and His glory, and His grace into our hearts,—to-day have we a right to rejoice: and the message which I bring to you is a message of exceeding great joy. Christ is risen! The Crucified has risen from the grave! Weakness has clothed itself with strength. Ignominy has clothed itself with glory. Death has been absorbed in victory; and the powers of hell are crushed and confounded for evermore. Is not this a message of great joy and triumph? And truly I may say to you, in the words of St. Paul, " *Gaudete in Domino ; iterum dico, gaudete*"—" Rejoice, therefore, in the Lord ! I say to you again, rejoice !"

Two reasons have we for our Easter joy and gladness. Two reasons have we for our great rejoicing. First of all, that of the friend to behold the glory of his friend: the joy of a disciple to see the glory of his master: a joy centering in Jesus Christ—rejoicing in Him and with Him, for His own sake. Was it not for His own sake we sorrowed? Was it not because of His grief and sufferings we shed our tears and cast ourselves down before Him? So, also, for His own sake let us rejoice. We rejoice to behold our God reassuming the glory of His divinity, and so participate in that glory to His sacred humanity, that the sunshine of the eternal light of God streams out from every member, sense, and limb of the sacred body of Jesus Christ our Lord. Pure light it seemed. With the transparency of Heaven it assumed all its splendor. All the glory was within Him in Almighty affluence, and sent itself forth, so that He was truly not only the light of grace for the world, but the light of glory. For this must every true believer in Jesus Christ rejoice.

But the second cause of our joy is for our own sake; for, although we grieve for Him and sorrow for Him, for His own sake, upon Calvary, we also grieve for ourselves. And it is, for us, the keenest and the bitterest sorrow, that the work of Calvary was the work of our doing by our sins; that if we were not what we were, He would never have been what He was on that Friday morning. That for us He bared His innocent bosom to receive all the sorrows and all the agonies of His Passion; that for us did He expose His virgin body to that fearful scourging and terrible crucifixion; that for our sins did He languish upon the cross;

that they put upon Him the burden of the iniquities of us all; and "He was afflicted for our iniquities and was bruised for our sins." It is for our own sorrows and for our own sins that the very deepest sorrow has a place in the Crucifixion. Well did He—He, who permitted that we should be the cause of His sorrow—wish us, also, for our own sake, to participate in His joy. And why? Because the resurrection of Christ from the dead was not only the proof of His divinity, the establishment of His truth, the conviction of His miracles, the foundation of His religion, but it was, moreover, the type and model of the glorious resurrection that awaits every man who dies in the love, and fear, and grace of Jesus Christ. Every man who preserves his soul pure, and every man who restores to his soul the purity of repentance,—to every such man is promised the glory of the resurrection, like unto that of our Lord Jesus Christ. For as Christ rose from the dead, so shall we rise; and as He clothed Himself with glory, so shall we pass from glory unto glory—to see Christ in the air—to be like unto Him in glory; and so shall we be with the Lord for ever. And that glory which comes to our Lord to-day, comes not only to His grand soul, returning surrounded by the Saints whom He had delivered from their prison, but it comes also to His body, wiping away and erasing every stain, every defilement, every wound, and communicating to that body the attributes of the Spirit; for "that which was laid down in dishonor rose in glory"—that which was laid down in weakness rose in power—that which was laid down subject to grief, if not to corruption, rose a spiritual and incorruptible body. Even so shall we rise:—for I announce to you a wonderful thing, that when the Angels sound the trumpet, and call the dead to judgment, they that are in Christ shall rise first. And as the soul of the Redeemer went back to the tomb, and entered into His body, to make that body shine in its spiritual glory,—so shall our souls return from the heights of heavenly contemplation, to find these bodies again—to reënter them—and to make them shine with the glory of God, if we only consent to live and die in the grace and favor of Jesus Christ. The eyes that now cannot look upon the sun in heaven without being blinded, these very eyes can gaze upon the face of God and not be blinded by His majesty. The ears that are now weary of the music of earth shall be so attuned to the music of Heaven, that the rapture of its hearing shall continue in all the ecstasy of delight, so long as God is God. The heart, now so circumscribed as scarcely to be able to rise to the dignity of the highest form of human love, will then be so purified and exalted that it will be filled with the fairest forms of divine love—purified, sanctified, animating every natural sentiment, every affection, until the body, growing into the soul's essence, shall all become spiritual and, as it were, divine. In a word, this gross, corruptible, material body of ours shall be so spiritualized—so glorified—so refined, as to be capable of the most exquisite pleasure of every spiritual sense; and yet pleasures purifying to the soul, in which every thought and every power of the soul and body shall be wrapped up into God.

But mark, dear brethren; the resurrection of our Lord is the pledge and promise that every soul shall realize; but two things are necessary in order to arrive at this glory. Two conditions are laid down in order to attain to this wonderful fulfilment of all the love of the redemption of Jesus Christ. And these two things are: First of all, we must keep a pure soul and a pure conscience. Mark how Jesus Christ came to His glory. He took a human heart, He took a human soul, He took a human conscience,—for He was true man. But He took every element of His humanity from a source so pure, so limpid, so holy, that in heaven or on earth nothing was ever seen, or ever shall be seen, until the end of eternity, that shall be compared with the Blessed Virgin's Son. Throughout His whole life of thirty-three years, nothing in it could have the slightest shadow of sin; —nothing that could have the slightest feature of sin upon it, ever was allowed to come near the blessed and most immaculate soul and heart of Jesus Christ. When, at last, He permitted the appearance of the sin that was not His own to come upon Him—to touch Him nearly—it so frightened Him—it so horrified Him—that the blood burst, as we know, from every pore of His body. It seemed as if His body, as it were, could not stand the sight. His was the grace of purity. Oh, my beloved brethren, that we might attain to that self-same purity, as far as our nature will permit us, that we might only know the beauty of that purity beaming from Him, as its author and creator! Christ our Lord laid out in His Church the path of purity—the path of innocence. But, for all those who fall, or stumble, or turn aside for a moment, He has built another royal road to salvation, namely, the road of penance. One or other of these must we tread; whether we tread the way of purity or the way of penance, we must suffer with Christ if we wish to be purified with Him. But, mark! All pure and holy as He was—infinite purity and holiness itself—no passion to disturb Him—no evil example to exercise its influence over Him—no secret emotion of pleasure,—even of that purely human pleasure, to come and interfere in the remotest degree with the perfect union with His divinity—yet with all this, He mortified that sacred body; He fasted; He humbled Himself; He prayed; and He ended by giving that body to be scourged and to be crucified! He shed His blood. What an example was this! That body of Jesus Christ was no impediment to His holiness. It only helped Him; for it was the instrument of His divine will in the salvation of men. Our bodies, on the other hand, impede us every day, and put between us and God. Every passion that dwells within us, rises from time to time to separate us from God. Every appetite that clamors for enjoyment would fain destroy the soul for ever, for a momentary pleasure. Every sense that brings thought and idea to the spirit, brings also in its train the imminent, the dangerous, the poisonous image of the evil example of sin. That which, with Christ, was a work of pleasure, is, with us, a work of toil. It is toil to deny ourselves somewhat; to put the sign of the cross, in penance and mortification, upon this flesh; to enter somewhat into the sufferings of our Lord—into His fasting—into His prayer—into His mortification—in order that our bodies may be chastened; for it is only chastened bodies that can contain pure and sinless souls. Those who are pure must chastise their bodies somewhat—must deny themselves—in order to preserve their purity. Those who are penitent must do it in order to appease the justice of God upon that body which, some time or other, has led them away from God by sin, and so tended to destroy the soul. And this is the reason why the Catholic Church commands us to fast: that it tells us we must not enjoy overmuch the pleasures of the theatre; the pleasures of gay and festive reunions. It tells us that we must, from time to time, be hungry, and yet not taste food, —that we must be thirsty, and yet refuse to refresh ourselves for a time with drink. And this, not only that these bodies may be chastened for a time, but that they may be transformed into fitness for the glory of Heaven. And here I would remark that, while every other religion, while every false religion puts away sadness and sorrow, puts away the precept of fasting, and says that men may pander to, and feed, and cherish their bodies,—the Catholic Church alone, from the very first day of her existence, drew the sword of the spirit—the sword of mortification—and declares through her monks, through her hermits, through her virgins, through her priesthood, that the body must be subdued, it must be abased, it must be chastened, in order that the soul may rise to God by purity and grace here, and through them, to the spiritual glory of the resurrection hereafter.

I say that there is a third motive for our joy this morning, and it is this: May I, dearly beloved, in this, which I may call the closing day of our Lent—may I congratulate those whom I see before me? The constant attendance of many amongst you, during the last forty evenings of Lent, has made your faces familiar to me. Over these Catholic countenances have I seen from time to time the expression— now of sorrow, now of delight;—but, whether of sorrow or of joy, always of sympathy with Jesus Christ. Of this am I a witness; and on this do I congratulate you. If it be true that the Christian man is, indeed, a man in whom Christ lives, according to the words of the Apostle: "I live no longer, I, but Christ lives within me,"—then, according to his words, you are lost to yourselves; you are dead; and your life is hidden with Christ in God. If, then, the Christian man be the man in whom Christ lives, well may I congratulate you upon every emotion of joy and of sorrow that has passed through your hearts and over your faces during these forty blessed days that you have passed; because these emotions were the gift of Christ, and the evidence of the life of Christ in you, and of your familiarity with Christ's image.

May I congratulate you on a good confession and a fervent communion? May I, in heart and spirit, bow down before every man among you to-day, as a man who holds in his bosom Jesus Christ; as a man whose heart is not an empty tomb, like that in the garden outside Jerusalem; not occupied merely by an Angel; but whose heart is the sanctuary wherein the risen and glorified Saviour dwells this morning? May I congratulate you on this? I hope so. I hope that the words that have been heard here have not been spoken in vain. It would fill me with fear if I thought there was one among the audiences who filled this church during the last Lent, whose hardened heart refused to make his Easter confession and communion; and to make it as the beginning of a series of more frequent—and, if possible, of monthly confessions and communions. It would fill me with fear if I thought there was such a one here; because then there would come upon me the conviction that it was my own unworthiness—my own unfitness—my own weakness that made the Word fall fruitless on my lips, and might, perhaps, make me a reprobate whilst I was preaching the Word. But, no. Nay, I will rather presume that God has done His own work—that the Divine Husbandman, who placed the seed of His Word in such hands as mine—most unworthy—that He has made that Word spring up; and that the fairest flowers of grace and sanctity already crown it in your hearts to-day. Upon this, therefore, I congratulate you as the third great motive of your joy; that not only is the Saviour glorified in Jerusalem, but He is glorified in your hearts. Not only has He conquered death in the Garden of Gethsemane, but He has conquered death in your souls. Not only has He driven the devil and all the powers of hell before Him, as He burst from the tomb, but He has driven him from your hearts, into which He has entered this morning. Oh, brethren, keep Him! Keep Him as your best and only friend! Keep Him as you would keep the pledge of that future glory which is to come, and of which, says the Apostle: "Eye hath not seen and ear hath not heard; nor hath it entered into the heart of man to conceive —what things the Lord God of heaven hath prepared for those who cease not to love Him!"

THE CATHOLIC MISSION.

[*A Sermon delivered by the Very Rev. T. N. Burke, O.P., on Sunday, April 7, 1872, in the Chapel of the "Xavier Alumni Sodality," attached to the Church and College of St. Francis Xavier, New York.*]

"Now, when it was late that same day, being the first day of the week, and the doors were shut, where the disciples were gathered together, for fear of the Jews, Jesus came, and stood in the midst, and said to them: 'Peace be to you.' * * * * The disciples, therefore, were glad when they saw the Lord: and He said to them again: 'Peace be to you.' Now, Thomas, the son of Didymus, was not with them. * * * Jesus came and stood in the midst of them, and said: 'Peace be to you!'" John xx: 19–31.

THIS mode of salutation was adopted by our Divine Lord after His resurrection and not before. Invariably, for the forty days that He remained with His own, after he had risen unto His glory, He saluted them with the words—" Peace be to you," as He had said elsewhere, "My peace I leave unto you; My peace I give unto you." After His resurrection, I say, He said these words. Before His Passion He could scarcely say them with truth; for, up to the moment that He sent forth His last cry upon the Cross,—saving us,—there was war between God and man; and how could the Son of God say, "Peace be to you?" But now, when He has reconciled all in Himself—*omnia reconciliavit, et in semet ipso pacem faciens*,—creating peace—that, which He Himself produced, He gave to His Apostles in the words which I have just read for you.

And now, my dear friends, let us consider what is that peace of which our Saviour speaks; what is that peace which He declares to be the inheritance of the elect,—the great legacy that He left to the world,—"the peace of God that surpasseth all understanding." In what does it consist? Do we know the meaning—the very definition—of it? It is a simple word, and familiar to us, this word peace; but I venture to say that it is one of those simple words that men do

7

not take the trouble to seek to interpret or to understand. In order, then, that we may understand what is this "peace of God which surpasseth all understanding," and in order that in our understanding of it by the light of faith, we may discover our own mission as Christian men, I ask you to consider what the mission of the Divine Son of God was, when He came and "was incarnate by the Holy Ghost of the Virgin Mary and was made man." What did He come for? What work did He have to do? I answer in the language of Scripture: "He came to effect many works of peace and reconciliation." In the day that man sinned and rebelled against God, he declared war against the Almighty; and God took up the challenge, and declared war against sinners. This war involved separation between God and man; and in this state of warfare did Christ our Lord find the world. He found the world separated from God, first of all by error and ignorance. "There is no truth and there is no knowledge of God in the land," was the complaint of the Prophet Isaiah. "Truth is diminished among the children of men," exclaimed, with sorrow, the royal Psalmist. "Nowhere is God known."

Before the Son of God came upon the earth, the nations had wandered away into a thousand forms of idolatry and of error. Every man called his own form of error by the name of "Religion." Some were "Epicureans;" sensualists—beasts—were made gods by them. They canonized the principle of impurity, and they called it by the name of a goddess; and they declared that this was their religion! Others there were, brutalized in mind, who worshipped their own passions of strife; and they canonized the principle of revenge and of bloodshed, and they worshipped it under the name of Mars. This thing went so far that even thieves, robbers, the dishonest, had their own god;—and the principle of dishonesty and of thievery was canonized, or, rather, deified, and called religion, and embodied under the name of the god Mercury! It is a trick of the devil, and it is a trick of the world,—to take up some form of error—some form of unbelief —and to call that "Religion." When He came who was "the Way, the Truth, and the Life," there was darkness over the whole earth. The world was "civilized" enough. Arts and sciences flourished. It was the "Augustan Era," which has given a name to the very highest civilization among the nations, from that day to this. But what was the awful want of their civilization? They ignored God; they took no account of God in their knowledge. They thought they could be wise without God. God nullified their wisdom, and abandoned them to a reprobate sense. Thus did mankind declare war against the God of Truth and of Wisdom. What followed from this? Another kind of war, more terrible, if you will,—the effect—the natural and necessary effect—of that separation of the human intellect from God. What was this? Every form of sin—nay, the vilest, the filthiest, the most abominable sin—was found among men. Not as an exception; not as a thing to be hidden; but as a thing to be acknowledged, as a matter of course. The husband was not faithful to the wife, nor the wife to the husband. Juvenal tells us that, in that flourishing society of paganism, as a man saw his wife growing old —and, accordingly, as the bloom of her youth passed away from her,—he began to despise her; until, in the words of the satirist, the day came when she saw a fair, blooming maiden come into the house, and herself, the mother of children, summoned to go out; because her eyes had lost their lustre, and her features the roses and the lilies of beauty; and a stranger was there to take her place. There was no principle of fidelity. There was no principle of honesty. No man could trust his fellow-man. No man knew who was to be trusted. Even the ancient, rugged virtues that the early Republics of Greece and Rome produced, had passed away. The world was over-civilized for them. They were the rough forms, with some semblance of that virtue upon them that the rugged, half-civilized man possessed, and were utterly laughed at, and scorned, and scoffed at by the civilized pagan, who was the very embodiment of sensuality and impurity.

Thus did the world declare war against God, and for sensuality. The God of Purity,—they knew Him not,—and therefore, they could not believe in Him. "There is no truth, and there is no knowledge of God in the land," says the Prophet. Then he immediately adds: "Cursing, lying, theft, and adultery have overthrown and blotted out much love: because my people, saith the Lord, have no grace."

The second kind of war which our Lord found upon the earth was the war between men: for they who had ceased to know God, had ceased to love or respect one another. Split up into a multitude of sects,—nation against nation, province against province, the very history of our race was nothing but a history of war, and strife, and bloodshed. Then came the Son of God Incarnate, with healing hand and powerful touch, to restore the world, and to renew the face of the earth. How did He do this? It could only be done by Him; and by Him could it be only done by His instituting, and leaving, and declaring the truth of God Himself, and leaving it in the midst of men; the unchangeable truth, the eternal truth, the pure, unmixed, bright light of truth as it beamed forth from the eternal wisdom of God. It was only thus that He could restore mankind to peace with the God of eternal truth. Then it was necessary that, having thus established the truth, He should wipe out the sin, by the shedding of His own blood, as a victim, and that He should leave behind Him, for ever in the world, the running stream of that sanctifying blood "unto the cleansing of the sinner and the unclean,—unto the strengthening of the weak, unto the encouraging of the strong, unto the revivifying of the dead." Did Christ do this? Yes, He lifted up His voice and spoke; and the voice of the Saviour was the voice of the eternal God. And mark, that, before He saved the world by the shedding of His blood,—before He redeemed the sin,—for three long years, night and day, in season and out of season, He was preaching and teaching; dispelling error, letting in the light; for mankind could not be prepared for redemption except through the light and through the truth of God. Wherefore we find Him, now on the mountain side, now on the lake; now among the Pharisees, now in the desert; now in the temple of Jerusalem, now in the by-ways of Judea; now in the little towns and villages; but everywhere—"*quotidie docens*," teaching every day, for three years; preparing the world for its redemption; reconciling the human intelligence with the light of God's truth; opening up the minds, and letting the stream of pure light from God into the intellect. Then, when the three years' preparation was over; then, when He had formed His disciples, and established His Apostolic College;—then did the eternal Victim go upon the Cross, and pour out His blood: and the shedding of that blood washed away the sins of the world, and left open those streams from His sacred wounds that were to flow through the sacramental channels, and that were to find every human soul, with all its spiritual wants, here, there, and everywhere, until the end of time,—according to that promise relating to the Church of the Lord: "You shall draw waters of joy from the fountains of sorrow!" He purified the world by the shedding of His blood. But well did He know our nature. "*Et naturam nostram ipse cognovit.*" He made us, and He knew us. Well did He know that the stream that He poured forth from His wounds on Calvary should flow for ever; because the sins which that blood alone could wipe away would be renewed, and renewed again, as long as mankind should be upon this earth. "For,"—and He said it with sorrowing voice—"it needs must be that scandal cometh."

Thus, in the Divine Truth and the sacramental grace which He gave, did He reconcile mankind to His Heavenly Father, and restore peace between God and man. Then, touching the other great warfare, He proclaimed the principle of universal charity—declared that no injuries, no insult, must obstruct it, or break it, or destroy it—declared that we must do good for evil,—declared that we must live for man; take an interest in all men, try to gain the souls of all men; and that this love, this fraternity, this charity must reign in our hearts at the very same time that we are upholding, with every power of our mind—and, if necessary, of our body, the sacred principles of Divine Truth, and of Divine grace.

Behold, then, my dear friends, the peace "that passeth all understanding;" the peace that He came to leave and to give. Peace means union. When nations are at war, they are separated from each other into two hostile camps; and they look upon each other with scowling eyes of hatred and anger;—but when the war is over, they come forth—they meet—and they join hands in peace. So, the meeting of the intellect of man with the truth of God—the admission of that divine truth into the mind—the opening of the heart to the admission of the grace of God, and of our Lord Himself by the Sacraments, establishes the meeting of peace between God and man. The charity of which I have spoken—the nobleness of Christian forgiveness, which is the complement of Christian humility—the grandeur of Christian patience and forbearance—establishes peace among all mankind. It was the design of Christ that that eternal peace of which I speak should also be represented by unity;—that all men should be one by the unity of thought in one common faith, by the unity of heart in one common charity. And it is worthy of remark that, just as our Lord saluted His Apostles with the words, "My peace be with you,"—after His Resurrection—so, before His Passion—on the night before He suffered—He put up His prayer to God—and over and over again, to the Father in Heaven—that all men might be one, even as He and the Father were one. "Father," He says, "Keep them one even, as thou and I are one." That is to say, a union of faith—a recognition of one undivided and unchanging truth,—a bowing down of all before one idea—and, then, a union of hearts springing from that union of faith. This was the design of Christ; and for this He labored. And this the Church has labored to effect. For this she has labored two thousand years. She has succeeded, in a great measure, in doing it;—but the work has been upset and destroyed in many lands by the hands of those who were the enemies of God in spoiling and breaking up the fair design of our Lord and Saviour.

Now, in this eternal and immutable truth preached to all men—recognized by all men—gathering in every intelligence—respecting all honest deviations—yet uniting all in faith;—in this truth and in this sanctifying peace which is in the Catholic Church, lies the salvation of the world—the salvation of society—the salvation of every principle which forms this highly commended and oft-praised civilization of ours. The moment we step one inch out of the Catholic Church and look around us, what do we find? Is there any agency on earth,—even though it may call itself a religion,—that will answer the purposes of society? Is there any of these sects—or religions, as they call themselves, that can make a man pure? No. They are unable to probe and sound the depths of the human heart. They do not pretend to legislate for purity of thought. Practically, they reduce the idea of purity to a mere saving of appearances before the world,—to a mere external respect and decorum. Are they able to shake a man out of his sins? No; there is no reality about them. They have no tribunal of conscience, even, to which they oblige a man to come after careful self-examination. They have no standard of judgment to put before him. They have no agency, divinely appointed, to crush a man,—to humble a man,—to break the pride in him,—to make him confess and avow his sin;—and then, lifting the sacramental hand over him,—by reason of his humility, his sorrow, and his confession,—to send him forth renewed and converted by the grace of God. There is no such thing. There is nothing so calculated to enable a man to keep his word faithfully. No. The first principle of fidelity—lying at the root of all society—the great fundamental principle of fidelity—is the Sacrament which makes the sanctity of marriage,—by which those whom it unites are sealed with the seal of God, and sanctified with the truth of God's Church. The man is saved from the treachery of his own passions. The woman is saved from the inconstancy of the heart of man. The family is saved in the assertion of the mother's rights,—in the placing on her head a crown that no hand on earth can touch or take away. The future of the world is saved by ennobling the Christian woman, and wife, and mother, with something of the purity of the Virgin Mother of God! Do they do this? Oh, I feel the heart within me indignant,—the blood almost boiling in my veins when I think of it!—when I see under the shadow of the Crucified,—nineteen hundred years after He had sanctified the world,—when I see men deliberately rooting up the very foundations of society, loosening the keystone in the arch, and pulling it down, in the day when they went back to their paganism,—in the day when they threatened that the bond that God had tied should be unloosed by the hands of men,—in the day when they gave the lie to the Lord Himself, who declared—"What God hath joined let no man separate;"—in the day when man is so flung out into his own temptations; and the woman, no matter who she may be,—crowned queen or lowly peasant,—the first or the last in the land,—is waiting in trepidation, not knowing the hour when, upon some infamous accusation, the writ of divorce may be put into her hand, and she, the mother of children, be ordered to go forth, that her place may be given to another!

Is there any agency to make men honest? No; they cannot do it. A man plunders, to-day; steals with privy hand; enriches himself unlawfully, unjustly, shamefully;—and, to-morrow, he goes to some revival, or some camp-meeting, and there he blesses the Lord in a loud voice, proclaiming to his admiring friends that he "has found the Lord!" But is there any agency to stop him, and say: "Hold, my friend, wait for a moment! Have you made restitution to the last farthing for what you unjustly acquired? Have you shaken out that Judas purse of yours, until the last dime—the very last piece of silver for which you sold your soul to hell—has gone back again to those from whom it was taken? If not, speak not of finding Christ!—speak not of leaning upon the Lord! Blaspheme not the God of justice!" Is there any agency outside of the Catholic Church to sift a man like this? Is there any such agency at all? No: we live in an age of shams—of pretences; and the worst shams of all—the vilest—the foulest pretences of all—are those we find in the so-called "religious world." Take up your religious newspapers; take up your religious publications, outside of the Catholic Church. I protest it is more than common sense or human patience can bear! If the great Church of the living God were not in the midst of you, unchanging in truth—ever faithful in every commission—clothed in the freshness of her first sanctity, and sanctifying all who come within her sacramental influence;—if she were not here as the city of God, this so-called "religious world" would bring down the wrath of God, calculated, as its antics are, to bring the Lord Himself into contempt; exciting the pity of angels, the anger of heaven, and the joy of hell.

A recent writer, who has devoted some attention to the consideration of the question of religious indifference, asks—"Why are the churches empty? How is it that the intellectual men of the day do not like to listen to sermons? How is it that they take no interest in the things of the Church? How is it that they have no belief?" And a wise voice—a pious voice—answers: "Because, my friend, you do not know how to preach to them. If you want to captivate the intellect of the men of our day;—if you want to interest them—if you want to convince them—do not be clinging to antiquated traditions;—do not rest upon these so-called doctrines of a bygone time. Read scientific books. Find there the problems that are bursting up continually from modern science, and try to reconcile your ideas of religion with those;—and, then, preach to them! Then will you show yourself a man of the age—a man of progress!" And so, henceforth, the subject-matter of our sermons is to be electric telegraphs, submarine cables, and flying ships. "If you want to learn how most effectively to preach," adds this wise and able voice, "read the latest novels, and try to learn from them all the by-ways and high-ways of the human heart." See how delicately they follow all the chit-chat of society,—all the little gossipings, and love-makings and the thousand-and-one influences that act upon the adulterous and depraved heart, of man—the wicked passions of man. This is the text from which the preacher of to-day is to preach if he wishes to attract the intellect of the world. And all this in the very sight, and under the shadow of the Cross of Christ, who died for man! Was ever blasphemy so terrible? And this is what is called "religion" by the world! Not a word about Divine truth; not a word about Divine grace! In one of the leading journals of New York—an able paper—a well-written paper—in a leading article of that paper, this very morning, I read a long dissertation on this very question of preaching and preachers;—and the word "truth" appeared only once in that article;—and then it came under the title of "scientific truth." The word "grace" did not occur even once. But never, even once, did simple "truth" occur—or even "religious truth" flash across the mind of the able, temperate-minded, judicious man that wrote it! And I do not blame him,—for he was writing for the age! He was giving a very fair idea of what the world is, and what the world is sure to come to, if the Almighty God, in His mercy, does not touch the hearts of men, and give them enough of sense to turn to the Catholic Church, and hear the voice of God—the Divine spouse of Christ in her teachings. Without this voice they cannot hear the voice of God. Without her teaching, this hardened, dried-up heart of man will never grow into purity or love.

Now we come to the mission that you and I have. Grand as is the vision that rises before our eyes, when we contemplate the heavenly beauty and graces of our great and mighty Mother, the Church, who has never told a lie, nor ever compromised or kept back the least portion of the eternal and saving truth which mankind should know; who has never tolerated the slightest sin, but to king and peasant has said alike: "Be pure, be faithful, or I will cut you off as a rotten branch, and cast you into hell,"—grand, I say, as is the spectacle of this glorious Church,—wonderful and convincing as are her claims to every man's faith and every man's obedience,—if the advocacy of these claims were left to me, and to such as I am, and to the Fathers, the world would scarcely ever be converted. You have your mission, my dear young friends,—children of the Church of God; you have your mission,—not as preachers, indeed; yet, far more eloquent than the voice of any preacher, in the silent force of example,—the example that you must give to those around you; forcing the most unwilling and reluctant to look upon you and to see in you, shining forth, the glories of your divine religion. "*Sic lux luceat omni mundo.*" He did not say to all, "Go and preach": only to the Twelve. But to all of them He said: "Let your light so shine before men, that, seeing your work, they may give glory to God who is in Heaven." And so I say to you, let your light shine calmly but brightly, that all men may see you, and thus give glory to your Mother the Church, triumphant in Heaven and militant for you on earth. It is your mission to avow, bravely, manfully,—however temperately, yet firm as the adamantine rock,—every sacred principle of Catholicity, and every iota of the teaching of that Church, when she teaches a law; because her destiny is to be the embodiment of truth in this world. "With the heart we believe unto justice." But that is not enough; with the mouth we must make loud confession unto salvation:—*loud confession!* Why? Because the devil is making a loud act of *his* faith, filling the world with it, bringing it out everywhere, in books, in newspapers, in speeches, in associations, in schools, in the public academies, in the universities, in the halls of medicine and of law; in the courts, in the senate;—it is the one cry—the harsh, grating cry by which the devil makes his act of detestable faith in himself, and denial of God;—an act of diabolical faith that meets us at every turn,—strikes and offends every sense of ours with its terrible language. We cannot take up a book that, if we do not find a satyr peering out from its pages, is not the bald, stark daub of some fool, who flings his smut or his infidelity into the sight of God. We cannot turn to a public journal that is not a record of plundering, of villany, of robbery, and murders and thefts and defalcations. Why, what would a dictionary of this day of ours look like? It would be filled with modern names,—page after page,—for these modern sins, of which our honest forefathers scarcely knew anything;—these sins, the embodiment of the practical immorality of the apostate monk of Wurtemburg. We must oppose this terrible exhibition of evil which the devil makes in our public streets, and throughout every organ that comes before us, not only by the strong assertion of our holy faith, but by the silent and eloquent example of our purity of life, our uprightness and cleanliness of heart. And therefore it is that, in truth, never perhaps before was the Word of the Lord so well fulfilled in the children of the Catholic Church, as to-day, when He said: "You are the salt of the earth." And so they are the salt of the earth throughout the world. How much more in this great country, where we are, as it were, in the Spring-time, only breaking up the ground and throwing in the seed from which, one hundred-fold, the fruit will come when we are lying in our cold, forgotten graves. The seedlings that we sow to-day of Catholic faith, of Catholic purity, of Catholic truth, will grow up into a fruit and an abundance so grand, so magnificent, that, perhaps, it is given to us that the ultimate glory of the Church of God shall be the work of our hands and of our lives to-day. It is a great thing to live in the Spring-time of a nation; it is a great thing to find one's self at the fountain head of a stream of mighty national existence that will swell with every age, gaining momentum as it rolls on with the flood of time. It is a great thing to lie at the fountain-head of that stream. It is said with truth—

"The pebble on the streamlet's brink
 Has changed the course of many a river;
The dew-drop on the acorn-leaf
 May warp the giant oak for ever."

The river of America's nationality and existence is only beginning to flow to-day; and we should endeavor to direct it into the current of Catholicity. The young oak which is planted to-day, and which will, in all probability, overshadow and overspread the whole earth, was but lately hidden in the acorn-cup. Ah, let us remember, that even a pebble in the hand of the youth David, hurled against Goliah, struck down the giant. Let us be the pebble in the hand of God that shall strike down this demon—this proud, presumptuous demon of infidelity that has entered into the land, and taking "seizing" of the whole continent of America, says: "This soil must be mine." Let us be as the pebble in the mountain brook, which turns the stream that will one day be a mighty river, into the great bed of Catholic truth and Catholic purity, that alone can save this land. Let us be as the dew-drop on the acorn leaf,—the dew-drop of Catholic faith, of Catholic intelligence, and Catholic morality; the tear, as it were, flowing from the pitying eye of the Saviour, upon the young, sprouting oak of human existence, training it towards heaven—sending it to heaven in the national aspiration, in the national action, and not permitting it to be dragged and warped, in this way and that, until it lies a stunted and misbegotten plant, clinging to the earth, into which it will fling its leaves; its trunk stunted and withered, conveying no sap but the sap of religious bigotry and intolerance, and the bitterest juices of foolish sectarianism; of absurd, blind folly, exciting the laughter of all sensible men upon the earth, the indignation of God, and the joy of hell. This is our mission. Say, will you fulfil it? Say, O Catholic young men, will you fulfil it? You cannot fulfil it without being thorough-going Catholics; you cannot fulfil it without being joined, heart and soul, with the Church, through the Church's head —through the immutable rock—the supreme governor—the infallible teacher of God's infallible Church. You cannot fulfil this mission until you join, with that rivalry of Christian self-denial, the rivalry of Christian purity, and a holy horror of every thing hollow and pretentious—a holy horror of shams. There are no shams in the Catholic Church; there is nothing but shams—religious shams—outside of her. You cannot fulfil this mission unless you seek to sanctify your hearts and your lives, and to sweeten those lives by prayer, by confession, and communion; and I congratulate you, that, in facing this mission, which lies before every Catholic man, you do it, not as individuals, but as a body, as an organization. We live in an age of organizations. There is nothing everywhere but organizations, for this thing, or for that: and nearly all of them belong to the devil. It is fitting that Christ, our Lord, should have His. It is fitting that the Church should have hers. You are banded together in the name of our Lord and Saviour. You remember that, in the Gospel of last Sunday, the Evangelist tells us—"These things are written that all men may believe that the Lord Jesus is Christ, the Son of God; and that, believing, they may have life in His name." In His name you are assembled together, bound by common hopes, by a common purpose, which, without interfering at all with your daily duties, or your individual liberty, still binds you together in a unity of thought, of opinion, and of purpose, to act on this great mass of society, in which our mission lies—yours and mine;—mine in the Word, mine in labor, mine in undivided thought, for that and nothing but that,—or else I also would be a sham;—yours in the manner of which I have spoken to you. And you are banded together under the guidance of those religious men whom the Church honors by permitting them to take the glorious name of Jesus as their own;—of those men who, for three hundred years, have led the van of the Holy Catholic Church in that mighty warfare that is going on, which makes the Church a militant church; —of those men whose fathers before them—the Saints— received first every blow that was intended to strike at the heart of the Church;—of those men who are known among the religious Orders of the Church, and represent the Saviour in His risen glory; for they rose again at the command of the Sovereign Pontiff;—of those men whose name is known in every land;—loved with the ardor of Catholic love; hated and detested with the first and most intense hatred of every man that hates the glorious and immaculate Church of Christ;—of those men who, for three hundred years, have trained and led the young intellect of Christendom,—have stamped upon every young heart that ever came under their hands, the sacred name and the sacred love which is their own title and their most glorious crown. And, therefore, I congratulate you with hope,—and a high and well-assured hope,—that all that God intends, all that the Church expects at your hands, in this glorious missionary Society;—that— all that—you will give to God and to His Church, so as to enable Him to repay you, ten thousand-fold, in glory, in the kingdom of His everlasting joy.

THE CONSTITUTION OF THE CATHOLIC CHURCH.

[*A Lecture delivered by Very Rev. T. N. Burke, O.P., in the Academy of Music, Brooklyn, April 24, 1872.*]

WE are assembled this evening, my dear friends, to contemplate the greatest work of all the works that the Almighty God ever created—namely, "The Constitution of the Holy Catholic Church." In every work of God it has been well observed that the Creator's mind shows itself in the wonderful harmony that we behold in it. Therefore the poet has justly said that "Order is Heaven's first law." But if this be true of earthly things, how much more does the harmony of God,—in the order which is the very expression of the Divine mind,—come forth and appear when we come to contemplate the glorious Church which Christ first founded upon this earth. The glorious Church I call her, and in using those words I only quote the inspired Scriptures of God: for we are told that this Church, which Christ, the Lord, established, is a glorious Church, without spot or wrinkle, or defect of any kind; but all-perfect, all-glorious, and fit to be what He intended her to be—the Immaculate Spouse of the Son of God.

Now, that our Divine Redeemer intended to establish such a Church upon the earth is patent from the repeated words of the Lord Himself; for it will appear that one of the strongest intentions that was in the mind of the Redeemer, and one of the primary conceptions of His wisdom, was to establish upon this earth a Church, of which He speaks, over and over again, saying: "I will build My Church so that the gates of Hell shall never prevail against it:" "He that will not hear the voice of the Church, let him be as if he were a heathen or a publican." And so throughout the Gospel, we find the Son of God again and again alluding to His Church, proclaiming what that Church was to be, and setting upon her the signs by which all men were to know her as a patent and self-evident fact among the nations of the world, until the end of time. And what idea does our Lord give us of His Church? He tells us, first of all,—and tells us over and over again,—that His Church is to be a kingdom; and He calls it—"My kingdom." And elsewhere, in repeated portions of the Gospel, He speaks of it as "the kingdom of God." One time He says, "The kingdom of God is like unto a city, which was built upon the mountain side, so that all men might behold it." And again: "The kingdom of God is like unto a candle set upon a candlestick, so that it might shed its light throughout the whole house, and that every one entering the house might behold it." And again: "The kingdom of God is like unto a net cast out into the sea, and sweeping in all that come in its way—both good and bad." And so, throughout, Christ always speaks of His Church as a Kingdom that He was to establish upon this earth. When, therefore, any meditative, thoughtful man reads the Scriptures reverently, dispassionately, without a film of prejudice over his eyes, he must come to the conclusion that Christ, beyond all, founded a spiritual kingdom upon this earth; and that that kingdom was so founded as to be easily recognized by all men.

Now, if we once let into our minds the idea that the Church of Christ is a kingdom, we must at once admit in the Church an organization which is necessary for every kingdom upon this earth. And what is the first element of a nation? I answer that the first element of a nation is to have a head or ruler,—call him what you will—elect him as you will. Is it a Republic? it must have a President. Is it a Monarchy? it must have its King. Is it an Empire? it must have its Emperor: and so on. But the moment you imagine a state or kingdom of any kind without a head, that moment you destroy out of your mind the very idea of a State united for certain purposes and governed by certain laws. That head of the nation must be the supreme tribunal of the nation. From him, in his executive office, all subordinate officers hold their power; and, even, though he be elected by the people and chosen from among the people, the moment he is set at the head of the state or nation, that moment he is the representative or embodiment of the fountain of authority. Every one wielding power within that nation must bow to him. Every one exercising jurisdiction within the nation must derive it from him. He, I say again, may derive it, even from the choice of the people; but, when he is thus elevated, he forms one unit, to which every thing in the State is bound to look up. This is the very first idea and notion which the word State or Kingdom involves.

It follows, therefore, that, if the Church founded by Christ be a kingdom, the Church must have a head; and, if you can imagine a Church without a head, yet retaining its consistency, its strength, its unity, and its usefulness, for any purpose for which it was created, you can imagine a thing that it is impossible to my mind, or to the mind of any reasonable man, to conceive. Luther imagined it, when he broke up the nations of the earth with his Protestant heresy; when he rent asunder the sacred garment of unity that girded the fair form of the holy Church, the spouse of God. Yet even he, when he broke up the Church, was obliged to maintain the principle of headship. The Church of England had her head; the Church of Denmark had her head; that is to say, her fountain of jurisdiction, her ruling authority, the existence of which, in all these States, we see, with at least the appearance of religion, kept up—the phantasm of a real Church. It is true, my friends, when you come to analyze these different heads that spring up in the different Protestant Churches in the various countries of Europe, we shall find some amongst them, that I believe here, in America, would be called "sore-heads." Henry the Eighth was a remarkable sore-head. Perhaps, if he had got a good combing from the Almighty God, in this world, he would not get so bad a combing as he is, in all probability, receiving where he now is.

We next come to the question: Who is the head of the Church of Christ? Who is the ruler? Before I answer this question, my friends, I will ask you to rise, in imagination, to the grandeur of the idea that fills the mind with the thought of the unfathomable wisdom of God, when He was laying, and sinking deeply into the earth, the foundations of His Church. What purpose had Christ, the Son of God, in view, that He should establish the Church at all? He answers, and tells us plainly, that He had two distinct purposes in view, and that it was the destiny of the Church which He was about to found, to make these purposes known and carry them out, and with the extension of them to spread herself, and be faithful to them unto the consummation of the world. What were these purposes? The first of these was to enlighten the world and dispel darkness by the light of her teachings. Wherefore He said to His Apostles: "You are the light of the world. Let your light so shine before men, that all men may see your works, and seeing you may give glory to your Father, who is in heaven." "You are the light of the world," He says. "A man does not light a candle and put it under a bushel; but sets it upon a candlestick, that it may illuminate the whole house, and that all men entering may behold it. So I say unto you, you are the light of the world and the illumination of all ages."

This was the first purpose for which Christ founded His Church. The world was in darkness. Every light had beamed upon it, but in vain. The light of pagan philosophy, even the highest human knowledge, had beamed forth from Plato, and from the philosophers; but it was unable to penetrate the thick veil that overshadowed the intellect and the genius of men, and to illumine that intelligence with one ray of celestial or divine truth. The light of genius had beamed upon it. The noblest works of art this earth ever beheld were raised before the admiring eyes of the pagans of the world. But neither the pencil of Praxiteles, nor the chisel of Phidias, bringing forth the highest forms of artistic beauty, was able to elevate the mind of the pagan to one pure thought of the God who made him. Every human light had tried in vain to dispel this thick cloud of darkness. The light of God alone could do it; and that light came with Jesus Christ in heaven. Wherefore He said: "I am the light of the world." And "in Him," says the Evangelist, "was Life, and the Life was the light of men."

The next mission of the Church was not only to illumine the darkness, but to heal the corruption of the world, which had grown literally rotten in the festering of its own spiritual ulcers, until every form that human crime can take was not only established amongst men, but acknowledged amongst them,—crowned amongst them; not only acknowledged and avowed, but actually lifted up upon their altars and deified in the midst of them; so that men were taught to adore as a god, the shameful impersonation of their own licentiousness, debauchery, and sin. Terrible was the moral condition of the world when the hand of an angry God was forced to draw back the flood-gates of heaven and sweep away the corruption which prevailed through the flesh, until the spiritual God beheld no vestige of His resemblance left in man! Terrible was the corruption when the same hand was obliged once more to be put forth, and down from heaven came a rain of living fire, and burned up a whole nation, because they were corrupt! Terrible was the corruption when the Almighty God called upon every pure-minded man to draw the sword, in the name of the God of Israel, and smite his neighbor and friend, until a whole nation was swept away from out the twelve tribes of Israel! Christ was sent as our head; and He came and found the world one festering and corrupt ulcerous sore; and He laid upon it the saving salve of His mercy, and declared that He was the purifier of society. And to His disciples He said: "You are not only the light of the world, to dispel its darkness; but you are the salt of the earth, to heal and sweeten and to preserve a corrupt and a fallen race and nature."

This is the second great mission of the Church of God, to heal with her sacramental touch, to purify with her holy grace, to wipe away the corruption of the world, and to prevent its return by laying the healing influence of Divine grace there. This is the mission of the Church of God— which was Christ's—to be, unto the end of time, the light of the world and the salt of the earth.

Now, from this twofold office of the Church of God, I argue that God Himself—the God who founded her, the God who established her in so much glory and for so high and holy a purpose, the God who made her and created her, His fairest and most beautiful work;—that God must remain with her, and be her true head unto the end of time. And why? Who is the light of the world? "I am," says Christ. Who is the purifier of the world? "I am," responds the same Christ. If then, thou, Christ, be the purifier of the earth and the light of the world, tell us, O Master, can light, or grace, or purity come from any other source than Thee? He answers: "No; the man who seeks it in any but in Me, finds, for his light, darkness; and for his healing, corruption and death. The man who plants upon any other soil than Me, plants indeed, but the heavenly Father's hand shall pluck out what he plants." Christ, therefore, is the true head of His Church, the abiding head of His Church, the unfailing, ever-watchful head of His Church; and is as much to-day the head of the Church as He was eighteen hundred years ago. Christ to-day is the real head, the abiding head. He arose from the dead after He had lain three days in darkness. He had said to His Apostles: "I am about to leave you; but it will only be for a little; a little while and you shall not see Me any more; but after a very little while you shall see me again. I will not leave you orphans; I will come to you again; and I will remain with you all days unto the consummation of the world." Oh! my friends, what a consoling thought is this unfailing promise of the words of the Redeemer! Oh! what a consolation has this world in Him who said: "Heaven and earth shall pass away, but My Words shall never pass away: I am with you all days unto the consummation of the world." And how is He with us? Is He with us visibly? No. Do we behold Him with our eyes? No. Do we hear His own immediate voice? No. Have any of you ever seen or heard Him, immediately and directly, as John the Evangelist saw Him when He was upon the Cross; as Mary Magdalen heard Him when He said to her: "I am the resurrection and the life!" No. Yet He founded a visible kingdom—a kingdom which was to be set upon the earth, as a candle set upon a candlestick. Therefore, if He is at the head of that kingdom,—if he is to preside over it,—if He is to rule and govern it, a visible kingdom, He must show Himself visibly. This He does not. In His second and abiding coming He hides Himself within the golden gates of the Tabernacle; and there He abides and remains: but when it was a question of governing His Church, Christ, our Lord, Himself appointed a visible head. And who was this? He called twelve men around Him; He gave them power and jurisdiction; He gave them the glorious mission of His Apostles; He gave them a communication of His own spirit; He gave them inspiration. He breathed His Holy Spirit, the Third Person of the Blessed Trinity, upon them; and He took one of the twelve, and He spoke to that one man three most important words. They were meant for that one man alone; and the proof is that on each occasion when Christ spoke to them, He called the twelve around Him, and He spoke to that one man alone in the presence of the other eleven, that there might be eleven witnesses to the privileges and the powers of the one. Who was that one man? St. Peter. St. Peter was chosen among the Apostles; St. Peter, not up to that time the one that was most loved; for John was "the disciple whom Jesus loved:" St. Peter who, more than any of the others, was reproved by his Lord, in the severest terms; St. Peter, who, more than any of the others, who were faithful,—showed his weakness until the confirming power of the Holy Ghost came upon him;—Peter was the one chosen; and here are the three words which Christ spoke. First of all He said: "Thou art Peter, and upon this Rock I shall build My Church." Christ heard the people speaking of Him, and He said: "Whom do they say I am?" And the Apostles answered: "Lord, some of them say you are Elias or Jeremias, and some of them say you are John the Baptist, and some say you are a prophet." Then Christ asked them solemnly: "Whom do you say I am?" Down went Peter on his knees, and cried out: "Thou art Christ, the Son of the living God." Then Christ, our Lord, said to him: "Blessed art thou, Simon, son of John, because flesh and blood hath not revealed it to thee, but My Father who is in Heaven. And I say to thee, thou art Cephas, and upon this rock I will build my Church." The man who denies to Peter the glorious and wonderful privilege of being the visible foundation underlying the Church of God and upholding it, is untrue to Christ, the head of the Church.

The second word the Son of God spoke to Peter was this: "To thee, O Peter," he said, in the presence of the others, "To thee, O Peter, will I give the keys of the kingdom of heaven. Whatsoever thou shalt bind upon earth shall be bound in heaven, and whatsoever thou shalt loose on earth shall be loosed, also, in heaven." He gave His promise to them all; but to Peter, singly, He said: "To thee do I give the keys of the kingdom of heaven." That is, the supreme power over the Church. On another occasion, Christ, our Lord, spoke to Peter; and the others were present; and He said to him: "Simon, Simon, the devil has asked for thee, that he might sift thee as wheat. But I have prayed for thee, that thy faith fail not; and thou, being once converted, confirm thy brethren." Now, any man who denies to Peter, in the Church, that eternal kingdom that is never to come to an end, and, to Peter and his successors, the power over his brethren, to confirm them in the faith which shall never fail,

—in the faith which was the subject of the prayer of the Son of God to His Father;—any man who denies this supremacy of Peter gives the lie to Jesus Christ.

On another solemn occasion, the Son of God spoke to Peter, when He was preparing to bid His Apostles and disciples a last farewell. They had seen Him crucified; they had seen him lie disfigured, mangled, in the silent tomb. From that tomb, with a power which was all His own, He rose, like the lightning of God, to the heavens, sending before Him, howling and shrieking, all the demons of hell, conquered and subdued. Now, His Apostles were gathered together. Suddenly a flash lights up the heavens, and He appears in their midst. Then He goes straight to Peter, and He says: Simon Peter, do you love Me more than these? Peter said: "Yea, Lord, Thou knowest that I love Thee." Then He said to Him: "Feed my lambs." A second time, after a pause, the Son of God said: "Simon, son of John, lovest thou Me?" Peter said: "Lord, Thou knowest that I love Thee." Again He said to him: "Feed my lambs." Another pause, and a third time He said to him: "Simon, son of John, lovest thou Me more than these?" And then Peter, bursting into tears, said: "Lord, Thou knowest all things— Thou knowest that I love Thee." Then said the Redeemer, "Feed My sheep." Elsewhere the same Redeemer had said, "There shall be one fold and one shepherd," and He laid His hand on the head of Peter and said: "Thou art Peter, the son of John, be thou the shepherd of the one fold:—feed My lambs; feed My sheep." He who denies, therefore, to Peter, and to Peter's successor, whoever he is, the one headship, the one office of shepherd in the one fold of God, gives the lie to Jesus Christ, the God of Truth.

The day of the Ascension came. For forty days did Christ remain discoursing with His Apostles, instructing them concerning the kingdom of God. And when the forty days were over, He led them forth from Jerusalem, into the silent, beautiful mountain of Olives; and there, as they were gathered around Him, and He was speaking to them and telling them of things concerning the Kingdom of God—that is, the Church,—slowly, wonderfully, majestically, they beheld His figure rise from the earth; and as it rose above their heads it caught a new glory and splendor that was shed down upon it from the broken and the rent heavens above. They followed

Him with their eyes. They saw him pass from ring to ring of light. Their ears caught the music of the nine choirs of heaven, of millions of angels, who, from the clouds, saluted the coming Lord. They strained their eyes and their hands after Him. They lifted up their voices, saying, as Eliseus did of old to Elias; "Oh! Thou chariot of Israel, and its charioteer! wilt Thou leave us?" And from the clouds that were surrounding Him He waved to them His last blessing; and their streaming eyes caught the last lustre and brightness of His figure, as it disappeared in the empyrean of heaven, and was caught up to the Throne of God. Then an Angel flashed into their presence, and said: "Ye men of Galilee, why stand ye here looking up to heaven? This Jesus, who is taken up into heaven, shall so come as you have seen Him going into heaven." And the other disciples bent their knees to Peter, the living representative of the supremacy, the truth, and the purity of Jesus Christ.

Henceforth the life of Peter, and of Peter's successors, became the great leading light around which, and towards which, the whole history of the world revolved. It became the central point to which every thing upon this earth must tend; because, in the designs of God, the things of time are but for the things of eternity; and Peter, in being the representative and viceroy of the Son of God upon earth—in the external headship and government of the Church—was the only man who came nearest to God, who had most of God in him, and most of God in his power—in the distribution of His grace, in the attributes that belong to the Saviour—and, consequently, became the first and highest and greatest of men, and the only man that was necessary in this world.

For many long and weary years Peter labored in his Master's cause, watering the way of his life with the tears of an abiding sorrow, because, in an hour of weakness, he had denied Jesus Christ; until, at length, many years after the Saviour's ascension into heaven, an old man was brought forth from a deep dungeon in Rome. There were chains upon his aged limbs, and he was bowed down, with care and austerity, to the very earth. The few white hairs upon his head fell upon his aged and drooping shoulders. Meekly his lips moved as in prayer, while he toiled up the steep, rugged side of one of the seven hills of Rome. And when he had gained the summit, lo! as in Jerusalem, many years

before, there was a cross and there were three nails. They
nailed the aged man to that cross, straining his time-worn
limbs, until they drove the nails into his hands and feet.
And then, when they were about to lift him, a faint prayer
came from his lips, and the crucified man said: "There was
One in Jerusalem whose royal head was lifted towards
heaven, upon a cross. And He was my Lord and my God,
Jesus Christ. I am not worthy," he said, "to be made like
Him, even in suffering; and therefore, I pray you, that you
crucify me with my head towards the earth, from which I
came." And so, thus elevated, he died; and THE FIRST
POPE passed away.

For three hundred years Pope succeeded Pope. Peter had
no sooner left the world than Linus took his sceptre and
governed the Church of God. Though, down in the Catacombs of Rome, he governed the Church of God, every
Bishop in the Church, every power in the Church recognized
him and obeyed him as the representative of God—the living
head, the earthly viceroy of the invisible but real Head—
Jesus Christ. For three hundred years, Pope after Pope died,
and sealed his faith in the Church of God with a martyr's
blood. And then, after three hundred years of dire persecution, the Church of God was free, and she walked the earth
in all the majesty and purity of her beauty.

In the fifth century, the Roman Empire yet preserved the
outward form of its majesty and power. All the nations of
the earth bowed to Rome. All conquered peoples looked
to Rome as their mistress, and as the centre of the world;
when, suddenly, from the forests and snows of the North,
poured down the Huns, the Goths, and Visigoths, in countless thousands and hundreds of thousands. The barbarian
hordes sallied from their fastnesses, and, led by their savage kings, broke in pieces the Roman Empire, and shattered
the whole fabric of Pagan civilization to atoms. They rode
rough-shod over the Roman citizens and their rulers, burned
their palaces, and destroyed their cities, leaving them a
pile of smouldering ruins. Every vestige of ancient Pagan
civilization and power, glory, and art, and science, went down
and disappeared under the tramp of the horses of Attila.
One power, alone, stood before these ruthless destroyers;
one power alone opened its arms to receive them; one
power arrested them in their career of blood and victory;

—and that power was the Catholic Church. "In that day," says a Protestant historian, "the Catholic Church saved the world, and out of these rude elements formed the foundation of the civilization, the liberty, and the glory which is our portion in this nineteenth century."

In the meantime, Rome was destroyed. The fairest provinces of Gaul, Spain, Italy, and Germany were overrun by the barbarians. The people were oppressed. Fathers of families were cut off, hearth-fires extinguished, and the blood of the young ravished maiden and of the weeping mother was wantonly shed. The people, in their agony, cried out to the only man whom the barbarians respected,—one whom the whole world recognized as, in a manner, tinged with divinity,—the Pope of Rome. The cry of an anguished people went forth from end to end of Italy; and in that hour of peril the cry was,—"Save us from ruin! Cover us with the mantle of your protection! Be thou our monarch and king! and then, and then only, can we expect to be saved." Then did the Pope of Rome clothe himself with a new power independent of that which he had received already, and which was recognized from the beginning,—namely, that temporal power and sovereignty, that crown of a monarch, that place in the council chambers of kings, that voice in the guidance of nations and in the influencing of the destinies of the material world which, for century after century, he exercised, but which we, in our day, have seen him deprived of by the hands of those who have plucked the kingly crown from his aged and venerable brow. How did he exercise that power? How did he wear that crown? What position does he hold as his figure rises up before the vision of the student of history, looking back into the past and beholding him as he passes among the long file of kings and warriors of the earth? O my friends, no sword dripping with blood is seen in the hands of the Pope-king, but only the sceptre of justice and of law. No cries of a suffering and afflicted people resound about him, but the blessings of peace and of a delighted and consoled world surround him. No blood follows, floating in the path of his progress. That path is strewn with the tears of those who wept with joy at his approach, and with the flowers of peace and of contentment. He used his power—and history bears me out when I say it—the power which was providentially put into his hands, by which he was made not only a king among kings, but the first recognized monarch in Christendom; the king, highest among kings; the man whose voice governed the kings of the earth, convened their councils, directed their course, reproved them in their errors, and restrained them from shedding the blood of their people, and from the commission of every other injustice;—all these powers he used for the good of God's people. He used that power for a thousand years for purposes of clemency, of law, of justice, and of freedom. When Spain and Portugal, in the zenith of their power, each commanding mighty armies, were about to draw the sword and devastate the fair plains of Castile and Andalusia, the Pope came in and said: "Mighty kings though you be, I will not permit you to shed the blood of your people in an unnecessary war." When Philip Augustus, of France, at the height of his power,—when he was the strongest king in Christendom,—wished to repudiate his lawful wife, and to take another one in her stead, the injured woman appealed to Rome; and from Rome came the voice of Rome's king, saying to him: "O monarch, great and mighty as thou art, if thou doest this injustice to thy married wife, and scandalize the world by thine impurity, I will send the curse of God and of His Church upon you, and cut you off like a rotten branch from among the community of kings." When Henry VIII, of England, wished to put away from him the pure and high-minded and lawful mother of his children, because his licentious eyes had fallen upon a younger and fairer form than hers, the Pope of Rome said to him: "If you commit this iniquity; if you repudiate your lawful wife; if you set up the principle that, because you are a king, you can violate the law; if no power in your own country is able to bring you to account for it, my hand will come down upon you; and I will cut you off from the communion of the faithful, and fling you, with the curse of God upon you, out upon the world." And I say that in such facts as these—and I might multiply them by the hundred —the Pope of Rome used his temporal sovereignty and his kingly power among the nations in establishing the sacred cause of human liberty. I speak of liberty—I speak of human liberty; I thank my God that I am breathing the air in which a free man may speak the language of freedom. I have a right to speak of freedom; for I am a child of a race that for eight hundred years have been martyred in the sacred cause of freedom. Never did a people love it, since the world was created, as the children of Ireland, who enjoy it less than any other nation. I can speak this night, but rather with the faltering voice of an infant, than with the full swelling tones of a man. For I have loved thee, O Mother Liberty! Thy fair face was veiled from mine eyes from the days of my childhood. I longed to see the glistening of thy pure eyes, O Liberty! I never saw it until I put my foot upon the soil of glorious young Columbia. And there, rising out of this great Western ocean, like Aphrodite of old from the foam of the rolling billows, I beheld the goddess in all her beauty; and as a priest, as well as an Irishman, I bowed down to her.

But what is liberty? Does it consist in every man having a right to do as he likes? No, my friends, this is not liberty. The quintessence of freedom lies, not in the power of every man to do what he likes, but that quintessence of freedom and liberty lies in every man having his rights clearly defined. No matter who he is, from the first to the last, from the humblest to the highest in the community, let every man know his own rights; let him know what power he has and what privileges; give him every reasonable freedom and liberty, and secure that to him by law; and then, when you have secured every man's rights and defined them by law, make every man in the State, from the highest to the lowest, from the President down to the poorest,—the greatest and the noblest, as well as the humblest and the meanest—let every man be obliged to bow down before the omnipotence of the law. A people that know their rights, a people that have their rights thus defined, a people that are resolved to assert the omnipotence of those rights—that people can never be enslaved. Now, this being the definition of liberty —and I am sure that it comes home like conviction to every man in this house—what is true freedom? That I know what rights I have, and that no man will be allowed to infringe them. Give me every reasonable right, and when I have these, secure them to me, and keep away from me every man that dares to impede me in the exercise of them, so that I may exercise them freely.

Now, I ask you, who is the father of this liberty that we enjoy to-day?—who is the father of it, if not the man who

stood between the barbarians, coming down to waste, with
fire and sword, to abolish the law, to abolish governments
and destroy the peoples—the man that stood between those
destroyers and the people, and said: "Let us make laws, and
you respect them, and I will get the people to respect them."
That man was the Pope of Rome. Who was the man that,
for a thousand years, as a crowned monarch, was the very
impersonation of the principle of law, but the Pope? Who
was the man that was equally ready to crush the poor man
and the rich man, the king and the people—to crush them
by the weight of his authority—when they violated that law
and refused to recognize that palladium of human liberty?
It was the Pope of Rome. Who was the man whose genius
inspired and whose ability contributed to the foundation and
the very institutions of the Italian Republics, and of the ancient liberties of Spain in the early Middle Ages? Who was
the man that protected them from the tyranny of the cruel,
lawless barons, fortified in their castles? He was the man
whose house was a sanctuary for the weak and persecuted,
and who surrounded that house with all the censures and
vengeance of the Church against any one who would violate its
sanctity. Who labored, by degrees, patiently, for more than
a thousand years, until he at length succeeded in elaborating
the principles of modern freedom and modern society from
out the chaotic ruin and confusion of these ages of barbarism? Who was he?—the father of civilization—the father
of the world? History asserts, and asserts loudly, that he
was the royal Pope of Rome. And now the gratitude of the
world has been to shake his ancient and time-honored throne,
and to pluck the kingly crown from his brow in his old age,
after seventy years of usefulness and of glory; and to confine him, a prisoner, practically, in the Vatican Palace in
Rome. A prisoner, I say, practically; for how can he be
considered other than a prisoner, who cannot go out of his
palace into the streets of the city, without hearing the
ribaldry, the profanity, the obscenity, and the blasphemy, to
which his aged, pure, and virgin ears had never lent themselves for a moment of his life. Yes—he is dethroned, but
not dishonored; uncrowned, but not dishonored; not uncrowned by the wish of his own people, I assert, for I have
lived for twelve years amidst them, and I know he never
oppressed them. He never drove them forth—the youth of

his subjects—to be slaughtered on the battle-field, because he had some little enmity or jealousy against his fellow-monarch. He never loaded them with taxes, nor oppressed them until life became too heavy to bear. Uncrowned, indeed, but not dishonored, though we behold him seated in the desolate halls of the once glorious Vatican, abandoned by all human help, and by the sympathy of nearly all the world! But upon those aged brows there rests a crown—a triple crown,—that no human hand can ever pluck from his brow, because that crown has been set on that head by the hand of Jesus Christ, and by his Church. That triple crown, my friends, is the crown of spiritual supremacy, the crown of infallibility, and the crown of perpetuity. In the day when Christ said to Peter, "Confirm thou thy brethren; feed my lambs, feed My sheep; to thee do I give the keys of the Kingdom of Heaven,"—in that day he made Peter supreme among the Apostles. His words meant this or meant nothing. Peter wielded that sceptre of supremacy; and nothing is more clearly pointed out in the subsequent inspired history of the Church, as recorded in the Acts of the Apostles, than the fact that, when Peter spoke, every other man, Apostle or otherwise, was silent, and accepted Peter's word as the last decision, from which there was no appeal. Never, in the Church of God, has Peter's successor ceased to assert broadly, emphatically, and practically this primacy. Never was a Council convened in the Catholic Church, except on the commands of the Pope. Never did a Council of Bishops presume to sit down and deliberate upon matters of faith and morals except under the guidance and in the presence of the Pope, either personally there, or there by his officers or legates. Never was a letter read at the opening of any Council,—and they were constantly sent to each succeeding Council,—that the Bishops of the Church did not rise up and proclaim; "We hear the voice of the Pope, which is the voice of Peter; and Peter's voice is the echo of the voice of Jesus Christ." Never did any man in the Church of God presume to appeal from the tribunal of the Pope, even to the Church in Council, without having the taint of heresy affixed to him, and the curse of disobedience and schism put upon him. For centuries it has been the recognized principle of the Catholic Church that no man can lawfully appeal to any tribunal from the decision of the Pope in matters spiritual or in matters touching faith and morality, because there is no tribunal to appeal to above him save that of God. He represents (as the visible head of the Church) the Invisible Head, who is none other than Jesus Christ. The consequence is that the Church, as a kingdom, like every other State, has its last grand tribunal, just like the House of Lords in England, or the High Court of Justice in Washington, from which there is no appeal. What follows from this? There is no appeal from the Pope's decision. There never has been. Is the Church bound to abide by that decision? Certainly; because the Church is bound in obedience to her head; one man alone can command the obedience of the Church and the duty of submission; and that man is the Pope. He has always commanded it; and no one has dared to appeal from his decision, because, as I said before, he is the Viceroy, the visible head of the Church, in whom, officially, is the voice of Jesus Christ present with His Church.

What follows from this, my friends? If it be true that the Church of God can never believe a lie; if it be true that she can never be called upon by a voice that she is bound to obey, to accept a lie; if it be true that nothing false in doctrine or unsound in morality can ever be received by the Church of God, or ever be imposed upon her;—for He who founded her said: "The gates of hell shall never prevail against My Church;"—then it follows that,—if there be no appeal from the Pope's decision, but only submission on the part of the Church,—it follows that the Pope, when he speaks as the head of the Church, when he preaches to the whole Church, when he bears witness to the Church's belief and the Church's morality, when he propounds a certain doctrine to her—upon a body that can never believe a lie, that can never act upon a lie, whose destiny it is to remain pure in doctrine and in morality—pure as the Son of God who created her;—it follows that when the Pope propounds that doctrine to the Church, he cannot propound a lie to her, or force that lie upon her belief—it follows that the same spirit of Divine Truth that preserves the body preserves also the head, and that the Pope, as head of the infallible Church, must be infallible. In other words, the Pope may make a mistake. If he write a book, as a private author, he may put something in it that is not true. If he propound certain theories, unconnected with faith and morals, he may be as mistaken as you or I. But the moment the Pope stands up before the holy Church of God, and says: "This is the Church's belief; this has been from the beginning her belief; this is her tradition; this is her truth;" then he cannot, under such circumstances, teach the Catholic Church —the spouse of Jesus Christ—a lie. Consequently, he is infallible. I do not give the Church's infallibility, as the intrinsic reason of Papal infallibility; but I say this, that if any reasoning man admits that Christ founded an infallible Church, it follows of necessity that he must admit an infallible head. It was but three or four days ago that I was disputing with an Unitarian minister, a man of intelligence and of deep learning, as clever a man, almost, as I ever met; and he said to me: "If I once admitted that the Church was infallible, that she could not err, that moment I would have to admit the infallibility of the Pope; for how on earth can you imagine a Church that cannot err, bound to believe a man that commands her to believe a lie! It is impossible; it is absurd upon the face of it." And so, my friends, it has ever been the belief and faith of the Catholic Church that the Pope is preserved by the same spirit of truth that preserves the Church.

But, you will ask me, "If this be the case, tell me how is it that it was only three or four years ago the Church declared that the Pope was infallible?" I answer that the Catholic Church cannot—it is not alone that she will not, but she cannot—teach any thing new, any thing unheard of. She cannot find a truth, as it were, as a man would find a guinea under a stone. She cannot go looking for new ideas and saying: "Ah! I find this is new! Did you ever hear of it before?" The Church cannot say that. She has from the beginning the full deposit of Catholic truth in her hand; she has it in her instinct; she has it in her mind; but it is only now and then, when a sore emergency is put upon her, and she cannot help it, that the Church of God declares this truth or that, or the other, which she has always believed, to be a revelation of God, and crystallizes her faith and belief and tradition in the form of dogmatic definition. Which of us doubts that the very foundation of the Catholic Church rests upon the belief that Christ, our Lord, the Redeemer, was the Son of God? It is the very foundation-stone of Christianity. This has been the essence of all religion since the Son of God became man. And yet, my friends, for three hundred years the Catholic Church had not said a single word about the divinity of Christ; and it was only after three hundred years, when a man named Arius rose up and said: "It is all a mistake; the Son of Mary is not the Son of God. He who suffered and died on the Cross was not the Son of God, but a mere man;"—then after three hundred years the Church turned round and said: "If any man says that Jesus Christ is not God, let that man be accursed as an infidel and a heretic." Would any of you say: "Then it seems that for three hundred years the Church did not believe it?" She always believed it; it was always her foundation-stone. "If she did believe it, why did not she define it?" I answer, the occasion had not arisen. It is only when some bold invader, when some proud, heretical man, when some bad spirit manifests itself among the people, that the Church is obliged to come out and say—"Take care! take care! Remember this is the true faith;" and then, when she declares her faith, it becomes a dogmatic definition, and all Catholics are bound to bow to it. Need I tell you, Irish maids, Irish mothers, and Irish men—need I tell you how St. Patrick preached of the woman whom he called *Muire Mhathaire*, "Mary Mother," the woman whom he called the Virgin of God? Need I tell you that the Church always believed that that woman was the Mother of God? And yet you will be surprised to hear that at the time that St. Patrick preached to the Irish people, the Church had not yet defined it as an article of faith. It was only in the fifth century that the Church, at Ephesus, declared dogmatically that Mary was the Mother of God. Did not she believe it before? Certainly! It was no new thing; she always believed it; but there was no necessity to assert it till heretics denied it. Then, to guard her children from the error which was being asserted, she had to define her faith. Did not the Church always believe in the presence of Christ transubstantiated in the Eucharist? Most certainly. All history tell us that she believed it. Her usages, her ceremonies, every thing in her, point to that divine presence as their life and centre; but it was sixteen hundred years before the Church defined transubstantiation as an article of faith; and then only because Calvin denied it. He was the first heretic to deny it. It was denied by Berengarius, a learned man, in the thirteenth century; but he immediately repented, and burned his book, and there was an end of it. But the first man to preach a denial of the **real presence of Christ was Calvin.** Luther never did. The Church of God declared that Christ was present, and that the substance of bread and wine was changed into the body and blood of the Lord. And so, in our day, the Church, for the first time, found it necessary to declare that her head, her visible head, cannot teach her a lie. It seems such an outrage upon common sense to deny this,—it seems so palpable and plain, from the very constitution of the Church, that it seems as if the definition of this dogma were unnecessary. Yet in truth it was to meet the proud, self-asserting, cavilling, questioning spirit of our day that the Church was obliged to do this. It was because, guided by a wise Providence,—scarcely knowing, yet foreseeing that which was to come,—that the Pope was to be deprived of all the prestige of his temporal power; that all that surrounded him in Rome was to be lost to Him for a time; that, perhaps, it was his destiny to be driven out and exiled, and a stranger among other men on the face of the earth; so that he might be unknown, lost sight of,—that the Church of God, with her eight hundred Bishops, rising up in the strength of her guiding spirit, fixed upon the brow of her Pontiff the seal of her faith in his infallibility, that wherever he goes, wherever he is found, whatever misfortunes may be his lot, he will still have that seal upon him which no other man can bear, and which is the stamp of the head of the Catholic Church.

And now, my dear friends, we come to the last circle of that spiritual tiara that rests upon the brow of Pius the Ninth. It is the crown of perpetuity. There is no man necessary in this world but one. We are here to-day; we die to-morrow, and others take our places. The kings of the earth are not necessary. Sometimes, Lord knows, it would be as well if they did not exist at all. The statesmen and philosophers of the earth are not necessary. My friends, the politicians of to-day are scarcely a necessity. We might manage by a little engineering—and above all by a little more honesty—to get on without them, and find perhaps a few dollars more in our pockets. One alone was necessary to this world from the beginning, and that was He whom we beheld upon the cross on Good-Friday morning—He alone. Without Him we were all lost; no grace, but sin; no purity, but corruption; no heaven, but hell. He was necessary from the beginning; and the only man that is now necessary upon the earth is the man that represents Him. We cannot get on without him. The Church must have her head; and He who declared that the Church was to last unto the end of time will take good care to keep her head. He is under the hand of God; and under the hand of the Ruler of the Church we can well afford to leave him. He will take good care of him. As a temporal ruler I assert still that the Pope is the only necessary ruler on the face of the earth. He is necessary, because, not establishing his power by the sword; not preserving it by the sword; not enlarging his dominions by the sword, or by injustice; as a monarch, as a king, he represents the principle of right unprotected by might, and of justice and law enthroned by the common consent of all the nations. In the day when might shall assume the place of right; in the day when a man cannot find two square feet of earth on which to build a throne, without bloodshed and injustice; in that day, when it comes, the Pope will no longer be necessary as a temporal sovereign;—but pray God, that before that day comes, you and I may be in our graves; for when that day comes, if ever it comes, life will be no blessing, and existence upon this earth will be a curse rather than a joy. The Pope is necessary because some power is needed to stand between the kings and the people; some power before which kings must bow down; some voice recognized as the voice not of a subject, not of an ordinary man, or an ordinary bishop; a voice as of a king amongst kings; some voice which will confound the jealousies, and passions, and scandals of the rulers of the earth, which only serve as so many means to shed the blood of the people. Our best security is the crown that rests upon the brow of a peaceful king. Our best security is the crown that rests upon the brow of a man who was always and ever ready to shield the weak from the powerful, and to save to woman her honor, her dignity, her place in the family, her maternity, from the treachery, and the villany, and the inconstancy of man; to strike off the chains of the slave, and to prepare him before emancipation for the glorious gift of freedom. This power is the Pope's, and he has exercised it honestly and well. Protestant historians will tell you that the Pope was the father of liberty; that he was the founder of modern civilization: and that the crown that was upon his head was the homage paid by the nations to clemency, and mercy, and justice, and law. And therefore he must come back; he must come and seat himself upon the throne again. The day will come when all the Christians in the world will be desirous of this. And when that day comes, and not till then, justice shall be once more tempered by mercy; absolutism shall be once more neutralized by the constitutional liberties and privileges of the people. When that day comes, the people on their side will feel the strong yet quiet restraining hand enforcing the law; while the kings, on their side, will behold once more the now-hated and detested vision of the hand of the Pontiff brandishing the thunders of the Vatican. That day must come, and with it will come the dawn of a better day, a day of peace. And I believe, even now, in this future day, in this coming year, when we shall behold the Pope advancing at the head of all the rulers of the earth, and pointing out, with sceptred hand, the way of justice, of mercy, of truth, and of freedom. We shall behold him, when all the nations of the earth shall greet his return to power, shall greet his entry into the council-chambers of their sovereigns, even as the Jews greeted the entry of Christ into Jerusalem, and hailed Him king. I behold him, when foremost among the nations that shall greet him, in that hour,—a sceptred monarch and crowned king, a temporal ruler, and, far more, a spiritual father,—amongst these nations, the mighty, the young, the glorious, and the free America shall present herself. When this land,—so mighty in its extent and the limits of its power, that it cannot afford to be any thing else than Catholic,—for no other faith can be commensurate with so mighty a nation;—when this land, this glorious America, developing her resources, rising into that awful majesty of power that will shake the world and shape its destinies, will find every other religious garb too small and too miserable to cover her stately form save the garb of the Catholic faith, the Christian garment in which the Church of God will envelop her; and she, strong in her material power, strong in her mighty intelligence, strong in that might that will place her at the front of the nations, shall be the first to hail her

Pontiff, her father and her king, and to establish him upon his mighty throne as the emblem and the centre of the faith and the glorious religion of an united people, whose strength—the strength of intellect, the strength of faith, the strength of material power—will raise up, before the eyes of a wondering and united world, a new vision of the recuperative power and majesty and greatness of the Almighty God, as reflected in His Church.

THE ATTRIBUTES OF CATHOLIC CHARITY.

[*A Lecture delivered by Very Rev. T. N. Burke, O.P., in St. Mary's Church. Hoboken, N. J., April 25, 1872, for the benefit of the Hospital under the charge of the Sisters of the Poor.*]

MY DEAR FRIENDS: We all read the Scriptures; but of the many who read them, how few there are who take the trouble of thinking profoundly on what they read. Any one single passage of the Scriptures represents, in a few words, a portion of the infinite wisdom of the Almighty God. Consequently, any one sentence of those inspired writings, should furnish the Christian mind with sufficient matter for thought for many and many a long day. Now, we, Catholic priests, are obliged, every day of our lives, in our daily "Office," to recite a large portion of the divine and inspired Word of God, in the form of prayer. Never was there a greater mistake than that made by those who think that Catholics do not read the Sriptures. All the prayers that we, priests, have to say—seven times a day approaching the Almighty God, —are embodied in the words of the Holy Scriptures; and not only are we obliged to recite them as prayers, but we are also obliged to make them the subject of our daily and our constant thought. I purpose, therefore, in approaching this great subject of the "Attributes of Christian Charity," to put before you a text of Scripture which many of you have, no doubt, read over and over again; viz.: the first verse of the fortieth psalm, in which the Psalmist says: "Blessed is the man that understandeth concerning the needy and the poor."

Now, if you reflect, my dear friends, you will find that, at first sight, it seems strange to speak of that man as "blessed" that understandeth concerning the needy and the poor; there seems to be so little mystery about them. They meet us at every corner: put their wants and their necessities before us; they force the sight of their misery upon our eyes; —and the most fastidious and the most unwilling are obliged to look upon their sorrows, and to hear the voice of their complaint and their sufferings. What mystery is there, then, in the needy and the poor? What mystery can there be? And yet, in the needy, and the poor, and the stricken, there is so profound a mystery that the Almighty God declared that few men understand it; and "blessed" is he that is able to fathom its depths. What is this mystery? What is this subject,—the one which I have come to explain to you? A deep and mysterious subject;—one that presents to us far more of the wisdom of the designs of God, than might appear at first. What is the mystery which is hidden in the needy and the poor, and in which we are pronounced "blessed" if we can only understand it thoroughly, and, like true men, act upon that understanding? Let me congratulate you, first, that, whether you understand this mystery or not, your presence here to-night attests that you wish to act upon it; that yours are the instincts of Christian charity, that the needy and the poor, and the stricken ones of God have only to put forth their claims to you, at the pure hands of these spouses of our Lord; and you are ready, in the compassion and the tenderness of heart which is the inheritance of the children of Christ, to fill their hands, that your blessings may find their way to the needy and the poor.

And yet, although so prompt in answering the call of charity, perhaps it will interest you, or instruct you, that I should invite your consideration to this mystery. What is it? In order to comprehend it, let us reflect. The Apostle, St. Paul, writing to his recently converted Christians, lays down this great rule for them: That, for the Christian man, there are three virtues which form the very life and essence of his Christianity; and these are,—not the virtues of prudence, nor of justice, nor of high-mindedness, nor of nobleness, nor of fortitude: no; but they are the supernatural virtues of Faith, Hope, and Love. "Now, there remain to you, brethren," he says, "Faith, Hope, and Charity,—these three; but the greatest of these is Charity." The life of the Christian, therefore, must be the life of a believer—a "man of Faith." It must be a hopeful life,—an anticipative life—a life that looks beyond the mere horizon of the present time into the far-stretching eternity that goes beyond it;—a life of Hope; but, most of all, it must be a life of divine love. Those are the three elements of the Christian character. Nowadays it is the fashion to pervert these three virtues. The man of faith is no longer the simple believer. Faith means a bowing-down of the intellect to things that we cannot understand, because they are mysteries of God. But the idea of religion, nowadays, is to reason and not to believe. The Apostle, if he were writing to the men of this nineteenth century, would be obliged to say: "Brethren, now there remain to you argument and reason," but not faith; for faith means, in words of the same Apostle, the humbling, unto full humiliation, of intelligence before the mystery which was hidden for ages with Christ in God. "Faith," says St. Paul, "is the argument of things that appear not." The Catholic Church, nowadays, is called the enslaver of the intelligence—the incubus upon the mind of man. And why? Because she asks him *to believe*. Mind,—men of intelligence who listen to me,—because she asks man to believe; because she says to him, "My son, I cannot explain this to you; it is a mystery of God;" and there is no faith where there is no mystery. Where there is the clear vision, the comprehensive conviction of the intelligence, arising from argumentation and reason, there is no sacrifice of the intellect;—there is no Faith.

Hope, nowadays, has changed its aspect altogether. Men put their hopes in any thing rather than in Christ. It was only a few days ago I was speaking to a very intellectual man. He was an Unitarian—a man of deep learning and profound research. Speaking with him of the future, he said to me: "Oh, Father, my future is the ennoblement of the human race; the grandeur of the 'coming man';—the perfect development, by every scientific attainment, by every grand quality that can ennoble him, of the man who is to be formed out of the civilization and the progress and the scientific attainments of this nineteenth century." That was his language; and I answered him and said: "My dear sir, my hope is to see Christ, the Son of God, shining forth in all my fellow-men here, that He may shine in them for ever hereafter. I have no other hope."

The Charity of to-day has changed its aspect. It has become a mere human virtue. It is compassionate, I grant you; but not with the compassion that our Lord demands from His people. It is benevolent, I am willing to grant you. We live in an age of benevolence. I bow down before that human virtue; and I am glad to behold it. I was proud of my fellow-men, seeing the readiness and generosity with which, for instance, they came to the relief of the great burned city on the shores of the northern lake. I am proud, when I come here, to hear New York and Jersey City and Hoboken called "cities of charities." It is the grandest title that they could have. But when I come to analyze that charity—when I come to look at that charity through the microscope that the Son of God has put in my hands, viz.: —the light of divine faith,—I find all the divine traits disappear; and it remains only a human virtue; relieving the poor, yet not recognizing the virtue that reposes in them; alleviating their sufferings, touching them with the hand of kindness or of benevolence; but not with the reverential, loving hand of faith and of sacrifice.

On the other hand, loudly protesting against this spirit of our age, which admits the bad and spoils the good; which lets in sin, and then tries to deprive of its sacramental nature the modicum of virtue that remains;—protesting against all this, stands the great Catholic Church, and says;—"Children of men, children of God, Faith, Hope, Charity must be your life: but your Faith and your Hope must be the foundation of your Charity; for the greatest of these virtues is Charity."

And why? What is Faith? Faith is an act of human intelligence; looking up for the light that cometh from on high—from the bosom of God, from the Eternal Wisdom of God. Recognizing God in that light, Faith catches a gleam of Him and rejoices in its knowledge. Hope is an act of the will, striving after God, clinging to His promises, and trying, by realizing the conditions, to realize the glory which is the burden of that promise. Charity, alone, succeeds in laying hold of God. The God of whom Faith catches a glimpse,—the God after whom Hope strains,—Charity seizes and makes its own. And, therefore, "the greatest of these is Charity." When the veil shall fall from the face of God, and when we shall behold Him in heaven, even as He is and as He sees us, there shall be no more Faith: it shall be absorbed in vision. When that which we strain after and hope for to-day shall be given us, there shall be no more Hope: it shall be lost in fruition. But the Charity that seizes upon God to-day, shall hold for all eternity. Charity, alone, shall remain, the very life of the elect of God. And, therefore, "the greatest of these is Charity."

Are there among you, this evening, any who are not Catholics? If there be, you may imagine that, because I come before you in the garb of a Dominican friar of the thirteenth century,—with seven hundred years not only of the traditions of holiness, but even of historic responsibility on my shoulders, in virtue of the habit that I wear,—you may imagine that I come among you, perhaps, with an alienated heart and embittered spirit for those without the pale of my holy, great, loving mother, the Church of God—for which, some day, God grant that it may be my privilege to die. But, no. If there be one here to-night, who is not a Catholic, I tell him that I love in him every virtue that he possesses. I tell him, "I hope for you, that you will draw near to the light, recognize it, and enter into the glorious halls illuminated by the Lamb of God—the Jerusalem of God upon earth, which needs not the sun nor the moon; 'for the Lamb is the lamp thereof.'" And most assuredly I love him. But I ask you, my friends, have you Faith? Have you simple belief, the bowing down of the intelligence to the admission of a mystery into your minds, acknowledging its truth,—while you cannot explain it to your reason? Have you Faith, my beloved?—the Faith that humbles a man—the Faith that makes a man intellectually as a little child, sitting down at the awful feet of the Saviour, speaking to that child, through His Church? If you have not this Faith, but if you go groping for an argument here or an argument there, trying to build upon a human foundation the supernatural structure of divine belief,—then, I ask you, how can you have Hope,—seeing that Almighty God stands before you and says: "Without Faith it is impossible to please Me; without Faith it is impossible to approach Me; without Faith you must be destroyed; for I have said it,—and My word cannot fail,—he that believeth not shall be condemned." And if you have not Faith and Hope,—the foundation,—how can you have the superstructure of divine Charity? How can we believe God, unless we know Him? How can we love Him, unless in proportion as we know Him? "O God," exclaimed the great St. Augustine, "let me know Thee, and know Thee well, that I may love Thee and love Thee well."

Now, these being the three virtues that belong to the Christian character, let us see how far the mystery which is in the needy and the poor, enters into these considerations of Faith, Hope, and Love. Certain it is that the Charity which the Almighty God commands us to have;—that is to say, the love which He commands us to have for Himself,—is united to the other commandment of the love that the Christian man must have for his neighbor. Certain, also, it is, that the poorer, the more prostrate, the more helpless that neighbor is, the stronger becomes his claim upon our love. Thirdly: it is equally certain from the Scriptures, that the Charity must not be a mere sentiment of benevolence, a mere feeling of compassion; but it must be the strong, the powerful hand extended to benefit, to console, and to uplift the stricken, the powerless, and the poor. "For," says St. John, "let us not love in word or in tongue; but in deed and in truth." And he adds: "If any man among you have the substance of this world, and shall see his brother needy, and poor, and in want, and shall give him not of those things that he hath, how doth the Charity of God abide in him?" Therefore your Charity must be a practical and an earnest Charity.

Such being the precept of God with respect to the needy and the poor, let us see how far Faith and Hope become the substratum of that Charity which must move us towards them. What does Faith tell us about these poor? If we follow the example of the world, building up great prisons, paying physicians, paying those whom it deems worth while to pay for attending the poor, the sick, and the sorrowful—if we consult the world, building up its workhouses, immuring the poor there, as if poverty were a crime,—separating the husband from the wife, and the mother from her children,—we see no trace here of divine Faith. And why? Because divine Faith must always respect its object. Faith is the virtue by which we catch a gleam of God. Do we catch a gleam of Him in His poor? If so, they enter into the arrangement of divine Charity. Now, I assert, that the poor of God, the afflicted, the heart-broken, the sick, the sorrowful—represent our Lord Jesus Christ upon this earth. Christ, our Lord, declared that He would remain upon the earth and would never leave it. "Behold," He said, "I am with you all days unto the consummation of the world." Now, in three ways Christ fulfilled that promise. First of all, He fulfilled it in remaining with his Church—the abiding Spirit of Truth and Holiness—to enable that Church to be, until the end of time, the infallible messenger of divine truth; that is to say, the light of the world—the unceasing and laborious sanctifier of all mankind. "You are the light of the world," says Christ; "you are the salt of the earth. You are not only to illumine, but you are to save and to purify. In order that you may do this, I will remain with you all days." Therefore, is He present in the Church. Secondly, He is present in the adorable Sacrament of the altar, and in the tabernacles of the Church—really and truly—as really and truly as He is upon the right hand of His Father. Therefore He said, "I will remain." And He indicated how He was to remain when, taking bread and wine, He transubstantiated them into His body and blood, saying, over the bread, "This is My body," and over the wine, "This is My blood." But in both these ways Christ, our Lord, remains invisibly upon the earth. No man sees Him. We know that He is present in the Church; and, therefore, when the Church of God speaks, we bow down and say, "I believe, because I believe and I know that the voice that speaks to me reëchoes the voice of my God, the God of Truth." When Christ, our Lord, is put upon that altar, and lifted up in the hands of the priest—lifted up in holy benediction, we bow down and adore the present God, saying: "I see Thee not, O Lord, but I know that behind that sacramental veil Thou art present upon Thy altar, for Thou hast said: Lo, I am here! This is My body! This is My blood!"

But, in a third way, Christ our Lord remains upon earth —visibly, and no longer invisible. And in that third way He remains in the persons of the poor, the sick, and the afflicted. He identifies Himself with them. Not only during the thirty-three years of His mortal life, when He was poor with the poor, when He was sorrowful and afflicted with the sorrowful, when He bore the burden of their poverty and the burden of our sins on His own shoulders;—not only was His place found among the poor,—He who said: "The birds of the air have their nests, the beasts of the field and the foxes have their holes;—but the Son of Man hath no place whereon to lay His head!" Not only was He poor from the day that He was born in a stable, until the day when, dying naked upon the cross, for pure Charity, He got a place in another man's grave;—but He also vouchsafed to identify Himself with His poor until the end of time, as though He had said: "Do you wish to find Me? Do you wish to touch Me with your hands? Do you wish to speak to Me words of consolation and of love? O Christian man, go seek the poor and the naked, the sick, the hungry, and the famishing;—seek the afflicted and the heart-broken; and in them you will find Me. For, amen, I say unto you, whatsoever you do unto them, that you do also unto me!" Thus does Christ, our Lord, identify Himself with the poor and the Church. He remains in the world, in His Church, commanding that we shall obey her:—for He is God. In His sacramental presence we may adore Him: He is God. In His poor,—in the afflicted, naked, hungry, famishing, we may bend down and lift Him up: He is God still. A most beautiful example of how the Saints were able to realize this, do we find recorded in the life of one of the beautiful saints of our Dominican Order—a man who wore this habit. He was a Spanish friar. His name was Alvarez of Cordova. He was noted among his brethren for the wonderful earnestness and cheerfulness with which he always sought the poor and the afflicted, to succor and console them. Well, it happened upon a day that this man of God, absorbed in God and in prayer, went forth from his convent to preach to the people, and, as he journeyed along the high-road, he saw, stretched helplessly by the roadside, a man covered with a hideous leprosy,—ulcerated from head to foot,—hideous to behold;—and this man turned to him his languid eyes, and, with faint voice, appealed to him for mercy and succor. The sun, in all its noonday fervor, was beating down fiercely upon that stricken man's head. He was unable to move. Every man that saw him fled from him. The moment the Saint saw him he went over to him and knelt down by his side, and he kissed the sores of the leprous man. Then, taking off the outer portion of our habit—this black cloak—he laid it upon the ground, and he tenderly took the poor man and folded him in the cloak, lifted him in his arms, and returned to his convent. He entered the convent. He brought the leper to his own cell, and laid him on his own little conventual bed. And, having laid him there, he went off to find some refreshments for him, and such means as he could for consoling him. He returned with some food and drink in his hands, laid them aside, went over to the bed, and there he found the sick man. He unfolded the cloak that was wrapped around him. Oh! what is this that he beholds? The man's head wears a crown of thorns; on his hands and his feet are the marks of nails; and forth from his wounded side streams the fresh blood! He is dead; but the marks of the Saviour are upon him; and then the Saint knew that the man whom he had lifted up from the roadside was Christ his Lord and his God! And so, with the eyes of faith, do we recognize Christ in His poor.

What follows from this? It follows, my friends, that the man who thus sees his God in the poor, who looks upon them with the eyes of Faith, who recognizes in them something sacramental, the touch of which will sanctify him who approaches them;—that that man will approach them with tenderness and with reverence: that he will consult their feelings—that he will seek to console the heart while he revives the body; and while he puts meat and drink before the sick man, or the poor man, he will not put away from his heart the source of his comfort. He will not separate him from the wife of his bosom or the children of his love. He will not relieve him with a voice unmindful of compassion; bending down, as it were, to relieve the poor. No; but he will relieve him in the truth of his soul, as recognizing in that man one who is identified, in the divinity of love and of tenderness, with his Lord and Master.

This explains to you the fact, that when the high-minded, the highly-educated, the noblest and best of the children of the Catholic Church—the young lady with all the prospects of the world glittering before her; with fortune and its enjoyments around her; with the beauty of nature and of grace beaming from her pure countenance;—when the young lady, enamored of heaven, and of the things of heaven, and disgusted with the world, comes to the foot of the sanctuary, and there, kneeling, seeks a place in the Church's holy places, and an humble share in her ministrations, the Church takes her—one of these—her holiest, her best, her purest, and she considers that she has conferred the highest honor upon the best of her children, when she clothes her with the sacred habit of religion, and tells her to go and take her place in the hospital, or in the poorhouse, or in the infirmary, or in the orphanage, and sit down and minister to the poor; not as relieving them, but as humbly serving them; not as compassionating them, but as approaching them with an almost infinite reverence, as if she were approaching Christ himself.

Thus, do we see how the Catholic virtue of Charity springs from heaven. All tenderness of heart, all benevolence, all compassion, must be there,—as no doubt it is,—in the hearts of the consecrated virgins, who, in order that they might love Christ and His poor all the more tenderly, all the more strongly, vowed to the Saviour, at His altar, that no love should enter into their bosoms, no emotions of affection should ever thrill their hearts, except love for Him; for Him, wherever they found Him: and they have found Him in His poor and in His sick. All the tenderest emotions of human benevolence, of human compassion, of human gentleness may be there. All that makes the good Protestant lady,—the good infidel lady, if you will,—so compassionate to the poor;—yet whilst the worldling, and those without the Church bend down to an act of condescension in their charity, these spouses of the Son of God look up to the poor, and in their obedience seek to serve them; for their compassion, their benevolence, their divinely tender hearts, are influenced by the divine faith which recognizes the Son of God in the persons of the poor and the needy, the stricken, and the afflicted.

This is the Catholic idea of Charity in its associations. What follows from this? It follows, that when I, or the like of me, who, equally with these holy women, have given our lives, and our souls, and our bodies to the service of the Son of God and of His Church, when we come before our Catholic brethren to speak to them on this great question of Catholic Charity, we do not come as preaching, praying, beseeching, begging. Oh, no! But we come with a strong voice of authority, as commanding you, "If you would see the Father's brightness, remember the poor, and, at your peril, surround them with all the ministrations of charity and of mercy."

And how does Hope enter into these considerations? Ah, my friends, what do you hope for at all? What are your hopes? I ask the Christian man, the benevolent brother, —I do not care what religion you are of: Brother, tell me your hope; because Hope from its very nature goes out into the future; Hope is a realizing, by anticipation, of that which will one day come and be in our possession. What are your hopes? Every man has his hopes. No man lives without them. Every man hopes to attain to some position in this world, or to gain a certain happiness. One man hopes to make money and become a rich man. Another man aspires to certain dignities, hopes for them, and labors assiduously until he attains them. Another man centres his hopes in certain passions, and immerses himself in the anticipation of sensual delights. But I do not care what your hopes are; this I ask you: are your hopes circumscribed by this world, or do they go beyond the tomb? Is all Hope to cease when the sad hour comes that will find each and every one of you stretched helpless on his bed of death, and the awful Angel, bearing the summons of God, cries out, "Come forth, O soul, and come with me to the judgment seat of Christ!" Is all Hope to perish then? No; no! but, for the Christian, the realization of Hope begins then. No, this life is as nothing compared with that endless eternity that awaits us beyond the grave; and there all our hopes are; and the Hope of the Christian man is that, when that hour comes that shall find his soul trembling before its impending doom, awaiting the sentence—that that sentence will not be, "Depart from me, accursed," but that it will be, "Come, my friend, my blessed one, come and enjoy the happiness and the delight which were prepared for thee!" This is our Hope. Accursed is the man who has it not. Miserable is the wretch that has it not! What would this life be—even if it were a life of ten thousand years, replete with every pleasure—every enjoyment —unmixed by the slightest evil of sickness or of sorrow,—if we knew that, at the end of those ten thousand years, the eternity beyond, that should never know an end, was to be for us an eternity of sorrow and of despair? We should be, of all men, the most miserable. "For," says the Apostle, "if in this life only we have hope in Christ, we are, of all men, the most miserable. But," he adds, "Christ is risen from the dead,—our hope;" and our hope is to rise with Him; translated from glory unto glory, until we behold His face, unshrouded and unveiled, and be happy for ever in the contemplation of God.

This is our Hope: yours and mine. But remember that, although the Almighty God has promised this, and our Hope is built upon the fidelity with which He keeps His word, no man can expect the reward, nor can build up his Hope on a solid foundation, unless he enters into the designs of God, and complies with the conditions that God has attached to His promises of glory. What are these conditions? Think how largely the poor and the afflicted enter into them! "Come," the Redeemer and Judge will say, "Come unto me, ye blessed of my Father! This is not the first time that you have seen me. I was hungry, and you gave me to eat! I was thirsty, and you gave me to drink! I was naked, and you clothed me! I was sick, and you visited me and consoled me!" And then the just shall exclaim: "Lord! when did we ever behold Thee—O powerful and terrible Son of God! when did we behold Thee naked, or hungry, or sick?" And He, answering, will call the poor,—the poor to whom we minister to-day; the poor whom we console to-day; whose drooping heads we lift up to-day,—He will call them, and say: "Do you know these?" And they will cry out: "Oh, yes; these are the poor whom we saw hungry, and we fed them; whom we saw naked, and we clothed them; whom we saw sick, and we consoled and visited them. These are the poor that we were so familiar with, and that we employed, Thy spouses, O Christ, to minister unto, and to console!" Then He will answer, and say: "I swear to you that, as I am God, as often as you have done it to the least of these, you have done it unto Me!" But if, on the other hand, we come before Him, glorying in the strength of our Faith,—magniloquent in our professions of Christianity,—splendid in our assumption of the highest principles,—correct in many of the leading traits of the Christian character,—but with hands empty of the works of mercy; if we are only obliged to say with truth: "Lord, I claim heaven; but I never clothed the naked; I never lifted up the drooping head of the sick and the afflicted—" Christ, our Lord, will answer and say: "Depart from me! I do not know you; I do not recognize you. I was hungry, and you would not feed me in my hunger; I was naked, and you would not clothe me in my nakedness; I was thirsty and sick, and you would not relieve me, or console me in my sickness." And the unjust will answer: "Lord, we never saw Thee hungry, or naked, or sick." And then, once more, will He call the poor, and say: "Behold these; to these did you refuse your mercy, your pity, your charity; and I swear to you that, as I am God, in the day that you refused to comfort, and to succor, and to console them, you refused to do it unto me. Therefore, there is no Heaven for you." The golden key that opens the gate of Heaven is the key of mercy; therefore, He will say: "As often as you are merciful to the poor, you are merciful to Me. I have said: blessed are the merciful, for they shall find mercy."

Who, therefore, among you, believing in these things, does not recognize that there is no true Faith that does not recognize Christ in His poor, and so succor them with veneration; who does not see that his Hope is built upon the relations which are established between him and the poor of God. Thus, out of this Faith and out of this Hope, springs the Charity with which we must relieve them.

Now, mark how beautifully all this is organized in the Catholic Church! There is a curious expression in the Scriptures. It is found in the Canticles of Solomon, where the Spouse of the King—that is to say, the Church of God —among other things, says: "My Lord and my King has organized charity in me"—"*Ordinavit in me caritatem.*" Thus it is not the mere temporary flash of enthusiasm; it is not the mere passing feeling of benevolence, touched by the sight of their misery, that influences the Catholic Church; but it is these promises and these principles of the Christian Faith, recognizing who and what the poor are, and our Christian Hope, building up all the conditions of its future glory upon this foundation. Therefore it is that, in the Catholic Church alone, is found the grand, organized Charity of the world. Nowhere, without her pale, do you find Charity organized. You may find a fair and beautiful ebullition of pity, here and there; as when a rich man dies and leaves, perhaps, half-a-million of dollars to found a hospital. But it is an exceptional thing, my dear friends; as when some grand lady, magnificent of heart and mind— like, for instance, Florence Nightingale—devotes herself to the poor; goes into the hospitals and the infirmaries for the wounded. It is an exceptional case, I answer. If you travel out of the bounds of that fair and beautiful compassion that runs in so many hearts, and if you go one step farther into the cold atmosphere of political or State charity, there is not one vestige of true Charity there; it becomes political economy. The State believes it is more economical to pick up the poor from the streets and lanes, to take them from their sick beds, transferring them into poorhouses and hospitals, and, while there, overwhelming them with the miserable pity that patronizes, making its gifts a curse and not a blessing, by breaking the heart while it relieves the body. Such is "State charity." I remember once, in the city of Dublin, I got a sick call. It was to attend a poor woman. I went, and found, in a back lane in the city, a room in a garret. I climbed up to the place. There I found, without exaggeration, four bare walls, and a woman seventy-five years of age, covered with a few squalid rags, and lying on the bare floor: not as much as a little straw had she under her head. I asked for a cup to give her a drink of water. There was no such thing to be had; and there was no one there to give it. I had to go out and beg among the neighbors, until I got a cupful of cold water. I put it to her dying lips. I had to kneel down upon that bare floor to hear that dying woman's confession. The hand of death was upon her. What was her story? She was the mother of six children, a lady, educated in a lady-like manner; a lady beginning her career of life in affluence and in comfort. The six children grew up. Some married; some emigrated; some died: the weak and aged mother was alone, abandoned, and forgotten: and now, she was literally dying, not only of the fever that was upon her, but of starvation! As I knelt there on the floor, and as I lifted her aged, greyhaired head upon my hands, I said to her: "Let me, for God's sake, have you taken to the workhouse hospital; at least, you will have a bed to lie upon!" She turned and looked at me. Two great tears came from her dying eyes, as she said: "Oh, that I should have lived to hear a Catholic priest talk to me about a poorhouse!" I felt that I had almost broken this failing heart. On my knees I begged her pardon. "No," she said, "let me die in peace!" And there, whilst I knelt at her side, her afflicted and chastened spirit passed away to God: but the taint of the "charity of the State" was not upon her.

Now, passing from this cold and wicked atmosphere of political economy into the purer and more genial air of benevolence, charity, and tenderness—of which there is so much, even outside the Church,—we enter into the halls of the Catholic Church. There, among the varied beauties, among the "consecrated forms of loveliness" with which Christ adorned His Church—we find the golden garment of an organized charity. We find the highest, the best, and the purest, devoted to its service and to its cause. We find every form of misery which the hand of God, or the malice of man, or their own errors can attach to the poor, provided for. The child of misfortune wanders through the streets of the city, wasting her young heart, polluting the very air that she breathes,—a living sin! The sight of her is sin—the thought of her is death!—the touch of her hand is pollution unutterable! No man can look upon her face and live! In a moment of divine compassion, the benighted and the wicked heart is moved to turn to God. With the tears of the penitent upon her young and sinful face, she turns to the portals of the Church; and there at the very threshold of the sanctuary of God, she finds the very ideal of purity,—the highest, the grandest, the noblest of the Church's children. The woman who has never known the pollution of a wicked thought,—the woman whose virgin bosom has never been crossed by the shadow of a thought of sin,—the woman breathing purity, innocence, grace, receives the woman whose breath is the pestilence of hell! Extremes meet. Mary, the Virgin, takes the hand of Mary, the Magdalene; and, in the organized charity of the Church of God, the penitent enters in—to be saved and sanctified.

The poor man, worn down and broken by poverty, exposed in his daily labor to the winds and rains of Heaven, with failing health and drooping heart, lies down to die. There by his bedside stands the wife, and round her, her group of little children. They depend upon his daily labor for their daily bread. Now, that hand that labored for them so long and so lovingly, is palsied and stricken by his side. Now his dying eyes are grieved with the sight of their misery. His ears are filled with the cry of the little ones for bread. The despair of their doom comes to embitter his dying moments. He looks from that bed of death out upon the gloomy world. He sees the wife of his bosom consigned to a pauper's cell, to await a pauper's grave; and, for these innocent faces that surround him, he sees no future but a future of ignorance and of crime;—of punishment without hope of amendment—and of the loss of their souls in the great mass of the world's crimes and misdeeds. But, while he is thus mournfully brooding with

sad and despairing thoughts, what figure is this that crosses
the threshold and casts its shadow on the floor of the house?
Who is this, entering noiselessly, modestly, silently, shrouded
and veiled, as a being of Heaven, not of earth? He lifts his
eyes and he beholds the mild and placid face of the Sister of
Mercy, beaming purity mixed with divine love upon him.
Now the sunshine of God is let in upon the darkness of his
despairing soul. Now he hears a voice almost as gentle,
almost as tender, almost as powerful as the voice of Him who
whispered in the ear of the Widow of Naim: "Oh, woman,
weep no more!" And she tells him to fear not; that her
woman's hand will ensure protection for his children—and
education, grace, virtue, Heaven and God! I once remember
I was called to attend a man, such as I have endeavored to
describe to you. There were seven little children in the
house. There was a woman, the mother of those children,
the wife of him who was dying there. Two years before
this man had fallen from a scaffold, and was so shattered that
he was paralyzed; and for two years he had lain upon that
bed starving as well as dying. When I was called to visit
this man, I spoke to him of the mercy of God. He looked
upon me with a sullen and despairing eye. "This is the first
time," he said, "that you have come to my bed-side." Said I,
"My friend, this is the first time that I knew you were sick.
Had I known it, I would have come to you before." "No
one"—this was his answer—"no one cares for me. And
you come now to speak to me of the mercy of God! I have
been on this bed for more than two years. I have seen that
woman and her children starving for the last two years.
And do you tell me that there is a God of Mercy above me?"
I saw at once it was a case with which I could not deal. I
left the house on the instant, and went straight to a convent
of the Sisters of Mercy that was near. There I asked the
Mother Superior, for God's sake, to send one or two of the
Nuns to the house. They went. Next day I visited him.
Oh, what a change I found! No longer the dull glance of
despair: he looked up boldly and cheerfully from his bed of
sorrow. No longer murmuring against the mercy of God,—
but with the deep thankfulness of a grateful heart: "Oh,"
said he, "I am so happy, Father, that I sent for you,—not so
much for any thing you can do for me; but you sent me two
angels of God from Heaven! They came into my house;

and, for the first time, in two long years, I learned to hope; to be sorry for my want of resignation; and to return with love to that God whom I dared to doubt!" Then he made his confession, and I prepared him for death. Patient he was, and resigned; and, in his last moments, when his voice was faltering,—when his voice became that of the departing spirit,—his last words were: "You sent to me the angels of God,—and they told me that when I should be in my grave they would be mothers to my children!"

O fair and beautiful Church, that knows so well how to console the afflicted, to bind up the wounds of the breaking heart, to lift up the weary and drooping head! Every form of human misery, every form of wretchedness, whether sent from God as a warning or a trial, or coming from men's own excesses and folly, and as a punishment for their sins,— every form of human misery and affliction, as soon as it is seen, is softened and relieved by the gentlest, the tenderest, the sweetest agency,—the touch of God through His consecrated ones. And it seems to the sufferer as if the word of the promise to come were fulfilled in time,—the word which says: "The Lord Himself will wipe away every tear from the eyes of His elect, and will bind up every bleeding and wounded heart."

And thus, my friends, we see how beautifully charity is organized in the Catholic Church. Not one penny of your charity is wasted. Every farthing that you contribute will be expended wisely, judiciously; and extended to its farthest length of usefulness in the service of God's poor and of God's stricken ones. And lest the poor might be humbled, while they are relieved; lest they might be hurt in their feelings, while consoled with the temporal doles that are lavished upon them, the Church of God, with a wisdom more than human, appoints as her ministers of the poor, those who, for the love of Christ, have become poor like them. Behold these nuns! They are the daughters of St. Francis. Seven hundred years ago now, almost, there arose in the city of Assisi, in Umbria, in Italy, a man so filled with the ineffable love of Christ,—so impregnated with the spirit of the Son of God, made man,— that, in the rapture of his prayer, the *stigmata*—the marks of the nails upon the hands and feet, of the thorns upon the brows, of the wounds upon the side of the Redeemer,—were given to Francis of Assisi. Men beheld him and started from the sight, giving glory to God that they had caught a gleam of the glory of Christ upon earth. He was the only Saint of whom we read, that, without opening his lips, but simply coming and walking through the ways of the city, all eyes that beheld him were melted into tears of tenderness and divine love: and he "preached Christ and Him crucified," by merely showing the mortification, and the spirit, and the love of Christ which was upon him and in him. These are the daughters of this Saint, inheriting his spirit; and he, in the Church, is the very ideal Saint of divine and religious poverty. He would not have a shoe to his foot. He would not have a second coat. He would not have in his bag provision even for to-morrow; but waited, like the Prophet of old, that it should come to him from God, at the hands of his benefactors,—the very ideal Saint of poverty; and, therefore, of all others, the most devoted in himself, and in having his children minister unto God's poor. When there was a question of destroying the religious Orders in Italy, and of passing a law that would not permit me, a Dominican, or these nuns, Franciscans, to dwell in the land,—just as if we were doing any harm to anybody;—as if we were not doing our best to save and serve all the people;—when it was a question before the Parliament, Cæsare Cantu, the celebrated historian, stood up in the assembly and said: "Men! before you make this law, abolishing all the religious men and women in the land, reflect for an instant. If any man among you, by some reverse of fortune, become poor,—if any man among you, in this enlightened age, be obliged to beg his daily bread; would not you feel ashamed—would not you feel degraded to have to go to your fellow-man to ask him for alms? For me, if God should strike me with poverty, I would feel it a degradation. But I would not feel it a degradation to go to a Dominican or Franciscan, and ask him, a brother pauper, to break his bread with me."

It is fitting that the voice which speaks to you this evening,—although it comes from one wearing the habit of St. Dominic,—should speak to you in the language of Saint Francis of Assisi, who was the bosom friend of the great Dominic of Guzman. United in life and in love as they were, their children are united in that spiritual love which is the inheritance of God's consecrated ones on earth. And, therefore, it is a privilege and a glory to me to speak to you this evening on behalf of my Franciscan sisters. Yet, not in their behalf do I speak, but in behalf of the poor; nor in behalf of the poor, but in behalf of Christ, who identifies Himself with the poor; nor in behalf of Him, but in your own behalf; seeing that all your hopes of the glory of Heaven are bound up with the poor of whom I speak. It is your glory, and the glory of this special charity, that it was the first hospital founded in this State; that at a time when men, concentrating their energies to amass wealth, immersed in their business, trying to heap up accumulations, and gather riches and large possessions, never thought of their poor; or, if the poor obtruded themselves, brushed them out of their path, and told them to begone; then there came the Church of Christ into the midst of you. She sought not money, nor land, nor possessions. She brought these poor nuns, vowed to poverty, despising all the things of the world, and leaving them behind them; she built up her hospital for the sick; she brought her children of St. Francis of Assisi, to minister to them, in mercy, in faith, and hope, and in the gentleness of divine charity. Do they not say to you: "Blessed is the man that understandeth concerning the needy and the poor"?

I hope I may have thrown some light into the minds of even one amongst you, this evening, and let him see how blessed is the man who knows his position concerning the needy and the poor. I hope that those to whom my words give no light, may, at least, be given encouragement to persevere. Persevere, Catholics of Hoboken and Jersey City, in maintaining these Sisters, in filling their hands with your benefactions; in enabling them to pursue their calm but glorious career of charity and of mercy. I know that in thus encouraging you, I am advancing the best interest of your souls; and that the mite that you give to-day, which might be given for pleasure or sinfulness,—that that mite shall return to you one day in the form of a crown, the crown of glory which will be set upon your heads, for ever and for ever, before the Throne of God, by the hands of the poor of Christ. Again, I say to you, will you hear the voice from the Throne: "Whatever you do to the poor, you do it unto Me"? Oh, may God send down His angel of mercy!—may the spirit of His mercy breathe amongst us!—may the charity

which guides your mercy, the charity springing from
an enlightened and pure faith, and from a true and substantial hope,—bring your reward:—that so, in the day
when Faith shall perish with time—when Hope shall be lost,
either in joy or in sorrow—either in the fruition of Heaven,
or in the despair of hell,—that on that day, you may be able
to exclaim, when you first catch sight of the unveiled glory
of the Saviour: "O Christ, of all the beauties of God, it is
true, 'the greatest is Charity.'"

THE CATHOLIC CHURCH THE TRUE EMANCIPATOR.

[*A Lecture delivered by Very Rev. T. N. Burke, O.P., in St. Stephen's Church, New York, April 30, 1872, for the benefit of the Mission to the Colored Race in America.*]

MY DEAR FRIENDS: I come before you this evening to assert a proposition which would require no proof, if all men were of one mind regarding the claims of the Catholic Church to be the Church of Christ. I assert for the Catholic Church that she is the true emancipator of the slave; and I say again, that, if men were of one mind touching her claims to be the true Christian Church, this proposition would require no proof; for any man who believes in the agency of Christ, as perpetuated in His Church, must at once conclude that one of the highest and greatest of the duties of that Church is the duty which her Divine Founder Himself came to accomplish, viz: the work of emancipation. He came and found, not this race, or that,—not this class or order of men, or that,—but all mankind, and all races of men, enslaved in the direst form of slavery;—a slavery that entered into their very souls; a slavery that not only destroyed their freedom of will, but also clouded, and thereby destroyed, the clearness of their intelligence; a slavery that bound them helpless at the feet of the most cruel of all masters;—for that master was no other than the devil, the prince and ruler of all mankind, the enslaver of the intellect, of the will, and of the soul of man. The Prophet of old had foretold of our Divine Lord and Redeemer, that He came to break the chains of man's slavery, to emancipate him, to take him from out that deep and terrible servitude into which he had fallen, and to endow him once more with "the freedom of the glory of the children of God." Therefore He came. Among all the other titles that belonged to Him is that, preëminently, of the emancipator of an enslaved and fallen race. And, if His action is to continue in the Church,—if His graces are to flow

on through that Church, and His light is to come forth, pure
and bright and radiant in the Church which He founded,—
all we have to do is to find that Church; and, bound to her
brows, we shall find the crown of the emancipator of the
human race. That Church we Catholics know and believe
to be the Mother that has begotten us unto God, through the
Gospel.

Now, my friends, how did Christ effect the work of His
emancipation? I answer that He emancipated or freed the
intelligence of man from the slavery of the intellect, which
is error; and that He emancipated the will of man from the
slavery of the will, which is sin. And He carefully defined
what manner of freedom He came to found and confer, when
He said to a benighted race, whom He enlightened: "You
shall know the truth, and the truth shall make you free!"
And, to a degraded and corrupt race, He said: "I am come
that, where sin hath abounded, grace might abound still more;"
and, in the abundance of His grace, He called us "unto the
freedom of the children of God."

Behold, then, the elements of emancipation, as found in
the actions and in the words of the Son of God, the Redeemer, the Saviour, and the Emancipator. Truth! Truth
broadly diffused; truth borne upon the wings of knowledge
unto every mind. Not speculation, but truth; not opinion,
but knowledge; not study of the truth, but possession of the
truth. There, says the Son of God, lies the secret of
your intellectual freedom. Therefore He lifted up His voice;
He flung abroad the banner of His eternal truth; He called
all men to hear the sound of His voice, and to rally round
the standard of His truth and of His knowledge. And the
word which He spoke was borne upon the wings of the Angels for all future time, unto the farthest ends of the earth,
upon the lips of the preaching and infallible Church which
He founded. I say the "preaching Church," which He
founded, for "Faith comes by hearing;" and the knowledge
which emancipates the intelligence must come by a living
voice. But I add:—as no other knowledge save that of the
pure truth, as it is in the mind of Jesus Christ, thus delivered
by a living voice, can emancipate the intelligence of man,
therefore the voice which He commanded to teach the world,
must bear the unfailing, and infallible, and unmixed message
of the truth of the Lord Jesus Christ. For, if that voice can

admit the slightest blending of error,— if that voice can falter in the delivery of the truth, or mix up the slightest distortion of error with that truth,— it ceases to be the voice of Jesus Christ, and it only, in its teachings, substitutes one form of slavery for another. Oh, if the men of our day would only understand this! if the men who boast of their civilization would only understand this,—that whatever is not the truth is not the voice nor the message of God;—whatever, by any possibility can be untrue, cannot be the voice of God;—if men would only understand this, that there is no greater insult than we can offer to a God of Truth than to take a religious lie—a distorted view—a false idea,—put it into our minds, and say; "This is the truth of God; this is religious truth!" But, no! We boast to-day of our liberality; we boast to-day of the multitude of our sects and of our religious institutions; we boast to day of an open Bible from which every man draws—not the word of God,—for I deny that it is the Word of God;—it is the Word of God only when it is taken from that page as it lies in the mind of God;—we boast to-day that that Bible is open to every man to look in it for the canonization of his own error, lying in the distorted meaning which he gives to that divinely-inspired page;—and then we pretend that all this is a mark of religion: and the man who would indignantly resent a lie, told him in the ordinary avocations and social duties of life;—the man who would resent, as a deep injury, being taken in in a matter of business, in the furnishing of an account, or any such transitory thing,—that man is precisely the one that is most indifferent, and careless, and most easily reconciled, when it is a matter that lies between him and the God of Truth, whether he possesses that truth or not. Yet, I say again, it is a disreputable thing to be taken in by a lie—to believe a lie. It is a mark of intellectual and moral imbecility to cling to a lie, and to uphold it as the truth. And remember that, when it is a matter between us and God—the interpretation of the message of God—the tone that the voice of God takes in falling upon our ear,—remember that whatever is not true as God, is the worst form of untruth—or, a lie; and that the truth of God is declared, by the Saviour of the world, to be the essential, primary element of that emancipation with which Jesus Christ came down to free us.

But, dear friends, grand and magnificent as is the possession of that truth,—luminous as is the light which is poured into the soul from Almighty God, through the eyes of the mind, opening, as it were, to the illumination of Divine truth,—it is not enough to accomplish the freedom of man. The soul of freedom lies not only in the mind possessing truth, and thus shaking off the chains of intellectual slavery, which is error; but it also lies in the will, sanctified, strengthened, and purified by the divine grace of Jesus Christ. Of what avail would it be to you, my fellowmen, or to me, that we should know all knowledge—that we should have all knowledge—if a man is a slave to his own passions—if every degrading passion and inclination of a base or an inferior nature has only to cry out imperiously to be instantly served and gratified at the expense of the soul's nobility and life, and at the expense of God's friendship and His grace? Of what avail is knowledge to a man, if that man be impure? Of what avail are the soundest principles or examples, moral or divine, to that man who, holding them, does not act up to them, but is dishonest? And therefore, there is another and a more terrible slavery, even than that of the intellect; and that is the slavery of the will. Now, to meet this, Christ our Lord, the divine healer, the divine physician of our souls, established certain means by which His grace, His strength, His purity, were to be communicated to us, to our wills, just as, by the preaching of the Gospel in the Church, her light is communicated to our intelligence. And these means are the sacred morality of the Church's laws; the sacred barriers that she uprears between the soul and sin; the sacramental graces that she pours forth to heal the soul, and purify it, and cleanse it again, if it be tainted and sullied by sin; the agencies that she holds in her hands to preserve that soul from a relapse into sin, strengthening it so that it is able to command all its passions, to repress all undue and corrupting inclinations, to give a triumph to the spirit over matter—to the soul over the body; —until the Lord Jesus Christ, who is not only the fountain of all truth, but the Creator of all holiness, and its representative, be reproduced in the souls of all His children, and a perfect people be reared up in sanctity to God.

Without this grace of the heart and the will, there is no freedom. Without the agency of the Church, I say, as a rule, there can be no grace. Without her Sacraments, the will of man—the will of man which may be enslaved—the will of man which is enslaved whenever man is in sin—can never be touched; for the sacramental hand of the Church alone can touch it. And, here, again, as the word of the Church's teaching must be no other than the word of Jesus Christ Himself,—not only as it is written in the inspired volumes, but as it lies in the mind of God, and, therefore, as the Church is bound to explain it;—so, also, the graces of the Church, and the agency that she has in her hands to touch the will, must be no other than the very power, the very action, the very grace of Jesus Christ. No other hand but His, no other power but His—no other influence but His—the Lord, the Redeemer, the Saviour,—coming home to every individual man,—can purify that man's soul, and strengthen him to gain the "victory which conquereth the world," the flesh, and the devil—the victory of Divine faith! For, of what avail to me, I ask you, of what avail to me is it that a priest should lift up his hand and say, "I absolve thee from thy sin," unless that word, that grace, that power to do it, come to that priest from Jesus Christ? Of what avail to me that a man pour water on my head and say, "I baptize thee in the name of the Father, and of the Son, and of the Holy Ghost," unless that baptism, that water had sacramental influence instituted by the Lord, endowed with a peculiar power for this purpose, —the cleansing of the soul,—and be tinged mystically with the saving blood of the Redeemer? Of what avail to me, if I come to this altar, open my mouth, and receive what appears to be a morsel of bread, unless the Redeemer of the world had said: "Without Me you can do nothing. And now I will come to you. Take ye—and eat of this;—for this is My body and My blood." Therefore, it is the action of Jesus Christ that must remain as powerful, as pure, as merciful in the dispensation of the Church's grace, as her words must be pure from error, and unmixed with error upon the lips of the Church's preaching?

Behold the two great elements of man's emancipation. Wherever these are not, there is slavery. He that believes a lie,—and, above all, a religious untruth,—is a slave. He that commits sin is the slave of sin. What avails it that you emancipate a man—strike the chains off his hands—send him forth, in name a free man,—send him forth with every constitutional right and civic privilege upon him,—send him forth, glorying in his freedom, without understanding it, and, perhaps, unprepared to use it as he should? If you leave that man's intelligence under the gloom of ignorance,—if you leave that man's will under the dominion of sin and of his own passions, have you made him a free man? You call him a free man. But God in Heaven does not so regard him; and, unfortunately, the devil in hell laughs and scoffs at your idea of freedom.

And, now, my friends, this being the mission, declared and avowed by our Divine Lord,—this, consequently, being the mission confided into the hands of the Church to be fulfilled by her, let us turn to the Church's history and see whether she has been faithful to her duty in thus applying the elements of emancipation to man. It is a historical question, and one that I must deal with, principally, historically. Now, in order to understand it, we are, first of all, to consider, what was the state of the world when the Church began her mission? How did she find society? Was it barbarous or civilized? I answer that the Church's mission, when she first opened her lips to preach the Gospel, was to a most civilized and highly intellectual people. Augustus was in his grave; but the "Augustan era," the proudest, the highest, and most civilized, yet shed its influence over the world. All the wisdom of the ancients, all the learning of Pagan philosophy, was represented in that august assembly before which, upon the hill of Athens, Paul the Apostle, stood up to preach "the Resurrection and the Life." All the light of ancient philosophy was there. All the glory of art was there in its highest perfection. All the resources then attained to in science were there. Men were glorying in that day, as they are in this, in their material progress and in their ideas. But, how was this society constituted with regard to slavery? Why, my friends, in that ancient Pagan world, we read that, at the time when there were sixty thousand inhabitants in the city of Athens, the capital of Greece, there were forty thousand slaves, and only twenty thousand freemen. We read how, in the society of Sparta, another city of Greece, the slaves had so multiplied that the masters lived in constant fear lest their servants—their bondsmen—should rise up in their power and destroy them. We read of Rome, that the slaves were in such numbers, that, when it was proposed in the Senate that they should wear a distinct dress, it was immediately opposed on the ground that, if they wore a distinct dress, they would come to recognize their own numbers and strength, and would rise and sweep the freemen from the soil. So much for the civilized nations. What do we know of the barbarous nations? Why, Herodotus the historian tells us, that, on one occasion, a nation of Scythians went forth and invaded Medea; and, when they returned, after a successful war, flushed with triumph and with victory, such was the number of the slaves that they had enslaved,—from the misfortunes of war and other causes,—that actually, when they returned in all their might, they found that, in their absence, their slaves had revolted; and they were chased by their own servants—their own slaves—from their own country. How were these slaves treated? They were treated thus: We read that when a certain Prefect of Rome, Pedanius Secundus, was murdered by one of his slaves, as a matter of course, following the law, there were four hundred of that man's bondsmen taken, and they were all put to death without mercy, without pity:—four hundred innocent men for the fault and the crime of one. Had the slave any rights? None whatever. Had the slave any privilege or recognition of any kind? None whatever. His life and his blood were accounted as of no value; and what was still worse, the highest philosophers of ancient Greece and Rome, writing on this subject, laid down as a principle, that these men were created by the gods, as they called them, for the purpose of slavery; that they came into this world for no other purpose; that they had no souls capable of appreciating any thing spiritual, no feelings to be respected, no eternal, or even temporal, interests to be consulted; so that a man who had the misfortune to fall into slavery, found himself not only enslaved but degraded.

Such was the state of the world when the Catholic Church began her mission. And now, what was the first principle that the Church preached and laid down? The first emancipating principle that the Catholic Church announced was this: She proclaimed that slavery was no degradation; that a man might be enslaved, and yet not be degraded. This was the first principle by which the Church of God recognized the nobility of the soul of man,—no matter from what race he sprang; no matter what misfortune may have fallen upon him;—that he might be enslaved; nay, more, that his very slavery might bring its own specific duties upon him; but that slavery, in itself, was no degradation. You may say to me, perhaps, this was a false principle. I answer, no; it is not a false principle. I am a slave; yet I am not a degraded man. I am a slave; for, many years ago, I swore away, at the foot of the altar, my liberty, my freedom, and my will, and gave them up to God. Am I therefore degraded? No. We are all slaves in this sense—that the Scriptures tell us that " we have been bought at a great price" by our Lord Jesus Christ; and, therefore, that we are the servants and bondsmen of Him who redeemed us. But who will say that such slavery as this is degradation? No, my friends. You may, perhaps, say to me, that we all admit our servitude to God. Well, this is precisely the point; and St. Paul, proclaiming the first elements of the Church's laws and doctrines touching slavery, declared that even a man who was enslaved by his fellow-man was no longer a slave,—that is, in the sense of a degraded slave; because Almighty God, through His Church, recognized that man's soul,—recognized his feelings, —and commanded him to be faithful, even as a slave,—not to the master as to a man, but to the master for the sake of Jesus Christ, and as reflecting authority and power over him. These are the express words of the Apostle; and mark how clearly they bring out this grand principle. He says: " Whosoever are servants under the yoke, let them account their masters worthy of all honor, lest the name of the Lord and His doctrines be blasphemed." He goes on to say: " You, slaves, obey those that are your masters according to the flesh, with fear and trembling, in the simplicity of your hearts, as to Jesus Christ Himself; not serving to the eye, as it were, pleasing men, but as the servants of Christ; doing the will of God from the heart, with a good will; serving as to the Lord, not to man." This was the first grand element of the Church's emancipation. She removed from the slave the degradation of his slavery, by admitting that, slave as he was, he could, in obeying his master, obey God;—transfer his allegiance, as it were, from the man to the principle of God's authority reflected in that man; and thus serve, not as to the eye of man, but to the eye of Jesus Christ.

Secondly, the Apostle declares that slavery ceased to be a degradation when the master and owner was as much a slave as his bondsman. And this he declares in this principle:

"And you, masters," he says, "do the same thing as your slaves; forbearing threatening, knowing that the Lord both of them and of you is in heaven, and that there is no respect of persons with Him." "Masters," he adds, "do to your servants that which is just and equal, knowing that you also have a Master who is in heaven." The pagan idea was that the master was the absolute governor and ruler of his slave,—the lord of life and death;—that that slave was created to do his will; and that, for his treatment of his servant, he was not responsible before God. The Apostle, in the name of the Church, imposes upon the master and slave the common servitude to the one God; and then he lays down the third great element, by which he relieves slavery of its degradation, when he says: "There is, in Christ, neither bondsman nor freeman, neither Jew nor Gentile, neither Barbarian nor Scythian; but Christ, the Lord, in all; and ye are all one in Jesus Christ."

These, my friends, were the first words of consolation, of hope, of manly sympathy with his fellow-men in slavery, that ever came from the lips of a teacher, religious or otherwise, from the world's creation. And these came from the lips of the Catholic Church, speaking through her divinely-inspired Apostle. Therefore I claim for her that, in the beginning, she was faithful to her mission; and that she proclaimed that she came to console the afflicted in his slavery, and to lift from him the weight of the degradation which was upon him. Then the history of the Church began. You all know, my dear friends, how, five centuries after the Church was established, the barbarians—the Goths, the Vandals, the Alans, and all these terrible nations from the north, swept down over the Roman empire, and destroyed every thing; broke up society; reduced it to its first chaotic elements: and slavery was the universal institution, all the world over. Every nation had it. The captive that was taken in war lost his liberty, not for a day, but for ever. The man who was oppressed with debt was taken for his debt and sold into slavery. The Church of God alone was able to meet these barbarians, to confront them, and to evangelize to them her gospel of liberation; and to soften, and gradually to diminish, until, at length, she all but destroyed, the existence of this unjust slavery. The Church of God—the Catholic Church—was the only power that these barbaric nations would respect. The Pope of Rome was the great upholder of the principles of liberty; because liberty means nothing more nor less than the assertion of right for every man, and the omnipotence of the law, which insures him his right, and defines that right.

And how did the Pope act? How did the Church carry out her mission? My friends, we find that, from the fifth century,—from the very time that the Church began to be known, and commenced to make her influence felt among the nations,—among the very first ordinances that she made, were some for the relief of the slave. She commanded, for instance, under pain of censure, that no master was to put his slave to death; and you may imagine under what depths of misery society was plunged, and from what a state of things the Catholic Church has saved the world, when I tell you that one of the ordinances of a Council in the sixth century was, that if any lady (now just imagine this to yourselves!)—being offended by any of her slaves, or vexed by them, put the slave to death, that she was to undergo several long years of public penance for the crime she had committed. What a state of society it was, when a delicate lady, arraying herself, perhaps, for an evening meeting,—a ball or a party,—with her maiden slaves around her, dressing her, adding ornament to ornament,—that, if one of them made a slight mistake, the delicate lady was able to turn round,—as we read in the Pagan historians, and as Roman ladies did,—and thrust her ivory-hilted dagger into the heart of her poor slave, striking her dead at her feet. The only power that was recognized on the earth, to make that lady responsible,—the only power that she would listen to,—the only representative of the law that was thus to fling its protection over the unhappy slave, was the power of the mighty Church, that told that lady, if she committed herself to such actions as these, that outside the Church's gates she should kneel, in sackcloth and ashes; that she should kneel far away from the altar and the sacrifice; that she should kneel there until, after long years of weeping and penitence, as a public penitent, she was to be permitted to crawl into the Church, and take the place of the penitent, nearest the door.

And so, in like manner, we find the Church, in the progress of ages, making laws, that, if any slave offended his master, and, if the master wished to punish him then and there, by some terrible form of aggravated punishment, and if that slave fled from his master, there was only one place where he could find security, and that was the Church. For the Church declared that the moment a slave crossed her door and entered into her sanctuary, that moment the master's hand was stayed, and the slave was out of his power, until the case was fairly tried, and a proportionate and just punishment imposed, as would be imposed on any other man who committed the same offence.

Again: we find the same Church, in the course of ages, imposing a threat of excommunication upon any man who should capture a manumitted or emancipated slave, and reduce him to slavery again. Further on, we find the same Church making a law that, when a Bishop, or a Cardinal, or a great ecclesiastic died, all those who were in servitude to him should be immediately freed. These were the freedmen of the Church, as they were called.

But you may ask, why did she not abolish slavery at once? And this is the accusation that is made against the Catholic Church, even by such a man as Guizot, the great French statesman and philosopher, who says: "I admit that the Catholic Church, in her action, in her genius, always tried to preach the subject of emancipation; but why did she not do it at once?" I answer, the Church of God is the only power upon earth which, at all times, has known how to do good, and to do it wisely and justly. It is not enough to do a good thing because it is good: it must be well done; it must be wisely done; there must be no injury accompanying the doing of it; nor no injustice staining the act. The Church of God could not, from the very beginning, have emancipated without doing a grave injustice to the society which she would disturb, to the owners of these slaves against whom she might be accused of robbery; but the greatest injustice of all to the poor slaves themselves, who were not prepared for the gift of freedom. And therefore, taking her own time, proclaiming her principles, acting upon them strongly yet sweetly, and drawing to her every interest; conciliating men's minds; creating public opinion among society; trying to save every man from injustice; and in the meantime, preparing mankind, by faith and by sanctity, for the gift of freedom,—she labored slowly, patiently, but most efficaciously in the great work of emancipation. For, my friends, there are two injustices, and grave injustices, which may accompany this great act of emancipation. There is the injustice which may affect the whole of society, may break up public order, may ruin interests; and that is the injustice which a sudden and a rash emancipation inflicts upon the society upon which it falls. For instance, as in Europe in the early middle ages, slaves who, according to St. Augustine, were enslaved, not from any inherent right of man over his fellow-man, but in punishment for their own sins,—these slaves formed a great portion of the public property. Nearly one-half of mankind were enslaved to the other half. The consequence was that the disposition of property was affected by them; that the tillage and cultivation of the land depended upon them; that in fact the status and condition of the half who owned the slaves would be affected; so that, by a sudden and rash emancipation, the freeman of to-day would become a slave, in the poverty and in the unlooked-for privation and misery that would come upon him by the loss of all that he possessed in this world. Was that injustice to be done? No; because it would defeat its own end. The end of all society is peace and happiness. The end of all society is concord and mutual straining to one end; each man helping his fellow-man: and the Church was too wise to throw such an element of universal discord among all the other dissensions that were tearing the heart of the world in those days—to throw in the element of dissension, and to set one half the world against the other.

But far greater is the injustice which is done to the poor slave himself, by a sudden, an unexpected, and a sweeping emancipation. For, my friends, next to Divine grace and faith, the highest gift of God to man is freedom. Freedom! sacred liberty!—within these consecrated walls,—even as a priest, I say that sacred freedom is a high gift of God: but the history of our race tells us that it is a gift that has at all times been most fatally abused; and the poet says, with bitter truth, that at an early age he was left

"Lord of himself—that heritage of woe."

Liberty,—lordship over one's self,—unfettered freedom is, in most cases, a "heritage of woe," and especially when a man does not understand what it means, and is not prepared for its legitimate exercise. What is liberty? that sacred word so often used, so frequently abused, so little understood? Ah! my friends, what is liberty? In our days men fall into two most fatal errors: they have a false idea of religious liberty, and they have a false idea of civil liberty. The false idea of religious liberty is, that it consists in unfettered freedom for every man to believe whatever he likes. A nation is said to have religious liberty when every man believes whatever notion of religion comes into his head; and consequently there are as many sects as there are religions. Men say, "Grand! glorious! this is religious liberty!" But yesterday there was only one faith in Italy, for instance; to-day we hear men boasting: "Thirty thousand hearers, ten thousand preachers," of some new creed; and in twenty years' time, if this goes on, we shall have Italy broken up into Quakers, and Shakers, and Baptists, and Anabaptists, and all sorts of religious sects. Is this religious liberty? Men say it is. Well, if this be religious liberty, all I can say is, that the definition that Christ our Lord gave of religious liberty is wrong; for He said: "You shall know the truth, and the truth shall make you free." Truth is one, and only one: it cannot contradict itself. You shall know the truth, and have it; and in that you shall find your freedom. It will follow from this that the more any nation or people approach to unity of thought, they approach to liberty, provided that one thought represent the truth of Jesus Christ.

Civil liberty is also misunderstood. Many imagine, nowadays, that the essence of civil liberty is the power to rise up at any time and create a revolution,—to rise up against the rulers and governors—against the fixed form of constitutional law,—and upset every thing. That is the idea, for instance—the popular idea, unfortunately—now in the minds of many in Europe. In France, for example, nearly every man that knows how to read and write has a copy of a constitution in his pocket, which he has drawn out himself to be the future constitution of France; and he is prepared to go out and stand on the barricades, and fight for his constitution, and kill his neighbor for it. The idea of liberty, too, which has taken possession of the minds of many, seems to lie in this,—that every man can do as he likes, and what he likes. Ah! if this were brought home to us; if it were brought home to us that every man could do as he liked; that we could be assaulted and assailed at every hand's turn; that every man should go out with his life in his hand; that there was no protection for a man against his neighbor who was stronger; and any man who, boasting of his power, says: "I want your money; I want your means; I am able to take it, and I am at liberty to take it; because liberty consists in every man doing as he likes;"—how would you like this liberty, my friends? No; the essence of liberty lies here: the essence of liberty lies in recognizing and defining every man's right, no matter what he is, from the highest to the lowest in the State. Let every man know his own rights, be they great or small, be they limited or otherwise; let every man have the rights that are just and reasonable; let him know his rights; do not keep him in ignorance of them; define them for him by law, no matter what position he holds in society: and when every man's rights are defined and recognized, and incorporated in law, let that law be put up on high: put it, if you will, upon the very altar; and let every man in the State,—President, King, Emperor, General, soldier, civilian,—let every man, high or low, bow down before the omnipotence and the supremacy of that law. Let that law be there to define every man's rights, and to secure them to him, and let every man know that, as long as he keeps himself within the exercise of his own rights, as defined by law, no power can touch him, no man can infringe upon him. Leave him free in the exercise of these rights: that is liberty; the supremacy of the law, the omnipotence of the law,—the law which is the expression of matured reason and of authority, respecting and defining every man's rights. Far more free is the man who is only able to do this thing or that, but knows that he can do them,—that knows that these are his rights, and that no man can prevent him from exercising them,—than the man who has an undefined freedom, which is not preserved or secured to him by any form of defined law.

This is civil liberty. And so it is as great a mistake to say, "I can do what I like; therefore I am free; I have civil liberty," as it is to say, "I can believe what I like; therefore I have religious liberty." No, it is not true. Dogma,—the truth of God,—does not leave us at liberty. It appeals to us, and we are bound to open our minds to let into our intelligence the truth of God. Any man who refuses it commits a sin. We are not at liberty to refuse it. The law appeals to us; we are not at liberty to disobey it. The quintessence of civil freedom lies in obeying the law; the quintessence of religious freedom lies in acknowledging the truth.

And now, my friends, this being the case, I ask you what greater injustice can you do to a man than to give him that liberty, that unlimited freedom, without first telling him his rights, defining his rights, establishing those rights by law, and without teaching that man that he must respect the law that protects him; that he must move within the sphere or circle of his rights, and content himself in this? What greater injustice can you do to society or to a man himself, than to give him freedom without defining what his rights are? In other words, is not the gift of liberty itself a misnomer? Is it not simply an absurdity to say to a man, "You are free," when that man does not know what is meant by the word freedom? Look at the history of emancipation, and will you not find this to be the case? The States have emancipated just as the Church has emancipated; but with this difference— that the Church prepared the slave before she gave him freedom; taught him his rights, taught him his responsibilities, taught him his duties; and then, taking the chains off his hands, said: "You are a free man. Respect your rights; move in the sphere of your duties, and bow down before the law that has made you free." The State has not said this. A few years ago England emancipated the black population of Jamaica;—a sweeping emancipation. The negroes were not prepared for it; they did not understand it. What was the first use they made of their liberty? The first use that they made of their liberty was to fling aside the hoe, the sickle, the spade, every implement of labor, and sit down idly, to famish and starve in the land. Now, among the duties of man, defined by every law, the first duty is labor, —work. The only respectable man in this world is the man who works. The idler is not a respectable man. If he were seated upon great Cæsar's throne, and there he would be an idler, I would have no respect, but only contempt for him. This was the first use that the negro population of Jamaica made of their freedom. What was the consequence? That their state to-day, after many years of emancipation, is one of absolute misery; while, during the time they were slaves, they were living in comparative comfort; because, small as the circle of their rights was, strictly defined as it was, still it had its duties : they knew their duties, they knew the law; they were protected in the exercise of their duties; and the consequence was they were a thriving people.

Look to the Southern States of this Union. You have emancipated your negro population, with one sweeping act of emancipation. I need not tell you that by so doing (I do not wish to speak politics; I do not wish to enter upon this question in any way that would be, perhaps, insolent in a stranger;—but this I do say)—that in that sweeping emancipation, though you did what the world may call a grand and a glorious thing, you know well how many you deprived of the very means of subsistence by it, and what misery and poverty you brought upon many families by it, and how completely, for a time, you shattered the framework of society by it. Have you benefited the slave population by it?—by this gift of freedom,—a glorious gift, a grand gift, provided that the man who receives it knows what it is; provided that the man who receives it is prepared to receive it and use it as he ought. But, either to the white man or the colored man, the gift of freedom is a fatal gift, unless he knows how to use it. Did you prepare these men for that freedom before you gave it to them? Did you tell them that they should be as laborious as they were in slavery? that labor was the first duty of every man? Did you tell them that they were to respect the rights of their fellow-men, to whom, slaves yesterday, they are made equals to-day? Did you tell them that they were not to indulge in vain, idle dreams of becoming a privileged class in the land, to govern and rule their fellow-men to whom the law only made them constitutionally and politically equal? Did you tell them that they were not to attempt instantly, forcibly, to overstep certain barriers that the God of nature set between them; but that they were to respect the race that manumitted and emancipated them? I fear you did not. I have had evidence of it. What use have they made of this gift of freedom? Ah! children as they were, though grown into the fulness of material manhood,—children as they were, without education, without knowledge,—what use could they make of their freedom? What use do you and I make of our freedom? we who are born free, we whose education and every thing surrounding us from our infancy, all tend to make us respect and use well that freedom. Is there that purity, that self-respect, that manly restraint over a man's passions, —is there that assertion of the dominion of the soul over the inferior nature stamped upon the Christian society and the white society of the world to-day, that would lead them to imagine that it is so easy for a poor child of slavery to enter into the fulness of his freedom? I fear not.

Well, my friends, still they are there before us. The dreams of the political economist will not teach them to use their freedom. The vain, ambitious, and I will add, impious purposes and theories propounded by those who would insinuate that the colored man was emancipated for the purpose of a commingling of races, will not teach them to use their freedom. The ambitious hopes of ascendency held out before them, will not teach them to use their freedom. The political parties that would make use of them for their own ends will never teach them to use their freedom. You have emancipated them; and I deny that they are free. I say that they are slaves. You have emancipated them. Tell me, what religious freedom have you given them? You have put an open Bible into the hand of a man who only learned to read yesterday; and you have told him, with bitter sarcasm, to go and find the truth of God in a book that has puzzled the greatest and wisest of the earth's philosophers. You have sent him in search of religion in a book that has been quoted by every false teacher, from the day that it was written, by prostituting that sacred, inspired word, and twisting it to lend a color to his arguments. You have sent teachers to them, teachers who began their lesson, began their teaching, by declaring that, after they had labored all day, they might have been mistaken all through; and that they had no fixed, immutable truths to give to the poor emancipated mind. You know it. What religious freedom have you given them? Have you touched their hearts with grace? You have given them, indeed, forms of religion, which you boast are suited to them, because you allow these overgrown, simple children to bellow and to cry out what seems to be the word of praise and of faith. Ah, my friends, it is not this corporeal exercise that will purify their hearts, strengthen their souls, subdue their passions, and make them, first of all, respect themselves and then respect their fellow-citizens of the land. You have emancipated them; but you have not freed them. They shall be free only in the day when these poor darkened intelligences shall have been led into the full light of God's knowledge, and when the strong animal passions of a race that, from whatever cause it be, seems to have more of the animal than many other races of mankind; when their strong passions are subdued, their hearts purified, their souls cleansed, graces received to be prized and to be retained;—then, and only then, will you have emancipated the negro. You have not done it as yet. But it is the Church's work to do it. It is her mission and her duty. She knows that He who came and died upon the cross, died not only for you but for these children of the mid-day sun. She knows that every soul of these colored people is as dear to the heart of God as the proudest and the best, the most learned and the most refined among you. She knows that if she can only make a truly faithful Catholic Christian out of the humblest of these children of the desert, that she will have made something more noble—grander and greater—than the best among you, if you be sinners; and she, therefore, sends to them her clergy, her consecrated children—priests and nuns. She says to the noblest and the best in the land: "Arise; go forth from house and home, from father and friends; go, seek a strange land and strange people; go in among them; go, seek the toil and the burning heat and the burden of the day; go seek the man whom many men despise; kneel down at his feet, and offer him Jesus Christ." We have been told by a high authority that this is an act of justice which England offers,—an act of reparation which Catholic England offers to America; for, great as has been the crisis of the late war, the slavery which was in America,—the highest ecclesiastical authority in England tells us, sanctioned by the voice of history,—has not been your creation, my American friends: it was England's creation. It was forced upon you; and, from having begun, it became a necessity. And, therefore, England to-day sends her children; and they come with humility, but with earnestness and zeal, and they say to you—to you, Catholics,—many—perhaps, a vast majority among you—of Irish parentage or Irish descent,—they say to you,—children of a faithful nation, children of a race that has always been intellectual enough to recognize the one truth, keen enough to know its value, energetic enough to grasp it with a firm hand,—lovers as you have been of freedom, worshippers at the shrine of your religious and your national liberty,—they ask you, children of a race of doctors, of martyrs, of apostles, to lend a helping hand to the Catholic Church to-day, and to aid her to emancipate truly those who have obtained only freedom in name, and to complete that work which can only be done by a touch of the hand of Jesus Christ.

Your presence here this evening expresses your sympathy with the high and noble purpose that has brought these children, the consecrated ones of the Church of God, to this country; and they appeal to you, through me :—and they have a right to appeal to you, through me, and I have a right to speak to you in this cause of freedom; for my brother, wearing this same habit, the venerable and holy Bartholomew Las Casas, the first Dominican that ever landed in America, in the very train of Christopher Columbus himself,—was the first man that raised his voice to proclaim to the poor Indian the birthright of that higher freedom that consists in the knowledge and the grace of Jesus Christ. We only ask you to help us to diffuse that knowledge and that grace—that knowledge which is the freedom of the intellect—that grace which is the freedom of the will, and without which double freedom there is no emancipation; for the fetters may fall from the hand, but the chain is still riveted upon the soul. Freedom is a sacred thing; but, like every sacred thing, it must be seated in the soul of man. Bodily freedom is as nothing unless the soul be emancipated by the holy Church of God. Your presence here this evening attests your sympathy with this great work; and, O my friends! as you have contributed materially, I ask you to contribute also intellectually and spiritually;—intellectually, by the sympathy of your intelligence with the labor of those holy priests; and spiritually, by praying to God, who came to emancipate the world, that He might make perfect the weak and inefficient action of mankind and of the State, by pouring forth His spirit of light and grace among these poor children and strangers who are in the land.

THE MONTH OF MARY.

[*A Sermon delivered by Very Rev. T. N. Burke, O.P., in the church of St. Vincent Ferrer, New York, May 1, 1872.*]

WE are commencing this evening the devotions to the Blessed Virgin, to which the Church invites all her children, during the month of May. The faithful, at all seasons, invoke the mercy of God through the intercession of the Blessed Virgin Mother. But more especially during this sweet month, the opening of the beautiful year, does our Holy Mother invite our devout thoughts and prayers to the Mother of God, and put before us the Blessed Virgin's claims and titles to our veneration and love. Guided by this Catholic instinct and spirit, we are assembled here this evening, my dear brethren, and it is my pleasing duty to endeavor to unfold before your eyes the high designs of God which were matured and carried out in Mary. And, first of all, I have to remark to you, as I have done before—that in every work of God we find reflected the harmony and the order which is the infinite beauty of God Himself. The nearer any work of His approaches to Him in excellence, in usefulness, in necessity, the more does that work reflect the beauty and harmony of God who created it. Now, dearly beloved, the highest work that ever God made—that it ever entered into His mind to conceive—or that He ever executed by His omnipotence—was the sacred humanity, or the human nature of Jesus Christ; and, next to Him, in grandeur, in sanctity, necessity, is the institution of, or the creation of, the Catholic Church of God. When, therefore, we come, as pious children of the Church, to examine her doctrines, to meditate upon her precepts, to analyze her devotions, we naturally find ourselves at once in the kingdom of perfect harmony and order. Every thing in the Church's teaching harmonizes with the works of the human intelligence; every thing in the Church's moral law harmonizes with the wants of man's soul. Every thing in the Church's liturgy, or devotions harmonizes with man's imagination and sense, in so far as that imagination and sense help him to a union with God. And so, every thing in the Church's devotion harmonizes with the nature around us, and within us, and with that reflection of nature in its highest and most beautiful form, which is in the spirit and in the genius of the Blessed Virgin Mary. I remember once speaking with a very distinguished poet—one of world-wide reputation and honorable name,—a name which is a household word wherever the English language is spoken;—and he said to me: "Father, I am not a Catholic; yet I have no keener pleasure or greater enjoyment than to witness Catholic ceremonial, to study Catholic devotion, to investigate Catholic doctrines; nor do I find," said he, "in all that nature or the resources of intellect open before me, greater food for poetic and enthusiastic thought than that which is suggested to me by the Catholic Church." And, so, it is not without some beautiful, harmonious reason that the Church is able to account for every iota and every tittle of her liturgy and of her devotions.

And, now, we find the Church, upon this the first of May, calling all her pious and spiritual-minded children, and telling them that this month is devoted, in an especial manner, to the Blessed Virgin Mary. What month is this, my dearly beloved? It is the month in the year when the Spring puts forth all its life, and all the evidences of those hidden powers that lie latent in this world of ours. You have all seen the face of nature at Christmas time, during Lent, even at Easter-time, this year: and, looking around you, it seemed as if the earth was never to produce a green blade of grass again. You looked upon the trees: no leaf gave evidence there of life; all was lifeless, all was barren, all was dried up. And to a man who opened his eyes but yesterday, without the experience of past years, and of past Summers, it would seem as if it were impossible that this cold, and barren, and winter-stricken earth could ever burst again into the life, the verdure, the beauty, and the promise of Spring. But the clouds rained down the rain of heaven; the sun shone forth with the warmth of Spring; and, suddenly, all nature is instinct with life. Now the corn-fields sprout, and tell us that in a few months they will teem with the abundance of the harvest. Now, the meadow, dried up, and burned, and withered, and yellow, and leafless, clothes itself with a green mantle, robing hill and dale with the beauty of nature, and refreshing the eye of man, and every beast of the field that feeds thereon. Now the trees that seemed to be utterly dried and sapless,—leafless and motionless, save so far as they swayed sadly to and fro to every wintry blast that passed over them,—are clothed with the fair young buds of Spring, most delicate and delightful to the eye and to the heart of man, promising in the little leaf of to-day the ample spread and the deep shade of the thick Summer foliage that is to come upon them. Now the birds of the air, silent during the Winter months, begin their song. The lark rises on his wing to the upper air; and, as he rises, he pours out his song in ether, until he fills the whole atmosphere with the thrill of his delicious harmony. Now every bud expands, and every leaf opens, and every spray of plant and tree sends forth its Spring-song, hailing with joy the Summer; and all nature is instinct with life. How beautiful is the harmony of our devotion and our worship: how delicate, how natural, how beautiful the idea of our Holy Mother the Church, in selecting this month—this month of promise—this month of Spring —this month of gladness—of serene sky and softened temperature—this month opening the Summer, the glad time of the year, and dedicating it to her who represents, indeed, in the order of grace, the Spring-time of man's redemption; opening the Summer of the sunshine of God, the first sign of the purest life that this earth was able to send forth under the eyes of God and man! Oh, how long and how sad was the Winter!—the winter of God's wrath—the winter of four thousand years, during which the sunshine of God's favor was shut out from this world by the thick clouds of man's sin and of God's anger! How sad was that Winter that seemed never to be able to break into the genial Spring of God's grace, and of His holy favor and virtue again! No sunbeam of divine truth illumined its darkness. No smile of divine favor gladdened the face of the spiritual world for these four thousand years. The earth seemed dead and accursed, incapable of bringing forth a single flower of promise, or sending forth a single leaf of such beauty that it might be fit to be culled by the loving hand of God. But, when the Summer-time was about to come—when the thick clouds began to part—the clouds of anger, the clouds of sin—the cloud of the curse was broken and rent asunder, and gave place to the purer cloud of mercy and of grace, that bowed down from heaven, overladen with the rain and dew of God's redemption. Then the earth moved itself to life in the sunshine, and the first flower of hope, the first fair thing that this earth produced for four thousand years, in the breaking of winter, before the summer, in the promise of spring, was the Immaculate Lily, the fairest flower that bloomed upon the root of Jesse, and in its bloom sent forth pure leaves, so fragrant, that their sweet odor penetrated heaven, and moved the desires of the Most High God to enjoy them, according to the word of the Prophet: "Send forth flowers as the lily, and yield a sweet odor, and put forth leaves unto grace." So bright in its opening was this spiritual flower—the first flower of earth—that even the eye of God, looking down upon it, could see no speck or stain upon the whiteness of its unfolding leaves. "Thou art all fair, my Beloved!" He exclaimed, "and there is no spot or stain upon thee." And this flower—this Spring flower—this sacred plant—that was to rear its gentle head, unfold its white leaves, and show its petals of purest gold, was Mary, who was destined from all eternity to be the mother of Jesus Christ. She was the earth's Spring, full of promise, full of beauty, full of joy; she was the earth's Spring that was to be the herald of the coming Summer, and of the full, unclouded light of God's own sun beaming upon her. And, just as the little leaf that comes forth in the cornfield to-day, holds in its tiny bosom the promise of a full ear of wheat, bending its rich, autumnal head, the staff of life to all men, so Mary's coming, from the beginning, was a herald and a promise of His appearance upon the earth,—was the announcement that that little plant was to grow and endure, until it was to be crowned with the purity of God, and to bring forth the bread of life, the manna of heaven, the bread of angels, Jesus Christ, the world's Redeemer, the Word made flesh.

How well, therefore, dearly beloved brethren, how well does not this fair Spring month of May, this opening of the Summer of the year, testify in nature what Mary was in the order of grace. And, just as the Almighty God clothes this month, in the order of nature, with every beauty, fills the fields with fragrance, clothes the hillsides with the varied garb of beauty that nature puts forth,—so tender, so fair in its early promise;—so, also, the Almighty God clothed the spiritual Spring of man's redemption, which was Mary, in every form of spiritual beauty, and robed her in every richest garb of divine loveliness of which a creature was capable; so that every gift in God's hand that a human creature was capable of receiving, Mary received. For in her the word of my text was to be fulfilled. It was a strange promise, beloved; a strange and a startling word that came from the inspired lips of the Psalmist, as he said, speaking of His chosen: "I have said, you are God's, and all of you the sons of the Most High!" That word was never fulfilled until the Son of the Most High became the son of a woman. This was the meaning of St. Augustine, when he says: "God came down from heaven, in order that He might bring man from earth to heaven, and make him even as God." Thus it was that man, in the Child of Mary, united with God, became the son of the Most High. Thus it was that, in virtue of the union of the human and divine which took place in Mary, we have all received, by the grace of adoption, the faculty to become children of God. "But to as many as received Him," says St. John, "to them did He give the power to be made the sons of God." And this was the essential mission, the inherent idea of Christianity,—to make men the sons of God; to make you and me the sons of God, by infusing into us the spirit of Jesus Christ, and bringing forth, in our lives, and in our actions, and in our thoughts, and in our inner souls, as well as in the outer man, the graces and glorious gifts that Jesus Christ brought down to our humanity in Mary's womb.

Never has this idea been lost to the Catholic Church. My friends and brethren, you are living now in the midst of strangers. You hear the wildest theories propounded every day, in philosophy, in science; but in nothing are the theories or the vagaries of the human mind so strange as when they take the form of religious speculation or religious doubt. The notion prevalent among all men outside of the Catholic Church, nowadays is, that man has within him, naturally, without the action of God, without the action of Christ, the seeds of the perfection of his life; that, by his own efforts, and by his own study, and by what is called the spirit of progress, a man may attain to the perfection of his own being without God, and become all that God intended him to become. That notion is antagonistic to and destructive of the very first vital principle of Christianity. The vital principle of Christianity is this: the Son of God came down from heaven and became man, and the child, the true child, of a woman, in order that mankind, in Him and through Him, might be able to clothe itself with His virtues, and so become like to God. And in that likeness to God lies the whole perfection of our being; and the end of Christianity is to bring every sufficient agency to bear upon man; to make that man like to God; to make him as the Son of God. "I have said, 'Ye are God's, and all of you sons of the Most High!'"

God is a God of truth. Man must be a man of truth in order to be like to God. God possesses the truth. He does not seek for it. He has it. He does not go groping, sophisticating, and thinking, and arguing in order to come at the truth. Truth is God Himself. And so, in like manner, man, to be a child of God, must have the truth, and not look for it. God is sanctity and purity in Himself. Man must be holy and pure, in order to be made the son of God. He must be free from sin, in order to be like to God, the Father. He must have a power over his passions to restrain them, to be pure in thought, in word, and in action, in soul and in body, before he can be made like to the Son of God. And that religion alone which has the truth and gives it; which has grace and gives it; which touches sin and destroys it; which enables the soul to conquer the body; which holds up in her sanctuaries the types of that purity which is the highest reflection of the infinite purity of Jesus Christ;—that religion alone can be the true religion of God. Every other religion is a lie. But the world is unable to believe this. Men compromise with their passions. Men go to a certain extent in satisfying their evil inclinations. Men refuse to accept the truth because the truth humbles them. Hence the Protestant maxim: "Read the Bible, read the Bible, and do not listen to any priest! These Catholics are a priest-ridden people! Whatever the priest says in the Church is law with the Catholics." They refuse the humility of this. They will not take the truth. They must find it for themselves; and the man who seeks it, by the very fact of seeking it, shows he is not the son of God. I say this much because, my dear friends, I wish you to guard against the wild, reckless spirit that is abroad in the world to-day; I wish to guard you in your fidelity to the Church of God, your mother, in your fidelity to her teaching, in your fidelity to her Sacraments; that word that she puts on my lips and on those of such as I am—that sacramental grace that she puts into the hands of the priest for you; these are the elements of your salvation; these are the means by which every one of you may become the child of God: and there is no perfection, no scheme of perfection, no secret of success, no plan of progress outside of this that is not an institution of the enemy, "a delusion, a mockery, and a snare." And all this we get through Mary, because Mary was the chosen instrument in the hands of God to give to Him that human nature in which man was made even to the Son of God.

Mary's coming upon the earth, therefore, was a Spring-time of grace. Mary's appearance in this world was like the morning star when, in the morning, after the darkness and tempest of the night, the sailor, standing on the prow of the ship, looks around to find the eastern point of the horizon, and he sees, suddenly rising out of the eastern wave, a silver star, beautiful in its pure beauty, trembling as if it were a living thing. And he knows that there is the east, for this is the morning star. He knows that precisely in that point, in a few moments, the sun will rise in all his splendor; and he knows that that sun is coming, because the herald that proclaims the sun has risen. The morning star proclaims to the wild wanderer on the deep, in the eastern horizon, the advent of the coming day. So with us, upon the wild and angry waves of sin and of error, and of God's anger and curse. Our poor humanity, shipwrecked in the garden of Eden; our poor humanity, without even the wreck left to us of the Sacrament of Penance; our poor humanity, groping in the sacrifices and in the oblations of the world, for the love of God, the Redeemer, the day-star whose light was to illumine the darkness of the world;—behold, suddenly, the Morning Star rises, the pale, trembling, silver beauty of Mary! Then it was known that speedily, and in a few years, the world would behold its Redeemer, and mankind would be saved in the fulness of Mary's time. Therefore it is that she enters so largely into the scheme and plan of redemption, that the Almighty God willed that, even as the name of Jesus Christ was to be made known to all men, was to be glorified of all men, was to be proclaimed as the only name under heaven by which man was to be saved; so, also, side by side with this purpose of God's declaration of the glory of His divine Son, came the prophecy of Mary, from the same spirit, that, wherever the name of Jesus Christ was heard and revered, there, and to the ends of the earth, all generations were to call her blessed. "He that is mighty hath wrought great things in me," she says: "wherefore, behold, henceforth all generations shall call me blessed."

And now, my friends, going back to the fountain-head of our Christianity, going back to the earliest traditions of the Church of God, examining, with the light of human scrutiny, her spirit, as manifested in the earliest ages of her being, in the earliest documents she presents us with, does not every man find that wherever the true religion of Christ was propagated, wherever there was the genius and the instinct of faith that adored Jesus Christ, there came the fellow-instinct and genius that loved, and revered, and venerated, and honored the woman who was His mother. If every other proof of this was wanting, there is one proof—a most emphatic proof—and it is this: that while the blessed Virgin Mary was yet living, during the twelve years that elapsed before her assumption into heaven, a religious Order was organized in the Catholic Church, devoted to the veneration, and the love, and the honor of the Blessed Virgin. A religious Order dating from the early times of the prophets—a religious Order founded by the sons of the prophets, under the Jewish dispensation, was converted to Christianity, and at once banded itself together and called itself "The Brethren of Our Lady of Mount Carmel." No sooner was Our Lady assumed into heaven, than these men spread themselves through Palestine and through the East; and the burden of their teaching and their devotion was the glory of the Mother of God; the woman who brought forth the Man-God, Jesus Christ. No sooner was the Gospel preached than the devotion to the Blessed Virgin Mary spread with the rapidity of thought, of sentiment, and of love, through all distant parts; and when, five hundred years later, a man rose up and denied that Mary was the Mother of God, we read that when the Church assembled at Ephesus, in General Council, the people came from all the surrounding countries, and the great city of Ephesus was overcrowded with the anxious people, all waiting for the result of the deliberations, and all praying; and when, at last, the Council of the Holy Church of God put forth its edict, declaring that Mary was the true Mother of God, we read of the joy that came from the people's hearts, the cry of delight that rang from their lips; the "All Hail!" that they gave to you, Mother in Heaven, spread throughout the universal Church; and, never, among the many conclusions of her Councils, for eighteen hundred years, never did the holy Catholic Church give greater joy to her children, than when she proclaimed, in the fifth century, that Mary was the Mother of God, and, in the nineteenth century, that Mary was conceived without sin.

But as we are entering upon this May's devotions, I wish, dearly beloved, to bring unto your notice this very devotion of the Month of Mary as a wonderful instance of the rapidity with which this devotion to the Mother of God spread throughout the Catholic Church.

It was at the beginning of this present century that this devotion of the Month of Mary sprang up in the Catholic Church: and the circumstances of its origin are most wonderful. Some seventy years ago, or thereabouts, a little child—a poor little child scarcely come to the use of reason,—on a beautiful evening in May, knelt down, and began to lisp with childish voice the Litany of the Blessed Virgin before the image of the Child in the arms of the Madonna, in one of the streets in Rome. One little child in Rome, moved by an impulse that we cannot account for—apparently a childish freak—knelt down in the public streets and began saying the Litany that he heard sung in the church. The next evening he was there again at the same hour, and began singing his little Litany again. Another little child, a little boy, on his passage, stopped, and began singing the responses. The next evening, three or four other children came, apparently for amusement, and knelt before the same image of the Blessed Virgin, and sang their Litany. After a time—a few evenings—some pious women, the mothers of the children, delighted to see the early piety of their sons and daughters, came along with them, and knelt down, and blended their voices in the Litany; and the priest of a neighboring church, said: "Come into the church, and I will light a few candles on the altar of the Blessed Virgin, and we will all sing the Litany together." And so they went into the church; they lighted up the candles, and knelt; and there they sang the Litany. He spoke a few words to them of the Blessed Virgin, about her patience, about her love for her Divine Son, and about the dutiful veneration in which she was held by her Son. From that hour the devotion of the month of May spread throughout the whole Catholic world; until, within a few years, wherever there was a Catholic church, a Catholic altar, a Catholic priest, or a Catholic to hear and respond to the Litany, the month of May became the Month of Mary, the month of devotion to the Blessed Virgin. Is not this wonderful? Is not this perfectly astonishing? How naturally the idea came home to the Catholic mind! With what love it has been kept up! How congenial it was to the soil saturated with the Divine grace through the intelligence, as illumined by Divine knowledge and Divine faith! Does it not remind you of that wonderful passage in the Book of Kings, where the prophet Elias went up into the mountain-top, when for three years it had not rained on the land, and the land was dried up; and he went up on the solitary summit of the mount, there to breathe a prayer to God to send rain upon the land? While he was praying, in a cave in the rock, he told his servant to stand upon the summit of the mountain, and to watch all round, and to give him notice when he saw a cloud. The servant watched, and returned seven times: "And at the seventh time, behold a little cloud arose out of the sea, like a man's foot. . . . . And while he turned himself this way and that way, behold the heavens grew dark with clouds and wind, and there fell a great rain."

The word, "Mary," means the sea—the Star of the Sea. A few years ago, a cloud of devotion, no larger than the foot of a little child, in Rome, was seen; and while men looked this way and that way, it spreads over the whole horizon of the Church of God, and over the whole world; and then, breaking in a rain of grace and intercession, it brings an element of purity, and grace, and dignity, and every gift of God to every Catholic soul throughout the world. Oh! when I think of the women that I have met in the dear old land of Faith!—the women oppressed from one cause or from another!—some with sickness in the house; some with, perhaps, a dissolute son; some with a drunken husband;

some with the fear of some great calamity, or of poverty, coming upon them; some apprehensive of bad news from those that they love;—how often have I seen them coming to me in the month of May, just in the beginning, and, brightening up, thank God, and say: "The month is come! I know she in Heaven will pray for me, and that my prayers will be heard!" And I have seen them so often coming before the end of the month, to tell me with the light of joy in their eyes, that the Mother heard their prayer, and that their petitions were granted. Then was I reminded of that mysterious cloud that broke out in the heavens, and rained down the saving rain. One have I before me—one whom I knew and loved—a holy nun who, for more than fifty years, had served God in angelic purity and in heroic sacrifice. For seven months she was confined to a bed of pain and of suffering that deepened into agony. And during those seven months, her prayer to God was, while suffering, to increase those sufferings;—not to let her leave the world until one, whom she loved dearly, and who was leading a bad and reckless life, should be converted unto God. Weeks passed into months, and month followed month; and most frequently did I sit at the bedside of my holy friend. Month followed month, for seven long, dreary months, and she spent that time upon the cross, truly with Jesus Christ. But when the first day of May came—the "Month of Mary,"—I came and knelt down by her bedside, to cheer her with prayer and sympathy. She said to me: "I feel that the month is come that will give me joy and relief. It is Mary's month; and it is the month when prayer grows most powerful in Heaven, because it is the month in which the Mother will especially hear our prayers." Before that month was over, he for whom she prayed was converted to God, with all the fervor of a true conversion; and when the month was drawing to a close, the sacrifice of pain and suffering was accepted; and she who began the month in sorrow, ended it with the joys of Jesus Christ and his Virgin Mother. So it is, all the world over. His secret graces are poured out at the instance of Mary's prayer. And even as she was the Spring-time of grace upon earth, so is she, even now in Heaven, by her prayers for us, the Spring-time of holy grace, obtaining for us the grace of repentance, the grace of prayer, the grace of temperance, the grace and power of self-restraint;—in a word, whatever grace we demand, that, springing up in our souls, will produce to-day the flower and leaf of promise—to-morrow, the fruit of maturity—and for eternity, the reward of grace which is the everlasting crown of God's glory.

THE POSITION AND DIGNITY OF THE MOTHER OF GOD.

[*A Sermon delivered by Very Rev. T. N. Burke, O.P., in the Church of St. Vincent Ferrer, New York, May 2, 1872.*]

"And to the disciple Jesus said : Son, behold thy mother."

DEARLY BELOVED: On last evening I endeavored to describe to you the beautiful harmony and analogy between the things of nature and the spiritual things of grace, so admirably developed and illustrated in the dedication of the month of May to the Blessed Virgin Mary; and I told you then that on this evening I should endeavor to unfold to you the place and the position which the mother of our divine Lord holds in the plan of man's redemption. Now, there are two great classes that occupy the world to-day,—two classes of men, who differ in their apprehension of the design of God as revealed in the redemption of man. The first are those who say, or seem to say, that we did not stand in need of redemption at all. They deny the fall of man; they deny the inherent sinfulness of man;—consequently, they deny the necessity of the Incarnation of Almighty God. They deny the necessity of the Sacraments, or their efficacy; and they say that man's constitution is such, that,—within himself, in the very elements of his nature,—by the mere development of his natural powers, he may attain to all the purposes of God, and to the full perfection of his being.

Such, for instance, is the doctrine of the wide-spread sect of Socinians. Such, in a great measure, are the ideas of a number of other sects; the Unitarians, the Humanitarians, believers in human nature alone; Progressists, men who look to this world and to its scientific attainments, and to its great developments as effected by man, and reflected in the spirit and in the intelligence of man, for all the perfection of humanity and of society. This class takes in all those who reject any definite form of religion at all; who put away from them all idea of the necessity of any fixed faith. This idea represents the vast multitude of mankind, to be found everywhere, and nowhere more numerous than here, in this very land, —the men who, with the most accurate ideas on business, on commercial transactions, on law, on politics, are only found to be following an inaccurate comprehension; careless, indefinite, and not only ignorant of, but willing to be ignorant of every specific form of defined faith, or belief in revelation at all. They do not give enough to God in their thoughts, in their minds, in the acknowledgments of their souls upon this question of man's redemption.

There are, on the other hand, a vast number who profess Christianity, who, if you will, give too much to God in this matter of redemption; who say that when the Son of God became man, He effected the redemption of mankind so completely,—that He wiped away the world's sin so utterly,— that all we have to do is to lean upon Him, to govern ourselves by faith, together with His justification, His merits; and that, without any concurrent labor of our own, without any work on our part, but only the easy operation of "believing in Christ," as they put it—that we can be saved. Hence we hear so much about justification by faith, and we hear so much ribald abuse of the Catholic Sacraments, of fasting, of the Holy Mass, of all the exterior usages and sacramental appliances of the Holy Catholic Church; all mocked at, all derided as contrary to the spirit of true religion, which simply is, according to them, to believe with all your soul in Jesus Christ, in His redemption, in His atonement,—and all your sins are cleansed! A man may have a thousand deeds of murder upon his soul: a man may have loaded himself with every most hideous form of impurity; a man may have injured his neighbor on the right hand and on the left, and may have enriched himself upon the spoils of his dishonesty—there is no law either of the relations of God to man, or of man to his fellow-man; but only "believe in God and you are saved!"

Hence, we hear of so many who go out to "camp-meetings" and "prayer-meetings," and there work themselves into a state of excitement, and say, "Oh, I have found the Lord Jesus! I have found him!" There is no more question about that; they are confirmed; they are "the elect;" they are the "perfect;" they are the "regenerated;" and there is an end to all their previous sins. They need not shed a tear of sorrow; but only believe in the Lord. They need not make an act of contrition, they need not mortify their bodies, but only believe in the Lord. It is a smooth and a very easy, a remarkably easy, doctrine; and, if it only led to Heaven, it would be, indeed, a sweet and an easy way, by which we could enjoy ourselves here as long as we liked, in the indulgence of every vile passion; and afterwards turn and "lean upon the Lord," and thus get into Heaven.

Between these two extremes,—the extreme of unbelief, and the mistaken view and zeal of what appears to be an over-fervent faith, but which in reality is not faith at all,—because faith means the apprehension of the truth, and not a distorted view of this text or that of Scripture;—between these two extremes stands the Holy Catholic Church of God; and she tells us as against the first class,—the "Humanitarians,"—that we are a fallen race; that sin is in our blood; that sin is in our nature; that that nature is deformed, disfigured by sin; that the very fountain-head of our humanity was corrupted in Adam; and just as, if you disturb the fountain-head of the stream,—if you poison it,—the whole current that flows from is muddy and disturbed, or poisonous; so the whole stream of our humanity that flows from the sin of Adam is tainted and disfigured and poisoned by sin; consequently that we stood in need of a Redeemer, who would atone for our sins, and would, by sacrificing Himself, and making Himself a victim, wipe away the sin of mankind.

On the other hand, the Holy Catholic Church teaches us, as against the second class, that two wills, two actions are necessary for man's salvation; namely, the will of God and the will of the man who is to be saved; that we must unite our will with God, and determine to be saved; otherwise that the will of God, which is never wanting, will not alone avail for the sanctification or the salvation of any man. That we must not only, with God, will our salvation, but that we must work with God in the work of our salvation, according to the words of St. Paul: "In fear and trembling we must work out our salvation." That although the gift of salvation comes from God, and is His, yet that He will not give it except to the man who strains himself to lay hold of it, according to that other word of the Apostle: "Lay hold of eternal life." God is amply sufficient to save us; God is willing to save us. We can only be saved by His graces. But if we do not lay hold of these graces, and correspond with them, there is no salvation for us. Just as if you saw a man who had fallen into the sea, and you threw him a rope, by which, if he lay hold of it, you can take him into your boat, or draw him on to the land;—you are willing to save him; you are anxious to save him; you have actually put into his hands the means by which he may be saved; but if he refuses to lay hold of that means of salvation, if he refuses the gift of life that you offer him, you cannot force him; and so he is lost by his own fault.

Now, as it requires, for the salvation of every man among us, two wills, two distinct actions,—the will and the action of God, our will and our action corresponding with His,—so also, in the Redemption, two things were necessary in order that man might be saved. First of all, it was necessary to find some victim whose very act was of such infinite value in the sight of God, that he might be available for the salvation of mankind, and capable of atoning to God's infinite honor and glory, which was outraged by sin. A victim must be found whose very act is of infinite value. And why? Because the atonement which he comes to make is infinite; because no creature of God, acting as a creature, with finite merit and power, and the circumscribed action of a creature, could ever atone to Almighty God for sin, which is an infinite evil. The first thing, therefore, that is necessary is an infinite power of atonement, an infinite power of merit in the victim for man's sin. The second thing that is necessary for redemption is a willingness and capability on the part of the atoner to suffer, and by his sufferings, and by his sacrifices, and by his atonement, to wash away the sin. Where shall this victim—of infinite merit, yet a victim,—be found! If we demand the first condition—namely, the power of restoring to God that infinite honor and glory which was outraged by sin; if we demand this, we may seek in vain throughout all the ranks of God's creatures; we may mount to the heaven of heavens, and seek throughout the choirs of God's holy angels; we shall never find him, because such a one is seated upon the throne of God Himself. God alone is infinite in His sanctity, in His graces; and, if He will consent to be a victim, in His power of atonement, God alone can do it. Man could place the cause there,—man could commit the sin; the hand of God alone can take that sin away by atonement. And yet, strange to say, dearly beloved brethren, God alone cannot do it; because God alone cannot furnish us with the second privilege of the atoner,—namely, the character of a victim. How can God suffer? How can God be moved? How can God bleed and die? He is happiness, glory, honor, and greatness itself; how can He be humbled who is above all things—infinitely glorious in His own essence? How can He be grieved who is the essential happiness of Heaven? He must come down from Heaven, and He must take a nature capable of suffering and pain and of the shedding of blood: He must take a nature capable of being abused and crushed and victimized, or else the world can never find its Redeemer. Yet He must take that nature so that every thing that He does as a victim, and every thing that He suffers as a victim, in that nature, must be attributed to God. It must be the action of God; it must be the suffering of God, or else it never can be endowed with the infinite value which is necessary for the atonement of man's sin.

Behold, then, the two great things that we must find, that God found in the plan of His redemption. God furnished one; the earth furnished the other. God furnished the infinite merit, the infinite grace, the infinite value of the atonement in His own divine and uncreated Word, the Second Person of the Holy Trinity; but when it was a question of finding a victim—of finding a nature in which this Word should operate, in finding the nature in which this Word was to be grieved, and to be bruised, and to bleed, and to weep, and to pray for man,—God was obliged to look down from Heaven and find that nature upon the earth.

Therefore, my dearly beloved brethren, Heaven and Earth united in producing Jesus Christ; and it is as necessary for us to believe in the reality of the divinity that, coming down from Heaven, dwelt in Him, as it is for us to believe in the reality of the humanity which was assumed and absorbed by Him into His Divine person. A man may exalt the divinity at the expense of the humanity, and may say: "He was divine, this man, Jesus Christ; but remember He was not a true man; He only took a human body for a certain purpose; and then, casting it from Him, went up into the high heaven of God." The man who says this is not a Christian; because he does not believe in the reality of the human nature of

Jesus Christ. Heretics have said this: and the Church cut them off with an anathema. Or we may exalt His humanity at the expense of His divinity, and say: "He was a true man, but he was not united to God by personal union; He was not a divine person but a human person: He was a true man, this man who was crucified for our sins—true and holy and perfect,—but not God." Heretics have said this, and say it to-day. Even Mahomet acknowledged that the Lord Jesus Christ was the most perfect of men, but He was not God. The man who says this is not a Christian; because he does not believe in the Divinity of Jesus Christ.

Now, I think that, from what I have said, you must at once conclude that, in the plan of man's redemption, the divinity was as necessary as the humanity; that the humanity was as necessary as the divinity: that the world could never be redeemed without the divinity; that man alone could not do it: that the world could never be redeemed without the humanity; for God alone could never suffer. What follows from all this? It follows, my dearly beloved, in logic and in truth, that, for the world's redemption, Mary on earth was as necessary as the Eternal Father in heaven. That in the decrees and councils of God—in the plan of God,—the Mother of His humanity was as necessary as the Father of His divinity; and that she rises at once, in the designs of God, to the magnificent part that was assigned to her in the plan of redemption, namely: that the world could not be redeemed without her, because she gave the human nature of Jesus Christ, without which there was no redemption for man. Who died upon the Cross? The Son of God. Whose hands were these that were nailed to that hard wood? The hands of the Son of God. What person is this that I behold, all covered with wounds, and bleeding and crowned with thorns? Who is this sorrow-stricken person? That is the Second Person of the adorable Trinity; the same God, begotten in Him, consubstantial to the Father, who was from the beginning, and by whom all things were made. And, if this be the Son of God, what right has that woman to look up to Him with a mother's eyes? What right have these dying lips to address her as mother? Ah! because, dearly beloved, He was as truly the Son of Mary as He was the Son of God.

And now, as I wish to take my own time, and to enter fully into all these things in successive meditations, let me conclude with only one remark. Since I came to the use of reason, and learned my catechism, and mastered the idea that was taught me of how God in heaven planned and designed the redemption of mankind,—the greatest puzzle in my life—a thing that I never could understand—has been, how any one, believing what I have said, could refuse their veneration, their honor, and their love to the Blessed Virgin, Mother of Jesus Christ. For it seems to me that nothing is more natural to the heart of man than to be grateful; and that in proportion to the gift which is received from any one, in the same proportion do we find our hearts springing with gratitude within us, and a strange craving, a strange, dissatisfied feeling to find out how we can express that gratitude that we feel. And is this a sacred feeling? Most sacred; natural, but most sacred. We find in the Scriptures the loud tone of praise, honor, and veneration, and the gratitude which the inspired writers poured forth towards those who were great benefactors of mankind, and especially to the women of the Old Testament. How loud, for instance, are the praises the Scriptures give to the daughter of Jephtha, because she sacrificed herself, according to her father's vow, for the people. How loud the praises which celebrated the glorious woman, Deborah, who, in the day of distress and danger, headed the army of Israel, drew the sword, and the Scriptures say that all the people praised her for evermore, and they sang, "Blessed be God, because a mother has arisen in Israel." How loud are the praises of Esther, of whom the Scriptures tell us that the Jews celebrated an annual festival in her honor, because she interceded with the King Ahasuerus, and saved the people from destruction. How loud the praises of Judith, who, coming forth from the city upon the rocky summit of the mountain, with her womanly hand slew the enemy of Israel and of Israel's God, Holofernes; and, returning in triumph, the ancients of the city came forth and cried out, "Blessed be the Lord God of Israel; and thou—thou art the glory of Jerusalem: thou art the joy of Israel; thou art the honor of our people." And yet, what did Deborah, or Esther, or Judith—what did any of these, or any other man or woman on the face of the earth, do for us compared with what Mary did? Judith cut off the head of Holofernes: Mary set her heel on the head of the serpent that was the destruction of our race. Esther pleaded for the people before the Assyrian monarch, and saved them from temporal ruin: Mary pleaded, and pleads, to the King of kings, to the King of Heaven, and saves the people from destruction. Jephtha's daughter gave her life: Mary brought down "the Life," indeed, from Heaven, and gave it to us. Yet, strange to say, those who are constantly talking about "the Bible; the open Bible; the Bible free to every man;" those who call themselves Bible men; those in whose oily mouths this Bible is always,—every text of it coming forth as if you taught a parrot in its cage to recite it,—understanding it as much as the bird would; these are the very people who tell us that we may join with the Jews of old in the praises of Esther and of Deborah; we may cry out in tones of admiration for Mary, the sister of Moses, or for Rachel; but we must not say a word to express our gratitude, our love, our veneration, and our honor for the woman, the woman amongst women, the spiritual mother of all our race, because her child was our first-born brother; the woman that gave us Jesus Christ; the woman that gave to Him the blood that flowed from His veins upon Calvary, and saved the world! For this woman no word, save a word of reproach, an echo of the hisses of hell, an echo of the sibilation of the infernal serpent that was crushed by God! Christ honored her; yet we must not unite with Him in her honor! Christ obeyed her; yet we must not unite with Him in obeying her! Christ loved her; yet we must not let one emotion of love for her into our hearts.

Who are the men that say this? I have heard words from their lips which they would not permit any man to say of their own mothers; and yet they had the infernal hardihood to say these words of the Mother of Jesus Christ, of the Mother of the Son of God!

And, now, my friends, I believe we can in nowise better employ this month of May, and its devotions, than in making reparation to our Lord and Saviour, and to His holy Mother, for the insults that fall upon Him when they are put upon her. The deepest insult that you could offer to any man would be to insult his mother; and the more perfect the child is, and the more loving, the more keenly will he feel that insult. He, with His dying lips, provided for Mary, His Mother, a second son, the purest and the most loving amongst men. It shows how He thought of her at His last moments; how she was the dearest object that He left upon this earth. And that which is dear to the heart of Jesus Christ should always be dear to your hearts and minds. Next to the love, eternal, infinite, essential, that bound Him in His divinity to His eternal Father,—next to that in strength, in intensity, in tenderness, was the love that bound Him to the Mother who came into closest relations with Him. And, O Lord Jesus Christ! teach us to love what Thou lovedst, and so revere and honor that which Thou didst condescend to honor.

MARY, THE IMMACULATE MOTHER OF GOD.

[*A Sermon delivered by Very Rev. T. N. Burke, O.P., in the Church of St. Vincent Ferrer, New York, May 3, 1872.*]

"Thou art all fair, O my beloved, and there is no spot or slightest stain in thee."

THESE words, beloved brethren, are found in the Canticles of Solomon; and the Holy Catholic Church applies them to the soul and body of the Blessed Virgin Mary. In the Scriptures, the King addresses his spouse by these words. The King represents no other than the Almighty God. And, surely, if, among all the daughters of men, we ask ourselves, who was the spouse of Almighty God? we must immediately answer, the Virgin Mother who brought forth the eternal God made man. Wherever, therefore, the Scriptures and the inspired writings of the Old Law speak words of love, and denote attributes belonging to a spouse, these are directly applicable to the Blessed Virgin Mary.

Now, among the many gifts and graces which the Prophet beheld in her,—and upon which he congratulates her,—are these; he tells us that he saw her "at the King's right hand, in golden garb, surrounded with variety;" that every thing of beauty and loveliness was upon her; but, in addition to this, he tells us that a vision of such perfect purity, such perfect immaculateness rose before his eyes, that, filled with the Holy Ghost and the joy of God, he exclaimed: "Thou art all fair, O my beloved! and there is no spot or slightest stain in thee." Behold, then, dearly beloved, the first great grace that the Virgin of virgins received at the first moment of her existence.

When we reflect upon the relationship which the Incarnation of our Divine Lord established between the Blessed Virgin Mary and the Almighty God—namely, that she should be the Mother of God,—that He, taking His sacred humanity from her, should be united to her, so as to be the flesh of her flesh, and the bone of her bone;—that He was to be altogether hers, as the child belongs to the mother at birth,—and in this new relation of His humanity He was not to suffer the slightest diminution of the infinite sanctity which belonged to Him as God;—when we reflect upon all this, and see the awful proximity in which a creature is brought to Almighty God in this mystery of man's redemption,—the very first thought that strikes the mind is, that God must have forfeited something of His holiness, or else the creature that He selected for His mother must have been all pure, all holy, and, so, fit to be the Mother of God;— either God must have forfeited some of His holiness, coming to one personally a sinner, taking tainted blood,—the nature that belonged to us that He took in her, and which was a broken, a disfigured, and a deformed nature, tainted with sin, and steeped, if you will, in sin;—for what, after all, is the record of man's history but a record of sin?—or, else, Mary must have been sinless.

But, if the Almighty God took that nature from one who bore in her own blood the personal taint of the universal sin, we must conclude that He thereby compromised His own infinite holiness;—nay, that He did more than this; that He contradicted His own word: for the word of God is, that nothing defiled, nothing tainted shall come near to Almighty God. The soul that departs from this world with the slightest taint of sin on it must pay to the last farthing, and purge itself into perfect purity before it can catch a glimpse of God in heaven. And if this immaculateness and purity be necessary in order even to behold God, think of the purity, think of the immaculateness that must have been necessary to Mary, in order to fit her not only to behold God, but to take Him into her bosom; to give Him the very human life that He lived; to give Him the very nature that He took and united to Himself in the unity of His own divine person;—to give him that humanity that He literally made Himself!

What infinite purity, what perfect innocence and immaculateness did these involve: unless, indeed, we are willing to conclude that the Almighty God came into personal contact with a sinner, and so allowed something not undefiled to come into contact with Him. But no; the mystery which brought so much suffering, so much humiliation, so much sadness and sorrow to the eternal Son of God, brought to Him no compromise with sin; brought to Him no defilement of His own infinite sanctity; did not in the least lower Him from that standard of infinite holiness which is His essence and nature as God. And, therefore, it was necessary that, coming to redeem a sinful race, the individual of that race from whom He took His most sacred humanity should be perfectly pure and immaculate.

More than this, we know that the Almighty God never yet called any creature to any dignity or to any office without bestowing upon that creature graces commensurate with the greatness, the magnificence, and the duties which He imposed upon him. Hence it is that we find when He was about to create the Prophet Jeremiah,—when He was about to make him a prophet, to put His divine inspiration into his mind;—when He was about to send this man to announce His vengeance to the people;—the Scriptures expressly tell us that He sanctified that man in his mother's womb, before he was born, and that the infant prophet came into this world without the slightest taint of sin. Hear the words of Scripture:—"The word of the Lord came to me, saying: Before I formed thee in thy mother's womb, I knew thee; and before thou camest forth out of the womb I sanctified thee, and made thee a prophet unto the nations." So, in like manner, when the Almighty God created the man who was to arrive at the highest dignity of the prophets—namely, not only to proclaim the coming of God, but to point out God amongst men in the person of our Saviour,—John the Baptist, created for the high and holy purpose,—created to be amongst men what Gabriel, the Archangel, was to Mary,—namely, the revealer of the Divine counsels,—God sanctified him in his mother's womb; and John the Baptist was born without sin.

If the Almighty God sanctifies a man before his birth, anticipates the sacramental regeneration of circumcision, sanctifies him before the sacrament, as in the case of Jeremiah and John the Baptist, simply because that man was called to the office of proclaiming the word of God, surely there must have been some distinctive sanctity, some especial grace in reserve for Mary, as much higher than the grace of the Prophet or of the prevision of the Baptist, as Mary's office transcends theirs. Jeremiah had but to announce the Word of God revealed to him: Mary it was who was to bring forth the Word of God incarnate in her immaculate womb. John the Baptist was to point Him out and say, " Behold the Lamb of God :" Mary was to hold Him in her arms and say to the world, "This Lamb of God, who is to save all mankind. is my Son." And, therefore, it is that,—as her office exceeded that of prophet, preacher, and precursor, as her dignity so far transcended any thing that heaven and earth could ever know or imagine in a creature,—so the Almighty God reserved her alone among all that He created upon this earth, that she should be conceived, as well as born, without sin :—that the stream of sin which touched us all, and in its touch defiled us, should never come near nor soil the immaculate Mary;— that the sin, which mixed itself up in our blood in Adam, and, upon the stream of that blood, found its way into the heart, into the veins, of every child of this earth, could never flow in the immaculate veins that furnished to Jesus Christ the blood in which He washed away the world's sin. Therefore, the Almighty God for this took thought and forethought from all eternity. "The Lord possessed me," says the Scripture, "in the beginning of His ways, before He made any thing from the beginning." That is to say, in the divine and eternal counsels of Almighty God, Mary arose in all the splendor, in all the immaculate whiteness of her sanctity and purity, the first, the grandest, and the greatest of all the designs of the eternal wisdom of God; because in her was to be accomplished the mystery of mysteries, the mystery that was hidden from ages with Christ in God,—namely, the Incarnation of the Eternal Word.

Thus did the Prophet behold her, as she shone forth in the eternal counsels of God, when he looked up in that inspired moment at Patmos, and saw the heavens opened and all the glories of God revealed, there in the midst of the choirs of God's angels, there in the full blaze and effulgence of the light descending from the Father of Light; and he exclaimed : " I beheld, and lo ! a great sign appeared in Heaven ; a Woman clothed with the sun, and the moon beneath her feet, and on her head a crown of twelve stars." Who was this woman ? Mark what follows, and you will know for yourselves. " And she brought forth a man-child, who was to rule all nations with an iron rod ; and her son was taken up to God and to His throne." Who can she be but the woman that brought forth the man-child, Jesus

Christ, the Son of God? Thus did the Prophet behold her, the sign of promise, of victory, and of glory. And how significant are the mysterious words that follow:—"And the Serpent cast out of his mouth, after the Woman, water, as it were a river, that he might cause her to be carried away by the river. And the earth helped the Woman; and the Earth opened her mouth and swallowed up the river which the Dragon cast out of his mouth." The earth, indeed, swallowed up those fatal waters; the whole world was saturated with them; but they never touched the Woman: and we behold in this the mystery of the Immaculate Conception, for I can call it nothing else than a mystery of divine grace, which is a triple triumph, namely, the triumph of God, the triumph of human nature, and Mary's own triumph and glory.

Consider these things, my friends. First of all, let us consider God's triumph in Mary. Recollect, dearly beloved, the circumstances that attended the fall and the sin of man. God made us in a perfect nature;—perfect in its organization, perfect in its beautiful harmony, perfect in its origin, perfect in its eternal destiny, perfect in the freedom and the glory with which He crowned the unfallen man. "Thou hast made him little less than the angels; thou hast crowned him with honor and glory." Then came sin into this world, and spoiled the beautiful work of God. All the fairest work of God was destroyed by Adam's sin. The integrity of our nature was injured. The harmony of creation was disturbed. Bad passions and evil inclinations were let loose; and the soul with its spiritual aspirations, its pure love and unshackled freedom, became their slave. But although the devil triumphed over God, in thus breaking, destroying, defiling, and spoiling God's work in man, yet his triumph was not perfect. God wished still to vindicate Himself. God would not give His enemy a total and entire triumph over Him, in the destruction and spoiling of His work. God set Mary aside and said: "For her, let there be no sin; for her, no soiling influence; for her, no taint." He took her, in His eternal designs, into the bosom of His own infinite sanctity and omnipotent power; and, while all our nature was destroyed, in her it retained its original purity, integrity, and beauty, in the one soul and body of the Blessed Virgin Mary.

Thus we see God's triumph. And here it is worthy of remark, dearly beloved, that, although in Scripture we often read of God's designs being frustrated, of God's work being overturned and spoiled by sin or some evil agency;—yet it is never totally spoiled. God never gives a complete triumph to His enemy. Thus, for instance, in the beginning, at the time of the Deluge, all mankind were steeped in sin; and God, looking down from Heaven, said: "I am sorry that I created this race; for My spirit is no longer among them." Yet, even then, did the Almighty God reserve to Himself Noah and his children; and, out of the whole race of mankind these were saved in purity and sanctity, that God might not be utterly conquered by the devil. Again, when the Almighty God prepared to rain down fire upon Sodom, He could not find ten holy men in the land. And yet, in the universal corruption, Lot and his family were saved. They were holy, where all else was unholy, and they preserved God in their hearts. Again, when the tribe of Benjamin was destroyed from among the other tribes of Israel, a few were saved, that God's work might not be utterly destroyed. And so the Prophet, speaking of the Jewish people, says: "If the Children of Israel were as the sands of the sea, yet a remnant shall be saved." Thus it is that we find, invariably, that the Almighty God allows, in His wisdom and in His vengeance, the devil to go to a certain point, and to revel in destruction so far; but yet, suddenly He stays him: God stretches out His hand and says: "Thus far shalt thou go, and no farther."

This ought to be a good lesson to us in our day. True, it seems to us, in this our day, that this devil of pride, this devil of infidelity, this devil of revolution, this devil of self-assertion, is let loose among the nations, to play riot with the Church of God, to strike the crown from off the Pontiff's head, to pervert the ancient, faithful nation which has upheld him for centuries, and make it the bitterest enemy of the Church, and to deprive the Head of the Church, for the time, of power. To-day, this devil runs riot in the world, shutting up Catholic churches, expelling Jesuits, tainting the fountains of education, loosening the sacred bonds of marriage and of society, blaspheming Christ in the Eucharist, persecuting His priests and bishops and representatives upon earth. But we know that, at some moment or other, and when we least expect it,—perhaps right in the mid career of its apparent glory,—the terrible, invisible hand will be put forth, and a voice will be heard : " No more—back ! So far in My vengeance, and so far even in My mercy, I have allowed you. Back ! Let there be peace." So the Almighty God triumphed even in the fall of Adam, which brought death into the world, polluted our blood, stirred up the passions, destroyed the equilibrium and harmony of human nature, and caused the very beasts of the forest to assume the savageness that they have to this day. All nature was tainted except that of Mary. Her the hand of the Omnipotent Lord held high above all attacks and attempts of her enemies: and in Mary God has triumphed, in that, in her His glory has been preserved, she never having been tainted with or spoiled by sin.

It is, also, the triumph of our nature, my friends. If Mary had not been conceived without sin, we might have been redeemed, we might have saved our souls, as we hope to do now; we might have gone up into the glory of Heaven; but a perfect human being we never could have seen. Heaven would be a congregation of penitents if Mary were not there: tears upon their faces; but no tears upon thine, O Immaculate Mother ! the blood of Christ upon the hands of all; but no blood of thy divine Son upon thy immaculate hands, O Mary ! The unfallen man would have been a thing of the past. Even in Heaven, the representative of what God had made in Adam would be wanting if Mary were not there. And, therefore, our nature has triumphed in her. We may all look up to her in Heaven ; we may all contemplate her; and we may glorify our humanity in Mary without the slightest fear of pride or blasphemy against God, because the humanity that is in Mary, being conceived without sin, is worthy of all honor and of all glory.

I will not compare her in her Immaculate Conception with sinners; I will compare her with the Saints, and behold how she towers above them. All sanctity,—whether it be wrought out by years of penance, by fasting and mortification, by laborious efforts for the conversion of souls, by utter consecration and sacrifice to God, by martyrdom, by any form of sanctity,—attains to but one thing ; and that is perfect sinlessness and perfect purity of soul. Perfect sinlessness and perfect purity of soul mean perfect union by the highest form of divine love with Almighty God. God so loves us, dearly beloved, that He wishes to have us all together united to Him by that intimate union of the strongest and most ardent love. How is it that that union is not effected? Because of some little imperfection, some little sinfulness, some little crookedness in our souls, which keeps us from that perfect union of love with God. Now, the aim of all the Saints is to attain to that ardent and perfect union with God, by purging from their souls, from their bodies, from their affections, and from their senses, every vestige or inclination or even temptation to sin. When they have attained to that, God crowns their sinlessness with a perfect union of love; and they have attained to the acme or summit of their desires. It is here—precisely where all the Saints have ended—here, precisely where all the Saints, tired and fatigued with the labors of their upward journey, knelt down in blessed rest, on the summit of Christian perfection—that Mary's sanctity begins; for, in her Immaculate Conception, she was conceived without sin. No thought, or shadow of thought "to sin allied," was ever allowed to fall upon the pure sunshine of her soul. No temptation to sin was ever allowed to quicken the pulsations of her sacred heart. Nothing of sin was ever allowed to approach her. Entrenched in the perfect sinlessness of her Immaculate Conception, the moment she was conceived, she surpassed in sanctity,—that is to say, in perfect sinlessness, and, consequently, in perfect union of love with God,—all of the Saints and Angels in heaven. This is the meaning of the words in Scripture, where the Prophet says: "Wisdom built unto itself a house; and the foundation thereof is laid upon the summits of the holy mountain. The Lord loveth the threshold of Sion more than the palaces and tabernacles of Judah." You know that every word of Scripture has a deep and Godlike meaning. What meaning can these words have? Apply this to Mary's sanctity; we find the first moment of her existence upon the summit of the holy mountain: that is to say, her very first step in life is dearer to the Lord than the palaces and tabernacles of Judah; that is, than all the edifices of sanctity that were ever built up on this earth. This was the beginning—the conception—of the woman who was destined to be the Mother of God made man.

But, you may ask me, in that case, if she never sinned, even in Adam, surely she stood in no need of a Redeemer; surely she was the only one for whom it was not necessary that God should become man. God became man to redeem sinners—to save them; if this woman did not require redemption or salvation, why does she say in the "Magnificat:" "My soul doth magnify the Lord, and my spirit hath rejoiced in God, my Saviour"? Well, my friends, she owes as much to the blood of Christ, shed on Calvary, as we do, and more. He was more her Saviour than ours. Whence came the grace of her immaculate conception?—whence came the power that kept her out of the way when all the rest of mankind were swept away into the current of sin? It was her divine Son, foreseen in the years of His humanity—foreseen by the eye of God's justice in the agony of His crucifixion; it was the blood that was shed upon Calvary to save us that saved Mary from ever being tainted with sin. Do you not know that the Almighty God may save in any way he likes? Do you not know, my friends, that the Almighty God is not bound to save this soul or that in this or that particular way? For instance, the Almighty God appointed circumcision as the only way by which original sin was to be removed under the Old Law. And yet we know that He saved and sanctified Jeremiah and John the Baptist without circumcision, and before; because, although circumcision was the ordinary way, Almighty God did not tie His own hands, nor oblige Himself never to apply an extraordinary way. And so, wherever there is a human spirit that is saved and made fit for Heaven, that saving and fitness are equally purchased by the blood of Christ, and by that alone. It saved Mary, as it saved us; only in a different manner. It saved us by falling upon our sinful heads in Baptism;—literally washing away the stain that was already there; it saved Mary by anticipating Baptism, by removing her from the necessity of the Sacrament, by anticipation. In us this blood of Christ is a cleansing grace; in Mary it was a preventing grace. She is saved as much as we are. For instance, suppose a wise prophet—a man that had a knowledge of the future—were to stand on the sea-shore, and see a number of persons about to embark on board a ship, leaving for a distant port; and that he said to one of them, "That ship is going to be shipwrecked; do not go on board," and the person followed his advice and was saved; the others went on the ship, and it is wrecked, as was foretold; the prophet is there, by some mysterious means, and saves them all;—he is as much the saviour of the person who stayed on shore as of those he saved on the vessel after it was wrecked. And so it is with God. He set Mary aside, and His spirit overshadowed her and saved her. Oh how gloriously did God save her!—how magnificently He vindicated Himself in her!—how kindly and mercifully He preserved one specimen of our pure and unbroken nature in her! Well might He hold her forth, as it were, in His omnipotent hand, to frighten the devil, even in the day of his triumph, when He said, "The woman, O spirit of evil, whom thou knowest well, shall crush thy head." Mary was the terror of hell from the beginning; because hell was afraid, from the beginning, of the pure, unfallen nature of man: and that was saved only in her.

Let us, therefore, meditate upon these things; and, giving thanks to God for all He did, for the greatest boon of mercy to our race—in that God so sanctified a creature that she might be worthy to approach Him;—and endeavor, in our own humble way,—by purifying our souls, putting away from us our sins, and weeping over the follies and errors that we have allowed to come upon our souls,—thus to fit ourselves, that, at some immeasurable distance we, too, may be able to approach Him, and Mary, the Immaculate Mother of God.

THE POPE'S TIARA—ITS PAST, PRESENT AND FUTURE.

[*A Lecture delivered by Very Rev. T. N. Burke, O.P., in the Academy of Music, New York, May 16, 1872, in aid of the " Catholic Union" Fund, for His Holiness, Pope Pius IX.*]

MAY IT PLEASE YOUR GRACE—LADIES AND GENTLEMEN: The subject on which I propose to address you is, "The Pope's Tiara, or Triple Crown; its Past, its Present, and its Future." We read of a celebrated orator of Greece, that the grandest effort he ever made was in a speech which he pronounced upon a crown. I wish I had, to-night, the genius or the eloquence of Demosthenes; for my theme, my crown, is as far beyond the glory of the crown of which he spoke, as my thoughts and my eloquence are inferior to his.

Among the promises and prophetic words that we read in Scripture concerning our Divine Lord and Redeemer, we read that it was prophesied of Him that He should be a King; that He should rule the nations; that He should wear a crown; and that His name was to be called "The Prince of Peace." He came; He fulfilled all that was written concerning Him; and He transmitted His headship and His office in the Holy Church, to be visibly exercised, and to be embodied before the eyes of men in the Pope of Rome. And, therefore, among the other privileges which He conferred upon His Vicar, He gave him that his brows should wear a crown. Therefore it is that, from the first day of the Church's history, her ruler, her Pope, her head rises before us, a sceptred man among men, and crowned with a glorious crown. Therefore it is that, encircling his honored brows, for ages the world has beheld the triple crown, or tiara, of which I am to speak to you this evening. Every other monarch among the nations wears for his crown a single circlet of gold. Ornament it as you will, there is but one circle, that would represent the meeting and the centring in the person of the sovereign of all the temporal interests and authority of the State. Upon the Pope's brows, however, rests a triple crown, called the tiara. It is made up of three distinct circles of gold. The first of these is symbolical of the universal episcopate of the Pope of Rome,—that is to say, of his headship of all the faithful in the Church; for, "there shall be but one fold and one shepherd," was Christ's word. The second of these circles that crowns the papal brows represents the supremacy of jurisdiction, by which the Pope governs not only all the faithful in the world at large, —feeding them as their supreme pastor,—but by which, also, he holds the supremacy of jurisdiction and of power over the anointed ministers, and the episcopacy itself, in the Church of God. The third and last circle of this crown represents the temporal influence, the temporal dominion which the Pope has exercised and enjoyed for more than a thousand years in this world.

Behold, then, what this tiara means. Upon those great festival days when all the Catholic world was accustomed to be represented by its highest, by its best and noblest, by its most intellectual representatives in Rome, the Holy Father was seen enthroned, surrounded by cardinals, patriarchs, archbishops, bishops, the priesthood, and the faithful. There he sat upon his high, and ancient, and time-honored-throne; and upon his head did he wear this triple crown, symbolizing his triple power.

Now, my friends, in the Church of God every thing is organized; every thing is arranged and disposed in a wonderful harmony which expresses the mind and the wisdom of God Himself. And, therefore, it is, that in every detail of the Catholic liturgy and worship, we find the very highest and the very holiest gifts symbolized and signified to the man of faith. What do those three circles of the Pope's tiara symbolize? They signify, first of all, the unity that God has set upon His Church. Secondly, they signify the power and jurisdiction that God has conferred upon His Church. And thirdly, they signify all these benefits of a human kind, which the Church has conferred upon this world and upon society.

The first circlet of this tiara represents the unity of the Church. For it tells the faithful, that although they may be diffused all the world over, although they may be counted by hundreds of millions, although they may be found in every clime, and speaking every language; although they may be broken up into various forms of government, thinking in varied forms of thought, having varied and distinguished interests in the things that should never perish, but abide with them for eternity; that moment, out of all these varied elements, out of these multiplied millions, out of these different nations, arises one thought, one act of obedience, one aspiration of prayer, one uplifting of the whole man, body and soul, in the unity of worship which distinguishes the Catholic Church, the spouse of Christ. This was the first mark that Christ, the Son of God, set upon the brows of His Church. He set upon her the glorious seal of unity in doctrine,—that all men throughout the world who belonged to her were to be as one individual man, in the one soul, and the one belief of their divine faith. He set upon her brows the unity of charity;—that all men were to be one, in one heart and in one bond, which was to bind all Christian men to their fellow-men, through the one heart of Christ. And, in order to effect this unity, the Son of God put forth, the night before He suffered, the tender but omnipotent prayer, in which He besought His Father, that the unity of the Church should be visible to all men, and that it should be so perfect as to represent the ineffable unity by which He was one with His Father, in that singleness of nature, which is the quintessence of the Almighty God. It was to be a visible unity. It was to be an unity that would force itself upon the notice of the world. It was to be an unity of thought and belief that would convince the world that the one mind, the one word of the Lord of all truth, was in the heart, and in the intelligence, and upon the lips of His Church. It would be in vain that Christ, the Son of God, prayed for that unity, if it was to be a hidden thing, not seen and known by men; if it was to be a contradictory thing, involving an outrage upon all logic and all reason; as, for instance, the Protestant idea of unity, which is, "Let us agree to differ." "Let us agree to differ!" Why, what does this mean? It means something like what the Irishman meant, when he met his friend, and said: "Oh, my dear fellow, I am so happy and glad to meet you! And I want to give you a proof of it." And he knocked him down! But, you remember, this was the sign of love. And so the Protestant logic of this world says;—"Let us agree to differ." That is to say;—let us create unity by making disunion!

Now, as the Divine, Eternal, Incarnate Wisdom determined that that crown and countersign of unity should be visible upon His Church, it was absolutely necessary for Him to constitute one man—one individual man—as the visible sign and guarantee of that unity in the Church for ever. It would not have answered to have left the twelve Apostles, equal in power, equal in jurisdiction. For, all-holy as they were, all-inspired as they were, if equal power and jurisdiction had been left to all, if no one man among them had been brought forth and made the head of all, with all their perfection, with all their inspiration, with all their love for Christ, they would not, being twelve, have represented the sacred principle of unity in the Church. Therefore did Christ, the Son of God, from among the Twelve take one: He called that man forth, He laid His hands upon Him, and said: "Hear him! hear his words!" That He did not say of any of the others, but took care that all the others should be present to witness these words and to acknowledge their chief. He took that man in the presence of the Twelve, and He said to him, to them: "Hitherto you have been called Simon; now I say your name is Cephas, which means a rock; and upon this rock I will build my Church." Again, in the plainest of language, He said to that man: "Thou—thou, O rock! confirm thy brethren!" In the presence of all, He demanded of that man the triple, thrice-repeated acknowledgment and confession of his love. "Peter," He said to him, "you know how dearly John, My virgin friend, loves Me. Do you love Me more? You know how well all these around Me love Me. Do you love Me more than all?" And until Peter three times asserted that he loved his Master with a love surpassing that of all others, Christ delayed His divine commission. But, when the triple acknowledgment was made, He said to Peter: "Feed thou My lambs; feed thou My sheep!" "There shall be one fold," said the Son of God, "and one shepherd." That was the visible unity of the Church; that was to be the countersign of the divine origin of the Church of God; and that was to be represented unto all ages by the one head and Supreme Pastor of all, the Pope of Rome.

Mark the splendid harmony that is here. The adorable Son of God is one with the Father by the ineffable union of nature from all eternity. The Son of God made man, still is man, and only man, in the hypostatical union in which the two natures met in one divine person. The Church that sprung from Christ,—the Lord God and man united,—is to be one until the end of time. And, therefore, the principle of unity passes, as it were, from Christ to Peter, and from Peter to each succeeding Pontiff; so that the Church of God is recognized by its union with its Head, and by that, the One Head, which governs all. Therefore did St. Ambrose say: "Show me Peter; for, where Peter is, there is the Church of God."

Now, you see at once the significance of that first circle of gold that twines round the papal crown. It speaks of the Pope as the supreme pastor of all the faithful. It speaks of him as the one voice, and the only one, able to fill the world, and before whose utterances the whole Christian and Catholic world bows down as one man. It speaks of the Pope as the one shepherd of the one fold; and it tells us that, as we are bound to hear his voice, and as that voice alone can resound through the whole Church, which cannot by possibility proclaim a lie,—when the Pope of Rome speaks to the faithful as supreme pastor, pronouncing upon and witnessing the faith of the Catholic Church,—it tells us that the self-same spirit that preserves that Church from falling into error, preserves her pastor, so that he can never propound to her any thing erroneous or unholy, or at variance with the sacred morality of the Christian law.

The second circle of gold represents the second great attribute that Christ, our Lord, emphatically laid upon His Church. As clearly as He proved that that Church should be one, so clearly did He pray and prophesy that that Church was to have power and jurisdiction. "All power," He said to His Apostles, "all power in heaven and upon earth is given unto Me." Behold the Head of the Church speaking to His Church. "Given unto me!" "I am the centre of that power." "As the Father sent me, thus endued with power, so do I send you." And then He set upon the brows of His Apostles, and, through them, on the Church, the crown of spiritual power. But, as all power is derived from God, it follows that, in the Church of God, whoever represents, as viceroy and vicar, supreme pastor and ruler of the Church,—whoever represents Christ, who is the source of all power, that man has supreme jurisdiction in the Church of God, not only over the Faithful, but over the pastors of the flock and the Episcopacy. James, and John, and Andrew, and Philip, and the others, were all Bishops. St. Ignatius of Antioch, and all the succeeding great names that adorn the episcopal roll in the Church,—all had power; all exercised power; and all were recognized, as the Church recognizes them and their successors still, as her Archbishops and Bishops; and all had that power by divine institution, and their episcopacy in the Church is of divine origin; and yet, that power is so subjugated and subordinated, that the Pope is the supreme Bishop of Bishops, to whom Christ said: "Feed not only My lambs," My faithful; but, "feed My sheep," the matured ones and holy ones in the sanctuary of the Church.

Finally, the third circle of gold twining around that time-honored crown of the tiara, represents the temporal power that the Pope has wielded for so many centuries, and which has been the cause of so many blessings, and so much liberty and civilization to the world. It was not in the direct mission of the Church of God to civilize mankind, but only to sanctify them. But, inasmuch as no man can be sanctified without being instructed, and thus having the elements of civilization applied to him, therefore, indirectly, but most powerfully, did Christ, our Lord, confer upon His Church that she should be the great former and creator of society; that she should be the mother of the highest civilization of this world; that she should be the giver of the choicest and the highest of human gifts; and, therefore, that she should have that power, that jurisdiction, that position, in her head, among the rulers of the nations, that would give her a strong voice and a powerful action in the guidance of human society. And as to the second circle of this golden crown—viz., the universal pastorate of the Church—and the supremacy, even in the sanctuary,—both of these did Peter receive from Christ; and these two have been twined round the Papal brow by the very hand of the Son of God Himself. The third circle, of temporal power, the Pope received at the hands of the world; at the hands of human society; at the hands of the people. And he received it out of the necessities of the people, that he might be their king, their ruler, and their father upon this earth.

Now, such being the tiara, we come to consider it in the past, as history tells us of it; in its present, as we behold it to-day; and in its future. How old is this tiara? I answer that, although the mere material crown and its form dates only from about the year 1340 or '42, and the Pontificate of Benedict the Twelfth, the tiara itself—the reality of it—the thing that it signifies—is as ancient as the Church of God, which was founded by Christ, our Lord. In the past, from the day that the Son of God ascended into Heaven, all history attests to us that Peter and Peter's successors were acknowledged to be the supreme pastors of the Church of God. Never, when Peter spoke, never did the Church refuse to accept his word, and to bow down before his final decision. In the very first Council of Jerusalem, grave questions that were brought before the Assembly were argued upon by various of the Apostles, until Peter rose; and the moment that Peter spoke and said: "Let this be done so; let such things be omitted; such things be enforced;"—that moment every man in the Assembly held his peace, and took the decision of Peter as the very echo of the Invisible Head of the Church, who spoke in him, by and through him. In all the succeeding ages, the nations bowed down as they received the words of the Gospel. The nations bowed down and accepted that message on the authority and on the testimony of the Pope of Rome. Where, among the nations, who have embraced the Cross,—where among the nations who have upheld the Cross,—where is there one that did not receive its mission and its Gospel message on the message and on the testimony of the Pope of Rome?

From the very first ages, while they yet lay hid in the Catacombs, we read of saintly missionaries going forth from under the Pope's hands, to spread the message of Divine Truth throughout the lands. Scarcely had the Church emerged from the Catacombs, and burst into the glory and splendor of her renewed existence, than we find one of the early Popes of Rome laying his hand upon the head of a holy youth that knelt before him, consecrating that youth into the priesthood, into the episcopacy,—and sending him straight from Rome to a mission, the grandest and most fruitful—the most glorious of any in the Church. That Pope was Celestine, of Rome; and the man whom he sent was Patrick, who, by the Pope's order, wended his way to Ireland. From the Pope of Rome did he (Patrick) receive his mission and his message. From the Pope of Rome did he receive his authority and his jurisdiction. The diploma that he brought to Ireland was attached to the Gospel itself. It was the testimony of the Church of Christ, countersigned by Celestine, who derived his authority from Peter, who derived his from Christ. And when, in his old age, he had evangelized the whole island; when he had brought Ireland into the full light of the Christian faith, and into the full blaze of her Christian sanctity, the aged Apostle, now drooping into years, called the bishops and priests of Ireland around him; and, among his last words to them, were these: "If ever a difficulty arises among you;—if ever a doubt of any passage of the Scripture, or of any doctrine of the Church's law—or of any thing touching the Church of God or the salvation of the souls of your people,—if ever any doubt arises among you, go to Rome—to the mother of the nations—and Peter will instruct you thereon." Well and faithfully did the mind and the heart of Ireland take in the words of its saintly Apostle. Never—through good report or evil report—never has Ireland swerved for one instant—never has she turned to look with a favoring or a reverential eye upon this authority, or upon that; but straight to Peter. Never has she, for an instant, lost her instinct, so as to mistake for Peter any pretender, or any other Pope. Never, for an instant, has she allowed her heart or her hand to be snared from Peter. It is a long story. It is a story of fourteen hundred years. But Ireland has preserved her faith through her devotion to Peter and to the Pope of Rome, Peter's successor; and she has seen every nation, during these fourteen hundred years—every nation that ever separated from Peter—she has seen them, one and all, languish and die, until the sap of divine knowledge,—until the sap of divine grace—was dried up in them; and they utterly perished, because they were separated from the Rock of Ages, the Pope of Rome.

Just as the people, in all ages and in all times, bowed down before their supreme pastor, so also has the Episcopate in the Church of God, at all times, recognized the supremacy of the Pope of Rome, and at all times bowed before the second crown that encircles his glorious tiara. Never did the Episcopacy of the Catholic Church meet in council except upon the invocation of the Pope of Rome. Never did they promulgate a decree until they first sent it to the Pope of Rome, to ask him if it was according to the truth, and to get the seal and the countersign of his name upon it, that it might have the authority of the Church of God before their people. From time to time, in the history of the Episcopate, there have been rebellious men that rose up against the authority, and disputed the power of the Church of Rome. But, just as the nations that separated from Peter separated themselves thereby from the unity of the truth, and of sanctity and of Christian doctrine, and of Christian morality, so, in like manner, the Bishop who, at any time, in any place, or in any age, disputed Peter's power, Peter's authority, and separated from him, was cut off from Peter and from the Church; the mitre fell, dishonored, from his head; and he became a useless member, lopped off from the Church of God, without power, without jurisdiction, without the veneration, or the respect, or the love of his people. Thus has it ever been in times gone by. The Pope of Rome commands the Church through the Episcopate. The Pope of Rome speaks and testifies to the Church's doctrine through the Episcopate. Whenever any grave, important question, touching doctrine, has to be decided, the Pope of Rome has always called the Episcopate about him;—not that he could not decide, but that he might surround his decision with all that careful and prudent examination, with all that weight of universal authority over the world which would bring that decision, when he pronounced it, more clearly and more directly home to every Catholic mind. And faithful has that Episcopate been,—since the day that eleven Bishops met Peter, the Pope, in Jerusalem, in the first Council,—down to the day when, three years ago, eight hundred Catholic Archbishops and Bishops met Peter's successor in the halls of the Vatican, and bowed down before the word of truth upon his lips.

Such in the past, as history attests, were the two circles of the supreme pastorate and supreme jurisdiction in the Church.

The Roman empire, as you all know, was utterly destroyed by the incursions of the barbarians, in the fifth century. A king, at the head of his ferocious army, marched on Rome. The Pope was applied to by the terrified citizens; and Leo the Great went forth to meet Attila, "the Scourge of God." He found him in the midst of his rude barbarian warriors, on the banks of the Mincio. He found him exulting

in the strength and power of his irresistible army. He
found him surging and sweeping on towards Rome, with the
apparent force of inevitable destiny, and with outspread
wings of destruction. He found him, in the pride and in
the supreme passion of his lustful and barbaric heart, sworn
to destroy the city that was the "Mother of Nations." And,
as he was in the very sweep of his conquest and pride,—
unfriended and almost alone,—having nothing but the
majesty of his position and of his glorious virtue around him,
—the Pope said:—"Hold! Rome is sacred, and your feet
shall never tread upon its ancient pavement! Hold! Let
Rome be spared!" And, while he was speaking, Attila
looked upon the face of the man; and presently he saw over
the head of St. Leo, the Pope, two angry figures, the Apostles St. Peter and St. Paul, with fire and the anger of God
beaming from their eyes, and with drawn swords menacing
him. And, even as the Angel stood in the Prophet's path of
old, and barred his progress, so did Peter and Paul appear in
mid-air and bar the barbarian. "Let us return," said he,
"and let us not approach this terrible and God-defended
city of Rome!" Attila fled to his northern forests; and Leo
returned, having saved the existence and the blood of ancient
and imperial Rome.

But army followed army; until, at length, Alaric conquered and sacked the city, burned and destroyed it, broke
up all its splendor and all its glory, overran and destroyed
all the surrounding provinces; and so the destruction that
he began was completed a few years later by the King
Odoacer, who wiped away the last vestige of the ancient
Roman empire. Then, my friends, all Italy was a prey to
and was torn with factions; covered with the blood of the
people. There was no one to save them. In vain did they
appeal to the distant Eastern Emperor, at Constantinople.
He laughed at their misery, and abandoned them in the
hour of their deepest affliction and sorrow; while wave after
wave of barbaric invasion swept over the fair land, until life
became a burden too intolerable to bear, and the people
cried out, from their breaking hearts, for the Pope of Rome
to take them under his protection, to let them declare him
King, and so obtain his safeguard and his protection for their
lives and their property. For many long years the Pope
resisted the proferred crown. It grew upon his brows

insensibly. It came to him in spite of himself. We know that, year after year, each successive Pope was employed sending letters, sending messengers to supplicate, to implore the Christian Emperor to send an army for the protection of Italy; and when he did send his army, they were worse, in their heretical lawlessness, more tyrannical, more bloodthirsty over the unfortunate people of Italy, than even the savage hordes that came down from the north of Europe. And so it came to pass that, in the dire distress of the people, the Pope was obliged to accept the temporal power of Rome, and of some of the adjoining provinces. History tells us that he might, in that day, have obtained, if he wished it, the sovereignty over all Italy. They would have been only too happy to accept him as their King. But no lust of power, no ambition of empire guided him; and the great St. Gregory tells us, that he was oppressed with the cares of the temporal dominion, and that it was forced upon him against his will.

However, now the crown is upon his head. Now he is acknowledged a monarch—a reigning king among monarchs. And now let us see what was the purpose of God in thus establishing that temporal power in so early a portion of the history of the world's civilization. At that time there was no law in Europe. The nations had not yet settled down or formed. Every man did as he would. The kings were only half-civilized, barbarous men, recently converted to Christianity, wielding enormous power, and only too anxious to make that power the instrument for gratifying every most terrible passion of lust, of pride, of ambition, and of revenge. Chieftains, taking to themselves the titles of Baron, Duke, Margrave, and so on, gathered around them troops, bands of mercenaries, and preyed on the poor people, until they covered the whole Continent with confusion and with blood. There was no power to restrain them. There was no power to make them spare their people. There was no voice to assert the cause of the poor and the oppressed, save one; and that was the voice of the monarch who was crowned in Rome, the ancient and powerful head of the Catholic Church. Whence came his influence or his power over them? Ah, it came from this: that, with all their crimes, they still had received from God the gift of faith; and they knew—the very worst among them knew—as history tells us, that, when the Pope spoke it was the echo of the voice of God. They acknowledged it as a supreme power over their consciences, over their actions,—as a power that could be wielded not only for their salvation, but even for their destruction, by the terrible sentence of excommunication, by which the Pope could cut them off from the Church. The faith that was in the hearts of these rude kings was also disseminated among their people; and so strong was it, that the moment the Pope denounced or excommunicated any monarch, that moment, no matter how great he was, as a warrior, as a statesman, as a writer,—that moment the people shrank from him as they would from the pest-stricken leper, and his voice was no longer heard as an authority, either on the battle-field or in the council chamber. Knowing this, the kings were afraid of the Pope. Knowing this, the people looked up to the Pope: and if any king overtaxed his people and ground them to the earth, or if any king violated the law of eternal justice by shedding the blood of any man without just cause, or if any king declared an unjust and unnecessary war, or if any king repudiated his lawful wife, and, in the strength and power of his passion, sought to scandalize his subjects, and to openly insult and outrage the law of God,—the people, the soldiery, society, the abandoned and injured woman, all alike, looked up to and appealed to the Pope of Rome as the only power that could sway the world, and strike terror into the heart of the greatest, the most powerful, and the most lawless king upon the earth.

History—from every source from which we can draw it—tells us what manner of men were the kings and dukes and rulers the Pope had to deal with. What manner of men were they? In the eleventh century, the Emperor Otho invited all his nobility to a grand banquet; and while they were in the midst of their festivity, in came one of the king's officers with a long list of the names of men who were there present; and every man whose name was called out had to rise from the banquet, and walk into a room adjoining, and there submit to an unjust, a cruel, and an instantaneous death. These were the kind of men the Pope had to deal with. Another man that we read of was Lothair. His lustful eye fell upon a beautiful woman; and he instantly puts away and repudiates his virtuous and honored wife, and he takes to him this concubine, in the face of the world, proclaiming, or suggesting that he could proclaim, that, because he was an emperor, or a king, he was at liberty to violate the law of God, outrage the proprieties of society, scandalize his subjects, and take liberties with their honor and with their integrity, which would not be permitted to any other man. How did the Pope, in these instances, deal with such men? How did he use the temporal power, so great and so tremendous, with which God and society had invested him? He made the murderers do public penance, and make restitution to the families of those whose blood they had shed. He called to him that Emperor Lothair; he brought him before him; he made him, in a public church, and before all the people, repudiate that woman whom he had taken to his adulterous embrace; take back his lawful empress and queen, pledge to her again, by solemn oath, before all the people, that he never would love another, and that he would be faithful to her as a husband and a man, until the hour of his death. Lothair broke his oath,—his oath taken at that solemn moment, when the Pope, with the ciborium in his hand, held up the body of the Lord, and said: "Until you swear fidelity to your lawful wife, I will not place the Holy Communion upon your lips." He took that oath; he broke it; and that day month—one month after he had received that Communion—he was a dead man; and the whole world—the whole Christian world,—recognized in that death the vengeance of God falling upon a perjured and an excommunicated sinner.

How did the Pope vindicate by his temporal power and authority the influence that it gave him among the kings and the nations? How did he operate upon society? When King Philip of France wished to repudiate his lawful wife and take another in her stead, the Pope excommunicated him, and obliged him, in the face of the world, to take back, and to honor with his love and with his fidelity the woman whom he had sworn before the altar to worship and to protect as long as she lived.

How did the Pope exercise his temporal power when Spain and Portugal, both in the zenith of their glory, were about to draw the sword, and to deluge those fair lands with the blood of the people? The Pope stepped in and said, "No war!—there is no necessity for war;—there is no justification for war; and if you shed the blood of your people," he said to both kings, "I will cut you both off, and fling you, excommunicated, out of the Church."

Thus did he preserve the rights—the sacred rights of marriage; thus did he preserve the honor, the integrity, the position of the Christian woman,—the Christian mother, who is the source, the fountain-head of all this world's society, and the one centre of all our hopes. Thus did he save the people, and curb the angry passions of their sovereigns. Thus did he tell the king: "So long as you rule justly, so long as you respect the rights of the humblest of your subjects, I will uphold you; I will set a crown upon your head, and I will fling around you all the authority, and all the jurisdiction and sacredness of your monarchy. I will preach to your people obedience, loyalty, bravery, and love; but, if you trample upon that people's rights, if you abuse your power to scandalize them, to injure them in their integrity, in their conscience,—I will be the first to take the crown from your head, and to declare to the world that you are unworthy to wear it." Modern historians say: "Oh, we admit all this: but what right had the Pope to do it? What right had he to do it?" What right? The best of right. Who, on this earth, had a right to do it, if not the man who represented Christ, the Originator and Saviour of the world? What right had he to do it? He had the right that even society itself and the people gave him; for they cried out to him: "Save us from our kings; save us from injustice; save us from dishonor, and we will be loyal and true as long as our leaders and our monarchs are worthy of our loyalty and our truth."

Such, in the past history of the world, was the third circle, that twines round the Papal Crown.

Now, passing from the past to the tiara of to-day, what do we find? We find a man in Rome, the most extraordinary, in some things, of all those that ever succeeded to the supremacy of the Church, and in the office of St. Peter;—most extraordinary, particularly in his misfortunes;—most extraordinary in the length of his reign; for he is the only Pope that has outlived "the years of Peter;"—most extraordinary in the ingratitude of the world towards him, and the patience with which he has borne it;—most extraordinary in the heroic firmness of his character, and in the singleness of his devotion to his God and to the spouse of God, the Church;— Pius IX, the glorious Pontiff, the man whom the bitterest enemies of the Church, the most foul-mouthed infidels of the day, are obliged to acknowledge as a faithful and true servant of the Lord, his God, a faithful ruler of the Church, and a man from whose aged countenance there beams forth upon all who see him, the sweetness, the purity of Christ. I have seen him in the halls of the Vatican; I have seen the most prejudiced Protestant ladies and gentlemen walk into that audience chamber; I have seen them come forth, their eyes streaming with tears; I have seen them come forth entranced with admiration at the vision of sanctity and venerableness that they have beheld in the head of the Catholic Church. He is extraordinary in that he has outlived "the years of Peter." Well do I remember, as he stood upon the altar, five and twenty years ago, fair and beautiful in his youthful manhood. Well do I remember the heroic voice that pealed like a clarion over the mighty square of St. Peter's, and seemed as if it was an Angel of God that was come down from Heaven, and, in a voice of melodious thunder, was flinging a pentecost of grace and blessing over the people. Five and twenty years have passed away, and more. Never during the long roll of Pontiffs—never did man sit upon St. Peter's chair so long; so that it even passed into a proverb, that no Pope was ever to see the years of Peter. That proverb is falsified in Pius. He has passed the mystic Rubicon of the Papal age. He has passed the bounds which closed around all his predecessors. He has passed the years of Peter upon the Papal throne. Oh! may he live, if it be God's will, to guide the Church, until he has doubled the years of Peter. He is singular in what the world calls his misfortunes, but what, to me, or to any man of faith, must absolutely appear as a startling resemblance to the last week that the Lord, our Saviour, spent before His passion in Jerusalem.

I remember Pius IX, surrounded by the acclamations and the admiration of the whole world. No word of praise was too great to be bestowed upon him. He was the theme of every popular writer. He was the idol of the people. The moment they beheld him, the cry came forth:—"*Viva, viva, il salvatore de la patria!*" Long live the saviour of his people and of his country! To-day he must not show his face in the very streets of Rome; and in the very halls of the deserted Vatican he hears the echoes of the shouts of those that cry: "Blessed be the hand that shall be imbrued in thy blood, O Pius!" Now, I ask any man on the face of the earth, what has this man done? What can the greatest enemy of the Pope lay his hand upon, and say he has done so and so, and he has deserved this change of popular friendship and of popular opinion? The greatest enemy that the Pope has on this earth is not able to bring a single charge against him, during these twenty-five years, to account for that change of opinion. What has changed blessings into curses? What has changed homage and veneration into contempt and obloquy? There is no accounting for it. It is like the change that came over the people of Jerusalem, who, on Palm Sunday, cried "Hosanna to the Son of David," and on Good-Friday morning cried, "Give Him to us! We will tear Him to pieces and crucify Him!" There is no accounting for it. Has he oppressed the Roman people? No. I lived many years in Rome, under his Pontificate. There was no taxation worth speaking of; there was no want, no misery. There was plenty of education for the children, plenty of employment, plenty of diversion. There was no forcible conscription of the youth, to send them into some vile cesspool of corruption, in the shape of a barrack, or to hunt them out to the battle-field, to be mown down and flung into bloodstained graves. No; every man possessed his house and his soul in peace. There was prosperity in the land. And over all this there was the hand ever waving a blessing, and a voice invoking benediction and grace for his people. Whence came the change? No man can tell. Therefore, I say, this man is extraordinary in his misfortunes, inasmuch as they bring out, in the most striking and terrible manner, his resemblance to his crucified Lord and Saviour, the Head of the Church. He is singular in the magnificence of his character. The student of history may read the lives of all the Popes that come down from Peter to Pius, and I make this assertion, that there is not a single feature of grandeur or magnificence in the character of any one of these Popes that does not shine out, concentrated, in the character of Pius IX. We admire the missionary zeal of St. Gregory the Great, or of St. Celestine. Pius the Ninth has sent from under his own hand, and from under his own blessing, men who have honored his Pontificate, as well as the Church, their mother, by shedding their blood in martyrdom, for the faith. From under his hand have gone forth those holy ones who have languished in the dungeons of China and of Japan. From under his hand have gone forth those heroic Jesuit sons of St. Ignatius, that have lifted the standard of the Cross, and uplifted the name— the name which forms their crown and their glory, even in the eyes of men,—unto the farthest nations of the earth. If we admire the love of Rome that shines forth in the character of St. Leo the Great, who was the Pope among them all that ever loved Rome and the Romans so tenderly as the heart of Pius IX loved them? When he came to the throne there were Romans in exile, and there were Romans in prison. The very first act of the Pontiff was to fling open the prison doors, and to say to these children of misfortune: "Come forth, Italians; breathe the pure air and feast your eyes upon the loveliness of your native land." There were Romans who were in exile: he sent them the message of manumission, and of pardon, and of love, in whatever land they were, and said: "Come back to me;—come back and sit down in peace and in contentment under my empire; for, O Rome and children of Rome, I love you." This was the language and these were the emphatic accents of the glorious Pius IX. Where was the Pope who ever embellished Rome as he did? I lived in Rome during the first year of his Pontificate: I lived there in the last. I might almost say that he found it a city of brick, and that he handed it over to Victor Emmanuel, the robber, a city of polished and shining marble. Orphanages, hospitals, public schools, model lodging-houses, public baths and lavatories, splendid fountains,—every thing that the Roman citizen could require, either for his wants or for his luxury, or, if you will, his pleasure,—the magnificent hand of Pius IX provided. For, for the last five-and-twenty years, that hand has never ceased in beautifying and embellishing his loved and imperial Rome.

We admire the glorious firmness, the magnificent, rock-like endurance of St. Gregory VII, whom history knows by the name of Hildebrand; how he stood in the path of the impious German Emperors. Like a rock against which the tide dashes, but dashes in vain,—so did he stand to stem the torrent of their tyranny and of their corruption. We admire Gregory VII, when, saying Mass before the Emperor, he took the blessed Eucharist into his hands, and turned round with the Holy Communion and said: "Oh! majesty, I am about to give you the Holy Body of Jesus Christ. I swear before my God," said the Pope, "in whose presence I now stand, that I have never acted save for the Church which He loves, and for the happiness of His people. Now, O King, swear thou the same; and I will put God upon thy lips!" The Emperor hung his head and said: "I cannot swear it, for it would not be true;" and the Holy Communion was denied him.

We admire that magnificent memory in the Church of God which upheld the rights of Peter and of the Church against king and kaiser; but, I ask you, does not the image of the sainted Gregory VII rise before our eyes from out the recesses of history, and come forth into the full blaze of the present generation, in the magnificent constancy and firmness of Pius IX, the Pope of Rome? It was a question of only giving up a little child that was baptized into the Christian Church, and engrafted, by Baptism, upon Christ, our Lord—a little child that was engrafted unto the Son of God and His Church—had received the rites, and claimed, in justice, to come to know and love that God on whom he had been engrafted by Baptism. All the powers of the world,—all the dukes and kings and governments in Europe,—came around the Pope and said: "You must give up that child; he must be taught to blaspheme and to hate that Lord upon whom he has been engrafted by Baptism. He must not belong to Christ or the Church, even though he is baptized into it." And they asked the Pope, by the surrender of that child, to proclaim the surrender of that portion of the Church's faith that tells us, on the authority of the inspired Apostle, that by Baptism, like a wild olive branch let into a good tree, we are let into Jesus Christ. They sent their fleets to Civita Vecchia; they pointed their cannon against the Vatican; and told the Pope that his existence and his life depended upon his giving up that child. And he declared, in the face of the world, and pronounced that word which will shine in characters of glory on his brow in Heaven,—he pronounced the immortal *non possumus*,—"I will not do it, because I cannot do it." If he wants an epitaph, the most glorious language that need be written on his tomb would be: "Here lies the man whom the whole world tried to coerce to commit a sin; and who answered the whole world '*non possumus*,'—I cannot do it." This is the man that to-day wears, and so gloriously wears, the time-honored tiara that has come down to him through eighteen hundred years of suffering and of glory, of joy and of sorrow.

The third circlet,—that of the temporal power,—for a time is gone. There is a robber, who calls himself a king, seated now in the Quirinal, in Rome. He had not the decency to tell the Pope that was he was coming to plunder him. He had not the decency, when he did come to Rome, to build a house for himself; but he must take one of the old man's houses. It was a question of bringing his women into these, the Pope's own chambers, which were always like sanctuaries, where ladies generally are not permitted to come in. There was a kind of tradition of holiness about them and exclusiveness, in this way; and he brings his Queen and his "ladies all" to these chambers, where, if they had a particle of womanly decency, and delicacy, and propriety, they would not enter. I do not believe there is a lady here listening to me, who would walk into the Quirinal, to-morrow, even if she was in Rome. The third circlet, for a time, is plucked from the Pope's brow; and, instead of a crown of gold, the aged man has bent down and has received from the hands of ungrateful Italy the present of a crown of thorns. But, as if to compensate him for the temporary absence of the crown of temporal rule; as if to make up to him for that which has been plucked, for a time only, from the tiara, the Almighty God has brought out, in our age, upon the pontificate of Pius IX, the other two circlets, that of supreme Pastorate and supreme Bishop of the Church, with an additional lustre and glory that they never had before. Never in the history of the Catholic Church, have the faithful, all the world over, listened with so much reverence, with so much love, with so much faith and joy, as the Catholics of the world, to-day, listen to the voice of Pius IX in Rome. Never have the Bishops of the Catholic Church shown such unanimity, such unity of thought, such profound and magnificent obedience. Never has the Episcopate of the Catholic Church so loudly, emphatically, and unitedly upheld the privileges and the glories of its head, as the Episcopacy of this day has upheld the glory of the Papacy of Pius IX. And it is no small subject of praise and of thankfulness to us, that, when eight hundred men among them, loaded with the responsibility of the Church,—eight hundred men representing all that the Church had, of perfection, of the priesthood, and of jurisdiction and power,—when these eight hundred men were gathered around the throne of the august Pontiff, they presented to the world in its hostility, in its infidelity, in its hatred, so firm a front, that they were all of one mind, of one soul. One voice only was heard from the lips of these eight hundred; and that voice said: "*Tu es Petrus!* O Pius, Peter speaks in thee; and Christ, the Lord, speaks in Peter." One of the most honored of these eight hundred,—one of the foremost in dignity and in worth,—now sits here in the midst of you, the Bishop and pastor of your souls. He can bear living witness to the fact which I have stated. Out of the resources of his learned mind,—out of his Roman experience, as an Archbishop,—will he tell you,—out of his historic lore will he tell you,—that never was the Church of God more united, both in the priesthood and episcopacy, and in the people,—more united in ranks cemented by faith and strengthened by love, than the Christian and Catholic world to-day is, around the glorious throne of the uncrowned Pontiff, Pius IX.

And what shall be the future of the Pope's tiara? We know that the crown of universal pastorship and the crown of supremacy are his; that no man can take from him that which has grown unto him under the hand of Jesus Christ. We know that he may be in exile to-morrow, that he may be without a home, persecuted and hunted from one city to another. But we know that God and the Church of God have set their seal upon him, and their sign that no other man upon this earth can wear, namely, that he is the head of the Church, and the infallible guide of the infallible flock of Christ. Will his temporal power be restored? Will the third circle ever again shine upon that tiara? It is a singular fact that the only man who can speak of the future with certainty is the Catholic. Every other man, when he comes to discuss any subject of the future, must say: "Well, in all probability, perhaps, it may come to pass; it may be so and so." But the Catholic man, when he comes to speak of the future, says, "Such and such things are to come:" he knows it as sure as fate. There is not a man among us that does not know that this usurpation of Rome is only a question of a few days;—that the knavish king may remain this year, next year; perhaps a few years more; but, as sure as Rome is seated upon her seven hills, so surely will the third circle of the tiara be there; so surely must there be a Pope-King there. And why? For the simplest of all reasons: that her empire, or her temporal power is very convenient, and very useful, and very necessary for the Church of God; and that whatever is convenient, or useful or necessary for her, God in Heaven will provide for her. That temporal power will return as it returned in the times of old, because it is good for the Church, and because the world cannot get on without it. The hand that has held the reins of society for a thousand years and more,—the hand that has held the curb tight upon the passions, and the ambition, and the injustice of kings;—the hand that has held with a firm grasp the reins that govern the people, is as necessary in the time to come, as it was in the times past: and, therefore, God will keep that hand, that holds the reins of the world, a royal hand. Hence it is that we, Catholics, have not the slightest apprehension, the slightest fear, about this. We know that, even as our Divine Lord and Master suffered in Jerusalem, and was buried and remained for three days in the grave, and undeniably rose again, all the more glorious because of His previous sufferings,—so, in like manner, do we know that, out of the grave of his present tribulation,—out of the trials of to-day,—Pius IX, or Pius the Ninth's successor,—for the Pope lives for ever,—will rise more glorious in his empire over the world, and in his influence and power,—all the more glorious for having passed through the tribulations of the present time. But, my friends, just as the most precious hours in the life of our Lord were the hours of His suffering, —just as that was the particular time when every loving heart came to Him,—the time when the highest privileges were conferred upon mankind, namely, to wipe the sweat and blood off his brow; to take the Cross off His shoulders; to lift Him from His falling and His faintness upon the earth; so, also, the present is the hour of our highest privilege as Catholics, when we can put out our hand to cheer, to console, to help our Holy Father the Pope. This hall is crowded; and, from my priestly, Catholic, and Irish heart, I am proud of it. It is easy to acclaim a man when he is "on the top of the wheel," as they say, and every thing is going well with him. It is easy to feel proud of the Pope when the Pope shines out, acknowledged by all the kings of the earth. Ah, but it is the triumph of Catholic and of Irish faith to stand up for him, to uphold him before the world, and, if necessary to fight for him when the whole world is against him! Therefore I hope, that when the proceeds of this lecture are sent to the man, who, although poor, and in prison to-day, has kept his honor, has kept his nobility of character; and when millions were put before him by the robber-king, said he would not dirty his hands by touching them;—but when the honest and the clean money of to-night shall be sent to him, I hope that some one of those officials here will also inform him that that money was sent to him with cheers and with applause, and from loving and generous Irish Catholic hearts; that it was given, as Ireland always has given when she gave,—given with a free hand and a loving and a generous heart. As a great author and writer of our day said: "I would rather get a cold potato from an Irishman, than a guinea in gold and a dinner of beef from an Englishman."

And, now, my friends, I have only to state to you that, from my heart, I thank you for your presence here this evening. I know that the sacredness of the cause brought you here as Catholics. I flatter myself a little, that, perhaps, some of you came, because, when I was last here before you, I told you, in all sincerity, that my heart and soul were in this lecture, and that I would take it as a personal favor if the hall were crowded this evening. The hall is crowded; and I am grateful to you for your attendance, and your patience in listening to me, and for the encouragement that you gave me by your applause.

THE IMMACULATE CONCEPTION.

[*A Lecture delivered by Very Rev. T. N. Burke, O.P., in St. Andrew's Church, New York, May 19, 1872.*]

"Thou art the glory of Jerusalem; thou art the joy of Israel; thou art the honor of our people."

THESE words, dearly beloved brethren, are found in the Book of Judith, and they commemorate a great and eventful period of Jewish history. At that time, the Assyrian King sent a mighty army, under his general, Holofernes, to subdue all the nations of the earth, and to oblige them not only to forego their own national existence, but also to conform to the religion and the rites of the Assyrians. This great army the Scriptures describe to us as invincible. Their horses covered the plains; their soldiers filled the valleys; there was no power upon the earth able to resist them; until at length they came before a city of Judea, called Bethulia. They summoned the fortress, and commanded the soldiers to surrender. Now, in that town there was a woman by the name of Judith. The Scriptures say of her that she was a holy woman; that she fasted every day of her life, and that, though young and fair and beautiful to behold, she lived altogether a secluded life, absorbed in prayer to God. When she saw the outlying army of the Assyrians;—when she heard the proud claims of their general,—that the people of her race, of her nation, should resign not only their national life, but also their religion, and forsake the God of Israel,—she arose, in the might of her holiness and in the power of her strength, and she went forth from the city of Bethulia; she sought the Assyrian camp; she was brought into the presence of Holofernes himself: and at the mid hour of night, while he was sunk in his drunken slumbers, she entwined her hand in the hair of his head; she drew his own sword from the scabbard that hung by the bed; and she cut off his head, and brought it back in triumph to her people. The morning came. The army found themselves without their general.

The Jewish soldiers and people rushed down upon them, and there was a mighty slaughter and a scattering of the enemies of God and of Israel. And then the people, returning, met this wonderful woman; and the High Priest said to her these words: "Thou art the glory of Jerusalem; thou art the joy of Israel; thou art the honor of our people."

Now, dearly beloved, this is not the only woman recorded in Scripture who did great things for the people and for the Church of God; and the word of Scripture, as applied to her, was meant in a higher and a greater sense: it was meant directly for Judith; but it was meant in a far higher and nobler sense for her of whom I am come to speak to you this evening,—the Virgin Mother, who brought forth our Lord Jesus Christ into this earth. To Mary does the word apply especially, as every great, heroic woman who appears in Scripture typified her. The sister of Moses, who led the choirs of the daughters of Israel; the daughter of Jeptha, who laid down her virgin life for her people; Deborah, who led the hosts of Israel; the mother of the Maccabees, standing in the blood of her seven sons;—these, and all such women of whom the Scriptures make mention, were all types of the higher, the greater, the real, yet the ideal woman, who was in the designs of God to be " the glory of Jerusalem, the joy of Israel, and the honor of our people;" namely, the Blessed and Immaculate Virgin Mary. It is of the first of her graces that I am come to speak to you. The first of her graces was her immaculate conception. Let us consider this, and we shall see how she is " the glory of Jerusalem, the joy of Israel," and the honor of our race and of our people.

Dearly beloved, we know that, before the eyes of God, before the mind of God, before the eternal councils of God, there is no such thing as past or future as we behold it in the course of time. All that we consider in the past, in this world's history, is before the Almighty God, at this moment, as if it were at this moment taking place. All that we consider in the future, even to the uttermost stretch of eternity, is before the mind of God now, as if it were actually taking place under His eyes; for the difference between time and eternity is this: that in time—that is to say, in the span of our life and of the world's history—every thing comes in succession; event follows event, and each moment of time follows the moment that went before it; but in eternity,—in time as viewed in relation to God, when time assumes the infinite dimensions of eternity,—there is neither past nor future, but all is present under the eye of God, circumscribed by His infinite vision and His infinite wisdom. Therefore, all that ever was to take place in time, was seen and foreseen by the Almighty God. He foresaw the creation of man, although that creation did not come until after the eternal years that never had a beginning. And so He foresaw the fall of man; how the first of our race was to pollute his own nature by sin, and in that personal pollution was to pollute our whole nature, because our nature came from Him. Just as when a man poisons the fountain-head of a river,—goes up into the mountains, finds the little spring from which the river comes, that afterwards, passing into the valley, enlarges its bed and swells in its dimensions, until it rolls a mighty torrent into the ocean;—if you go up into the mountain;—if you poison the fountain-head of the little stream that comes out from under the rock;—all the waters that flow in the river-bed become infected and poisoned; because the spring and the source of the river is tainted. So also, in Adam, our nature sinned. He lay at the fountain-head of humanity; and the whole stream of our nature that flowed from him came down to you and to me with the taint and poison of sin in our blood and in our veins. Therefore does the Apostle say that "we are all born children of the wrath of God;" therefore did the Prophet of old say, "For, behold I was conceived in iniquity and in sin did my mother conceive me." God saw and foresaw all this from eternity; He saw that His creature, man, whom He made so pure, so perfect, so holy, was to be spoiled and tainted by sin. In that universal corruption, the Almighty God reserved to Himself one, and only one, of the race of mankind, and preserved that one specimen of our race unpolluted, untainted, unfallen. That one was the Blessed Virgin Mary. Certainly such a one must have existed: because the Scripture,—the inspired word of God,—speaks of such a one when it says, in the language of the Psalmist: "Thou art all fair, O my beloved, and there is no spot nor stain in thee." Who is she? Is she multiplied? Is she found here and there among the daughters of men? No; she is one and only one. Therefore the Scripture says: "My beloved, my love, my dove is one and only one." That one was the Blessed Virgin Mary. God took her and preserved her from the stream of corruption that infected our whole nature. God folded His arms of infinite sanctity around her, and took her in the very first moments of her existence,—nay, in the eternal decree that went before that existence. He folded her in the arms of His own infinite sanctity; and she is the one to whom shade or thought of sin or evil has never been allowed to approach. Why is this? Because, dearly beloved, she was destined from all eternity to be the Mother of God, who was made incarnate in her. The language of the Church is: "He was incarnate of the Holy Ghost, of the Virgin Mary, and was made man." She was destined from all eternity to be the Mother of God,—to give to the Almighty God that humanity, that body, that flesh and blood which He was to assume in His own divine person, and to make one with God by the unity of one divine person, the Second Person of the Blessed Trinity. Reflect upon this.

The Scriptures expressly tell us that nothing defiled can approach to God—that nothing with the slightest speck or stain of sin upon it can come near God. Therefore it is that, in proportion as men approach to God, in the same proportion are they immaculate. Almighty God tells us, in the Scripture, expressly, that, although all men were to be born in sin, yet there were a few, a very few, who were excepted from that general rule, because they were allowed to approach so near God. The Prophet Jeremias was excepted from that rule; and he was sanctified before he came forth from his mother's womb. "Before thou camest forth from thy mother, I sanctified thee," said the Lord. And why? Because he was destined to be a prophet, and to propound the word of God to the people. John the Baptist was sanctified in his mother's womb, and came forth in his birth free from the original sin of Adam, because he was destined to be the one among men to say: "Behold the Lamb of God who takes away the sins of the world." And if these men,—one because he was to preach the word of God, another because he was to point out God to man,—if they, because of this high function, were born without sin, surely, dearly beloved, we must conclude that the woman who was to give God His sacred humanity, the woman who was to be the Mother of God, the woman who was to afford to the Almighty God that blood by which

He wiped out the sin of the world, that woman must receive far more than either John the Baptist or Jeremias received; and the grace that she received must have been the grace of her conception without sin. And, in truth, as nothing defiled, nothing tainted, was ever allowed to approach Almighty God, the woman who approached Him nearest of all the daughters of the earth, who came nearer to God than all His Angels in Heaven were allowed to approach Him, must be the only one of whom the Scripture speaks when it says: "My beloved is one and only one, and she is all fair, and there is no spot nor stain in her."

What follows from this? It follows that the immaculate woman who was destined to be the Mother of Jesus Christ, received at the first moment of her being a grace inconceivably greater than all the grace that was given to all the Angels in heaven, to all the Saints upon the earth, because the dignity in which she was created was inconceivably greater than theirs. The highest Angel in heaven was made but to be the servant of God; Mary was created to be the Mother of God. What was that grace? Perfect purity, perfect sinlessness, perfect immaculateness, and consequently perfect love of God and highest union with Him. For, reflect, my dear friends, wheresoever the human soul is found perfectly free from sin, without spot or stain of sin, without the slightest inclination or temptation to sin,—wheresoever such a soul is found, that soul is united to the Almighty God by the highest, by the most perfect and the most intimate union of divine love. God loves all His creatures; God loves the soul of man; so that wherever He finds that there is no impediment of sin, no distortion of inclination, nothing to hinder that union, He gives himself to that soul in the most intimate and the highest form of love; and He gathers that soul to him by a most perfect union. Hence it is that perfect union with God and perfect sinlessness mean one and the same thing.

The Blessed Virgin Mary, conceived without sin, was kept and held aside to let the stream of sin flow by without touching her. The only one in whom our nature was preserved in all its pristine beauty and perfection, the blessed Virgin Mary, in that sinlessness of her conception, attained at the moment of her conception the most perfect and intimate union with God. And this,—for which all the Saints and all holy souls strive on the earth,—the very highest climax of saintly perfection,—was the first beginning of her sanctity. The saint who wearies himself during the sixty or seventy years of his life, the hermit in the desert, the martyr in the arena, all aim at this one thing,—to purge their souls most perfectly from sin, from every mortal and venial sin; to rise above their passions and their lower and sinful nature; and, in proportion as they attain to this, do they climb the summit of perfection and attain to closer union with God. That which all the saints tend to,—that which all the virgins and saints in the Church thirst for,—that which they consider as the very summit of their perfection,—that is the grace that was given to Mary at the first moment of her being;—namely, to be perfectly pure, perfectly sinless, perfectly immaculate, consequently, perfectly united to God by supreme and most intimate union. And this is the meaning of the word of Scripture: "The foundations of her are laid upon the holy mountain. The Lord loves the threshold of Zion more than all the tabernacles and tents of Judah;" more than all the accumulated perfection of all the Angels and Saints of God. Where they end is the beginning of Mary's perfection in His sight.

And now let me apply the text: "Thou art the glory of Jerusalem; thou art the joy of Israel; thou art the honor of our people." Whenever the Scriptures speak figuratively or spiritually of Jerusalem, they always allude to the Kingdom of Heaven, the kingdom of the just made perfect. The Church of God, dearly beloved, consists of three great elements or portions. There is the Church that purges, in Purgatory, the elect of God, by the slow action of divine justice, cleansing them from every stain and paying the last farthing of their debt. That is the Church Suffering. There is the Church on earth, contending against the world, the flesh, and the devil; fighting a hard and weary battle, which you and I are obliged to fight every day of our lives. We are obliged to fight against our passions and subdue them. We are obliged to fight against the powers of darkness seeking our destruction, and subdue them. We are obliged to fight with the world, surrounding us with its evil maxims, with its loose principles, with its false ideas of morality, with its bad example; and, despising all these, to conquer them. We are obliged to fight the battle of our faith. We are obliged to enter upon this, that, and the other questions, and upon these questions to take our stand as Catholics, and to fight the good fight of faith. The question of Sacraments, the question of Education, the question of the Church, the question of the Pope, the question of the injustice of the world in robbing him of all his power and of his dignity; these, and a thousand others, are the burden of the Church's battle on this earth; and, therefore, she is called the Church Militant. But the Suffering Church or the Militant Church is still the Church of God. Having passed through the battle-field of earth, having passed through the purgation of Purgatory, and having attained to the vision of God, there she triumphs; there she rejoices in the undiminished glory and the uncreated brightness of God;—and that is the Church Triumphant. Now, the Scriptures, speaking of that Kingdom of Heaven, or of the Church Triumphant, mentions it under the name of Jerusalem. For instance: "I saw," says the inspired Evangelist, "the New Jerusalem descending from Heaven, as a bride arrayed for her bridegroom." St. Paul, speaking of the same Kingdom, says: "Thou art come to Mount Zion, and to the city of the living God, the heavenly Jerusalem, and to the kingdom of the just made perfect." Jerusalem, therefore, as expressed in the words of my text, "Thou art the glory of Jerusalem," means the Church Triumphant. It means the glorious assemblage of all the Angels of God; it means the glorious society of all the Saints of God; it means all that Heaven or earth ever held or had of noble, generous, self-sacrificing and devoted, now crowned with the everlasting glory of the presence of God. And of that assemblage of the Church Triumphant Mary is the glory. She is the glory: and why? Because, as the Scripture tells us expressly, the Angels of God are interested in the affairs of this world. Our Lord, speaking of little children, says: "Woe to you who scandalize them; because their Angels see the face of my Father." Elsewhere He says: "There is more joy in Heaven for one sinner doing penance than for ninty-nine just who need not repentance." If, then, the Angels in Heaven rejoice at every new manifestation of the glory and omnipotence of God; if their glory is to contemplate the Almighty God in His works; it follows that, whenever they see these works destroyed, whenever they see the purposes of the Almighty God frustrated, whenever they see the work and the mercy of God ruined, they must grieve, as far as they are capable of grieving, because they rejoice when that work is restored by repentance. They, therefore, looking down from their high places in Heaven, beheld with great joy the new-born race of men; they beheld the work of God, most perfect in our first parents, Adam and Eve. They saw in the first woman that was created the woman who was destined in her progeny to people Heaven with saints, and to fill the thrones that were left vacant there by the defection of the rebel angels. Their glory was that their choirs before God might be filled, and that the chorus of Heavenly music might be perfect in its harmony by the filling of their places. They saw that one-third of their angelic brethren had fallen into hell, and left the halls of Heaven more or less empty by their fall. They waited,—they waited for many years,—we know not how long: we know not but that that time of waiting may have extended for thousands of years;—until, at length, they beheld the Creator make the new creature, man. They knew the destinies of man; they knew that this woman, who was created upon the earth, was to be the mother of the race that was to fill up their choirs, and to fulfil and make perfect their glory in Heaven. Oh, how sad was their disappointment!—oh, how terrible was their grief, when they saw Eve fall into sin, and become the mother of a race of reprobates, and not of saints, and her destiny change; that she should people hell with reprobates rather than fulfil her high destiny and people Heaven with saints. Mary arose. The earth beheld her face. Her coming was as the rising of the morning star, which, trembling in its silvery beauty over the eastern hills, tells the silent and the darkened world that the bright sun is about to follow it and dispel the darkness of the night by the splendor and the brightness of its shining. Mary arose; and when the Angels of God beheld her, their glory was fulfilled; for now they knew that the mother of the Saints was come, and that the woman was created who was to do what had failed in Eve,—to people Heaven and fill Heaven's choirs with the progeny of saints in everlasting glory. Therefore did they hail her coming with angelic joy. Oh, what joy was theirs when they looked down upon the earth and beheld the fallen race of man restored in all its first integrity in Mary! Oh, what joy was theirs who rejoiced when Magdalen arose in all the purity of her repentance;—they who rejoice and make the vaults of Heaven ring with their joy when you or I make a good confession, and do penance for our sins! Oh, what must their joy have been, and the riot of their delight and of their glory, when Mary arose, and they beheld, in her, the mother of all those who are ever to be saved, the mother of all true penitents, the mother of all the elect of God; for, becoming the mother of Jesus Christ, she has become the mother of all the just. Therefore, she is the glory of the heavenly Jerusalem. Therefore did these Angels, on the day of her assumption, joyfully come to Heaven's gate, and fill the mid-air with the sound of their triumph, when Heaven's Queen, the Mother of God, was raised to the place of her glory. "The morning stars praised the Lord together, and all the suns of God made a joyful melody." The glory of Jerusalem, the Angels' glory is concentrated in the glory of God. Whatever gives glory to God glorifies them. Now, in all the works of God, He is most glorified in Mary, as we shall see; and therefore Mary is the glory of the heavenly Jerusalem, and the delight of God's blessed Spirits and Angels in His everlasting kingdom.

But she is more; she is "the joy of Israel." What is this Israel? Jerusalem was the summit of Israel's triumphs. Israel had to fight for many a weary year before the foundations of the Holy City were laid. Israel, that is to say, the Jewish people, passed through the desert, crossing the Red Sea, fighting with their enemies, there to wait for many a long and weary year, until the Holy City of Jerusalem was raised up in all its beauty, and until the temple of God was founded there. And just as that city, Jerusalem, represents the Church Triumphant, so by the name of Israel the inspired writer meant the Church Militant, the Church in the desert of this earth, the Church passing through the Red Sea of the martyrs' blood, the Church crossing swords with every enemy of God, and fighting and bearing the burden and heat of the day. Of that Church Militant, of that Israel of God, Mary is the joy. Why? Dearly beloved, Christ, our Lord, founded His Church for one express purpose, and it was that, where sin had abounded, sin might be destroyed and grace abound still more. "For this I am come," He says, "that where sin hath abounded grace might abound still more." Wherever, therefore, there is a victory over sin by Divine grace, there is the joy of the Church Militant, because there is her work accomplished. Wherever the sinner rises out of his sin, and does penance and returns to God, there the Church triumphs, her mission is fulfilled, the purpose for which she was created is accomplished, and her joy is great in proportion. Now where has grace so triumphed as in Mary? Sin abounded in this world. Christ came and shed His blood that grace might take the place of sin, and superabound where sin had abounded before. Where has grace so triumphed over sin as in Mary! Great is the triumph of grace when it expels sin from the sinner's soul and makes that which was impure to be purified, and makes that which was unjust to be glorified by sanctity before God. Oh, still greater is the triumph when grace can so anticipate sin as never to allow it to make its appearance! The most perfect triumph of grace is in the utter exclusion of sin. Therefore, it is that Christ, our Lord, in His sacred humanity, was grace itself personified in man; because in Him there was essential holiness, and an utter impossibility of the approach of sin. If, therefore, the joy of the Church be in proportion to the triumph of grace over sin, surely she must be "the joy of Israel," and the first fruits of the Church, the only one that this mystical body of Christ can offer to God as perfectly acceptable; the only soul, the only creature that the Church can offer to God and say: "Lord, look down from Heaven upon this child and daughter of mine; she is Thy beloved in whom there is no spot nor stain. She is the joy of Israel."

Oh, my dearly beloved, need I tell you,—you who were born in the faith like myself; you who come from Catholic stock, who come from Catholic blood; you in whose veins, in whose Irish veins, hundreds of years of Catholic faith and Catholic sanctity are flowing,—need I tell you of the woman whose name, preached by Patrick, fourteen hundred years ago, has been, from that hour to this, Ireland's greatest consolation in the midst of her sorrows? In the loss of fortune, in the loss of property, in the loss of liberty, in the loss of national existence, every Irish Catholic has been consoled in the midst of his privations, by the thought that the Mother of God loved him, and that he had a claim upon Mary Mother. Well do I remember one whose expression embodied all of Irish faith and Irish love for Mary; an old woman whom I met, weeping over a grave, lying there with a broken heart, waiting only for the kind hand of Death to put her into the dust where all she had loved had gone before her; forgotten by all, abandoned by all, the hand of misery and poverty upon her; and when I would console and speak to her of heaven and of heaven's glory; when I endeavored to lighten the burden of her sorrow by consolation; she turned to me and said: "Oh, Father, you need not speak to me. The cross may be heavy, but the Virgin Mary's cross was heavier than mine." She forgot her sorrows in her great love for Mary. Nay, that love, even in her sorrow, was as a gleam of hope, one ray of joy let in upon the soul that otherwise might have despaired. And thus it is that Mary,—the knowledge of her love for us, the knowledge of our claim upon her, through her divine Son, and the knowledge of the divine commission that He gave her upon the Cross, to be the Mother of all that were ever to love Him,—is the one ray of joyful and divine consolation that Christ, our Lord, lets in upon every wounded spirit, and every loving, grieving heart.

Finally, she is "the honor of our people." Dear friends, the Almighty God when He created us made man in perfection: "*Deus fecit hominem rectum.*" He gave to man a mighty intelligence, a high and a pure love, and a freedom of will asserting the dominion of the soul over the body, and through that body the dominion of man over all creatures. Every thing on this earth obeyed him. The eagle, flying in the upper air, closed his wings and came to earth to pay homage to the unfallen man. The lion and the tiger, at the sound of his voice, came forth from their lairs to lick the feet of their imperial master, the unfallen man. As every thing without him was obedient to him, so every thing within him was obedient to the dictates of his clear reason and to the empire of his will. In this was the honor of God reflected as it was invested in man. God gave him intelligence. God is wisdom: His wisdom was invested in man. God gave him love. God is love: and the purity of that love was reflected in the affections of unfallen man. God is power, empire, and freedom: and the empire of God, and the freedom of God, were reflected in the free will of man, in the imperial sway in which he commanded all creatures. Thus was the honor of God invested in us. Now, sin came and destroyed all this. The serpent came and whispered his temptation in the ears of the vain and foolish woman, who, unmindful of all that she had, risked all and lost all for the gratification of her appetite and of her womanly curiosity. The serpent came and told Eve to rebel against God. Eve rebelled; she induced Adam to rebel; and, in this two-fold rebellion, man lost all that God had given him of grace and of supernatural gifts. All of divine honor that God Almighty had reflected in man, all of divine glory that he had imparted to man, all was lost. The intelligence was darkened; the affections were depraved; the freedom of the soul was enslaved; and man was no longer the high, and pure, and perfect image of his Creator.

Now, as we have seen in that sin of Adam, not only was that man himself destroyed and corrupted, but the whole race of mankind was corrupted in him. How is Mary the honor of our people? She is the honor of our people in this, that where all was ruined, she alone was preserved; that, but for her and her immaculate conception, neither God in Heaven, nor Saint nor Angel in Heaven, nor man upon the earth would ever again look upon the face of unfallen man. The work of God would have been completely destroyed; not a vestige would remain of what man was as he came from his Creator's hand, but that the Almighty preserved one unfallen specimen of our race, to show His Angels and His Saints in Heaven, and to show all men upon the earth, what a glorious humanity was the untainted nature which God had invested in man. She is the solitary boast of our fallen nature. Take Mary away; deprive her of the grace of her immaculate conception; let the slightest taint of sin come in;—she is spoiled like the rest of us: and the Almighty God has not retained, in the destruction of our race, one single specimen of unfallen nature. But not so; for God in all His works may allow **His enemy to** prevail against Him; He may allow the spirit of **evil to** come **in, and spoil** and taint and destroy His works; but He **never** allows His works to be utterly destroyed: never. When mankind fell from God and from grace, so that the image of God disappeared, and the spirit of God from among them; and the Almighty found it necessary to destroy the whole race of man in the Deluge,— He preserved Noah, and his sons, and his daughters. Eight souls were preserved, while hundreds of millions were destroyed; but God, in these eight souls, preserved the race, and did not allow the spirit of evil to utterly destroy His work. When God drew back again the bolts of heaven, and allowed the living fire of His wrath to fall upon Sodom and Gomorrah, and destroyed the whole nation, yet even then He saved Lot and his family; and a few were saved, where all the rest were lost. When the Almighty resolved to destroy, for their impurity, the race of Benjamin, yet He preserved a few, lest the whole tribe might be utterly destroyed.

And thus it is that we find the Almighty God always preserving one or two specimens of His work, lest the devil might glory overmuch, and riot in his joy for having utterly destroyed the work of God. Our nature was destroyed in Eve. One fair specimen of all that could be in us,—of all that was in Adam before his sin,—of all that God intended us to be,—one fair specimen of all this was preserved in Mary, who, in her immaculate conception, enshrined in the infinite holiness of God, was preserved untainted and unfallen, as if Adam had never sinned. It may be asked, if, then, this woman was without sin, if she was conceived without sin, how is it that she calls Christ her Saviour, saying: "My soul doth magnify the Lord, and my spirit hath rejoiced in God, my Saviour." Oh, my friends, need I tell you that Christ, our Lord, is as much the Saviour of Mary as He is your Saviour or mine? Need I tell you that, but for His incarnation, but for His suffering and passion and death, Mary could not have received the grace of her immaculate conception, any more than you or I could have received the grace of our baptism? Baptism has done for us, as far as regards the removal of original sin, all that her immaculate conception did for Mary. For the four thousand years that went before the incarnation of the Son of God, every child of Adam that was saved, was saved through the anticipated merits of the blood that was shed upon Calvary. Adam himself was saved, Moses was saved, Abraham, Isaac, and Jacob, Daniel, all the Prophets, all the Saints were saved by their faith in the Son of God, and by the prevision of His merits before His Eternal Father. The merits of the Son of God, as yet unincarnate, yet foreseen and applied, thousands of years before their time, to the souls of the Patriarchs and the Prophets,—the self-same merits were applied to the soul of Mary in the eternal design of God, in her immaculate conception. He is as much her Saviour as He is ours; only He saved her in a way quite different from that in which we were saved. You may save a man, for instance, by keeping him from going into the way of danger; you may save a child by taking it out of the street, when some dangerous procession is passing, or when some railway engine is passing—something that may endanger its life; or you may save the same child, when in immediate danger, by the touch of your powerful and saving hand, and restore it to life. So, the Almighty God saved Mary by preventing the evil, just as He saves us by cleansing us from the evil which has already fallen on us. Hence it is that she, more than any of us, had reason to call Christ, her Son, her Lord and her Saviour. "My soul doth magnify the Lord," she said, "and my spirit hath rejoiced in God my Saviour." Truly He was her Saviour. Truly He shows His power in the manner in which He saved her. He did not permit her to be immersed in the ocean of sin. He did not take her, as something filthy and defiled, and wash her soul in the laver of Baptism; but he applied the graces of Baptism to her conception; so that she came into this world all pure, all holy, all immaculate, just as the Christian child comes forth from the baptismal font.

Behold, then, how she is the glory of the heavenly Jerusalem, the joy of the earthly Church of Israel, and the honor of our people; seeing that, if Mary were not as she is in Heaven, immaculate and unstained, that Heaven would be, after all, only a congregation of penitents. Every other soul that enters Heaven enters as a Magdalen—at least, as Magdalen rising from original sin. Mary alone entered Heaven, as Eve would have entered if she had resisted the evil and conquered the temptation of sin. Thus do we behold the Mother of God as she shines forth before us in the prophecy of Scripture—an honor and a triumph and a symbol of God's complete victory. The victory that God gains over sin is not complete when He has to come to remedy that evil after it has fallen upon the soul. The complete triumph of God is when He is able to preserve the soul from any approach of that evil, and to keep it in all its original purity and immaculateness and innocence.

Such was the woman whom the Prophet beheld: "And a great sign appeared in Heaven—a woman clothed with the sun, and the moon under her feet, and on her head a crown of twelve stars." Of what was this woman a sign? She was the sign of the victory of God; for he adds: "And I saw another sign in Heaven, a great dragon coming to devour the woman and to destroy her; but it was cast forth and there was no room for him nor place for him any more in Heaven." And Mary shone forth, in the eternal council of God, the very sign and type, promise and symbol of God's victory over sin. God's victory over sin was complete, as every victory of God is; and the completeness of that victory was embodied in the immaculate conception of Mary.

What wonder, then, my dearly beloved, that we should honor one whom God has so loved to honor! What wonder that we should hail her as all-pure; hail her from earth, whom God hailed from Heaven, saying: "Thou art all fair, my beloved, and there is no stain in thee!" What wonder that we should rejoice in her who is the joy and the glory of the heavenly Jerusalem! What wonder that we should sing praises to her; put her forth as the very type of purity, innocence, and virtue, whom the Almighty God so filled with all his highest gifts, that Heaven and earth never beheld such a creature as Mary; that the very Angel, coming down from before the throne of God, was astonished when he beheld her greatness; and, bending in his human form before her, said: "All hail to thee, O Mary, for thou art full of grace;" and when she trembled at his words, he assured her, saying: "Fear not, O Mary, for thou hast found grace before the Lord." Oh, how grand was her finding! Grace was lost by the first woman, Eve: and every daughter of earth sought it for four thousand years, and found it not. How could they find it? They came into this world without it. How could they find that grace which Eve had lost? They came tainted by Eve's sin upon this earth. Mary alone found it—the grace of immaculate creation, the grace of primeval purity. Therefore, the Angel said to her:—"Fear not, I tell thee thou shalt be the mother of God, and that He that is to be born of thee shall be called the Son of the Most High. Yet, O woman, fear not, for I say to thee, that thou hast found grace before the Lord." Therefore do we honor her, my dearly beloved; therefore do we rejoice that she, being such as she is, is still our mother and regards us with a mother's love; and we can look up to her with the unsuspecting and all-confiding love of childhood. O mother mine!—O mother of all the nations!—O mother that kept the faith in that land of our mothers, that through temptation and suffering never lost her love for thee,—that, famished and famine-stricken, never lost the faith,—I hail thee! As thou art in Heaven to-night, clothed with the sun of divine justice, with the moon reflecting all earthly virtues beneath thy feet, and upon thy head a crown of twelve stars,—God's brightest gift,—I hail thee, O mother! And in the name of the Catholic Church, and in the name of my Catholic people, and in the name of the far-off and loved land that ever loved thee, I proclaim that "thou art the glory of Jerusalem, thou art the joy of Israel, and thou art the honor of our people!

CATHOLIC EDUCATION.

[*A Lecture delivered by the Very Rev. T. N. Burke, O.P., in St. Peter's Church, New York, May 23, 1872.*]

I PROPOSE to speak to you, my dear friends, this evening, on the question of "Catholic Education." My attention was attracted, this morning, to a notice in one of the leading papers of this city, in which the writer warned me, that, if I was not able to find a solution for this difficult question of Education, which would be acceptable to all classes, I might please my co-religionists, but that I could not please the public. While I am grateful to the writer of that article, or to any one else that gives me advice, I have to tell you, my friends, and the writer of that notice, and everybody else, that I am not come to this country, nor have I put on this habit to please either the public or my co-religionists, but to announce the truth of God, in the name of His holy Church. He who accepts it, and believes it, and acts upon it, shall be saved: he that does not choose to believe, Christ, our Lord, Himself says shall be condemned. God help us! God pity the people whose religious teachers have to try and "*please their co-religionists and the public!*" Great Lord! how terrible it is when the spirit of farce and of unreality finds its way, even into the mind of the man who is to proclaim the truth by which alone his fellow-men and himself can be saved! But it was remarked, and truly, in the same article, that "this is one of the most—perhaps, *the* most,—important questions of the day." No doubt, it is. I do not suppose I could have a more important theme for the subject of my thoughts or of my words, than that of Education. This is a question that comes home to every man among us. No man can close his mind against it. No man can shut it out from his thoughts. No man in the community can fold his arms and say, "This is a question which does not concern me, consequently upon which I am indifferent." No: and why? Because every man among us is obliged to live in society: that is to say, in inter-communion with his fellow-men. Every man's happiness or misery depends, in a large degree, upon the state of society, in which he lives. If the associations that surround us are good, and holy, and pure; if our children are obedient; if our servants are honest; if our friends are loyal, and our neighbors are peaceable; if the persons who supply us with the necessaries of life are reliable,—how far all these things go to smooth away all the difficulties, and annoyances, and anxieties of life! And yet, all this depends mainly upon education. If, on the other hand, our children be rude, disobedient, and wilful; if those around us be dishonest, so that we must be constantly on our guard against them; if our friends be false, so that we know not upon whose word to rely; if every thing we use and take to clothe ourselves be bad, and adulterated, or poisonous; how miserable all this makes life! And yet, these issues, I say again, depend mainly upon education. Therefore, it is a question that comes home to every man, and from which no man can excuse himself, or plead indifference or unconcern.

Now, first of all, my friends, consider, that the greatest misfortune that Almighty God can let fall upon any man is the curse of utter ignorance, or want of education. The Holy Ghost, in the Scriptures, expressly tells us that this absence of knowledge, this absence of instruction and education, is the greatest curse that can fall upon a man, because it not only unfits him for his duties to God, and for the fellowship of the elect of God, and for every Godlike and eternal purpose, but it also unfits him for the society of his human kind; and therefore the Scripture says so emphatically,—"Man, when he was in honor," (that is to say, created in honor,) "lost his knowledge." He had no knowledge. What followed? He was compared to the senseless beasts,—made like to them. What is it that distinguishes man from the brute? Is it strength of limb? No! Is it gracefulness of form? No! Is it acute sensations—a sense of superior sight, or a more intense and acute sense of hearing? No! In all these things many of the beasts that roam the forest exceed us. We have not the swiftness of the stag;—we have not the strength of the lion;—we have not the beautiful grace of the antelope of the desert;—we have not the power to soar into the upper air, like the eagle, who lifts himself upon strong pinions and gazes on the sun. We have not the keen sense of sight of many animals, nor the keen sense of hearing of others. In what, then, lies the difference and the superiority of man. Oh, my dear friends, it lies in the intelligence that can know, and the heart which, guided by that intelligence, is influenced to love for intellectual motives, and in the will which is supposed to preserve its freedom by acting under the dominion of that enlightened intellect and mind. For, mark you, it is not the mere power of knowing that distinguishes man from the brutes, and brings him to the perfection of his nature. It is the actual presence of knowledge. It is not the mere power of loving that distinguishes man from the lower creatures. No. For if that love be excited by mere sensuality,—by the mere appeal to the senses,—it is not the high human love of man, but it is the mere lust of desire and passion of the brute. It is not the will that distinguishes man in the nobility of his nature from the brute; but it is the will, preserving its freedom, keeping itself free from the slavery and dominion of brute passions, and answering quickly—heroically—to every dictate of the high, and holy, and enlightened intelligence that is in man. What follows from this? It follows that if you deprive man of intelligence or knowledge;—if you leave him in utter ignorance, and withdraw education, you thereby starve, and, as far as you can, annihilate the very highest portion of the soul of man; you thereby dwarf all his spiritual powers; you thereby leave that soul, which was created to grow, and to wax strong, and to be developed by knowledge,—you leave it in the imbecility and the helplessness of its natural, intellectual, and spiritual infancy. What follows from this? It follows that the uneducated, uninstructed, ignorant, dwarfed individual is incapable of influencing the affections of the heart with any of the higher motives of love. It follows that, if that heart of man is ever to love, it will not love upon the dictate of the intelligence guiding it to an intellectual object, but, like the brute beast of the field, it will seek the gratification of all its desires upon the mere brutal, corporeal evidence of its senses. What follows moreover? It follows that the will which was created by the Almighty God in freedom, and which, by the very composition of man's nature, was destined to exercise that freedom under the dictates of intelligence, is now left without its proper ruler,—an intelligent, instructed intellect; and, therefore, in the uninstructed man, the allegiance of the will—the dominion of the will—is transferred to the passions, to the desires and depraved inclinations of man's lower nature. And so we see that, in the purely and utterly uninstructed man, there can be no loftiness of thought, no real purity of affection; nor can there be any real intellectual action of the will of man. Therefore, I conclude that the greatest curse Almighty God can let fall upon a man is the curse of utter ignorance, unfitting him thereby for every purpose of God and every purpose of society.

First, then, my dear friends, I assert that want of education, or ignorance, unfits a man for his position, no matter how humble it be, in this world and in society. For all human society exists among men, and not among inferior animals, because of the existence in men of intelligence. All human society or intercourse is based upon intellectual communication;—thought meeting thought; intellectual sympathy corresponding with the sympathy of others. But the man who is utterly uninstructed; the man who has never been taught to read or write; the man who has never been taught to exercise any act of his intelligence;—the poor, neglected child that we see about our streets, growing up without receiving any word of instruction,—that child grows up,—rises to manhood utterly unfit to communicate with his fellow-men, for he is utterly unprepared for that intercommunion of intelligence and intellect which is the function of society. What follows? He cannot be an obedient citizen, because he cannot even apprehend in his mind the idea of law. He cannot be a prosperous citizen, because he can never turn to any kind of labor which would require the slightest mental effort. In other words he cannot labor as a man. He is condemned by his intellectual imbecility to labor merely with his hands. Mere brute force distinguishes his labor; and the moment you reduce a man to the degree and amount of corporeal strength,—the moment you remove from his labor the application of intellect,—that moment he is put in competition with the beasts; and they are stronger than he; therefore he is inferior to them. Take the utterly uninstructed man: he it is that is the enemy of society. He cannot meet his fellow-men in any kind of intellectual intercommunion. He is shut out from all that the past tells him in the history of the world: from all the high present interests that are pressing around him: from all his future he is shut out by his utter destitution of all religious as well as civil education. What follows from this? Isolated as he is, flung back upon his solitary self,—no humanizing touch, no gentle impulse, no softening influence even of sorrow or trouble,—no aspiration for something better than the present moment,—no remorse for sin,—no consolation for pain,—no relief in affliction,—nothing of all this remains to him. An isolated, solitary man, such as you or I might be, if in one moment, by God's visitation, all that we have ever learned should be wiped out of our minds,—all our past lost to us,—all the aspirations of the future cut off from us;—such is the ignorant man; and such society recognizes him to be. If there be a man who makes the State and the government of the State to tremble, it is the thoroughly uninstructed and uneducated man;—it is the class neglected in early youth, and cast aside and utterly uninstructed and undeveloped in their souls, in their hearts, and in their intellects. It is this class that, from time to time, comes to the surface, in some wild revolution,—swarming forth in the streets of London, or the streets of Paris, or in the streets of the great Continental cities of Europe;—swarming forth, no one knows from whence; coming forth from their cellars; coming forth from out the dark places of the city; with fury unreasoning in their eyes, and the cries of demons upon their lips. These are the men that have dyed their hands red in the best blood of Europe, whether it came from the throne or the altar. It is the thoroughly uninstructed, uneducated, neglected child of society that rises in God's vengeance against the world and the society that neglected him;—that pays them back with bitter interest for the neglect of his soul in his early youth. Therefore it is that statesmen and philosophers cry out, in this our day, " We must educate the people." And the great cry is education. Quite true!

And if the world demands education, much more does the Catholic Church. She is the true mother, not merely of the masses, as they are called, but of each and every individual soul among them. She it is to whose hands God has committed the eternal interests of man: and therefore it is with a zeal far greater than that of the world, the Catholic Church applies herself to the subject and question of education. Why so? Because if, as we have seen, all human society is based upon knowledge—upon inter-communion of intellect,—of which the uninstructed man is incapable,—the society which is called the Church—the supernatural and divine society,— is also much more emphatically founded upon the principles of knowledge. What is the foundation, the bond, the link, the life and soul of the Catholic Church? I answer—faith. Faith in God. Faith in every word that God has revealed. Faith, stronger than any human principle of belief, opinion, or conviction. Faith, not only bowing down before God, but apprehending what God speaks; clasping that truth to the mind, and informing the intelligence with its light, admitting it as a moral influence into every action and every motive of a man's life. It is the soul and life of the Catholic Church. Faith! What is faith? It is an act of the intelligence whereby we know and believe all that God has revealed. Faith, then, is knowledge? Most certainly! Is it an act of the will? No; not directly—not essentially—not immediately. It is, directly, essentially, and immediately, an act of the intellect, and not of the will. It is the intellect that is the subject wherein faith resides. The will may command that intellect to bow down and believe; but the essential act of faith is an act of the intelligence, receiving light and accepting it; and that light is knowledge; therefore the Catholic Church cannot exist without knowledge.

More than this, the world has many duties which it imposes upon man, which require no education, little or nothing of instruction;—for instance, the duty of labor, where one man, educated and instructed, taking his position at the head of the works, or the engineering, is able to direct ten thousand men: there, among these ten thousand, no great amount of instruction or education is necessary or required. But the Catholic Church, on the other hand, imposes a great many tasks upon her children, every one of them requiring not only intellect, but highly trained and well-educated intellect. Look through the duties that the Church imposes upon us. Every one of these duties is intellectual. The Church commands us to pray. Prayer involves a knowledge of God; a knowledge of our own wants, and a knowledge how to elevate our souls to God; for prayer is an elevation of the soul; and the uninstructed soul cannot elevate inself to the apprehension of a pure spiritual being. The Church commands us to prepare for confession. That involves a knowledge of the law of

God, in order that we may examine ourselves, and see wherein we have failed;—that involves a knowledge of ourselves, in order to study ourselves that we may discover our sins. Preparation for confession involves a knowledge of God's claim to our love, in order that we may find motives for our sorrow. The Church commands us to approach the Holy Communion. That approach involves the high intellectual act whereby we are able with heart and with mind to realize the unseen, invisible, yet present God, and to receive Him. We see the strong act of the intellect realizing the unseen, and transcending the evidence of the senses, so as to make that unseen, invisible presence act upon us more strongly,—agitate us more violently,—than the strongest emotion that the evidence of the senses can give. The Church commands us to understand what her Sacraments are; and that is a high intellectual act, whereby we recognize God's dealings with man through the agency of material things. In a word, every single duty the Catholic Church imposes is of the highest intellectual character.

Again: though the world demands knowledge and education as the very first elements in its society, still the motive-power that the world proposes to every man is self-interest; the appeal that the world makes through the thousand channels through which it comes to us, is all an appeal to self. All the professions, all the mercantile operations, all the duties and pleasures of life, appeal to the individual to seek his own self-aggrandizement—his own self-indulgence;—to make life happy and pleasant to himself. Not so with the Church; faith is her foundation; and the motive she puts before every man is not self, but charity. Just as self concentrates the heart of man, narrows his intellectual and spiritual horizon, makes him turn in upon his own contracted being, and so narrows every intellectual and spiritual power within him; charity, on the other hand, which is the motive propounded by the Church, enlarges and expands the heart of man, enlarges the horizon of his intellectual view, and lifts him up above himself. Like a man climbing the mountain side, every foot that he ascends he beholds the horizon enlarging and widening around him. So, also, every Catholic, the more he enters into the spirit of his holy religion, the more does he perceive the intellectual, moral, and spiritual horizon enlarging,—taking in more interests and manifesting more beauties of a spiritual order. So it is with the Church of God. She depends more upon education than even the world, both upon the fundamental principle of faith, which is an act of the intellect, and the motive of action, which is charity, which is an expansion of the intellect; and also upon the nature of the duties which she imposes upon her children, and which are all of the highest intellectual character.

And yet, my friends, strange to say, among the many oddities of this age of ours, there is a singular delusion which has taken hold of the Protestant mind, that the Catholic Church is opposed to education: that she is anxious to keep the people ignorant; that she is afraid to let them read; that she does not like to see schools opened, and that she is afraid of enlightenment. They argue so blindly and yet so complacently, that when you find a good-natured and good-humored Protestant man or woman calmly talking about these things, it is difficult to keep from laughing;—it is easy enough to keep your temper, but very hard to keep from laughing. For instance: talking about Spain or Mexico; calmly and complacently telling how the whole country is to become Protestant as soon as the whole people "learn how to read, you know!" and "begin to reason, you know!" "If we can only get good schools amongst them." Then they believe the infernal lies told them; for instance, the lie is told that, in Rome, since Victor Emmanuel entered it, thirty-six schools had been opened,—taking it for granted there were no schools there before! I lived twelve years in Rome, under the Pope, and there was a school in almost every street: not a child in Rome was uneducated. Nay more; the Christian Brothers and the Nuns went out in the streets of Rome, regularly, every morning, and went from house to house, and up stairs in the tenement houses, among the poor people, picking up the children; or if they found a little boy running in the streets, he was taken quietly to school. They went out regularly to pick up the children out of the streets. And yet these men who are interested in blinding the foolish Protestant mind, come with such language as this; for it is the popular idea, which they wish to perpetuate, that the Catholic Church is afraid of education. No, my friends: the Catholic Church is afraid of one man more than any other, and that is the man who is thoroughly ignorant. The man who brings disgrace upon his religion is the thoroughly ignorant man, if he is a professed Catholic; and the man impossible to make a Catholic of, is the thoroughly ignorant Protestant. The more ignorant he is, the less chance there is of making a Catholic of him. The truth is, in this day of ours, the great conversions made to the Catholic Church, in this country and Europe, from Protestantism, all take place among the most enlightened, and highly educated, and cultivated people. Why? Because the more the Protestant reads,—the more he knows,—the nearer he approaches to the Catholic Church, the true fountain-head and source of education. Why is this accusation brought against the Catholic Church, that she is afraid of this and afraid of that? I will tell you. Because she insists, in the teeth of the world, and in spite of the world's pride, and ignorance, and bloated self-sufficiency,—the Catholic Church insists, as she has insisted for eighteen hundred and seventy-two years, on saying: "I know how to teach; you do not: you must come to me;—you cannot live without me. Do not imagine you can live by yourselves, or you will fall back into the slough of your own impurity and corruption." The world does not like to hear this. The Catholic Church insists that she alone understands what education means: the world does not like to hear that. But I come here to-night to prove it, not only to you, my Catholic friends, my co-religionists, but, if there be one here who is not a Catholic, to him also; and so to please the public if they choose to be pleased. But if my co-religionists or the public choose to be displeased, the truth is there, personified in the Church; and that truth will remain after the co-religionists and the indignant public are all swept away.

There are three systems of education that are before us in this country. There are three classes of men that are talking about education; namely,—those who go for what is called a thoroughly secular system; those who go for a denominational system, as far as it is Protestant; and the Catholic, who goes in for Catholic education. Let us examine the three. There is a large class, in England and in America, who assume the tone of the philosopher, and who, with great moral dignity and infinite presumption, lay down the law for their neighbors, and tell them:—"There is no use quarrelling, my dear Baptists and Methodists,—and you, pestering Catholics, on the other hand; you want your schools; every one wants his own school; let us adopt a beautiful system of education, that will take in every one, and leave your religious differences among yourselves: let us do away with religion altogether. The child has a great deal to be taught independent of religion. There is history, philosophy, geography, geology, engineering, steam works; all these things can be taught without any reference to God at all. So let us do this: let us adopt *non-sectarian* education." Now, my friends, these are two big words: non-sectarian,—a word of five syllables,—and education,—nine syllables altogether. Now, when people adopt great, big words in this way, you should always be on your guard against them; because if I wanted to palm off something not true, I would not set it out in plain English, but try to involve it in big words; for, as the man in the story says,—" If it is not sense, at least, it is Greek." So, these two words, non-sectarian education, if you wish to know what they mean,—turn it into English—non-sectarian education, in good old Saxon English, means *teaching without God:* five syllables. Teaching your children, fathers and mothers, and educating them without God! Not a word about God, no more than if God did not exist! He can be spoken of in the family; He may be preached in the temple or in the church; but there is one establishment in the land where God must not come in; where God must not be mentioned; and that establishment is the place where the young are to receive the education that is to determine their life, both for time and eternity:—the place where the young are to receive that education upon which eternity depends. The question of heaven or hell for every child there depends upon that education; and that education must be given without one mention of the name of the God of heaven!

Try to let it enter into your minds what this amiable system is. This beautiful system is founded upon two principles —those two principles lie at the bottom of it—namely:— The first principle is, that man can attain perfection without the aid of Jesus Christ at all. This system of education does not believe in Christ. It is the Masonic principle; the principle of the Freemasons over again;—namely, that God has made us so that, without any help from Him at all, without any shadow of grace, or sacrament, or religion, we can work out perfection in ourselves; therefore, we are independent of

God. It is the last result of human pride; and hence the secular education which does not take cognizance of God says, we can bring up these children to be what they ought to be, without teaching them any thing about God. The second principle upon which it is based is, that the end of human life, under the Christian dispensation, is not what Christ our Lord, or St. Paul, supposed it be, but something else. The Scripture says, that the end of the Christian's purposes, in this life, should be to incorporate himself with the Lord Jesus Christ, and to grow into the fulness of his age and his manhood in Christ; to put on the Lord, the unity, the love, the generosity, and every virtue of our divine Lord and Saviour. This is to be the end of the Christian man; the purpose of his life, on which all depends. Now, these principles are expressly denied on the part of those who teach without God. Can they teach without God—the Almighty God, who has them in the hollow of his hand? The principle is absurd in itself. To teach human sciences without God, is an impossibility. For instance, can you teach history without God. The very first passage of history says:—" In the beginning, God created the heavens and the earth:" and, therefore, in this system of education, the professor of history, the teacher, must say: "My dear children, I am going to teach you history; but I must not begin at the beginning; for there we find God, and He is not allowed in the school!" Can you teach philosophy without God? Philosophy is defined to be the pursuit after wisdom. It is the science that traces effects to their causes; and the philosopher proceeds from the existence of the first cause; and that first cause is God; therefore, the philosophy that excludes God must begin with the second cause; just as if a man wanted to teach a little boy how to cast up sums, and he said—"We will begin with number two; there is no number one." The child would turn round and say:—"Is not number two a multiplication of number one?—how can there be a number two unless there is a number one to be multiplied?" Can a man teach the alphabet and leave out the first letter *A*, and say, let us begin with the second letter *B*? Such is the attempt to teach philosophy or history without God. Can they teach geology without God? Can they exclude from their disquisitions upon the earth, and the earth's surface, and the soil of the earth,—can they exclude the

Creator's hand? They attempt to do it; but in their very attempt they preach their infidelity. Hence, no man can teach geology without being either a profound and pious believer in Revelation, or an avowed and open Infidel. In a word, not one of these human sciences is there that does not, in its ultimate result and analysis, fall back upon the first truth—the fountain of all truth—the cause of all certainty;—and that is God.

But, putting all these considerations aside, let us suppose we gave our children to these men to instruct them; they say, the parents can teach, at home, any form of religion they like. Let us suppose we give our children to the instruction of these men. Do they know how to educate them? They do not know what the word education means. What does it mean? It means, in its very etymology, to bring forth, to develop, to bring out what is in the mind. That little child of seven years is the father of the man. It is only seven years of age; but it is the father of the man that will be, in twenty years time. Now, to educate and bring out in that child every faculty, every power of his soul that he will require for the exercise of his manhood to-morrow; that is the true meaning of the word education. In the human soul there are two distinct systems of powers, both necessary for the man, both acting upon and influencing his life. First of all, is the intelligence of a man; he must receive education. But there is, together with that pure intellect or intelligence, there is the heart that must also be educated; there are the affections; there is the will; and as knowledge is necessary for the intellect, divine grace is necessary for the heart and for the will. If you give to your child every form of human knowledge, and pour into him ideas in abundance, and develop, and bring forth every faculty of his intellect, and let nothing be hid from him in the way of knowledge, but do not mind his heart, and do not educate his affections; how is he to subdue his passions? Do not speak to him of his moral duties, which are to be the sinews of his life, and do not attempt at all to strengthen, and teach the will to bow to the intellect; do not speak to him of his duties, nor the things that he must practise: what will you have at the end of the education? An intellectual monster. Fancy a little child, five or six years old. Suppose all the growth was turned into his head, and the rest of his body remained fixed;

in a few years you would have a monster; you would have a little child with the head of a giant upon him. Do not attempt to purify the affections, and you will develop, indeed, the intellect, but the other powers will be in such disproportion that you have made an intellectual monster. You have made something worse,—you have made a moral monster! It is quite true, knowledge is power. You have given that man power by giving him knowledge. But you have not given him a single principle to purify and influence, or restrain that power, so as to use it properly. Therefore, you have made a moral monster! And, now, that man is all the more wicked, and all the more heartless, and all the more remorseless and impure, in precisely the same proportion as you succeed in making him cultured and learned. This is the issue of this far-famed system of "non-sectarian" education.

There is another system of education, and it is that of our separated brethren in this land, who say that they are quite as indignant and as horrified as we are at the idea of an utterly godless education: that they do not go in for a godless education; on the contrary, they mean to have God everywhere. They are trying now to put Him in the American Constitution, if they can succeed. They also build their schools; and they think that Catholics are the most unreasonable people in the world because we do not consent to send our children to them. They say,—"What objection can you have to the Bible? do you not believe in it as well as we do?" They say:—"Cannot you send your children to us on the platform of our common Christianity? There are a great many things that we believe together." They say:—"We will not ask to teach the children one iota against the Catholic worship; nor ask them to participate in any religious teaching, only as far as they hold that general truth in common with our Protestant children." So, they ask us to stand with them "*on the platform of a common Christianity.*" Well, my friends, a great many Catholics are taken by this; and think it is very unreasonable, and that it is almost bigotry in the Catholic Church to refuse it. Well, let us examine what the "platform of our *common Christianity*" allows. What does it mean? Here is a Protestant school, carried out on Protestant principles. Let us suppose that they shut up the Protestant Bible, and put it aside, but carry on the school on Protestant principles as far as they go in common with the Catholic faith. The Catholic is invited to share the school with them. First of all, my friends, how far do we go together? I do not know if there be any Protestants here; if there be, I do not wish to say a harsh, disrespectful, or unpleasant word; but let us consider how far we can go together,—the Protestants and Catholics! Well, they answer, first of all, "We believe in the existence of God." Thanks be to God, we do!—the Protestants and Catholics are united on that; both believe that there is a God above us. The next great dogma of Christianity is—"We believe in the divinity of Christ." Stop, my friends! I am afraid that we must shake hands and part. I am afraid the platform of "our common Christianity" is too narrow. Are you aware that it is not necessary for a Protestant to believe in the divinity of Jesus Christ? A great many Protestants do believe it, most piously and most fervently; a great many Protestants believe in it as we do. It is most emphatically true, however, that there are clergymen of the Church of England preaching in Protestant churches throughout England, who deny the divinity of Jesus Christ; and it is emphatically true that at this very moment the whole Protestant world is trying to get rid of the Athanasian creed, because that creed says whoever does not believe in the divinity of Jesus Christ cannot enter into the kingdom of Heaven. Therefore, I must fling back this assertion. I cannot grant it. I wish to God I could. No, my friends: if, to-morrow, the Anglican clergy who have written against the divinity of our Lord, and against the inspiration of the Scriptures, and against all forms of religion, in works that are printed, asking all the pious Protestants of England to believe in their ideas; —Professors of England, enjoying their yearly salaries; preaching *religion* (God save the mark!)—if one of these men were to appear on trial to-morrow, the Queen and her Council would decide that the divinity of Christ is not a *necessary* doctrine. You go one step beyond the existence of God, and the platform is overthrown; and the Catholic and the Protestant child can no longer stand side by side. Into that Protestant school goes a Protestant child, to be taught his religion,—to be taught all that his religion requires him to learn; but the Catholic child, before he can go in to receive his instruction, must leave behind him, outside the door, his belief in the Sacraments, Confession, the Holy Communion, prayers for the dead, the Blessed Virgin, all the Saints, the duty of self-examination and of prayer; in a word, all the specific duties, all the principles of the Catholic religion must be forgotten and ignored by that Catholic child before he can come down low enough to take a seat on the platform with his little Protestant brother. Is it any ·wonder that we should not like to do it? If you should live in a beautiful house, well furnished, with every convenience; and your neighbor was living in a damp cellar, where it was cold and dark; and if he asked you to come down and live with him, you would answer: "I am much obliged, my dear friend; but I prefer not." If you had a good dinner of roast beef, and your neighbor had only a salt herring; and he requested you to eat with him, you would answer: "No; I cannot do it." And so when they ask us to come down from the heights of our Catholic knowledge; to go out of the atmosphere of the Sacraments and of the divine presence of Jesus Christ, the atmosphere of responsibility to God, realized and asserted in Confession and Communion; and from the intercessory prayer of Mary, the Mother of Jesus Christ; and of the Saints; and ask us to forget our dead; ask us to give up every thing that a Catholic holds dear, that we may have the privilege of standing upon the miserable platform of "our common Christianity," with our Protestant brethren; we must say that we are much obliged to them, but beg to decline. I say it is a meagre meal that they offer us; but inasmuch as we have something a great deal better and more luxurious at home, we beg leave to be excused; and if they choose to come to us, let them step up to our Catholic schools and find all that they can find in their Protestant schools, and a great deal more; but if they choose not to do it, we cannot help it. We cannot go down to them; never!

Now, on the principle of Catholic education, the Catholic Church says: "I know how to educate; there is no single power in that child's soul, not a single faculty, either intellectual, moral, or spiritual, that I will not bring forth into its full bloom. That child requires knowledge for its intelligence; and every form of human knowledge; so that we can compete with every other teacher in the world." Some time ago, there was a Commission issued by the British Government to examine the schools of Ireland. They thought to convict our Catholic schools of inefficiency; at least, they thought that we paid so much attention to religion, that we did not give the children enough of secular knowledge. Their Commissioners went through the country, and solemnly reported, in the House of Commons, that they found that no schools in Ireland imparted so much secular knowledge as the Christian Brothers' and the Nuns'. They had to say it. The teachers in the other schools declared that secular knowledge was their first object, and religion, if admitted at all, was only a secondary thing. The Christian Brothers said—Religion first, and secular knowledge afterwards. The other schools admitted a miserable modicum of religion, in order to induce the child to receive secular education; but the Christian Brothers admitted secular knowledge, in order to induce in the child's heart and soul religion. And yet, in the rivalry, the Catholic Church was so completely ahead,—even in imparting secular knowledge,—that our enemies on this question of secular education were obliged to acknowledge that there is nothing at all in Ireland like the schools of the Christian Brothers and of the Nuns.

The Church says, " Let no fountain of human knowledge be denied. Let every light which human knowledge and science can bring be thrown upon that intelligence. I am not afraid of it. I desire that the child may have intelligence. The more I can flood that intellect with the light, the surer guarantee I have that that man will be a true and fervent, because an eminently intellectual, Catholic." But, the Church adds : " That child's heart requires to be instructed ; that child's affections require to be trained; that child's passions must be purified ; that child must be made familiar with the things and joys of Heaven before he becomes familiar with the sights and joys of earth." Therefore she takes the child before he comes to the age of reason, and makes his young eyes to be captivated with the images and sweetness and spiritual beauties of Jesus and Mary; and draws and makes that young heart full of love for the Redeemer before the appeal of passion excites the earthly love, before the "mystery of iniquity" that is in the world is revealed to his reason. Therefore, she draws that child and familiarizes his mind with the words of faith, and the language of Heaven and prayer; intermingling with his amusements and studies an element of devotion and of religion. Because she recognizes, that, as much as the world stands in need of intellectual men, far, far more does it stand in need of honest men, pure men, high-minded men. Because she knows that, if knowledge is not intermingled with grace, knowledge without grace becomes a curse, instead of a blessing. It was the curse of the world that it was so intellectual in the era of Augustus; because, says St. Paul, "They refused to admit God into their knowledge; and God gave them up to a reprobate sense." What follows? Every faculty of the mind, of the affections, as well as of the intellect, is brought out in that Catholic child; so that the whole soul is developed, and has fair play, and is brought forth under the system of Catholic Education.

Which of these three systems, think you, is the most necessary for the world? Ah! my friends, I was asked to please the public as well as my co-religionists. I wish to God I could please the public with such a doctrine as this, and propound the truth and say to the public; to every father and mother in America, Protestant and Catholic:—When God gave you that child, it was only that, by your action and by your education, that child might grow into the resemblance of Jesus Christ; it was only that Christ, the Son of God, might be multiplied in men that men are born at all. What do you imagine we come into this world for? To become rich? It is hard for the rich man to be saved. To become great and wondrous before the world's eyes? Oh, this greatness is like the mist which the rays of the morning sun dispel. No. God made us for eternity; and our eternity depends upon our bringing out in our hearts, in our affections, in the interest and harmony of our lives, in the simple faith and belief of our souls, in every highest virtue,—bringing out within us, and clothing ourselves with the Lord Jesus Christ.

And, now, I ask again, which of the three systems of education is likely to do this? Would to God that I could please the public of America when I preach Jesus Christ and Him alone. Now, surely, it is to our schools we can apply the words of Him who said, "Suffer little children to come unto Me." And if the public are not pleased when they hear His name, when they hear how they are to implant Him in their children's lives,—all I can do is to pray for the public, that the Almighty God may open their blind eyes and let in the pure light into their darkened intellects.

I know, my friends, that it is hard upon the Catholics of

this country to be constantly called upon to build one set of schools for Catholics, and to be obliged as citizens to build another set and furnish them for persons wealthier or better off than themselves. It is a hardship; and I do not think the State—with great respect to the authorities—ought to call upon you to do it. But still, great as the hardship is, when you consider that your children receive in the Catholic schools what they cannot receive elsewhere; when you consider that your own hopes for Heaven are bound up in these children, and that the education they need they can receive only in the Catholic school, and nowhere else, you must put up with this disadvantage, and make this sacrifice, among many others, to gain Heaven. For it is written: "The kingdom of Heaven suffers violence, and the violent shall bear it away."

THE BLESSED EUCHARIST.

[*A Sermon delivered by Very Rev. T. N. Burke, O.P., in St. Michael's Church, New York, June 2, 1872.*]

DEARLY BELOVED BRETHREN: In this wonderful age of ours, there is nothing that creates in the thinking mind so much astonishment and wonder as the fact that the Catholic Church stands before the world in all the grandeur of her truthfulness, and that the intellect of this age of ours seems incapable of apprehending her claims, or of acknowledging her grandeur. Men in every walk of life are in pursuit of the true and the beautiful. The poet seeks it in his verse, the philosopher in his speculations, the statesman in his legislation, the artist in the exhibition of his art. And, while all men profess thus to pursue the true and the beautiful, they wilfully shut their eyes against that which is the truest and most beautiful of all things upon the earth,—the Holy Catholic Church of Jesus Christ. I do not know whether there be any Protestants among you here to-day; I believe there are not. But whether they be here, or whether they be absent, I weep, in my heart and soul, over their blindness and their folly,—that they cannot recognize the only religion which is logical, because it is true;—the only Church which can afford to stand before the whole world, and bear the shock of every mind and the criticism of every intellect, because she comes from God?

Now amid the many features of divine beauty and grandeur and harmony that the Almighty God has set upon the face of the Catholic Church, the first and the greatest of her mysteries,—the greatest of her beauties, both intellectual and spiritual,—is the awful presence of Jesus Christ, who makes Himself, really and truly, here, an abiding and present God in the Blessed Eucharist. I have chosen this presence as the subject and theme of my observations to you to-day, because we are yet celebrating (within the octave) the festival of Corpus Christi. We are yet in spirit, with our holy mother, the Church, at the foot of the altar, adoring, in an especial manner, Him who is here present at all times; and rejoicing, with a peculiar joy, for that grace, surpassing all graces, which the Almighty God has given to His Church, in the abiding presence of Jesus Christ among us.

Most of you, I dare say, know that what I propose to you to-day is to consider that presence as the fulfilment of the designs of God, and the fulfilment of all the wants of man. If I can show you what these designs are, and what these wants are, and if I can sufficiently indicate to you that they are fulfilled only in the Blessed Eucharist—then, my brethren, I conclude without the slightest hesitation, that, in no form of religion,—in no Church,—can the designs of God and the wants of man meet their fulfilment, save in that one Church, in that one holy religion, in which Christ is substantiated, under the form of bread and wine in the Blessed Eucharist. In order to do this, I have to ask you to reflect with me what are the designs of God upon man.

There are three remarkable and magnificent epochs that mark the action of the Almighty God upon His creature, man. The first of these was the moment of creation, when God made man. The second was the time of redemption, when God, becoming incarnate, offered Himself as the victim for man. The third epoch was the institution of the Blessed Sacrament, when God left himself to be the food of His children, and to be made one with them by the highest and the most intimate communion of a present God, through all ages. To each of these three epochs I shall invite your attention when I attempt to explain to you the designs of God.

In the first of these,—that is to say in the act of creation,—we find God stamping His image on man, in order that in man He might see the likeness of Himself. In the second of these epochs,—that of redemption, we find God assuming and absorbing our human nature into Himself; so that God and man became one and the same divine person, in order that God might see no longer *the image* of Himself in man; but that He might see Himself actually and truly in man. In the third of these epochs, the institution of the Blessed Sacrament, we have God coming home to every individual; entering into our hearts and souls; bringing all that He is and all that He has to each and every man among us; that the Man-God, in whom God and man were united, might be visible before the Father's eyes in the heart, in the soul, in the life of every man. The Creation, therefore, was a design of mercy, which produced only an image or likeness; the Redemption was a higher design of mercy, which produced God in man. The Holy Communion was the consummation of these designs of mercy, which propagated that God until He was made present in every man. Behold the designs of God! First, then, is the creation. God, in the beginning, created all things, heaven and earth. He made the earth, with all its beauty. He made the firmament of heaven, with all its wonderful harmony and order. At His creative word, —"*fiat*,"—let it be,—light sprang forth from darkness; order came forth in silent beauty from chaos and confusion; every star in heaven took its place in the firmament of God; the sun blazed forth in his noonday light and splendor; the moon took up her reflected light, and illumined with her silver rays the shades of night. All the spheres of God began their revolution through space, to that exquisite harmony of the Divine commandment and the Divine law. And they all surrounded that spot of creation which was earth, and destined to be the habitation of man. This earth the Almighty God clothed with its manifold forms of beauty. He gave to it the revolving seasons—the freshness of the Spring—the deep shade of the Summer,—the fruitful overteeming of the Autumn;—and every season took up its strain of joy, abundance and delight, at the command of God. But all these things, every form of life that existed, existed by the one word, "*fiat*," of the Almighty God. But now, when the heavens above are prepared; now, when the spheres are all in their places; now, when every creature of God has received its commission, its faculty of life, light, splendor, and beauty;—the whole earth, heaven, and the firmament are made: yet no image of God is there; for there is no intelligence there; and God is knowledge: there is no power of love there; and God is the highest and most intimate love. There is no freedom there, but only the necessity of nature's law and instinct. The whole world,—in all its beauty, in all its harmony,—still wants its soul: for that soul, wherever it is to be, must be something like to God. Finally, when all things were prepared, God took of the slime of the earth, and made and fashioned with His hands a new creature,—a creature that was to rise and to uplift his eyes and behold the sun; a creature whose every form of material existence was to remain perfectly distinct from all other forms of creation. Into this creature's face the Almighty God breathed His own image and likeness, in an imperishable spirit, an immortal soul. Before He made this soul, the mirror of Himself, He took thought with Himself, and said no longer—"Let it be!" but —counselling with His own Divine wisdom, He said: "Let Us make man to Our own image and likeness." And unto His own image and likeness, therefore, He made him, for He breathed upon him the inspiration of spiritual life,—a living soul into the inanimate clay;—and upon that soul He stamped His own divine image. He gave to that soul the light of an intelligence capable of comprehending the power of love, capable of serving Him and loving Him. He gave to that soul the faculty of freedom, that by no necessary law, by no iron instinct, was this new creature to act; but with judgment, and with thought, and with intellectual inquiry. He was to act freely, and every action of his life was to flow from the fountain of unfettered freedom, like the actions of the Almighty God Himself, whose very essence is eternal freedom.

Thus was man created. Behold the image of God stamped upon him! Oh, how grand, how magnificent was this creature! The theory has been mooted in our day:—"Was it worth God's while to create the sun, moon, and stars, and untold firmaments which no eye of man has yet discovered;— those stars far away exceeding our earth in their magnitude, in their splendor, in their attractive power and beauty;—was it worth God's while,"—the astronomer asks,—"for the sake of giving light to one of the smallest of the planets, to create so many others to revolve around her in space?" Yes, I answer, it was worth God's while; for one man, if He had created but one;—it was worth His while to create all these material beauties; because man alone,—that one man,—would reflect in his soul the image of God—the uncreated and spiritual loveliness of his Maker. How grand was this first man when he arose from the green mound out of which the Lord created him! when he opened his eyes and beheld before him, shrouded in some dazzling form of material beauty, the presence of God! He opened his eyes; and seeing this figure of light and transparency before him, hearing from his lips the harmony of his Creator's voice, he knelt in adoration. He alone, of all the creatures in the world, was able to appreciate the infinite beauty of the Maker; and springing to that Maker, with all the energy of his spirit, he bowed down before Him, and offered the sacrifice of intellectual praise. He alone, of all the creatures of God, was able to appreciate the infinite eternity of His existence; His omnipotence; His infinite goodness, grandeur, and beauty. He alone, of all God's creatures, was capable of appreciating with soul;—that, out of the appreciation of his mind, his heart was moved to love, and he strained towards his God with every higher aspiration and affection of his spirit. He alone, of all the creatures of God, was able to say, out of the resources of a free and unshackled will: "I will love Thee! I will serve Thee, O God! for Thou alone art worthy of all love and all service for all time!" So, freely and deliberately weighing the excellencies of God against all created beauty; calculating with the power of his intelligence the claims of God upon him,—he acknowledged these claims; he acknowledged in his intellect the infinite beauty of God; because of his intellectual appreciation, he decided freely to serve God in his life. That free decision from the intellect was a godlike act, of which no other creature upon this earth was capable. Therefore, the Almighty God appealed to that act as the test and proof of man.

Thus we see in the beginning that Almighty God stamped His image upon His people. And in this He showed the design of His creation;—the greatness of His mercy and of His love. He had prepared all things for man. He had made all things for him. All things pointed to him; all nature, newly created in all its beauty, still cried out for that crowning beauty, the beauty of intelligence, the beauty of the power of love, the grandeur of freedom. And man was created as the very apex, the very climax of God's creation; the crown and the perfection of all. Behold the mercy of God! God might have left this world in all its material, yet unintellectual beauty. He might have left all His creatures to enjoy the life that He gave them, and to fulfil the limited and necessary sphere of their duties,—and yet never have sent intelligence and love and freedom upon them. But no; God wished to behold Himself in His creation. He wished to be able to look down from Heaven and see His image in His creation. God wished that all nature should hold up the mirror of its resemblance to Him in man. God's design was that, wherever the child of man existed, there He, looking down, should behold His own image in the depths of that pure intelligence, in the depths of those pure affections, in that unshackled, magnificent, imperial freedom of man's will.

This was the first design. Far greater was the second design of God's mercy. God knew and foreknew, from all eternity, that man, by the abuse of his free will, would turn against his God. The Almighty God knew and foreknew, as if it were present before His eyes,—for there is no past, no future to the eyes of God; all things are present to Him;—He knew and foreknew that, in the day when He placed Himself and His own divine perfection and His own claims on one side, and the devil made the appeal to the passions and pride of man on the other side,—He knew that His free creature would decide against Him,—would abandon Him,—tell Him to begone, and take all His gifts with Him, and would clutch the animal and base gratifications of a sensual pride. God knew this. He knew that, in that act, man was destined to cloud his clear intelligence, so that it would no longer reflect the image of God;—that man was destined, in that act, to pollute his pure affections, so that they should no longer reflect the image of God in love. God foresaw and foreknew that man was destined, in that act of rebellion, to fetter and enslave his free will, and to make it no longer a servant and minister of his intelligence, but of his passions and of his desires. In a word, God saw His own image broken and spoiled in man by the sin of Adam.

Then, my dearly beloved, in these eternal designs of love, God said, in His own decrees, from all eternity: "My image is gone; My likeness is shattered; My spirit is no longer among them; and I must provide a remedy greater than the evil. I will send—in the second plan of My mercy and the design of My love,—I will make no longer a renewed image in man; I will not restore what they have broken and destroyed; but I will send My Eternal Son. He, the reality, whom no evil can touch, whom no temptation can conquer,—I will put Him into man; and I shall behold, no longer the fallen man, but I shall behold, in the redeemed man, Myself restored in the person of Jesus Christ." O my beloved brethren! does not the infinite mercy,—the all-extending, all-grasping love of God,—come in here? He might, in His designs of mercy, have restored His broken image in man. He might have given man the power of repentance. He might, in the largeness of His mercy, wipe away sin, undo that most fatal work, and give back to man, in the unclouded intelligence, and in the pure heart, and in the free will, all that man had lost of the divine image by sin. He might have done this without at all descending Himself; without at all coming down from the throne of His greatness and uncreated majesty and glory. But no! God resolves to do more for the reparation of man than man had ever done in the ruin of himself by sin. God resolves to send His only begotten Son, who, incarnate by the Holy Ghost of the Virgin Mary, was made man. The Lord Jesus Christ is born of the Virgin Mary: an infant wails upon His Mother's bosom: an Infinite God, looking down from heaven, beholds not only His own image in man, but beholds Himself in Him, His only begotten, coëqual, and consubstantial Son. Therefore, He is no longer the image, but the Man-God. He is no longer the likeness of God, but the reality of God,—according to the Scriptures of old: "I have said ye are gods, and all of you the sons of the Most High."

God made us to be His servants. When man refused to be a servant, God, in His mercy, lifted him up, and made him a son. Instead of taking the children of men and binding us together, as a bundle of faggots, and flinging us into hell, and in His greatness and glory forgetting us all;—instead of doing this, when God saw that we were fallen, and that not even His image remained in man, in the destruction of grace, and in the partial destruction of the perfection of his nature,—He sent His only begotten Son; so that the creature, instead of being punished by eternal ruin and banishment, is raised by redemption, and made a son of God. "To those who received Him, He gave the power to become the sons of God." Can you comprehend this mercy? Do you ever reflect upon it? I sinned in Adam. Sinning thus in Adam, I deserved to be cast away from God, and never to see His face again. I sinned in Adam. Sinning thus, I lost all that God gave me of grace, and a great deal that He gave me of nature. Instead of flinging me aside, Almighty God

comes down from Heaven, becomes my brother, and says:—
"Brother, all that I am in Heaven,—the Son of God,—I am
willing to make you by adoption. My Father is willing to
take you in as My younger brother. My father is willing to
acknowledge that all I am by nature you are by the grace of
adoption." So, in the work of redemption,—in the second
design of God,—we rise to the grandeur and dignity of a
more sublime position than in Adam. We become the
younger brethren of God Himself. We become members of
the household and of the family of Jesus Christ.

But, you will say to me, what connection has this with
the Blessed Eucharist? You engage to show us that the
designs of God were fulfilled in the Real Presence. You
speak of the design of creation,—of the design of redemption;
—but what have these two designs to do with the institution
of the Blessed Sacrament? the transubstantiation of Christ
upon the altar? It has this: The first design of creation
was intended by the Almighty God to be, that man, preserving the graces in which he was created,—preserving the image
in which he was made,—should remain faithful to God, free
from sin, the conqueror of his own passions, and of every
temptation that could come upon him; and so, living in the
light of purity, in the fervor of love, in the strength of freedom, that he might journey on through happiness and peace
upon the earth, until he attained to the fulfilment of his perfection, and laid hold of the eternal crown of glory. This
was the design of God. This was marred by sin. Man sinned;
and the design of God could no longer be fulfilled. He
let evil into his soul; he destroyed the integrity of his nature;
he violated the virginity of his soul; he came to the knowledge of evil; and, with the knowledge, he came to the love
of evil. Understand this well; it is a deep thought; it enters
into the designs of God. Every individual man born into
this world was born a sinner. Defilement was upon him:
the seeds of future evil were in him. All that was necessary
for him was to let that infant grow into a youth; and, of
necessity, he became an individual sinner, because the root
of evil was in him. The seeds of corruption were implanted
in him; his blood was impure and defiled. All that was
necessary was the dawn of reason and the awakening of passion. The former made him an infidel; the latter made him
a debauched, licentious, and impure sinner. This was the

consequence of Adam's sin. Therefore, my dearly beloved, it was not only our nature that sinned in Adam, but every individual of our nature sinned in him, save and except the Blessed Virgin Mary. Put her aside, and at once the whole race of human beings are individual sinners in Adam:—not actual sinners, but individually tainted by sin. This, to be sure, is one of those things that people overlook. They do not understand that the curse of Adam came down to each and every one of us,—this sin of Adam, which was written upon our foreheads in characters of defilement. When it was a question of remedying that evil, it was necessary that the Almighty God should exercise His mercy individually upon each and every one of us.

Two things, therefore, were tainted by the sin of Adam,—the nature and the individual. The nature, common to all, was tainted; man's nature was broken; man's nature was corrupted; that which was common to us all,—the universal nature,—was defiled and injured by Adam's sin; and in that defilement and injury every single, individual child of Adam participated; so that every one of us, personally and individually, was defiled in our first parent. Now, it follows from this, that when the Almighty God, in His second design of mercy,—namely the Redemption,—when He resolved to undo all the evil that Adam had done,—when He resolved to bind up and heal the wound that Adam had made,—it was necessary that God should take thought for the nature that was corrupted, and for the individuals that had fallen in Adam. If He had taken thought only for the nature, it would not be sufficient for us; for our nature may be restored, and, unless that restoring power come home to us, we ourselves may remain in our misery. God provided a remedy for the nature,—the universal nature,—in the Incarnation. He sent His own Divine Son, who took our nature—our human nature,—who took a human body, a human soul, human feelings, a human heart, a human mind, human intellect, human will;—every thing that belonged to the nature of man, Christ, our Lord, took; but He did not take the individual. Mark it well! You Catholics ought to know the theology of your divine religion;—mark it well. Christ, our Lord, took every thing that was in man except the individuality,—personality. That He did not touch. He took our nature, and absorbed it into His own person; but He never took a human person.

No man could say of our Lord, pointing to Him: "He is an individual man." No! He was a divine man. When He spoke, His words were those, not of man, but of God; because the person who spoke was divine. If He suffered, it was the suffering, not of man, but of God; because the person was divine. This was necessary; because, unless the Divine Person,—that is to say, God,—consented to suffer and to die, the sin of man's nature could never have been wiped out. When, therefore, the Eternal Father, in His love for mankind, sent His co-Eternal Son upon the earth, He, in that act of Incarnation of the Second Person of the Blessed Trinity, provided a remedy for the evil of Adam's nature—for the human nature that was spoiled. Again I assert that Christ, our Lord, never took the human personality; that He left the individuality of every man to himself; that He did not take the individuality or personality of the man; but only the nature. In order to remedy the nature it was necessary, in the designs of God, that God should unite Himself with that nature. Mark this,—that God should unite Himself with man's nature was necessary in the designs of God, in order that man's nature might be purified and restored. Was this necessary to the designs of God? Absolutely necessary. The Virgin Mary,—on that day in Nazareth, when Gabriel stood before her,—represented the human race. She represented human nature, in her alone unfallen; and to that all-pure and unfallen one the Angel said: "Mary, a child shall be born to you, and He shall be called the Son of the Most High God." Mary paused; and until Mary, of her own free will, answered: "Behold the handmaid of God; be this thing done unto me according to thy word;" until Mary said that word, the mystery of the Incarnation was suspended, and man's redemption was left hanging upon the will of one woman. But, when Mary said the word, human nature, distinct from man's personality, was assumed by God. If Almighty God had not consented to unite Himself with our nature, that nature never could have been redeemed. But, thus we see that one great portion of Adam's evil was remedied in the Incarnation,—namely, that our nature was purified.

But what about the individual? It is not so much the purification of my nature—our common nature—that concerns me. I am an individual man,—the son of my mother; I am a human person: Christ, our Lord, had nothing to say to the human person in the Incarnation. How then am I,—a human person,—to enter into the graces and purity of God? Oh, behold, my brethren, how the two previous designs culminate! Christ, our Lord, multiplied Himself. Christ, our Lord, changed bread and wine into His own divine body and blood. Christ, our Lord, made Himself present in the form of man's food. That food is broken. Every child that cries for that divine bread shall have it. That human individual, that personal creature is united to God; and the individual is sanctified as the nature was sanctified. The nature could not be redeemed or sanctified except by union with God: the individual is sanctified by the same means—union with God in the blessed Eucharist. Thus, then, we see how the design of creation,—spoiled in Adam, —spoiled not only in the nature, but in the individual,—is made perfect in Jesus Christ, as far as regards the mystery of the Incarnation. Well, therefore, He says: "Unless you eat of the flesh of the Son of Man, and drink His blood, you shall not have life in you." He was speaking to the individual. He did not say, "You cannot have life in your nature." He put life into human nature by taking that nature upon Himself. There was life there already,—life eternal,—in the person of Jesus Christ. But He was speaking to individuals, and He said to them: "Unless you bring Me home unto yourselves, individually, you cannot have life in you; for I am the life;—life indeed;—life eternal, that came down from heaven; and unless you eat of My flesh and drink of My blood, you cannot have life in you. But, if you do this,—if you eat of this flesh and drink of this blood, then you shall abide in Me and I in you."

Behold, therefore, dearly beloved, how the mystery of the Incarnation, affecting, as it did, our nature, is brought home in its wonderful expansion to each human person in the Holy Communion. Oh, how sad and terrible—how dreadful is the thought that the devil has succeeded the second time in destroying us! First, he destroyed our nature in Adam; now he succeeds in destroying the person in heresy, in Protestantism. He came and whispered,—"Christ is not in the Blessed Eucharist! He is not there!" He cut off—by that denial of Protestantism of the Real Presence—the last great design of God, in which the creation and the redemption were to be made perfect in their remedy and brought home to every individual man. Suppose, my children, that some dreadful epidemic came in among you,—some fearful irruption of Asiatic cholera :—that a sailor landed from a ship in New York with the cholera, and from him it spread through the city;—we would look upon that man as the origin of the evil, because he brought it, as Adam brought evil and sin and misery into this world. Then suppose some great physician arose,—some mighty sage,—and said he held in his hand the great remedy; said to the whole city of New York —" Behold, I am come from a foreign land, where we have never known disease or complaint, with this sovereign remedy in my hand: no one that partakes of this shall ever suffer from this hideous disease." Would we not take the remedy out of his hands? Would we not eat of that medicine, which is life out of death to us? So, Christ, Our Lord, represents that great physician, coming with a sovereign remedy in His hand, and with that remedy we will remedy our nature in His Incarnation. Then He says: "I am come from a foreign land that has never known disease or death. I came from Heaven. I bring the remedy against Adam's corruption and Adam's sin. I am the head of your nature: now I am one with you. So I say to you all : whoever wishes to escape this dire disease, must partake of this miraculous food. It is the self-same food brought down to elevate your nature, that is, My own self." What would you think of a man that said, "Do not go near Him! do not take that food from His hand! do not believe in Him"?—thus clinging to disease and death. Why, you see clearly, my brethren, as we Catholics believe and know that the Almighty God has sufficiently revealed in His designs that it is absolutely necessary for every man who wishes to be saved and sanctified, to come into personal contact with our Lord Jesus Christ, by opening his mouth and receiving the Body and Blood, Soul and Divinity, of the Lord in the Holy Communion.

Such is the design of God. Now it remains for us to see whether that, which so completely fulfils the designs of God, fulfils also the wants of man. O my brethren! before we leave these designs, let us consider how magnificent they are! The Father loved man. First, in the beginning, when as God He loved His own image. What great love have you for the likeness of your own face in the looking-glass? Every feature is there, every expression is there, but it is only an image. What love would a man have for his own portrait, even though designed by a master hand? Every tint and beauty of color may be there, every delicate trait most true to nature, and to the person represented. But, after all, it is only a piece of canvas, overlaid with a little paint and skilfully arranged; only an image. God, in the second design, beholds in man His own adorable and beloved Son: the Eternal Word, that from all eternity rested in the Father's bosom; the very figure of His substance, and the splendor of His glory, equal to Him in all things, knowing and loving Him, and loved by Him with a substantial love, which is the third person of the Blessed Trinity—the Holy Ghost. He came down from Heaven, became man; and the Eternal Father no longer looks upon man, as a man would look upon his own picture, as an image. He looks down, as a loving father of a family looks down on the face of his eldest son. How different the love of a man is for his own image, reflected in a mirror, or perpetuated by the painter's hand,—cold, lifeless, inanimate,—and his own image seen in every feature, in every lineament of his child; the child of his own manly love; the child growing and displaying every perfection, and returning the love of the father; the child surrounding all the graces of ordinary infancy with a peculiar grace and shining beauty in his father's eyes, until he draws every chord of that father's heart, entwining around him so closely, that, if the child should die or disappear, the father would seem to have lost every purpose of life, and be ready to lie down and die upon the grave of his first-born. So the Almighty and Eternal God, looking down in the second design of His redemption, beheld one who was not a human person, but the second Divine Person of the adorable Trinity; not merely human, though truly human; but man and God united in one. And that union consummated, not in man, not in the human person, but in God the Divine person: and just as that image of Jesus Christ so captivated the Father's love, that twice He rent the Heavens miraculously, and sent down His voice,—once when Christ was standing in the Jordan; and another time when He was transfigured on Mount Tabor;—on both occasions, the miraculous voice—as if God could no longer contain His love—saying, "This is My beloved Son, in whom I am well pleased. Hear ye Him:" that image so captivated the

Father's love, that He wished to reproduce it in all the children of men,—that He wished to multiply it. It was so fair, so beautiful, that the Eternal Father, whenever He cast His eyes upon the earth, wished to see it multiplied in every man personally. He wished to see every man another Jesus Christ, His Son. He wished to be able to say to you and to me:—"He is also my beloved child, in whom I am well pleased." In order to do this, His Divine Son multiplied Himself, and remained upon earth,—broke, as it were, His existence, His perfect existence, His inseparable existence;— broke it; separated it into a thousand forms; became present upon your lips and mine, and on those of the little child that comes up to this altar: so that the mere image of God receives the Holy Communion, goes down from this altar; and the Father of Heaven looks down and says:—"Behold, My beloved Son, Jesus Christ, is there!" The Angel Guardian that conducts the child to the altar, prostrates himself before the figure of that child as he returns from the altar again. For now, he is, indeed, a human person; but God is in him.

And this is the supreme want of man. That which is the fulfilment of the Divine design is the supreme want. What is that which we want? Christian believers as you are, tell me your great want in this world. Every man has his own wants and hopes, and desires and purposes of life. What is it that you want? What do we aspire to? Tell me. One man says:—"Well, I hope to become a wealthy man; to be the founder of a grand family in the land." Do your hopes stop here, my friend? The grand family you found will follow you to the grave. Have you brought no hopes with you? Another says:—"I hope to obtain some distinguished position, the first position in the land." I suppose you may be one day President of the United States. But the day will come when they will carry the President, and consign him, also, to his grave. What is your hope and mine? O friends and brethren, is it not my hope to bring out in my soul, here by grace, and hereafter by glory, the image of the Eternal God, which is stamped upon it? My hope is to live in the light of divine grace, to walk in the beaming of divine purity. My hope is to keep my will unfettered, that freely I may devote it to the service of my God. My hope is to rise by divine help into all the majesty of Christian holiness. And the majesty and the glory of the Christian man lie here,—that Jesus Christ, the Son of God, may be brought out in him. No great one in Heaven, but the greatest of all—the Eternal God and man, Jesus Christ. He stamped the God upon our humanity in the Incarnation. He stamped the God upon our nature; and that stamp He left on our nature; and we must stamp it upon our person. And the true want of every Christian man, and the true purpose of his existence, is to bring out the Christ that is in him, and to become a son of God. Nothing short of this. If we fail in this, then all our hopes perish from us. If we fail in this, it is in vain that we have achieved every other purpose of life; it is in vain that we have written our names, even in letters of gold, upon the foremost page of our country's history; it is in vain that we have left a name to other times, built up upon the solid foundation of every higher quality that is enshrined in the temple of man's immortality. It is in vain that we have accumulated all the world's riches. If we fail to bring out the Christ that is in us, then we are, of all men, the most miserable; because we have failed in realizing the only true hope, the only true want of the Christian man. What follows? Says the Saviour—"If a man gain the whole world,"—the world's places, the world's honors—"and lose his own soul, what profiteth it him?" And the loss of his soul is effected in man by neglecting to bring Christ out in him. For it is written—our vocation, our calling, our justification—that is to say, our sanctification—our ultimate glory,—all depend upon one thing,—making ourselves, by divine grace, conformable to Jesus Christ. For God foreknew and predestined that we might be made like to the image of Jesus Christ: and "those whom He called He justified, and those whom He justified He glorified."

This being the want of man, how is it to be supplied? Can man alone supply the want? No! There are three enemies that stand before us. Powerful and dreadful is each and every one of these enemies, saying to us—"I am come to destroy the Christ in you!" The first of these is the world—the world with its evil maxims; the world with its pride, with its avarice, with all its false ideas; the world with its newspapers and periodicals; with all its theories not stopping short of theorizing upon God;—the world that tells us its influence is elevating, although the Almighty

God tells us it is not; and that mocking buffoonery of religion, dissolving the matrimonial tie, the most sacred of all bonds; the world, flooded with impurity, evil examples, and its evil maxims and principles,—comes before the Christian man hoping to be made like unto Jesus Christ, and says: " I tell you you must not be a Christian. I will surround you by my influence; I will beset you with evil examples; I will pollute the moral atmosphere you live in with my false principles, and work the Christ out of you!" Will any man be able, of his own power, to resist this influence and conquer it? Ah! it has captivated and enslaved the best intellects of our age; the grandest minds of our age have been utterly debauched by worldly principles; for we know the very best intelligences of our age, at this moment, are writing the sheerest nonsense about religion;—these men who write articles in the newspapers with so much wisdom upon commercial subjects;—these men whose wits are keen as a razor in philosophical speculation;—quick to perceive a flaw in an argument; —when these men come to write about religion, they are fools,—as you will see in looking at any of the leading newspapers of New York to-morrow morning,—what this man and that man said in the various conventicles and churches to-day:—you will find a Quaker standing up,—a holy man,—humming, hawing, and rocking himself; lifting up his languid eyes to Heaven; and then, after a long pause, you will find him denying the Divinity of Jesus Christ and declaring that He was not the Son of God at all! This happened last Sunday in New York. You will find another man coming out with the theory and the belief that man never fell; and therefore does not need any remedy. This —in the face of the moral and social corruption and guiltiness of our age, that is revolting to the eyes of God and man!

Thus it is the world blinds the very best intellects, and the shrewdest and strongest minds. And do you expect to resist this? No! You cannot do it. You must say with St. Paul: "Of myself I can do nothing; but I can do all things in Him." In Him we can do all things. He is here for you and me.

The next great enemy is the flesh;—the domestic enemy. The blood in our veins, the passions and the senses of our bodies rise up against us to enslave us, and say: " You must not become like to the Son of God! The Son of God was infinite purity. I will not allow you to possess your soul in purity! I will not allow you to develop the spiritual existence that is within you; you must follow the dictates of your passions; you must become a drunkard, a licentious and impure man! I will fill that eye with the flaming, lustful glances of desire; I will make the absorbing desire for every thing base throb in your veins, till it becomes a necessity of your nature." Thus says the flesh. Can we conquer it? The greatest and the grandest of earth's sons have been the meanest slaves to their own passions. The grandest names upon the rolls of history,—the greatest heroes,—the greatest philosophers—have all attached to them—when we turn the leaves of history and look at their lives—the foul stain of their impurity, running through their lives and covering all their existence with the vilest of all earthly passions. No! We cannot conquer this flesh of ours, but in Him,—the Lord our God,—who of old bound up the demon and cast him forth into the desert of Ethiopia. So can we bind, with Him, these unruly passions, and stem the flood of desire in our corrupt and polluted natures, and deny ourselves for Him, who will enable, while He commands us to do it; and to cast forth the demon into the outer world that is so fitted for him.

Finally comes the pride of life;—the third enemy. Ambition, the self-reliance, the pride of man, the pride that refuses to be dictated to. "Why"—that pride says—"why should I submit to the commands of religion? Why, it tells me I should go like a little child, and prepare myself, and go to confession! Why, it tells me I should go through these devotions that are only fit for women and nuns! Why should I fast and suffer hunger? I have all things around me. Do not I find such and such texts in Scripture that tell me, 'All things are good?' Why shall I abstain from any thing? Why should I not have my own way, and reject all authority, human and Divine? and, first of all, the law that man must bear the obedience, humility, and mortification of Jesus Christ in him if he would be saved?" Will you be able to contend against this pride? this pride that carries away the best and highest of earth's children? No! You will never be able to contend against it, to keep the humility of your intellect, the fidelity of your faith, unless you feed upon Him who is the source of all virtue and all life. And thus, it is only by the same means that Christ has effected in the Incarnation,—by God uniting Himself in our nature in Christ,—that He also effects our sanctification in the Holy Communion. Therefore it accomplishes at once all the designs of God.

I have done my duty. I have finished my theme. Nothing remains for me but to remind the Catholics who are here,—the Catholics of this city,—the Catholic men who were nourished in the Catholic faith, and derived that faith from Catholic—and many amongst them from Irish—mothers,—to remind you that, for three hundred years of persecution and death, it was the Holy Communion, and Ireland's devotion to it, that kept the faith alive in our fathers. They resisted that pride of life. The world came and declared to them that they should give up their faith. They said no, against the whole world. They kept their faith through Jesus Christ, in the Holy Communion. They resisted their passions and restrained them; so that Ireland's purity, in the purity of her daughters and the manliness of her sons,—(a virtue that always accompanies personal purity and purity of race), was unexcelled. They resisted even when titles and honors were ready to be showered upon them. And when high intellect was challenged to disprove the faith in which they believed, they bowed down before their time-honored altars; and Ireland's faith in her religion was never stronger than in the days when she suffered most for it. I say to you, Catholics of New York, that no man can be saved from the world around him, from the flesh within, and the Devil that is beneath him, unless Jesus Christ be with him. I tell you, Catholics of New York,—men of New York, who only go once a year to Holy Communion,—that it would be almost better for you if you did not know the truth. If you want to know the explanation of your sins,—of the drunkenness around you,—of the impurity and savage assaults committed; of all the quick, hasty crimes of which our Irish nature is more capable than of the meaner and more corrupt crimes.—the reason of it all is this,—that you are not frequent and fervent communicants. If you ask me for a rule, I find, although I go to Communion every day of my life, I have enough to do still to conquer my spiritual enemies. And, if I, a priest, have enough to contend with to be saved after receiving the Holy Communion every morning,—how can you be saved? If you ask me for a rule I will give it in a few words: I believe every man who wishes to have the peace of Christ, and live in His Christian holiness, and have Christ brought forth in him,—that man should be, at least, a monthly communicant.

THE DIVINE COMMISSION OF THE CHURCH.

[*A Sermon delivered by Very Rev. T. N. Burke, O.P., in the Church of St. Vincent Ferrer, June 16, 1872.*]

"At that time it came to pass that, when the multitude pressed upon him to hear the word of God, he stood by the lake of Genesareth. And he saw two ships standing by the lake; but the fishermen were gone out of them, and were washing their nets. And going up into one of the ships that was Simon's, he desired him to draw back a little from the land. And sitting, he taught the multitude out of the ship. Now when he had ceased to speak, he said to Simon: Launch out into the deep, and let down your nets for a draught. And Simon answering said to him: Master, we have labored all the night, and have taken nothing; but at thy word I will let down the net. And when they had done this, they enclosed a very great multitude of fishes, and their net broke. And they beckoned to their partners that were in the other ship, that they should come and help them. And they came and filled both the ships, so that they were almost sinking. Which when Simon Peter saw, he fell down at Jesus' knee, saying: Depart from me, for I am a sinful man, O Lord. For he was wholly astonished, and all that were with him, at the draught of the fishes that were taken. And so were also James and John, the sons of Zebedee, who were Simon's partners. And Jesus saith to Simon: Fear not; from henceforth thou shalt catch men. And having brought their ships to land, leaving all things, they followed him."—LUKE V, 1–11.

WHEN we read the positive doctrines laid down in the Gospel, we are bound to open our minds to the utterances of the Almighty God. We are also bound to meditate upon even what appear to be the most trifling incidents recorded in the actions and sayings of Jesus Christ. Every word that is recorded of Him has a deep and salutary meaning. There is not one word in the Gospel, nor one incident, that is not full of instruction for us: and the evidence that this Gospel gives of the divinity of the Christian religion, and of the divine origin of the Church, lies not only in the broad assertion,—such, for instance, as where Christ says: "I will build my Church upon a rock; and the gates of hell shall not prevail against it;" or, elsewhere: "He that will not hear the Church, let him be to thee as a heathen and a publican;" but these evidences lie also in the minor incidents which are so carefully and minutely recorded, from time to time, by the Evangelists. Now I ask you to consider, in this spirit, the Gospel which I have just read to you. St. Peter,—who was afterwards the Pope of Rome,—began life as a fisherman, on the shores of the Sea of Galilee. He had his boats, he had his nets; he swept those waters, pursuing his humble trade in company with James and John, the sons of Zebedee, and with Andrew, his own elder brother. These men had passed the night upon the bosom of the waters, toiling and laboring; but they had taken nothing. Sad and dispirited for so much time and labor lost, they landed from their boats in the morning; and they took out their nets to wash them. While they were thus engaged, a great multitude appeared in sight, —men who followed the Lord Jesus Christ, and pressed around Him, that they might hear the words of divine truth from His lips. He came to the shores of the lake, and He entered into one of the boats; and the Evangelist takes good care to tell us that the boat into which the Saviour stepped was Simon Peter's boat. He then commanded Peter to push out a little from the land that He might have a little water between Him and the people, and yet not remove Himself so far from them but that they might hear His voice. There, —while the people stood reverently listening to the law of the divine Redeemer,—sat the Saviour in Peter's boat, instructing the multitude. After He had enlightened their minds with the treasures of the divine wisdom which flowed from Him, He turned to Peter and said to him : "Launch out into the deep, and let down your nets for a draught of fishes." Said Peter, answering: "Master, we have labored all night; and we have taken nothing. However," he replied, "in Thy word I trust; and at Thy command I will let down the net." No sooner does he cast that net into the sea, under the eyes, and at the command of Jesus Christ, than it is instantly filled with fishes, and Peter's boat is filled until it is almost sinking. This is the fact recorded. What does it mean ? What is the meaning of this passage in the Gospel? Has it any meaning at all ? Was it prophetic of things that were to be? Oh, my brethren, how significant and how prophetic, in the history of this Christian religion, and in the Church, was the action of Jesus Christ as recorded in the Gospel. "He sat in Peter's boat, and from that boat He taught the people." What does this mean ? What is this barque of Peter? Need

I tell you, my Catholic friends and beloved brethren, what this barque of Peter meant? Christ our Lord built unto Himself His Church! He made her so that she was never to be shipwrecked upon the stormy waves of this world. He built her so that He Himself shall be always present in her, although Peter sat at the helm. He built her so that it was her fate to be launched out upon the ever-changing, ever-agitated, and stormy sea of this world and its society. He declared that Peter should be at the head of this ship, when He said to him: "Feed thou My lambs; feed thou My sheep;" "Confirm thou thy brethren;" "I will make you to be fishers of men;" "Launch out into the deep, and let down your nets for a draught."

St. Peter himself, inspired of the Holy Ghost, in after times taught that the Church of God is like a goodly ship, built by Jesus Christ, in which were to be saved all those that are to be saved unto the end of time; for he compares this ship to the Ark of Noah, in which all who were saved in the great Deluge found their refuge; for, he says, all were destroyed and perished, save and except the eight souls who received shelter in the Ark of Noah; and the rest were tossed upon the stormy, tumultuous billows of the Deluge;—thrown upon the tide;—and as the waters rose up around them in a mighty volume, the strong man went down into the vasty deep, the infant sent forth a cry, and presently its cry was stifled in the surging waves. All was desolation; all was destruction, save and except the Ark, which rode triumphant over the waters, passed over the summits of the mountains, braving the storms of heaven above and the angry waves beneath, until it landed its living freight of eight human souls in safety and in joy. So, also, Christ our Lord built unto Him a ship— His Church; He launched this Church forth upon the stormy waves of the world, and it is a matter of surprise that this ocean of human society has not welcome for the Church of God. Men ask, "Is Christianity a failure? Why are so few saved? Why are so few found to comply with the conditions which the Holy Church commands? Why, if she received the commission to command the whole world, and to convert them, why is it that this Church of God seems to have always been persecuted and abused?"

Oh! my friends, there is a deep and profound analogy between the things of nature and the things of grace. The goodly ship is built upon the stocks; she is strongly built, of the very best material; she is sheathed and plated with every thing that can keep her from the action of the seas; she is built so that, in every line, she shall cleave through the waters and override them; and, when she is all prepared, she is launched out into the deep; and her mission is to spread her sails, and navigate every sea to the farthermost end of the world. Through all of them must she go; over them all must she ride; a thousand storms must she brave; and that ocean that receives her in its bosom, apparently receives her only for the purpose of tossing her from wave to wave, of trying her strength, of trying every timber and every joint, opening its mighty chasms to swallow her up and, failing in that, dashing its angry waves against her, as if, in the order of nature, the ship and the sea were enemies, and that the ocean that received that vessel was bent upon her destruction. Is it not thus in the order of nature? is it not this very stormy ocean, these mighty, foam-crested billows, these angry, roaring waves, the thunder that rolls, and the lightnings which flash around her,—is it not all these that try and prove the goodness of the ship; and if she outlive them, if she is assuredly able to override them all, and to land her freight and her passengers in the appointed port,—is it not a proof that she is well built? If the ocean were as smooth as glass; if the winds were always favorable; if no impediment came upon her; if no waves struck her and tried to roll her back, or no chasm opened to receive her into its mighty watery bosom; what proof would we have that the ship was the making of the master hand, under the care of master minds? And so Christ, our Lord, built the ship of His Church, and launched her out upon the world; and from the very nature of the case it was necessary that, from the very first day that she set forth until the last day, when she lands her freight of souls in the harbor of Heaven, she should meet, upon the ocean of this world of human society, the stormy waves of angry contradiction on every side. This was her destiny; and this, unfortunately, is the destiny that the world takes good care to carry out.

Men say, Christianity is a failure, because this Church has not been enabled to calm every sea, and ride triumphant, without let or hindrance, upon every ocean. I answer, my friends, Christianity would have been a failure if the ship had been wrecked; Christianity would be a failure if there was any ocean into which that ship was afraid to enter; Christianity would be a failure if that ship were known at any time, at any moment of her existence, since the day she was built and rigged by Divine wisdom and the Divine Architect, Christ,—if she were known for an instant to have gone down; for a moment to have let the angry waters of persecution and error close over her head: then would Christianity be a failure. But this could not be, for two reasons. First of all, because the helmsman, whom Christ appointed, is at the wheel; and he is Peter, and Peter's successor. Second, because, in the ship,—Himself seated in her, and speaking in her, casting out the nets that are to gather in all those who come on board, and are to be saved,—is Christ, the Lord, that God. The great lessons that are in this Gospel are, our Peter's boat cannot be wrecked, because Christ, our Lord, us in her; Peter's boat cannot be emptied of the living freight of souls, because He is in her who commanded the net to be cast out until the boat was filled. Peter's boat cannot be destroyed, because Peter himself, in his successor, is at the helm. And this boat of Peter's is the Holy Roman Catholic Church. In no other ship launched out upon this stormy ocean of the world is the voice of God heard. In every other vessel it is the voice of man that commands the crew; it is the hand of man that turns the ship's prow to face the storm; it is the hand of man that built the ship, and, consequently, every other ship of doctrine that has ever been launched out on the waves of this world has gone down in shipwreck and in destruction; whereas, the oldest of all, the holy Catholic Church, lives upon the waves to-day, as fair to the eye, floating as triumphantly the standard, spreading as wide a sail, as in the days when she came forth from the master hand of Jesus Christ, our Lord. In her the word and voice of God are heard. Christ sat in Peter's boat; and Christ sits in Peter's boat to-day; we have His own word for it: "And Heaven and earth," He says, "shall pass away, but My word shall not pass away; and My word is this; I am with you all days, until the consummation of the world." But, for what purpose, did we ask, "Art Thou with us?" He answers and says: "I am with you to lead you to all truth; to keep you in all truth; to teach you all truth; and to command you, that even as I have taught you, so go you and teach all nations whatsoever things I have taught you."

The voice of Christ is in the Church; the voice of God has never ceased to resound in her; the voice of God has never been silent, from the day that Mary's Child first opened His infant lips upon Mary's bosom, until the last hour of the world's existence. That voice is misinterpreted; that voice is sometimes misunderstood. Men say, here is the voice of God, and there is the voice of God; the people lift up their voices with loud demands, sometimes against law, sometimes against right and justice; and the time-serving politician and statesman says: "It is the voice of the people; it is the voice of God. *Vox populi, vox Dei.*" But the voice of the people is not the voice of God. There is, indeed, the voice of God resounding on the earth; but it is only heard in the unerring Church: therefore we may say with truth, "*Vox ecclesiæ, vox Dei;*" the voice of the Church is the voice of God. Wherever the voice of God is, there no lie can be uttered, no untruth can be taught, no falsehood can be preached; wherever the voice of God is, there is a voice that never for an instant contradicts itself in its teachings; for it is only enunciating one truth, derived from one source, the mind, the heart of the infinite wisdom of the Almighty. Where is the evidence in history of a voice that has ever spoken on this earth, which has never contradicted itself, except the voice of the Catholic Church? I defy you to find it. There is not a system of religion which pretends to teach the people at this moment upon the earth, that has not flagrantly contradicted itself, save and except the holy Catholic Church of Jesus Christ. Take any one of them and test it. Where is the voice that teaches with authority save and except in the Catholic Church? Remember wherever the voice of God is, there that voice must teach with authority; wherever the voice of God is it must teach with certainty and clearness and emphasis, not leaving any thing in doubt, not allowing the people to be under any misapprehension. Where is that voice to be heard to-day save and except in the holy Catholic Church?

Men ask, "Is Christianity a failure?" I answer, No! It will be a failure as soon as that voice of the Catholic Church is hushed; it will be a failure as soon as some King or some Emperor or some great statesman, successful in war and in council, is able to bend the Catholic Church and make her teach according to his notions or his views. Where, in her history, has she ever bowed to king or potentate? Where has she ever shaped her doctrines to meet the views of this man, or to further the designs of this other man because they were able to persecute her, as they are persecuting her to-day? The most powerful man of the world says to the Catholic Church, "You must remodel your teachings; you must alter some of your dogmas and some of your material principles; you must admit that the State has a right to educate the children; that you have no right; you must admit that religion is not a necessary element of education; I will make you do it." Thus speaks Von Bismarck. He imagines because he has put his foot upon the neck of the bravest and most heroic race upon earth, that now he can trample upon the Church of God. Oh! fool that he is! oh, foolish man! He thinks, because he has trampled upon a nation, that he can trample upon Christ and His holy Spouse. He says to the Church: "I will make a decree, and I will expel every Jesuit in Germany: I will persecute your Bishops: I will take your churches; I will alienate your people; I will persecute and imprison your priests; I will put them to death if necessary." But the Church of God stands calmly before him, and says: "You can do all this, but you cannot make me change my teaching; I am God's messenger, and God is truth!" Christ speaks in Peter's boat. It is true there are many who will not hear His voice. I ask you what is their fate? What is their fate who refuse to hear the voice of the true Church? They appeal to the Scriptures. In this morning's New York *Herald*, there is a letter from a man who denies the immortality of the soul: and he proves it by "five texts from Scripture." The very truth that Plato, the pagan philosopher, wrote a book to prove,—a man who had never heard the name of God; who had never known the light of God;—by the natural light of his benighted, pagan intellect arrived at the conclusion that the soul was immortal, and that its immortality was inherent, and belonged to it as its nature. That which the pagan philosopher discovered and proved, the Christian of to-day denies; and he quotes "five texts of Scripture" to prove that the soul of man is not immortal; and that men when they die, even in their sins, cease to exist; that there is no judgment, no consequences, no vengeance; for them no torments; they have no hell. He proves it by the Scripture, and gives the lie to Him who said: "Depart from me, ye accursed, into everlasting flames." That is the fate of all those outside the Catholic Church. They are tossed about by every whim and caprice of doctors, who now start one theory and then another; who now dispute the inspiration of the Scripture, and again the divinity of Jesus Christ; who now deny the immortality of the soul, and then come and abuse me, and the like of me, because I tell them that, until they step on board of Peter's boat, they have no security, no certainty, no true light, no true religion, and that they must go down. We are called bigots, because we preach the Word of God, and refuse to change our teaching to suit the varying views of men. If the Church preach not the truth, then where is the use of having a Church at all? But if the Church teach the truth, if she come with a message from God, it is not in her power, nor in my power, nor in any man's power, to change it. I come to preach to you the very words of Christ: "He that will not hear the Church, let him be as a heathen and a publican." If I come, then, and say, "It is not necessary to hear the Catholic Church; if you love the Lord and believe, it is all right;" if I say that, I am telling a lie, and I am damning my own soul. I cannot do it. I must preach the message which Christ our Lord has given me. I should be glad to preach a wider faith, if God would let me; but I must preach the message of God. If they steel their hearts and turn their ears against our doctrines, God will hold them accountable, for He has said: "**He that believeth not shall be condemned.**"

Not only, my brethren, is the voice of Christ heard in that Church in the truth which has never changed nor contradicted itself; but the second great action of the Church of God is prefigured in our Divine Lord's action in this day's Gospel. "Peter," He said, "launch out thy boat into the deep, and let down thy nets for a draught." It is no longer a question of preaching. The people have heard the Lord's voice; they have retired from the shores of the lake, and scattered themselves to their homes, each one taking with him whatever of that word fell upon the soil of a good heart. Now, the next operation begins; and it is between Christ and Peter. "Launch out into the deep," He says;

"cast forth thy net." Peter cast out his net, and he filled his boat with fishes. What does this mean? It means the prefiguration of the saving and sacramental action of the Church of God; for not only is the voice of Christ heard, but the action of Christ is at work in her, taking you, and me, and all men who will submit to that action, out of the waters of passion and impurity, and vain desire, and every form of sin, and lifting us up by sacramental action, out of those waters, and placing us in the the ship under His very eyes,—in the light of His sanctity and the brightness of His glory. His action lies in the Catholic Church; and she alone can draw forth from the stormy, destructive waters of sin, the soul that will submit to be so drawn. A man falls into that sea;—a man,—like Peter, in another portion of the Gospel,—the Christian man,—treading upon the fluctuating waves of his own passion, of his own evil desire and wickedness, can scarcely keep his footing, and can only do it as long as he fixes his eye upon Jesus Christ, and adheres to Him. But a moment comes, as it came to Peter, when the waves seem to divide under our feet, when man is sinking, sinking into the waves of his own passions, of his own baseness, into the waves of his own corrupt nature, when he feels that these waves are about closing over him. He is lost to the sight of God; and he sees Him no more. God sees him no more with the eyes of love; God sees him no more with the eyes of predilection. He has lost his past with all its graces, and his future with all its hopes; he has gone down in the great ocean of human depravity and human sin; and he has sunk deeply into these waters of destruction. Oh! what hand can save him? what power can touch him? The teacher of a false religion comes with his message of trust and confidence; comes with message of glozing and flattery; comes to tell this fallen, sinful man: "You are an honest man; you are an amiable man; you have many good gifts; be not afraid; trust in the Lord; it is all right;" while the serpent of impurity is poisoning his whole existence.

Oh! that I had the voice of ten thousand thunders of God, that I might stifle the false teachings, and drown the voice of those who are poisoning the people by pandering to their vices and flattering their vanity, and not able—nor willing, even if able—to teach the consequences of their sins! The Catholic Church alone, ignoring whatever of good there may be in a man, if she finds him in mortal sin, lays her hand upon that sin; she makes the man touch himself with his own hand, look at himself, and realize his miseries. She tears away the bandages with which his self-love conceals the wound; and then, with her sacramental power, she cuts out all that proud and corrupt flesh; she cleanses the wound with the saving blood of Jesus Christ; she brings him forth from out that slough, that cesspool of impurity and wickedness, and cures him, and brings him forth with the tears of sorrow on his face, with a new-born love of God in his heart, in the whiteness of his baptismal innocence; and he is now no longer in the wiles of hell, but he takes his place and lifts up his eyes in gladness before the Lord. What other Church can do that? What other religion even pretends to do it, and does it? In her Sacraments she does it. Her sacramental hand will, though sin be sunk into his blood, go down and sweep the very bottom of the deep lake of iniquity, and take even those who lie there, fossilized in their sin, and scrape them up from out the very depths of their misery, and make them fit for God once more. As they are out of the way of salvation who hear not the voice of the Church—the voice of Christ—so, also, these Catholics are outside of the way of salvation who will not come and submit to her cleansing and sacramental power, who refuse to open their souls to her, who refuse to come frequently and fervently to her confessional, and to her communion table. To do that is as bad as if they refused even to hear her voice, even as if they disputed her testimony. The bad Catholic is in as bad a position, and in even a worse position, than that of the poor man who disputes and raises questions as to whether the soul is immortal, and as to whether Jesus Christ is God.

Oh, my brethren, let us be wise in time; let us have the happiness to know and to hear the voice that speaks in the Church. Oh, let us lay ourselves open to her sacramental power and bare our bosoms to her sanctifying touch and cleansing hand, that so we may be guided into the treasures of her choicest and best gifts; that so, if we have not the ineffable gift of purity, if we have sinned, we may at least have our robes washed in the waters of grace, and restored to their first brightness through Jesus Christ, who is our Saviour; and, in this hope, let us pass the few remaining days of our lives here, sharing in our mother's struggles; taking a hand in her quarrels; weathering with her every storm that bursts over us, in the confidence that she is destined to triumph and to ride in safety over the crest of every opposing wave. It will not always be so. The haven is at hand. The Church Militant passes from the angry ocean of her contests into the calm and quiet haven of her triumph. Oh, in that harbor, no stormy winds shall ever blow; no angry waves shall ever raise their foaming crests; there and only there, when the night, with its tempests and storms of persecution and of difficulty—the night with its buffetings upon the black face of the angry ocean,—when all that has been passed through, in the morning shall the Christian come to catch a glimpse of his eternity. Then will he hear the voice of Him who was present in the storm, saying to the waves: "Be still! Be calm!" and to the stormy winds howling around, "Depart. Leave us in peace." Then the clouds shall fade, and every ripple shall cease; and there on that ocean, which was so stormy, every angry gust of wind shall die away into perfect calm; and, in the distant horizon before us, we shall behold the Church Triumphant,—while, like the spread of the illimitable ocean, we see that pacific ocean of God's eternity illumined by the sunshine of His blessedness. And there shall be every beauty and happiness. All that shall be ours if we only fight the good fight, if we only keep the faith, and the commands of God delivered to us by His holy Church.

www.ingramcontent.com/pod-product-compliance
Lightning Source LLC
Chambersburg PA
CBHW030006240426
43672CB00007B/846